Collins

Published by Collins
An imprint of HarperCollins Publishers
Westerhill Road
Bishopbriggs
Glasgow G64 2QT

www.harpercollins.co.uk

First Edition 2018

10 9 8 7 6 5 4 3 2

© HarperCollins Publishers 2018
All quizzes copyright Puzzler Media – www.puzzler.com

ISBN 978-0-00-829028-3

Collins® is a registered trademark of HarperCollins Publishers Limited

www.harpercollins.co.uk

Typeset by Puzzler Media

Printed and bound by CPI Group (UK) Ltd, Croydon, CR0 4YY

A catalogue record for this book is available from the British Library.

If you would like to comment on any aspect of this book, please contact us at the above address or online.
E-mail: puzzles@harpercollins.co.uk

Introduction

What makes a good quiz? A witty and amusing host and a choice of interesting categories are good places to start.

You could combine the hosting talents of Alexander Armstrong and Jeremy Paxman but you need a great set of questions too.

That's where *Collins Quiz Night* comes in. We've taken the hassle out of creating the perfect quiz by providing 10,000 questions on all manner of subjects in an easy-to-use format.

There's something on offer for everyone, too, from easy questions for those taking their first tentative steps from quizzing base camp right up to super-tricky testers for those experienced trivia travellers heading for the highest peaks of general knowledge.

Let's get going.

The quizzes

The book is divided into two parts, each with 250 quizzes. Half of the quizzes are based on themes ranging from biology to buildings, geography to golf, nature to numbers and a whole host of subjects in between. The rest of the quizzes are pot luck and contain a little bit of everything.

The quizzes in each part of the book are grouped together depending on how tricky we think they are. The easy ones come first, followed by medium and finally hard.

Easy

With a wide range of themes on offer in our easy section, you're bound to find some questions and quizzes easy and others a bit harder. It's not all straightforward in this section though: watch out for a few themes that aren't quite as obvious as the title suggests. Quiz 251 marks the start of the second easy section.

Medium

You'll get a good general knowledge workout when you tackle our medium quizzes. Classic themes that appeared in the easy section are repeated here, but you'll most likely need some extra thinking time to complete the quizzes at this level. The second medium section starts at Quiz 401.

Hard

You'll really need to work those little grey cells when you venture into our hard quiz section, so set aside plenty of time. An enthusiast's knowledge would be a definite advantage on some of the themed quizzes. When you've toiled your way through the first section, the second hard section begins at Quiz 476.

The answers

Each quiz header tells you where the answers are printed. They're mostly just a couple of pages away, for example the answers to Quiz 1 appear at the bottom of Quiz 3. The exceptions are the last two quizzes in each part of the book, which appear at the bottom of the first two quizzes in that part.

Running a quiz

When you're running a quiz night, there's a great sense of satisfaction to be had in doing a job well, and a little bit of effort beforehand will go a long way to making sure that your quiz goes without a hitch.

❖ Plan: consider how many questions you want to ask in the time available, making sure you leave enough thinking time between questions. Once you've done that, pick a good range of subjects so that there's something for everyone.

❖ Rehearse: Go through all the questions you're going to be asking beforehand, checking any potentially tricky pronunciations and making sure your timings work. Note down all the questions (notes look better in a quiz environment than reading from a book) and answers. Every effort has been made to ensure that all the answers in *Collins Quiz Night* are correct. Despite our best endeavours, mistakes may still appear. If you see an answer you're not sure is right, or if you think there's more than one possible answer, then do check.

❖ Paper and writing implements: make sure you prepare enough sheets of paper for everyone to write on, including scrap paper, and have plenty of pens to hand for those who need them.

❖ Prizes: everyone likes a prize. No matter how small, it's best to have one on offer.

Good luck! We hope you enjoy *Collins Quiz Night*.

Contents

Easy Quizzes

1. Pot Luck
2. Food and Drink
3. Pot Luck
4. Geography
5. Pot Luck
6. Films
7. Pot Luck
8. History
9. Pot Luck
10. Music
11. Pot Luck
12. Nature
13. Pot Luck
14. Sitcoms
15. Pot Luck
16. UK Politics
17. Pot Luck
18. Human Biology
19. Pot Luck
20. Sport
21. Pot Luck
22. Communications
23. Pot Luck
24. Film Music
25. Pot Luck
26. Maths
27. Pot Luck
28. Art
29. Pot Luck
30. Celebrity
31. Pot Luck
32. At the Double
33. Pot Luck
34. Science Fiction
35. Pot Luck
36. France
37. Pot Luck
38. George
39. Pot Luck
40. Trees
41. Pot Luck
42. Literature
43. Pot Luck
44. Crime
45. Pot Luck
46. Football
47. Pot Luck
48. Television
49. Pot Luck
50. Mythology
51. Pot Luck
52. Royalty
53. Pot Luck
54. Yellow
55. Pot Luck
56. Scotland
57. Pot Luck
58. Animal World
59. Pot Luck
60. Transport
61. Pot Luck
62. Nursery Rhymes
63. Pot Luck
64. Third Place
65. Pot Luck
66. Astronomy
67. Pot Luck
68. Television Costume Drama
69. Pot Luck
70. Also Known As
71. Pot Luck
72. Notable Occasions
73. Pot Luck
74. Harry Potter
75. Pot Luck
76. Formula 1
77. Pot Luck
78. Organisations
79. Pot Luck
80. Video Games
81. Pot Luck
82. Mountains
83. Pot Luck
84. The Romans
85. Pot Luck
86. Classic Novels
87. Pot Luck
88. Superheroes
89. Pot Luck
90. Rock Music
91. Pot Luck
92. Points of the Compass
93. Pot Luck
94. Animated Films
95. Pot Luck
96. Science
97. Pot Luck
98. Golf
99. Pot Luck
100. Horses
101. Pot Luck
102. Diamonds and Pearls
103. Pot Luck
104. London
105. Pot Luck
106. Famous Buildings
107. Pot Luck
108. Dance
109. Pot Luck
110. James
111. Pot Luck
112. Technology
113. Pot Luck
114. Musicals
115. Pot Luck
116. Footwear
117. Pot Luck
118. Action Films
119. Pot Luck
120. Europe
121. Pot Luck
122. Money
123. Pot Luck
124. Shades of Grey
125. Pot Luck
126. Music Used in Adverts
127. Pot Luck
128. Games

129. Pot Luck
130. Legal Dramas
131. Pot Luck
132. Prequels and Sequels
133. Pot Luck
134. Sweet Things
135. Pot Luck
136. Bridges
137. Pot Luck
138. Architects and Architecture
139. Pot Luck
140. Months
141. Pot Luck
142. Italy
143. Pot Luck
144. World History
145. Pot Luck
146. Television Presenters
147. Pot Luck
148. Theatre
149. Pot Luck
150. Kate

Medium Quizzes

151. Pot Luck
152. Television Crime Drama
153. Pot Luck
154. Sport
155. Pot Luck
156. 1980s Music
157. Pot Luck
158. Science
159. Pot Luck
160. Dogs
161. Pot Luck
162. Loves and Fears
163. Pot Luck
164. Classical Music
165. Pot Luck
166. Literature
167. Pot Luck

168. World History
169. Pot Luck
170. Blue
171. Pot Luck
172. Food and Drink
173. Pot Luck
174. Famous Roads
175. Pot Luck
176. Television
177. Pot Luck
178. Rivers
179. Pot Luck
180. Ball Sports
181. Pot Luck
182. Germany
183. Pot Luck
184. Planet Earth
185. Pot Luck
186. Plays and Playwrights
187. Pot Luck
188. Education
189. Pot Luck
190. James Bond
191. Pot Luck
192. Park and Ride
193. Pot Luck
194. XYZ
195. Pot Luck
196. Famous Relatives
197. Pot Luck
198. History
199. Pot Luck
200. Television Quizzes
201. Pot Luck
202. 1950s Music
203. Pot Luck
204. Films
205. Pot Luck
206. Diaries
207. Pot Luck
208. Pink
209. Pot Luck
210. The Olympic Games

211. Pot Luck
212. Sea Creatures
213. Pot Luck
214. 1920s
215. Pot Luck
216. Days
217. Pot Luck
218. Arts and Crafts
219. Pot Luck
220. England
221. Pot Luck
222. Physics
223. Pot Luck
224. Andrew
225. Pot Luck

Hard Quizzes

226. Literature
227. Pot Luck
228. Pop Music
229. Pot Luck
230. History
231. Pot Luck
232. Science
233. Pot Luck
234. Flags
235. Pot Luck
236. Sailing
237. Pot Luck
238. Film
239. Pot Luck
240. Birds
241. Pot Luck
242. Sport
243. Pot Luck
244. John
245. Pot Luck
246. Television
247. Pot Luck
248. World Politics
249. Pot Luck
250. Europe

Easy Quizzes

251. Pot Luck
252. Literature
253. Pot Luck
254. Oscar Winners
255. Pot Luck
256. Science
257. Pot Luck
258. Cricket
259. Pot Luck
260. US Sitcoms
261. Pot Luck
262. History
263. Pot Luck
264. Green
265. Pot Luck
266. The Arts
267. Pot Luck
268. Classical Music
269. Pot Luck
270. Animal World
271. Pot Luck
272. Vegetables
273. Pot Luck
274. Chemistry
275. Pot Luck
276. Castles
277. Pot Luck
278. Greece
279. Pot Luck
280. Money
281. Pot Luck
282. Films
283. Pot Luck
284. Paper
285. Pot Luck
286. 1940s
287. Pot Luck
288. 1960s Music
289. Pot Luck
290. Sport
291. Pot Luck
292. Superstitions

293. Pot Luck
294. Technology
295. Pot Luck
296. Natural World
297. Pot Luck
298. Modern Fiction
299. Pot Luck
300. Children's Television
301. Pot Luck
302. Steps
303. Pot Luck
304. Comedians
305. Pot Luck
306. Desserts
307. Pot Luck
308. Disney Films
309. Pot Luck
310. Up and Down
311. Pot Luck
312. World Politics
313. Pot Luck
314. Theatre
315. Pot Luck
316. Languages
317. Pot Luck
318. Michaels
319. Pot Luck
320. Fashion
321. Pot Luck
322. Flowers
323. Pot Luck
324. Pop Music
325. Pot Luck
326. Athletics
327. Pot Luck
328. Stars
329. Pot Luck
330. Tom Tom
331. Pot Luck
332. Geography
333. Pot Luck
334. Television
335. Pot Luck
336. Little Things

337. Pot Luck
338. Gardening
339. Pot Luck
340. Insects
341. Pot Luck
342. The Bible
343. Pot Luck
344. Space
345. Pot Luck
346. Sport on Wheels
347. Pot Luck
348. Musicals
349. Pot Luck
350. 1930s
351. Pot Luck
352. Spain
353. Pot Luck
354. Environment
355. Pot Luck
356. Long-Running Television Series
357. Pot Luck
358. Numbers
359. Pot Luck
360. Pick and Mix
361. Pot Luck
362. Susan and Friends
363. Pot Luck
364. Business and Commerce
365. Pot Luck
366. Fantasy Films
367. Pot Luck
368. Musicians
369. Pot Luck
370. Devon
371. Pot Luck
372. Kings and Queens
373. Pot Luck
374. Snacks
375. Pot Luck
376. Pantomime
377. Pot Luck
378. Wales

379. Pot Luck
380. Waterbirds
381. Pot Luck
382. Bells and Whistles
383. Pot Luck
384. Chefs and Cooks
385. Pot Luck
386. First and Last
387. Pot Luck
388. Clothing
389. Pot Luck
390. 1970s Television
391. Pot Luck
392. DIY and Decorating
393. Pot Luck
394. Musical Goodbyes
395. Pot Luck
396. The UK
397. Pot Luck
398. Co-Stars
399. Pot Luck
400. Weather

Medium Quizzes

401. Pot Luck
402. Art
403. Pot Luck
404. Animal World
405. Pot Luck
406. Air Travel
407. Pot Luck
408. Foreign Language
     Television
409. Pot Luck
410. European History
411. Pot Luck
412. Time
413. Pot Luck
414. Geography
415. Pot Luck
416. Film
417. Pot Luck
418. Literature

419. Pot Luck
420. Food and Drink
421. Pot Luck
422. Pop Music
423. Pot Luck
424. Fictional Doctors
425. Pot Luck
426. Sport
427. Pot Luck
428. Hands and Feet
429. Pot Luck
430. Ballet
431. Pot Luck
432. Cats
433. Pot Luck
434. Science
435. Pot Luck
436. Television
437. Pot Luck
438. History
439. Pot Luck
440. Technology
441. Pot Luck
442. Peter
443. Pot Luck
444. Africa
445. Pot Luck
446. Numbers
447. Pot Luck
448. Lakes and Lochs
449. Pot Luck
450. Water Sports
451. Pot Luck
452. Red
453. Pot Luck
454. Talent Shows
455. Pot Luck
456. Classical Music
457. Pot Luck
458. Royalty
459. Pot Luck
460. Scandinavia
461. Pot Luck
462. Glass

463. Pot Luck
464. Golf
465. Pot Luck
466. Biopics
467. Pot Luck
468. Words
469. Pot Luck
470. Human Biology
471. Pot Luck
472. World Politics
473. Pot Luck
474. The UK
475. Pot Luck

Hard Quizzes

476. Football
477. Pot Luck
478. Television
479. Pot Luck
480. Planet Earth
481. Pot Luck
482. Literature
483. Pot Luck
484. Inventors and
     Inventions
485. Pot Luck
486. Film
487. Pot Luck
488. Rock Music
489. Pot Luck
490. Mythology
491. Pot Luck
492. Also Known As
493. Pot Luck
494. Geography
495. Pot Luck
496. Communications
497. Pot Luck
498. Car Makes and
     Models
499. Pot Luck
500. Science

x

1   What is the French word for "water"?

2   Who had hits with *Rock DJ* and *Radio*?

3   Which musical term means "quickly"?

4   A nonagon has how many sides?

5   Which actor played nine members of the same family in the 1949 black comedy *Kind Hearts and Coronets*?

6   What name is given to a baby kangaroo?

7   What is the Earth's only natural satellite?

8   In which street did the Great Fire of London start?

9   Which group had a hit in 1978 with *Night Fever*?

10 Midsummer Day falls in which month?

11 Which cartoon bear lives in the village of Nutwood?

12 How many cents are there in a Canadian dollar?

13 Which is the world's largest desert?

14 Which Jewish greeting means "peace"?

15 Who played Gary Strang in the TV series *Men Behaving Badly*?

16 What term is given to a small bar of gold bullion?

17 Which actor was known as "Duke"?

18 Sir Arthur Conan Doyle created which detective?

19 What was the given name of America's President Lincoln?

20 Who was the "doubting" apostle?

Easy

Medium

Hard

Answers to QUIZ 249 – Pot Luck

1	Togo	11	Tobias Smollett
2	1896	12	Cretaceous
3	Maurice Ravel	13	The Sheaf
4	Aar (or Aare)	14	Aragon
5	Van Morrison	15	Saturn
6	Hardwick Hall	16	Amos
7	Absorbed radiation dose	17	Guarani
8	Arthur Balfour	18	Jean-Jacques Rousseau
9	The Weeknd	19	Bayview
10	Dis Pater (or Pluto)	20	Emilia

ANSWERS ON PAGE 4

Easy

1 Cheddar cheese is named after a village in which county?

2 What term is used to describe food that is served set alight?

3 Which herb is traditionally served with lamb?

4 What do Americans call jam?

5 Which Indian side dish is made from cucumber, mint and yoghurt?

6 Which insect lends its name to a cocktail made from crème de cacao and crème de menthe?

7 What is the British name for the eggplant?

8 Comice is a variety of which fruit?

9 What style of Indian food is cooked in a clay oven?

10 Which popular pasta sauce is made with bacon, egg and cream?

Medium

11 What type of food can be served sunny side up?

12 Which patty of fried minced meat is named after its German city of origin?

13 Bara brith is a traditional tea bread from which country?

14 What does a barista serve?

15 Which French term describes a dry wine?

16 Which salad plant is usually grown with mustard?

17 From which flower is saffron obtained?

18 What is a Chinese cooking pan called?

19 What is the name of the Russian metal urn used for making tea?

20 Which Middle Eastern dip is made from chickpeas and sesame seeds?

Hard

Answers to QUIZ 250 – Europe

1	Mainz	11	Avignon
2	Liège	12	North Utsire
3	Avernus	13	Iceland
4	Portugal	14	La Fenice (The Phoenix)
5	Andorra	15	Suir
6	Have a nice day!	16	Livy
7	Vienna	17	Warsaw
8	Ennis	18	Strait of Messina
9	Bulgaria	19	1956
10	Unter den Linden	20	Robert Louis Stevenson

1   What colour is the flag that traditionally denotes surrender?

2   Who wrote the 1967 novel *Where Eagles Dare?*

3   Flamenco dancing is associated with which country?

4   What type of food is lollo rosso?

5   At which historical landmark would you find Traitor's Gate?

6   What is a school's shared occupancy bedroom called?

7   What is the county town of Cornwall?

8   Which actress played Clara Oswald in *Doctor Who*?

9   What decoration is known in the USA as "frosting"?

10 Which group's hits include *Holding Back the Years* (1985) and *Stars* (1991)?

11 What type of creature is a house martin?

12 What name is given to the spike of a fork?

13 Which metal has the symbol Fe?

14 Which town in south-east Ireland is famed for its crystal?

15 What is the currency unit of Mexico?

16 What word describes a musical note played slightly lower than it should be?

17 Who presented the TV series *Time Team*?

18 How is 2018 written in Roman numerals?

19 What is the penultimate radio alphabet code letter?

20 Who was the leader of the Soviet Union during WWII?

Answers to QUIZ 1 – Pot Luck

1	*Eau*	11	Rupert
2	Robbie Williams	12	100
3	Presto	13	Sahara
4	Nine	14	Shalom
5	Sir Alec Guinness	15	Martin Clunes
6	Joey	16	Ingot
7	The Moon	17	John Wayne
8	Pudding Lane	18	Sherlock Holmes
9	The Bee Gees	19	Abraham
10	June	20	Thomas

QUIZ 4 – Geography

ANSWERS ON PAGE 6

1   Which mountainous principality lies between France and Spain?

2   In which city is the Taj Mahal?

3   What is the name of modern-day Persia?

4   Which city is the capital of Romania?

5   The shamrock is the emblem of which country?

6   What are the native inhabitants of New Zealand known as?

7   Which language is spoken in the south-western part of Cyprus?

8   What is the longest river wholly in France?

9   "The Windy City" is the nickname of which US city?

10 Which sea lies between Italy and Croatia?

11 Which international airport is located in Bedfordshire?

12 Giza is a city in which country?

13 In which Australian state is Brisbane?

14 In which North American mountain range are Banff and Jasper located?

15 What is the capital of Vietnam?

16 Which Portuguese island is famous for its dessert wine?

17 What is the currency unit of Switzerland?

18 The World Heritage site of Ephesus is in which modern country?

19 In which English county is Ross-on-Wye?

20 Which South American country has Lima as its capital?

Answers to QUIZ 2 – Food and Drink

1	Somerset	11	Fried egg
2	Flambé	12	Hamburger
3	Mint	13	Wales
4	Jelly	14	Coffee
5	Raita	15	Sec
6	Grasshopper	16	Cress
7	Aubergine	17	Crocus
8	Pear	18	Wok
9	Tandoori	19	Samovar
10	Carbonara	20	Hummus

ANSWERS ON PAGE **7**

1 Who was the lead singer with The Police?

2 Who starred in the TV series *Murder, She Wrote*?

3 Which Biblical character was betrayed by Delilah?

4 What is the name for toasted Italian-style sandwiches?

5 What name is given to a gnawing mammal such as a rat or mouse?

6 Who is the patron saint of England?

7 What is the common name of sodium chloride?

8 Who was the first president of the USA?

9 What does the "A" of "VAT" stand for?

10 Which chess pieces move in L-shapes?

11 The cartoon character Popeye is associated with which vegetable?

12 Which Canadian police go on horseback?

13 Which classic film and book series includes *The Two Towers*?

14 Charles I and James I belonged to which royal House?

15 Which type of ship flies the Jolly Roger flag?

16 Which Welsh singer's debut hit was *Lost in France* in 1976?

17 A Manx cat is missing which feature that most cats have?

18 What is the national airline of Australia?

19 What term is given to a plant that lives for one year?

20 Which ocean is the world's largest?

Easy

Medium

Hard

Answers to QUIZ 3 – Pot Luck

1	White	11	A bird
2	Alistair MacLean	12	Tine
3	Spain	13	Iron
4	Lettuce	14	Waterford
5	Tower of London	15	Peso
6	A dormitory	16	Flat
7	Truro	17	Sir Tony Robinson
8	Jenna Coleman	18	MMXVIII
9	Icing	19	Yankee
10	Simply Red	20	Joseph Stalin

Easy

1. Who voiced the title character in the 2009 film *Fantastic Mr Fox*?

2. What does the second M in the film company MGM stand for?

3. Which actor starred in the 1959 film *Ben-Hur*?

4. Which film was mistakenly announced as the winner of the Best Picture Oscar at the 2017 ceremony?

5. Which 1960 Sir Alfred Hitchcock film is famed for its shower scene?

6. Who found fame as Bella Swan in the *Twilight Saga*?

7. Which creature featured in the 1975 film *Jaws*?

8. Who starred as a prison guard in the 1999 film *The Green Mile*?

9. What was the name of the Volkswagen in the 1968 Disney film *The Love Bug*?

10. What is the subtitle of the second *Terminator* film, released in 1991?

11. The 1955 film *Rebel Without a Cause* starred which actor?

12. Which film is based on the life of the Trapp Family Singers?

13. Who starred in the 2010 film *Black Swan*?

Medium

14. Which *Toy Story* character has the catchphrase "To Infinity, and Beyond!"?

15. Who co-starred with Robert Redford in *Butch Cassidy and the Sundance Kid*?

16. Which actress played Bobbie in the 1970 film *The Railway Children*?

17. What is the nickname of India's film industry?

18. How does James Bond like his martini?

19. Ryan Gosling starred in a 2017 sequel to which 1982 sci-fi film?

20. Who played Gandalf in *The Lord of the Rings* trilogy?

Hard

Answers to QUIZ 4 – Geography

1	Andorra	11	Luton
2	Agra	12	Egypt
3	Iran	13	Queensland
4	Bucharest	14	The Rockies
5	Republic of Ireland	15	Hanoi
6	Maori	16	Madeira
7	Greek	17	Franc
8	Loire	18	Turkey
9	Chicago	19	Herefordshire
10	The Adriatic	20	Peru

1   Which museum houses the *Mona Lisa*?

2   In which town is the Royal and Ancient Golf Club?

3   What term is given to the heating process which destroys disease-producing bacteria in milk?

4   What is the name given to the Central Criminal Court in London?

5   A kumquat is what colour?

6   What is the capital of the US state of Hawaii?

7   What title was traditionally given to the most senior nurse in a hospital?

8   Harry Potter was played on screen by which actor?

9   Who wrote the play *Blithe Spirit* (1941)?

10 What was the language of ancient Rome?

11 What, according to the proverb, gathers no moss?

12 Cheddar Gorge is part of which range of hills?

13 Who topped the UK singles chart in 1999 with *Baby One More Time*?

14 Which sign of the zodiac is represented by the Ram?

15 Which group's first chart-topper was 1995's *Some Might Say*?

16 The New Zealand rugby team perform what ritual before a match?

17 What, proverbially, is the mother of invention?

18 Which 1942 Disney film featured Thumper the rabbit?

19 Who is the patron saint of travellers?

20 What unit is used in measuring the height of a horse?

Easy

Medium

Hard

---

1. The euro was first adopted as an official currency on New Year's Day in which year?
2. Which spa town was founded by the Romans as Aquae Sulis?
3. Which Elizabethan seaman was captain of the *Golden Hind*?
4. Where were the Hanging Gardens, one of the Seven Ancient Wonders of the World?
5. Which was originally the tenth month in the Roman calendar?
6. During which battle was Horatio Nelson (Viscount Nelson) killed?
7. What nickname was given to a Parliamentary soldier in the English Civil War?
8. What acronym denoted the forces' showbiz organisation in WWII?
9. What was the profession of "Capability" Brown?
10. Which civilisation inhabited Peru before the Spanish conquest?
11. Who was the first person to fly the Atlantic solo?
12. Which organisation was founded by William Booth?
13. In which year did the *Titanic* sink?
14. Which 19th-century movement is associated with William Morris?
15. Which Italian volcano destroyed Pompeii in AD 79?
16. What type of transport was a penny-farthing?
17. Which king succeeded Elizabeth I?
18. Which medal was awarded to Malta in 1942?
19. Who was the last president of the Soviet Union?
20. What was the name of the census commissioned by William the Conqueror in 1085?

Easy

Medium

Hard

Answers to QUIZ 6 – Films

1	George Clooney	11	James Dean
2	Mayer	12	*The Sound of Music*
3	Charlton Heston	13	Natalie Portman
4	*La La Land*	14	Buzz Lightyear
5	*Psycho*	15	Paul Newman
6	Kristen Stewart	16	Jenny Agutter
7	Great white shark	17	Bollywood
8	Tom Hanks	18	Shaken, not stirred
9	Herbie	19	*Blade Runner*
10	*Judgment Day*	20	Sir Ian McKellen

1   What name is given to the central aisle of a church?

2   Where were the 2016 Summer Olympics held?

3   In which county is St Albans?

4   With which band did Ronan Keating find fame?

5   Who is the god of mischief in Norse mythology?

6   What is the fourth book of the New Testament?

7   To which side of a boat does the term starboard refer?

8   Who released the album and single *Let's Get It On* in 1973?

9   What is Paddington Bear's sandwich of choice?

10 Someone born on August 1 has which birth sign of the zodiac?

11 Which river flows through Dublin?

12 Who is Bart Simpson's father in *The Simpsons*?

13 What name is given to the central tower of a castle?

14 What do milliners produce?

15 Who wrote *Charlie and the Chocolate Factory* (1964)?

16 Rickets is caused by the lack of which vitamin?

17 What is the currency unit of South Africa?

18 Which large vein is found in the neck?

19 What is the name of Jack's hill-climbing companion in the nursery-rhyme?

20 Which wading bird was worshipped by the ancient Egyptians?

Easy

Medium

Hard

Answers to QUIZ 7 – Pot Luck

1	The Louvre	11	A rolling stone
2	St Andrews	12	Mendips
3	Pasteurisation	13	Britney Spears
4	Old Bailey	14	Aries
5	Orange	15	Oasis
6	Honolulu	16	Haka
7	Matron	17	Necessity
8	Daniel Radcliffe	18	*Bambi*
9	Sir Noël Coward	19	St Christopher
10	Latin	20	Hand

Easy

1. Ziggy Stardust was the alter ego of which singer?
2. Which character on a musical stave determines pitch?
3. Which duo wrote the opera *Trial by Jury*?
4. What is the name of Elvis Presley's Memphis estate?
5. Which singer's backing band were called The Wailers?
6. What was the title of Lady Gaga's first UK chart-topper?
7. Which singer/songwriter had an early hit with *Crocodile Rock*?
8. Which song title was a hit in 1993 for Mariah Carey and in 2002 for Enrique Iglesias?
9. The video to which 2012 song by Psy became the first YouTube video to reach a billion views?
10. Which Bizet opera, first performed in 1875, is set in Spain?

Medium

11. Who had a hit in 1982 with *Come on Eileen*?
12. Jason Orange was a member of which group until 2014?
13. Which musical term means "smoothly flowing"?
14. Who had 1984 hits with *Penny Lover* and *Stuck on You*?
15. Roger Daltrey founded and fronted which band?
16. What type of instrument is a bongo?
17. What name is given to the final passage in a musical work?
18. Which Britpop band had a 1994 hit with *Parklife*?
19. Which group topped the charts in 1966 with *Paperback Writer*?
20. What cry for help has been a hit for both Abba and Rihanna?

Hard

Answers to QUIZ 8 – History

1	1999	11	Charles Lindbergh
2	Bath	12	The Salvation Army
3	Sir Francis Drake	13	1912
4	Babylon	14	Arts and Crafts
5	December	15	Vesuvius
6	Trafalgar	16	A bicycle
7	Roundhead	17	James I
8	ENSA	18	The George Cross
9	Landscape designer	19	Mikhail Gorbachev
10	Inca	20	The Domesday Book

ANSWERS ON PAGE 13

1   With which town is Brighton joined to make an official city name?

2   What was Archimedes' famous cry of discovery?

3   Which band had a hit in 1982 with *Save a Prayer*?

4   Of which country is Damascus the capital?

5   Which engineer built the Great Western Railway?

6   What is a young lion called?

7   Who played Gordon Gekko in the *Wall Street* films?

8   Of which English county is Chelmsford the county town?

9   Which figure of Greek myth flew too close to the Sun?

10   Which misnamed war lasted from 1337 until 1453?

11   Which disorder is marked by difficulty in recognising written words?

12   What is the principal ingredient of chow mein?

13   Lex Luthor is the enemy of which comic-book hero?

14   What is the capital of the US state of Georgia?

15   Who composed the 1812 *Overture*?

16   What term is given to two under par for a hole in golf?

17   Dennis Quaid and Jake Gyllenhaal starred in which 2004 disaster film?

18   What is the name of the slender tower on a mosque?

19   Which is the largest continent?

20   What is the name of the dog in *Peter Pan*?

Easy

Medium

Hard

Answers to QUIZ 9 – Pot Luck

1	The nave	11	The Liffey
2	Rio de Janeiro	12	Homer
3	Hertfordshire	13	The keep
4	Boyzone	14	Hats
5	Loki	15	Roald Dahl
6	John	16	Vitamin D
7	Right	17	Rand
8	Marvin Gaye	18	Jugular
9	Marmalade	19	Jill
10	Leo	20	Ibis

Easy

1 Which soft-bodied crustacean lives in the empty shells of other molluscs such as whelks?

2 Which Australian marsupial feeds on eucalyptus leaves?

3 Which type of elephant has the largest ears?

4 How many limbs do squid have?

5 What term is used to describe the vast treeless plains of the Arctic?

6 Which fish is associated with the Sargasso Sea?

7 What type of creature lives in a holt?

8 Which flower yields digitalis?

9 Which chemical element is found in kelp?

10 Which is the world's largest antelope, native to South Africa?

11 Zephyr, sirocco and chinook are all types of what?

12 Which oil, derived from flax, is used in putty?

13 Which type of lizard has the ability to change its colour?

14 What is an insect called in the early stage of development?

Medium

15 What is "Old Faithful" in Yellowstone National Park?

16 Which African carnivore has a call that sounds like laughter?

17 Which type of amphibian has varieties including crested, fire belly and spotted?

18 In which direction does the sun rise?

19 Which wild cat has tufts on its ear tips?

20 Which river runs through America's Grand Canyon?

Hard

Answers to QUIZ 10 – Music

1	David Bowie	11	Dexys Midnight Runners
2	Clef	12	Take That
3	Gilbert and Sullivan	13	Legato
4	Graceland	14	Lionel Richie
5	Bob Marley	15	The Who
6	Just Dance	16	Drum
7	Sir Elton John	17	Coda
8	Hero	18	Blur
9	Gangnam Style	19	The Beatles
10	Carmen	20	SOS

1   What is a level or grade in judo called?

2   Which fish has varieties including brown and rainbow?

3   Who directed the 2008 film *Slumdog Millionaire*?

4   What was the title of ABBA's first UK chart-topper?

5   What is the French word for "thank you"?

6   What title is given to the supreme commander of the British navy?

7   *Dinnerladies* was created by and starred which comedienne?

8   What does the Richter scale measure?

9   Which vitamin is most abundant in carrots?

10   What is a baby swan called?

11   Which Womble was named after a Siberian city?

12   Proverbially, which reptile cries insincere tears?

13   In which county is Bexhill?

14   What is the American term for a holiday?

15   What familiar short name is used for London's police force?

16   Which retired athlete's autobiography is entitled *Faster than Lightning*?

17   What is the *Flying Scotsman*?

18   Which animated pair had *A Grand Day Out* in 1989?

19   Which river flows through Stoke?

20   Who wrote the play *The Winter's Tale*?

Easy

Medium

Hard

Answers to QUIZ 11 – Pot Luck

1	Hove	11	Dyslexia
2	Eureka!	12	Noodles
3	Duran Duran	13	Superman
4	Syria	14	Atlanta
5	Isambard Kingdom Brunel	15	Tchaikovsky
6	A cub	16	Eagle
7	Michael Douglas	17	*The Day After Tomorrow*
8	Essex	18	Minaret
9	Icarus	19	Asia
10	The Hundred Years War	20	Nana

QUIZ 14 – Sitcoms

Easy

1 Who played Pam in *Gavin & Stacey*?

2 In which London borough was *Only Fools and Horses* set?

3 What was the name of Ricky Gervais' character in *The Office*?

4 Which part-improvised series featured siblings Ben, Karen and Jake?

5 Which actress played Grace in *Will & Grace*?

6 In which sitcom did Simon Bird play the character Will McKenzie?

7 Which sitcom was set on Craggy Island?

8 Who played Manuel in *Fawlty Towers*?

9 Who co-starred with Zoë Wanamaker in *My Family*?

10 In which city was *Bread* set?

Medium

11 Which profession features in *Damned*?

12 Which US medical sitcom starred Zach Braff and Sarah Chalke?

13 Which series starred Dame Judi Dench and Geoffrey Palmer as Jean and Lionel?

14 David Hyde Pierce played which character in *Frasier*?

15 Which country is the setting for the TV sitcom *Two Doors Down*?

16 What was the name of Paul Eddington's character in *The Good Life*?

17 What was the nickname of the company clerk in *M*A*S*H*?

18 Officer Crabtree, famed for his French mispronunciation, appeared in which sitcom?

19 Which actor provided the narration for *Twenty Twelve* and *W1A*?

20 Who played Miranda's mother in the sitcom *Miranda*?

Hard

Answers to QUIZ 12 – Nature

1	Hermit crab	11	Wind
2	Koala	12	Linseed
3	African	13	Chameleon
4	Ten (eight arms, two tentacles)	14	Larva
5	Tundra	15	A geyser
6	Eel	16	Hyena
7	Otter	17	Newt
8	Foxglove	18	East
9	Iodine	19	Lynx
10	Eland	20	Colorado

1   What colour is turmeric?

2   Which creature is said to be caught by the early bird?

3   Who wrote *The Three Musketeers*?

4   What was the name of the Soviet space station launched in 1986?

5   The Shambles is a street in which English city?

6   Who was the chief Greek god on Mount Olympus?

7   What substance makes up the outer layer of a tooth?

8   Yaffle is a dialect name for which bird?

9   "Simian" refers to which type of animal?

10 Which section of an orchestra includes flutes?

11 "The Gunners" is the nickname of which football team?

12 What term is given to a bishop's high hat?

13 In which county is Sherwood Forest?

14 Which actress starred in the TV series *Hannah Montana*?

15 Which singer was originally named Anna Mae Bullock?

16 In the PG Wodehouse novels, who is Bertie Wooster's manservant?

17 Who had a 1978 hit with *Song for Guy*?

18 What is a Scottish water sprite in the form of a horse called?

19 Who were the Rockers' 1960s rivals?

20 The Woolpack pub is featured in which long-running TV series?

Easy

Medium

Hard

Answers to QUIZ 13 – Pot Luck

1	Dan	11	Tomsk
2	Trout	12	Crocodile
3	Danny Boyle	13	East Sussex
4	*Waterloo*	14	Vacation
5	*Merci*	15	Met
6	Admiral of the Fleet	16	Usain Bolt
7	Victoria Wood	17	Steam locomotive
8	Magnitude of earthquakes	18	Wallace and Gromit
9	Vitamin A	19	Trent
10	Cygnet	20	William Shakespeare

Easy

1. What is the title of the official printed record of Parliamentary proceedings?
2. Who was the first female Speaker of the House of Commons?
3. Who was Prime Minister at the outbreak of WWII?
4. On which day of the week are British elections usually held?
5. Who became the UK's first Green Party MP in 2010?
6. Who was Gordon Brown's Chancellor of the Exchequer?
7. In which Lincolnshire town was Baroness Margaret Thatcher born?
8. Which former Prime Minister is associated with the country house of Chartwell?
9. What exclamation is heard in the House of Commons to signal Members' agreement?
10. Which former MP was elected Mayor of Greater Manchester in May 2017?
11. What is the maximum period between general elections in the UK?
12. Which London street is home to the Ministry of Defence?
13. What term is given to a seat in the House of Lords for an independent or minor party member?

Medium

14. Who was Prime Minister from 1990 to 1997?
15. In the House of Commons, what colour are the seats?
16. What was the nickname of the 1940s Labour politician Aneurin Bevan?
17. What are the initials of the government's industrial mediation body?
18. What is the name of the Speaker's seat in the House of Lords?
19. On which occasion does the Chancellor traditionally brandish a red case?
20. In 2017 who became leader of the Liberal Democrats for the second time?

Hard

Answers to QUIZ 14 – Sitcoms

1	Alison Steadman	11	Social work
2	Peckham	12	*Scrubs*
3	David Brent	13	*As Time Goes By*
4	*Outnumbered*	14	Niles (Crane)
5	Debra Messing	15	Scotland
6	*The Inbetweeners*	16	Jerry Leadbetter
7	*Father Ted*	17	Radar
8	Andrew Sachs	18	*'Allo, 'Allo!*
9	Robert Lindsay	19	David Tennant
10	Liverpool	20	Patricia Hodge

ANSWERS ON PAGE 19

1   What is the capital of Portugal?

2   Who were Gladys Knight's backing group?

3   What term is given to a blacksmith's iron block?

4   What is a grinding tooth called?

5   Which soft, bland foodstuff is made from soya beans?

6   In a limerick, which lines should rhyme with the second line?

7   What is the longest river in South America?

8   Which Cumbrian town is famous for its mint cake?

9   In which month is Armistice Day?

10   What is the name of the Marquess of Bath's stately home in Wiltshire?

11   Which ballet features the *Dance of the Sugar Plum Fairy*?

12   How many fiddlers does Old King Cole have in the nursery rhyme?

13   Who wrote *Far from the Madding Crowd* (1874)?

14   Which fictional village is the setting for *The Archers*?

15   What is the largest planet in our solar system?

16   Toxteth is an area of which English city?

17   What is the musical term for a range of eight notes?

18   Which actor starred in the 1984 film *Footloose*?

19   What is the Irish name for Ireland?

20   What are young goats called?

Easy

Medium

Hard

Answers to QUIZ 15 – Pot Luck

1	Yellow	11	Arsenal
2	The worm	12	Mitre
3	Alexandre Dumas (père)	13	Nottinghamshire
4	Mir	14	Miley Cyrus
5	York	15	Tina Turner
6	Zeus	16	Jeeves
7	Enamel	17	Sir Elton John
8	Green woodpecker	18	Kelpie
9	Monkey	19	The Mods
10	Woodwind	20	*Emmerdale*

Easy

1. What is the name of the red pigment in blood?
2. Which hormone, secreted by the pineal gland, induces sleepiness?
3. Which of the five senses might be impared as a result of laryngitis?
4. In which organs of the body would you find aqueous and vitreous humour?
5. Which muscle is found at the front of the upper arm?
6. Which molecule, in the form of a double helix, transfers genetic characteristics?
7. Which parts of the body are technically called the nares?
8. Which condition occurs as a result of alopecia?
9. Which vital organ neutralises harmful substances in the blood?
10. Which disease, also called infantile paralysis, is prevented by swallowing a vaccine-treated sugar cube?

Medium

11. The umbilicus is the clinical name for what part of the body?
12. Which nerve transmits visual information from the retina to the brain?
13. What is the "soft spot" on a baby's head called?
14. Which is the outermost layer of the skin?
15. What is the common name for the scapula?
16. What is the science of the structure of the body?
17. Encephalology is the study of disorders of which part of the body?
18. What is the medical term given to low blood sugar?
19. Which word meaning "dog-like" applies to a human tooth?
20. What do the letters BMI stand for in the context of personal health?

Hard

Answers to QUIZ 16 – UK Politics

1	Hansard	11	Five years
2	Baroness Betty Boothroyd	12	Whitehall
3	Neville Chamberlain	13	Crossbench
4	Thursday	14	Sir John Major
5	Caroline Lucas	15	Green
6	Alistair Darling	16	Nye
7	Grantham	17	ACAS
8	Sir Winston Churchill	18	The Woolsack
9	Hear, hear	19	Budget Day
10	Andy Burnham	20	Sir Vince Cable

1   Which medical instrument is used to listen to the heart?

2   *Firework* was a 2010 hit for which singer?

3   Who co-starred with Jodie Foster in the 1991 film *The Silence of the Lambs*?

4   Which northern Italian town is famous for its cured pork and cheese?

5   Which pre-decimal British coin was worth twelve old pence?

6   What is the capital city of Turkey?

7   Which Sunday precedes Easter by a week?

8   Which is Amsterdam's airport?

9   What is the study of disease called?

10   Which is the world's largest bird?

11   Which legendary musician led children from Hamelin?

12   In the TV series *Dallas*, who played Bobby Ewing?

13   Which elite regiment's motto is "Who Dares Wins"?

14   What do Americans call a full stop?

15   Who was Eric Morecambe's comedy partner?

16   Which Latin word is the "A" of "AD"?

17   In which Scottish city would you find the Royal Mile?

18   What is a period of six balls in cricket?

19   Which imaginary line around the Earth is at Latitude 0°?

20   Which car company has a rampant lion as its logo?

Easy / **Medium** / **Hard**

Answers to QUIZ 17 – Pot Luck

1	Lisbon	11	*The Nutcracker*
2	The Pips	12	Three
3	Anvil	13	Thomas Hardy
4	Molar	14	Ambridge
5	Tofu	15	Jupiter
6	First and fifth	16	Liverpool
7	Amazon	17	Octave
8	Kendal	18	Kevin Bacon
9	November	19	Eire
10	Longleat	20	Kids

Easy

1   What name is given to the New Zealand international rugby team?

2   Who was the first man to run the mile in under four minutes?

3   Which of the grand slam tennis tournaments is played on clay?

4   Which country failed to qualify for the FIFA World Cup in 2018, its first absence since 1958?

5   The Henley Regatta takes place on which river?

6   Which name is applied to the Wolverhampton and Bolton football teams?

7   Which indoor game is played with a shuttlecock?

8   Which famous cricket venue is in St John's Wood, London?

9   Which part of a dartboard is worth 50 points?

10 What is the thrower called in a game of baseball?

11 How many players are there in a rugby union team?

12 Where were the 2014 Winter Olympics held?

13 What is the home ground of Liverpool FC?

14 What are the final odds offered before a horse race?

Medium

15 Strikes and spares feature in which indoor sport?

16 Which athletics contest comprises ten events?

17 Which winter sport is associated with the Cresta Run?

18 Who won the Masters Snooker title for a record seventh time in 2017?

19 Which cricketing trophy is played for every two years by England and Australia?

20 What is the name of the rubber disc used in ice hockey?

Hard

Answers to QUIZ 18 – Human Biology

1	Haemoglobin	11	The belly button
2	Melatonin	12	Optic nerve
3	Speech	13	Fontanelle
4	The eyes	14	Epidermis
5	Biceps	15	Shoulder blade
6	DNA	16	Anatomy
7	The nostrils	17	The brain
8	Baldness	18	Hypoglycaemia
9	The liver	19	Canine
10	Polio	20	Body Mass Index

1   In which London borough is Heathrow Airport situated?

2   Who had a hit in 1977 with *When I Need You*?

3   Which ornamental fabric has a Chantilly variety?

4   Which large body of water surrounds the North Pole?

5   In the TV series *Happy Days*, who played the Fonz?

6   What yarn is derived from the Angora goat?

7   Who invented the miner's safety lamp?

8   What is the English name of the Catholic prayer to Our Lady?

9   Which infectious viral disease causes inflammation of the face's salivary glands?

10   Which sauce is traditionally eaten with roast beef?

11   A plant of the genus *Urtica* has what common name?

12   Which species of eel shares a name with a Scottish firth?

13   Where in the human body is the patella?

14   Who was Arthur of Camelot's wife?

15   Chestnut and oyster are varieties of which food item?

16   What is the capital of Finland?

17   With which musical instrument is Vanessa Mae associated?

18   What, according to the proverb, is better than no bread?

19   Which actress played Lucy in the 1985 film *A Room With A View*?

20   What is a trumpet-quietening device known as?

Easy   **Medium**   **Hard**

Answers to QUIZ 19 – Pot Luck

1	Stethoscope	11	Pied Piper
2	Katy Perry	12	Patrick Duffy
3	Sir Anthony Hopkins	13	SAS
4	Parma	14	Period
5	Shilling	15	Ernie Wise
6	Ankara	16	*Anno*
7	Palm Sunday	17	Edinburgh
8	Schiphol	18	Over
9	Pathology	19	Equator
10	Ostrich	20	Peugeot

Easy

1 What does the "C" stand for in the initials BBC?

2 Who invented the World Wide Web?

3 Which word represents the letter "T" in the standard radio phonetic alphabet?

4 Which was the first programme to be broadcast on Channel 4?

5 What was the name of the world's first adhesive postage stamp?

6 What does DAB stand for in relation to radios?

7 Which is the most frequently used letter in the English language?

8 What was the world's first teletext information service, started by the BBC in 1974?

9 In which year did the UK complete the switch to digital television?

10 By what system is a letter sent if labelled "par avion"?

11 What does SMS stand for in relation to texting?

12 Who invented the telephone?

13 What does "fax" stand for?

14 Which country developed emojis?

Medium

15 Which letter is represented in Morse Code by a single dash?

16 How much did a standard first class stamp cost in the UK at the beginning of 2018?

17 Who was the first person to produce a printed book in English?

18 On a standard keyboard, what is the topmost left letter?

19 Which London thoroughfare was traditionally associated with newspapers?

20 In 1973, which company became the first to mass-produce the handheld mobile phone?

Hard

Answers to QUIZ 20 – Sport

1	The All Blacks	11	15
2	Sir Roger Bannister	12	Sochi (Russia)
3	The French Open	13	Anfield
4	Italy	14	Starting price
5	The Thames	15	Tenpin bowling
6	Wanderers	16	Decathlon
7	Badminton	17	Bobsleigh
8	Lord's	18	Ronnie O'Sullivan
9	The bull	19	The Ashes
10	Pitcher	20	Puck

1 Which city is the capital of India?

2 Who was the Greek goddess of retribution?

3 What term is given to the central part of a wheel?

4 In which Welsh county is Bangor?

5 Who had a hit in 2009 with *Bad Romance*?

6 What title is given to a person who owns a large estate in Scotland?

7 Which English naval hero was commander of *HMS Victory*?

8 The football ground of Elland Road is in which city?

9 What is the term for an official who leads prayers in a mosque?

10 What is the American term for a narrow rocky valley?

11 Who was the composer of *The Planets* suite?

12 What is the state capital of Tennessee?

13 In the 2012 film *Les Misérables*, who played Jean Valjean?

14 Where does an arboreal creature live?

15 In which county is Loughborough?

16 What is the medical term for short-sightedness?

17 Which Ealing comedy was remade in 2004 with Tom Hanks in the starring role?

18 What is the word of Indian origin for an equestrian show?

19 Which peach variety has a smooth yellow and red skin?

20 What is the capital of Japan?

Easy

Medium

Hard

Answers to QUIZ 21 – Pot Luck

1	Hillingdon	11	Nettle
2	Leo Sayer	12	Moray
3	Lace	13	The knee
4	Arctic Ocean	14	Guinevere
5	Henry Winkler	15	Mushroom
6	Mohair	16	Helsinki
7	Sir Humphry Davy	17	Violin
8	Hail Mary	18	Half a loaf
9	Mumps	19	Helena Bonham Carter
10	Horseradish	20	Mute

Easy

1   Who sang *Gangsta's Paradise*, featured in the 1995 film *Dangerous Minds*?

2   Who won an Oscar for the score to the film *ET: the Extra-Terrestrial*?

3   Who sang the theme song to the 1984 film *Ghostbusters*?

4   The song *Bright Eyes* was the theme tune to which 1978 animated film?

5   The 1945 film *Brief Encounter* featured which composer's *Concerto No 2 in C Minor*?

6   Which film theme song was a hit for Phil Collins in 1984 and Steve Brookstein in 2005?

7   Who had a second hit with *Unchained Melody* in 1990 as a result of the film *Ghost*?

8   Who composed *The Pink Panther* theme?

9   Which group topped the charts for 15 weeks in 1994 with *Love is All Around*, from *Four Weddings and a Funeral*?

10 Who wrote *I Will Always Love You*, Whitney Houston's hit from *The Bodyguard*?

11 Which song used in *Despicable Me 2* was a 2014 hit for Pharrell Williams?

12 Who sang *My Heart Will Go On*, the theme song to *Titanic...*?

13 ...and who composed the score?

Medium

14 Berlin's *Take My Breath Away* featured in which 1986 film?

15 Which 2002 James Bond film had a theme tune performed by Madonna?

16 *Let It Go* is a song from which 2013 animated film?

17 Who composed the score for the 1966 film *The Good, The Bad and The Ugly*?

18 *Everything is Awesome* by Tegan and Sara was from which 2014 film?

19 Which song used in *Robin Hood: Prince of Thieves* topped the UK charts for 16 weeks?

20 Vangelis won an Oscar for which 1981 British film's soundtrack?

Hard

Answers to QUIZ 22 – Communications

1	Corporation	11	Short Message Service
2	Sir Tim Berners-Lee	12	Alexander Graham Bell
3	Tango	13	Facsimile
4	*Countdown*	14	Japan
5	Penny Black	15	T
6	Digital Audio Broadcasting	16	65p
7	E	17	William Caxton
8	Ceefax	18	Q
9	2012	19	Fleet Street
10	Airmail	20	Motorola

1   Which ship famously sank off the Portsmouth coast in 1545?

2   In which country was Russell Crowe born?

3   What was the name of the first "talkie" film, released in 1927?

4   What modern measurement of length is equivalent to just over a yard?

5   The city of Hull lies on which estuary?

6   What term describes lines lying in the same plane and not intersecting?

7   What is the French term for the South of France?

8   The Gurkhas hail from which mountainous Asian country?

9   What is the collective noun for a group of owls?

10 Of which European country is The Hague the seat of government?

11 Which group had a hit in 1992 with *November Rain*?

12 Which author created the character of Tom Sawyer?

13 What name is given to a female horse?

14 In which city is Central Park?

15 Who was the god of war in Roman mythology?

16 What is the common name for the tiny piece of silicon used in circuits?

17 Who was the lead singer with The Jam?

18 Of which country is Budapest the capital?

19 Which salad is made from tuna, French beans, olives and eggs?

20 Which screen legend starred in the film *The Seven Year Itch*?

Easy

Medium

Hard

Answers to QUIZ 23 – Pot Luck

1	New Delhi	11	Gustav Holst
2	Nemesis	12	Nashville
3	The hub	13	Hugh Jackman
4	Gwynedd	14	In a tree
5	Lady Gaga	15	Leicestershire
6	A laird	16	Myopia
7	Horatio Nelson (Viscount Nelson)	17	*The Ladykillers*
8	Leeds	18	Gymkhana
9	Imam	19	Nectarine
10	Gulch	20	Tokyo

1   How many sides does an octagon have?

2   What unit of time is 1440th of a day?

3   What term is given to the distance from the centre of a circle to its outside edge?

4   What is 0.025 expressed as a fraction?

5   What unit of land is ten thousand square metres?

6   Which mathematical diagram of intersecting circles was invented by British logician, John?

7   What term is given to the mathematics of shapes?

8   What name is given to a triangle that has two equal sides?

9   Which imperial length measurement is equal to 2.54 centimetres?

10 How many degrees are there in a right angle?

11 What term is given to an angle of between 90 and 180 degrees?

12 What is the square root of 169?

13 Which metric unit of weight is equivalent to 1000 kilograms?

14 How many sides are there on a rhombus?

15 Which branch of mathematics is concerned with theoretical rather than practical aspects?

16 Which shape has long straight sides and two equal-sized circular ends?

17 What term is given to a graph shown as a circle divided into sections?

18 What is the decimal equivalent of the binary number 110?

19 Which unit of quantity is equal to twelve dozen?

20 What term is given to the top line of a fraction?

Answers to QUIZ 24 – Film Music

1	Coolio	11	*Happy*
2	John Williams	12	Celine Dion
3	Ray Parker Jr	13	James Horner
4	*Watership Down*	14	*Top Gun*
5	Rachmaninov	15	*Die Another Day*
6	*Against All Odds*	16	*Frozen*
7	Righteous Brothers	17	Ennio Morricone
8	Henry Mancini	18	*The Lego Movie*
9	Wet Wet Wet	19	*(Everything I Do) I Do It for You*
10	Dolly Parton	20	*Chariots of Fire*

Easy

Medium

Hard

1   Who was the original host of the TV series *QI*?

2   Proverbially, what is it that blows nobody any good?

3   Bangkok is the capital of which south-east Asian country?

4   Which syrupy liqueur is an ingredient of the cocktail Kir Royale?

5   What is the modern name for Ceylon?

6   What is the term for money paid to the courts as security?

7   The Blockheads were the backing band for which singer?

8   Which town in Warwickshire is associated with Shakespeare?

9   Who was the Greek god of pastures and nature?

10 In rounders, which player stands behind the batter?

11 Which is the largest cathedral in the world?

12 Which English conflict lasted from 1642 to 1646?

13 Who was the director of *2001: A Space Odyssey*?

14 *Mrs Brown's Boys* was created by which comedian?

15 The Serpentine is in which area of London?

16 What was Jack's surname in the TV series 24?

17 What is the highest award at the Cannes Film Festival?

18 Who won the men's singles title at Wimbledon in 1974 and again in 1982?

19 Which motor-racing circuit is situated near Swanley in Kent?

20 What is a solution of water strongly impregnated with salt called?

Easy

Medium

Hard

Answers to QUIZ 25 – Pot Luck

1	The *Mary Rose*	11	Guns N' Roses
2	New Zealand	12	Mark Twain
3	*The Jazz Singer*	13	A mare
4	Metre	14	New York
5	The Humber estuary	15	Mars
6	Parallel	16	Microchip
7	Midi	17	Paul Weller
8	Nepal	18	Hungary
9	Parliament	19	Niçoise
10	Netherlands	20	Marilyn Monroe

Easy

1 Which art museum is located in London's Bankside area?

2 Who decorated the ceiling of the Sistine Chapel in the 16th century?

3 Who created the art installation *My Bed* in 1998?

4 Which pop artist said that everyone would be famous for 15 minutes?

5 Which 18th-century artist painted the satirical sketches *A Rake's Progress*?

6 Which colour is obtained by mixing red and blue paint?

7 *The Angel of the North* sculpture is near which town?

8 What brownish-orange hair colour is named after a Renaissance painter?

9 What was Picasso's first name?

10 *The Monarch of the Glen* (1851) is a painting by which British artist?

Medium

11 Which French painter was famed for his pictures of water lilies?

12 Which artist painted *The Night Watch* (1642)?

13 What is the support for an artist's canvas called?

14 Which artist painted *The Fighting Temeraire* (1838)?

15 In which city can Leonardo da Vinci's *The Last Supper* be seen?

16 Which Cornish seaside town has a branch of the Tate gallery?

17 George Stubbs is famous for his paintings of which type of animal?

18 Who sculpted *The Kiss* (1882)?

19 In which city is the Uffizi gallery?

20 Which French artist (b.1848) is famous for his paintings of Tahiti?

Hard

Answers to QUIZ 26 – Maths

1	Eight	11	Obtuse
2	Minute	12	13
3	Radius	13	Tonne
4	Fortieth	14	Four
5	Hectare	15	Pure maths
6	Venn	16	Cylinder
7	Geometry	17	Pie chart
8	Isosceles	18	Six
9	An inch	19	Gross
10	90	20	Numerator

1 Which female rank is equivalent to a knight?

2 What is the national bird of the USA?

3 What is the fourth letter of the Greek alphabet?

4 Which Italian dish consists of slices of raw meat or fish?

5 For what type of comedy plays was dramatist Georges Feydeau famous?

6 Which is the second largest of the Great Lakes by surface area?

7 Which southern county gave its name to a geological period?

8 Which wild flower has a seed head known as a clock?

9 What is the Spanish word for "donkey"?

10 Epiphany is celebrated in which month?

11 What is the capital city of Belgium?

12 What was the surname of the butler in *Downton Abbey*?

13 On which river does Chester stand?

14 Linen is obtained from which plant?

15 What is the lowest male singing voice?

16 Vulpine refers to which animal?

17 What is the nickname of Norwich City FC?

18 Of which family did John Galsworthy write a series of novels between 1906 and 1921?

19 *Tapestry* was a 1971 album by which singer/songwriter?

20 What, according to the proverb, is the sincerest form of flattery?

Easy

Medium

Hard

Easy

1. Which TV scientist played in the 1990s band D Ream?

2. Who is the youngest of the Kardashian sisters?

3. Which girl group was formed as a result of the programme *Popstars: The Rivals*?

4. In which US state was Nicole Kidman born?

5. Which reality TV star won the 2017 series of the winter sports competition *The Jump*?

6. Angelina Jolie is the daughter of which actor?

7. Which intrepid TV presenter first found fame on *Castaway 2000*?

8. Which guitarist graduated with a physics PhD in 2008, having originally begun his studies in the 1970s?

9. The TV series *Cradle to Grave* is a biopic of which TV and radio presenter's early life?

10. What is the name of David and Victoria Beckham's second son?

11. What is the surname of Oscar-winning film-making brothers Joel and Ethan?

12. Which comedian featured on the 2005 version of Tony Christie's *Is This the Way to Amarillo*?

Medium

13. In which country was Cate Blanchett born?

14. Which Oscar-winning actor is a founder member of the band Thirty Seconds to Mars?

15. On which talent show did Simon Cowell first appear as a judge?

16. Which group was Beyoncé part of before going solo?

17. Dakota Johnson is the daughter of which actress?

18. Which Hollywood actress was Miss USA runner-up in 1986?

19. By what name is Stefani Germanotta better known?

20. Arnold Schwarzenegger was Governor of which US state from 2003 to 2011?

Hard

Answers to QUIZ 28 – Art

1	The Tate Modern	11	Claude Monet
2	Michelangelo	12	Rembrandt
3	Tracey Emin	13	An easel
4	Andy Warhol	14	JMW Turner
5	William Hogarth	15	Milan
6	Purple	16	St Ives
7	Gateshead	17	Horses
8	Titian	18	Auguste Rodin
9	Pablo	19	Florence
10	Sir Edwin Landseer	20	Paul Gauguin

1   Who wrote the 1936 novel *Jamaica Inn*?

2   What term is used to describe sloping type?

3   What alias does Superman use?

4   The Isle of Dogs is part of which area of London?

5   Which US state has Denver as its capital?

6   In Roman numerals, what number is represented by LXXV?

7   Which bird is traditionally seen as an emblem of peace?

8   What is the common name for the crane fly?

9   What was the title of Phil Collins and Philip Bailey's 1985 no.1 hit?

10   What is a gavotte?

11   Wales has which patron saint?

12   What general disorder does the suffix "itis" indicate?

13   What, according to the proverb, should you not look in the mouth?

14   Which was the only one of Disney's Seven Dwarfs without a beard?

15   Which TV series is set in the fictional Cornish village of Portwenn?

16   In which year did Concorde make its first flight?

17   Who starred in the 2003 film *School of Rock*?

18   What was the name of Victor's wife in the TV series *One Foot in the Grave*?

19   Which member of a rowing team is responsible for steering?

20   The cities of Glasgow and Edinburgh are linked by which motorway?

Answers to QUIZ 29 – Pot Luck

1	Dame	11	Brussels
2	Bald eagle	12	Carson
3	Delta	13	Dee
4	Carpaccio	14	Flax
5	Farces	15	Bass
6	Huron	16	Fox
7	Devon	17	Canaries
8	Dandelion	18	Forsyte
9	Burro	19	Carole King
10	January	20	Imitation

Easy

1 What name is given to the short stiff skirt worn by a ballerina?

2 Who is Yogi Bear's best friend?

3 What term is given to a ditch used as an invisible garden boundary?

4 In which decade did the ra-ra skirt first become popular?

5 Couscous is made from which type of grain?

6 How many wheels are there on a tuk-tuk?

7 Who wrote the 2012 novel *Me Before You*?

8 Which bird has the Latin name *Troglodytes troglodytes*?

9 What was the name of the frog in the 1960s children's series *Hector's House*?

10 The can-can dance originated in which country?

11 Who had a 1974 hit with *Rebel Rebel*?

12 Tête-à-Tête is a dwarf variety of which flower?

13 Which radio alphabet code word follows "papa"?

14 Which group had a 1983 hit with *Mama*?

Medium

15 Which long-extinct bird was native to Mauritius?

16 What type of transport might be described as "ro-ro"?

17 What type of creature is the cartoon character Pepé Le Pew?

18 In the TV series *Teletubbies*, what colour is Laa-Laa?

19 Which group had a 1965 hit with *California Dreamin'*?

20 "Toto, I've a feeling we're not in Kansas anymore" is a quote from which film?

Hard

Answers to QUIZ 30 – Celebrity

1	Brian Cox	11	Coen
2	Khloé	12	Peter Kay
3	Girls Aloud	13	Australia
4	Hawaii	14	Jared Leto
5	Spencer Matthews	15	*Pop Idol*
6	Jon Voight	16	Destiny's Child
7	Ben Fogle	17	Melanie Griffith
8	Brian May	18	Halle Berry
9	Danny Baker	19	Lady Gaga
10	Romeo	20	California

1   In which US state is Disney World?

2   What word represents the letter "F" in the radio phonetic alphabet?

3   Which sport is played at Headingley and The Oval?

4   Which versatile pungent bulb is said to ward off vampires?

5   What term is given to a female deer?

6   What is the German word for "Mrs"?

7   *Joey* was a spin-off from which TV series?

8   St Austell can be found in which English county?

9   Which imperial liquid measure is equivalent to eight pints?

10   In which country was porcelain first made?

11   Which group topped the UK charts in 1978 with *Dreadlock Holiday*?

12   What word is used in the US for a lift that travels between floors?

13   Which long-running drama series is set in Weatherfield?

14   In the Bible, which archangel foretells the birth of Jesus to Mary?

15   Which period covers the years 1901-10 in Britain?

16   Which British fashion designer launched the miniskirt?

17   In the nursery rhyme, how many men did the Grand Old Duke of York have?

18   Which alcoholic drink is produced from fermented honey?

19   In the TV series *CSI*, what does the "I" stand for?

20   Which author created the character Tracy Beaker?

Easy

Medium

Hard

Answers to QUIZ 31 – Pot Luck

1	Dame Daphne du Maurier	11	St David
2	Italic	12	Inflammation
3	Clark Kent	13	A gift horse
4	Docklands	14	Dopey
5	Colorado	15	*Doc Martin*
6	75	16	1969
7	Dove	17	Jack Black
8	Daddy-long-legs	18	Margaret
9	*Easy Lover*	19	Cox
10	An 18th-century dance	20	M8

1 Which 2004 Will Smith film is based on short stories by Isaac Asimov?

2 What is the name of the villainous computer network in the *Terminator* films?

3 Who played the lead role in the 2015 film *The Martian*?

4 What was the title of the 2016 film released as part of the *Star Wars* franchise?

5 The 1990 film *Total Recall* features a mining colony on which planet?

6 Who played the hero Galen in the TV series *Planet of the Apes*?

7 What giant creatures featured in the 1954 film *Them!*?

8 The 1968 film *Barbarella* featured which famous actress?

9 Who played Jean-Luc Picard in the TV series *Star Trek: the Next Generation*?

10 Which actor starred in the 2002 film *Minority Report*?

11 The Cylons featured in which TV series of the 1970s and 2000s?

12 Which famous author wrote *The Time Machine* and *The War of the Worlds*?

13 Who wrote *The Hitch-Hiker's Guide to the Galaxy*?

14 Which famous sci-fi character was played by Sylvester Stallone and later by Karl Urban?

15 How did the extra-terrestrials communicate in *Close Encounters of the Third Kind*?

16 What colour were the tall humanoids in *Avatar*?

17 Which actress starred in the 2016 sci-fi film *Arrival*?

18 Which TV series has featured the alien Sontarans, Ice Warriors and Silurians?

19 Which rock group provided the soundtrack to the 1980 film *Flash Gordon*?

20 What does Babylon 5 refer to in the title of the TV series?

Answers to QUIZ 32 – At the Double

1	Tutu	11	David Bowie
2	Boo-Boo	12	Daffodil
3	Ha-ha	13	Quebec
4	1980s	14	Genesis
5	Semolina	15	The dodo
6	Three	16	A ferry (roll-on, roll-off)
7	Jojo Moyes	17	A skunk
8	Wren	18	Yellow
9	Kiki	19	The Mamas & the Papas
10	France	20	*The Wizard of Oz*

1   Sicily and Cyprus lie in which sea?

2   On which course is the classic horse race the Oaks run?

3   What was the name of the cow in *The Magic Roundabout*?

4   Which point is the southernmost tip of Britain?

5   What type of fruit is an ogen?

6   Which Caribbean island has Havana as its capital?

7   What name is given to a pale, dry sherry?

8   Which girl's name is the French word for "she"?

9   According to the song, who sold "cockles and mussels, alive, alive-o"?

10 Which of Handel's oratorios contains the "Hallelujah" chorus?

11 What title is given to the head of a monastery?

12 Who is Charlie Brown's blanket-carrying friend?

13 Which sign of the zodiac is represented by the Archer?

14 Which German city hosted the 1972 Olympic Games?

15 Who recorded the 1990 hit *Unbelievable*?

16 Ancient poets gave which name to the drink of the gods?

17 Which of the Cinque Ports shares its name with a cereal crop?

18 What is the line behind which darts players stand?

19 What is the given name of Ms Harker, the heroine of *Dracula*?

20 Where is the headquarters of London's Metropolitan Police?

Answers to QUIZ 33 – Pot Luck

1	Florida	11	10cc
2	Foxtrot	12	Elevator
3	Cricket	13	*Coronation Street*
4	Garlic	14	Gabriel
5	Doe	15	Edwardian
6	Frau	16	Dame Mary Quant
7	*Friends*	17	10,000
8	Cornwall	18	Mead
9	Gallon	19	Investigation
10	China	20	Dame Jacqueline Wilson

Easy

1 On which river does Paris stand?

2 What is the term for a French police officer?

3 Which French stew of fish and vegetables originated in Marseille?

4 Which French port is linked to Newhaven by ferry?

5 *Jaune* is French for which colour?

6 Which former French royal house is also the name of a variety of American whiskey?

7 What name is given to the Parisian underground?

8 Of which former duchy and province of France was William the Conqueror a duke?

9 On which Parisian thoroughfare does the Tour de France finish?

10 Which novelist wrote *Les Misérables* (1862)?

11 What is the French phrase for the dish of the day in a restaurant?

12 Which town in the north of the country is associated with racing and lace?

13 What is the French word for "snail"?

14 In which year of the late 20th century did France host the FIFA World Cup?

Medium

15 Which singer (b.1915) was nicknamed the "Little Sparrow"?

16 Which Parisian landmark was begun by Napoleon to celebrate his victories?

17 Which French wine classification is the highest level for Burgundy?

18 The "little black dress" was popularised by which French fashion designer?

19 Which French term means "baked in a pastry coating"?

20 At which venue is the French Grand Slam tennis tournament played?

Hard

Easy

1   Which element combines with oxygen to make water?

2   Which fairy-tale character met the three bears?

3   In which county is the seaside town of Cromer?

4   What is the eastern Mediterranean flaky pastry used to make strudel?

5   Who is Popeye's girlfriend?

6   Which group released *The Lexicon of Love II* album in 2016?

7   According to the rhyme, on what day was Solomon Grundy born?

8   Pumpernickel bread is from which country?

9   What is the colour of the ball worth three points in snooker?

10 Which unit of weight is used for gems and gold?

11 What is the name of Sherlock Holmes' housekeeper?

12 What term is given to a fish's breathing organs?

13 Who played the Prime Minister in the 2003 film *Love Actually*?

14 What is the dead skin at the base of a nail called?

15 According to the saying, what die hard?

16 In which TV series did Lea Michele play Rachel Berry?

17 Portland is the capital of which US state?

18 Who was the main presenter of the long-running consumer series *That's Life*?

19 Which constellation is known as the Hunter?

20 Des Moines is the capital of which US state?

Medium

Answers to QUIZ 35 – Pot Luck

1	Mediterranean	11	Abbot
2	Epsom	12	Linus
3	Ermintrude	13	Sagittarius
4	Lizard Point	14	Munich
5	A melon	15	EMF
6	Cuba	16	Nectar
7	Fino	17	Rye
8	Elle	18	Oche
9	Molly Malone	19	Mina
10	*Messiah*	20	New Scotland Yard

Hard

Easy

1   Winston Smith and Emmanuel Goldstein are characters in which George Orwell novel?

2   George Cole played Flash Harry in which series of films?

3   George the pink hippo appeared in which childrens' TV series?

4   In which month is the feast day of St George?

5   Who duetted with George Michael in 1991 on *Don't Let the Sun Go Down on Me*?

6   Which British monarch's reign saw the American War of Independence?

7   Which actor's only outing as James Bond was in *On Her Majesty's Secret Service*?

8   What was George and Mildred's surname in the 1970s sitcom?

9   Which English engineer was known as "the Father of Railways"?

10 Which English spymaster features in John le Carré's *Tinker, Tailor, Soldier, Spy*?

11 Who was French president from 1969 to 1974?

12 What was the surname of George Takei's *Star Trek* character?

13 In which 1946 film did James Stewart star as George Bailey?

14 Georges Simenon created which fictional detective?

15 Which actor played TV's Inspector George Gently?

16 Who played the title role in the 1994 film *The Madness of King George*?

17 What was the name of George Wendt's character in the TV series *Cheers*?

18 Which 1980s TV series starred George Peppard as Hannibal Smith?

19 Which type of instrument did George Formby play?

20 What is the capital of the country Georgia?

Answers to QUIZ 36 – France

1	The Seine	11	*Plat du jour*
2	Gendarme	12	Chantilly
3	Bouillabaisse	13	*Escargot*
4	Dieppe	14	1998
5	Yellow	15	Édith Piaf
6	Bourbon	16	Arc de Triomphe
7	Métro	17	Grand cru
8	Normandy	18	Coco Chanel
9	Champs-Élysées	19	En croute
10	Victor Hugo	20	Roland Garros (Paris)

1   In which county is Henley-on-Thames?

2   What was the nickname of rock 'n' roll pianist Antoine Domino?

3   What is toxicology the study of?

4   Who hosted *Ready Steady Cook* before Ainsley Harriott?

5   What is a cutting tooth called?

6   What term is given to a tennis serve that cannot be returned?

7   Which Cornish town is the home of Gilbert and Sullivan's pirates?

8   The 1986 film *Crocodile Dundee* starred which actor in the title role?

9   What is the official language of Chile?

10   What is the US equivalent of "Ltd"?

11   What term is given to the scientific study of birds?

12   Which New Testament book precedes Romans?

13   The 1974 novel *Jaws* was written by which author?

14   Which cup was sought by King Arthur's knights?

15   What is a dried plum called?

16   Which trophy is contested by male US and European golfers every two years?

17   *Nutbush City Limits* was a hit for which separating duo in 1973?

18   What is the chess term for a deadlock?

19   Which is the largest living primate?

20   What metal is an alloy of iron and carbon?

Answers to QUIZ 37 – Pot Luck

1	Hydrogen	11	Mrs Hudson
2	Goldilocks	12	Gills
3	Norfolk	13	Hugh Grant
4	Filo	14	Cuticle
5	Olive Oyl	15	Old habits
6	ABC	16	*Glee*
7	Monday	17	Oregon
8	Germany	18	Dame Esther Rantzen
9	Green	19	Orion
10	Carat	20	Iowa

1   What is the popular name given to the fruit of the horse chestnut tree?

2   The oil from which tree native to Australia has medicinal uses including clearing congestion?

3   What name is given to a botanical tree garden such as Westonbirt?

4   The berries of which tree are used to flavour gin?

5   Which tree shares its name with a US ski resort?

6   Which tree traditionally provides the leaves used for making honorary wreaths?

7   What is the term given to a tree's liquid?

8   Which country has a cedar tree on its national flag?

9   The wood of which tree is traditionally used to make cricket bats?

10 What term is given to a tree that is leafy all year round?

11 Which Californian tree has a seven-letter name that contains all five vowels?

12 The branch of which tree signifies an offer of reconciliation?

13 Which tree is also known as the rowan?

14 What term is given to a fruit tree trained on stakes?

15 For what use is the Norway Spruce tree most well-known?

16 Acorns are the fruit of which tree?

17 Which tree "bears the crown" in the lyrics of a well-known seasonal song?

18 What name is given to the cylindrical flower cluster that forms on trees such as birch or hazel in spring?

19 What is the maple tree genus?

20 What term is given to the concentric marks on a tree trunk?

Answers to QUIZ 38 – George

1	*Nineteen Eighty-Four*	11	Georges Pompidou
2	St Trinian's	12	Sulu
3	*Rainbow*	13	*It's a Wonderful Life*
4	April	14	Maigret
5	Sir Elton John	15	Martin Shaw
6	George III	16	Sir Nigel Hawthorne
7	George Lazenby	17	Norm
8	Roper	18	*The A-Team*
9	George Stephenson	19	Ukulele (or banjolele)
10	George Smiley	20	Tbilisi

1 Which period of fasting precedes Easter?

2 Which mushroom-like organisms are studied by mycologists?

3 In which year did Madonna have her first UK top ten hit with *Holiday*?

4 What is the canine symbol of Great Britain?

5 Which bloodsucking worm was once used in medicine?

6 In the name of the charity ROSPA, what does the "A" stand for?

7 Which musical centres around the character of Sally Bowles?

8 What title is given to an army chaplain?

9 Which number is written as XC in Roman numerals?

10 Where were the summer Olympic Games of 1980 held?

11 What jelly is made from seaweed and used in glue-making?

12 What was the middle name of the poet Shelley (b.1792)?

13 Which French wine-growing region is also a deep red colour?

14 Jacob Marley is a character in which Dickens novel?

15 Which US city suffered a massive earthquake in 1906?

16 What type of creature is a painted lady?

17 What term is given to the highest part of a tropical rainforest?

18 Who was elected Mayor of London in 2016?

19 Which band had a hit in the mid-1980s with *Take On Me*?

20 What is the name of the Royal Military Academy near Camberley in Surrey?

Easy

Medium

Hard

Answers to QUIZ 39 – Pot Luck

1	Oxfordshire	11	Ornithology
2	Fats	12	Acts
3	Poisons	13	Peter Benchley
4	Fern Britton	14	The Holy Grail
5	An incisor	15	Prune
6	Ace	16	Ryder Cup
7	Penzance	17	Ike and Tina Turner
8	Paul Hogan	18	Stalemate
9	Spanish	19	Gorilla
10	Inc	20	Steel

Easy

1. How many lines are there in a sonnet?

2. For what type of book is Samuel Pepys best known?

3. Which author created the Secret Seven?

4. Who wrote the 1899 novel *Heart of Darkness*?

5. Whom did Gepetto the woodcarver create?

6. In which Dickens novel does Miss Havisham, who was jilted on her wedding day, appear?

7. Who is Scotland's national poet?

8. Which creature raced against the hare in Aesop's fable?

9. Who wrote *Salem's Lot, Cujo* and *It*?

10. Which bear admitted to "having very little brain"?

11. What is Sherlock Holmes' address?

12. What is the name of the girl who flies to Neverland with Peter Pan?

Medium

13. Who wrote the 1961 novel *The Prime of Miss Jean Brodie*?

14. Which Tennyson poem begins "Come into the garden"?

15. Elizabeth Bennet is the main character in which 1813 novel?

16. What is the family's surname in the 1868 novel *Little Women*?

17. Which classic novel features the character of Catherine Earnshaw?

18. Which novel by Richard Adams was made into an animated film in 1978?

19. CS Lewis penned stories set in which imaginary land beyond the wardrobe?

20. Which author created Inspector Wexford?

Hard

Answers to QUIZ 40 – Trees

1	Conker	11	Sequoia
2	Eucalyptus	12	Olive
3	Arboretum	13	Mountain ash
4	Juniper	14	Espalier
5	Aspen	15	Christmas tree
6	Laurel	16	Oak
7	Sap	17	Holly
8	Lebanon	18	Catkin
9	Willow	19	*Acer*
10	Evergreen	20	Growth rings

1   *Smooth Operator* was a 1980s hit for which singer?

2   What name is given to a male goose?

3   What was the first name of French philosopher Sartre (b.1905)?

4   Which kind of building can be found at Westminster, Woburn and Whitby?

5   Which offence in the US might be "grand" or "petty"?

6   Who starred in the 2003 film *Hulk*?

7   In which county is Preston?

8   In which month is Twelfth Night?

9   Which salad is made from romaine lettuce, croutons and Parmesan?

10 What name is given to a Freemasons' meeting place?

11 Who played Carrie in *Sex and the City*?

12 Which word can be an island, a coffee bean or a computer language?

13 *The Catcher in the Rye* (1951) was written by which novelist?

14 Which city, near the Pyramids, is the capital of Egypt?

15 Which fatty substance is found in wool?

16 What nickname is given to a private in the Royal Engineers?

17 Which ex-*Neighbours* actor had a hit in 1991 with *Any Dream Will Do*?

18 What is the German equivalent of the title "Miss"?

19 Which Spanish Surrealist painted *The Persistence of Memory* (1931)?

20 How many pounds are there in a stone?

Easy

Medium

Hard

Answers to QUIZ 41 – Pot Luck

1	Lent	11	Agar
2	Fungi	12	Bysshe
3	1984	13	Burgundy
4	Bulldog	14	*A Christmas Carol*
5	Leech	15	San Francisco
6	Accidents	16	A butterfly
7	*Cabaret*	17	Canopy
8	Padre	18	Sadiq Khan
9	90	19	A-Ha
10	Moscow	20	Sandhurst

Easy

1 The 1995 film *Rogue Trader* was based on whose autobiography?

2 Which Scottish legal officer performs the functions of public prosecutor and coroner?

3 For what crime was Al Capone jailed in 1931...?

4 ...and what was the nickname of the team of agents, led by Eliot Ness, who investigated his crimes?

5 What name is given in the UK to an establishment where criminal cases are tried by a judge and jury?

6 What were Bonnie and Clyde's surnames?

7 In which city was John F Kennedy assassinated?

8 Which former UK politician unsuccessfully attempted to fake his own death in 1974?

9 In which year did the Great Train Robbery take place in the UK?

10 Which criminal organisation is known in the USA as Cosa Nostra?

Medium

11 What term is given to the likeliest perpetrator of a crime?

12 Who has responsibility for maintaining the law in a US county or independent city?

13 Which murderer was the subject of the 1985 film *Dance with a Stranger*?

14 What did Colonel Thomas Blood famously steal in 1671?

15 Which phrase describes a court case held behind closed doors?

16 What term is given to the head of a prison in the UK?

17 Who played OJ Simpson in the 2016 *American Crime Story* dramatisation *The People v. O.J. Simpson*?

18 Which term describes evidence which may not be brought before a court of law?

19 Which Roman statesman was murdered on the Ides of March?

20 The term "Triad" is used to describe criminal gangs in which country?

Hard

1	14	11	221b Baker Street
2	A diary	12	Wendy
3	Enid Blyton	13	Dame Muriel Spark
4	Joseph Conrad	14	*Maud*
5	Pinocchio	15	*Pride and Prejudice*
6	*Great Expectations*	16	March
7	Robert Burns	17	*Wuthering Heights*
8	Tortoise	18	*Watership Down*
9	Stephen King	19	Narnia
10	Winnie-the-Pooh	20	Baroness Ruth Rendell

1 Who presented the long-running children's series *Animal Magic*?

2 Which is the second-largest city in Pakistan?

3 The Goat represents which star sign?

4 What term is given to a grotesquely carved water-spout found on churches?

5 What is the common name for the delphinium?

6 Where are the headquarters of Surrey County Cricket Club?

7 What is the measurable unit of work or energy in the CGS system?

8 Which London hotel was built by theatrical impresario Richard D'Oyly Carte?

9 In which US state is San Francisco?

10 Which red gem is January's birthstone?

11 Which beetle was sacred to the ancient Egyptians?

12 Who directed the 1946 film *It's a Wonderful Life?*

13 What reaping tool is associated with Old Father Time?

14 What was Mel B's Spice Girls' nickname?

15 What kind of animal is a dromedary?

16 Which waters separate Anglesey from the Welsh mainland?

17 Merino is a breed of which animal?

18 What is the family name of Juliet in Shakespeare's *Romeo and Juliet*?

19 What is the currency unit of Israel?

20 "Bob" was a slang term for which pre-decimal coin?

Answers to QUIZ 43 – Pot Luck

1	Sade	11	Sarah Jessica Parker
2	Gander	12	Java
3	Jean-Paul	13	JD Salinger
4	Abbey	14	Cairo
5	Larceny	15	Lanolin
6	Eric Bana	16	Sapper
7	Lancashire	17	Jason Donovan
8	January	18	Fräulein
9	Caesar	19	Salvador Dali
10	Lodge	20	14

Easy

1. Who was the manager of Manchester United from 1945 until 1969?

2. Which club, nicknamed "The Seagulls", made their Premier League debut in 2017?

3. What term is given to the scoring system where the first goal scored in extra time wins the match?

4. Which European team plays its home games at Camp Nou?

5. How many points are awarded for a win in an FA league game?

6. What name is given to a match between two local teams?

7. Who captained England to victory in the 1966 FIFA World Cup?

8. What colour shirts and shorts do Chelsea players usually wear?

9. In football, what is another name for an upright?

10. In which year did the infamous "Hand of God" incident occur?

11. Where was the home ground of Arsenal FC until 2006?

12. For which football club did Gary Lineker play professionally from 1978 to 1985?

13. Which stadium is the home of Rangers FC?

Medium

14. In which Italian city is the football club Juventus based?

15. Who was the first non-Englishman to manage the England national team?

16. Which football team is known as "the Toffees"?

17. Which hymn is traditionally sung at the FA Cup final?

18. Who captained Portugal to their UEFA European Championship win in 2016?

19. Which Premier League team played home games at Wembley during the 2017-18 season?

20. Which colour card does a football referee show as a warning?

Hard

Answers to QUIZ 44 – Crime

1	Nick Leeson	11	Prime suspect
2	Procurator fiscal	12	Sheriff
3	Tax evasion	13	Ruth Ellis
4	The Untouchables	14	Crown Jewels
5	Crown court	15	*In camera*
6	Parker and Barrow	16	Governor
7	Dallas	17	Cuba Gooding Jr
8	John Stonehouse	18	Inadmissible
9	1963	19	Julius Caesar
10	The Mafia	20	China

1 Which cocktail is mainly made from gin and cherry brandy?

2 Who won the men's singles title at Wimbledon in 1981, 1983 and 1984?

3 Sudoku puzzles originate from which country?

4 Matt LeBlanc starred as himself in which sitcom with Stephen Mangan and Tamsin Greig?

5 In the Bible, which city's walls were blown down by trumpets?

6 In which body of water is the island of Mustique?

7 What is the term given to a speculative opening move in chess?

8 What is the name of Postman Pat's black and white cat?

9 What initials denote the index of the top 100 UK companies?

10 Which yobbish plasterer was an early Harry Enfield TV creation?

11 Which Turkish dish has doner and shish varieties?

12 To which family of fish does the barbel belong?

13 Who first played Ripley in the 1979 film *Alien?*

14 What surname is shared by former *EastEnders* actors Martin and Ross?

15 Which lasagne-loving ginger cartoon cat is friends with a dog named Odie?

16 What was Thailand's name until 1939?

17 In which county is the seaside town of Whitstable?

18 Which author's novels include *Polo* and *Riders?*

19 What is a potter's oven called?

20 Which Cambridge college is famed for its choir's Christmas carol-singing?

Easy

Medium

Hard

Answers to QUIZ 45 – Pot Luck

1	Johnny Morris	11	Scarab
2	Lahore	12	Frank Capra
3	Capricorn	13	Scythe (or sickle)
4	Gargoyle	14	Scary
5	Larkspur	15	Camel
6	The Oval	16	Menai Strait
7	Erg	17	Sheep
8	Savoy	18	Capulet
9	California	19	Shekel
10	Garnet	20	Shilling

Easy

1. In which fictional town is the soap *Home and Away* set?
2. Who was the original host of the quiz show *Blockbusters*?
3. Who starred as Jonathan Pine in the 2016 TV series *The Night Manager*?
4. Which animated canine graduated from Dogwarts University?
5. Who played Lady Mary in *Downton Abbey*?
6. Which celebrity won the first series of *Strictly Come Dancing*?
7. Fozzie Bear featured in which series?
8. Who replaced Margaret Mountford on the TV series *The Apprentice*?
9. Which charity benefits from Red Nose Day?
10. Who returned as the main *Gardeners' World* presenter for the second time in 2011?
11. Peter Dinklage is best known for playing Tyrion Lannister in which TV show?
12. Who was Andy Pandy and Looby Loo's companion in the children's series?
13. What was the first name of Ricky Tomlinson's character in *The Royle Family*?
14. Who played Nicholas Brody in the TV series *Homeland*?

Medium

15. Which series starred James Gandolfini as the boss of a crime family?
16. Who played Mr Big in *Sex and the City*?
17. *Holby City* is a spin-off from which other TV drama?
18. Which 1970s TV detective was played by Telly Savalas?
19. Who starred in the TV series *House*?
20. Whom did Rachel Riley replace as the maths expert on *Countdown*?

Hard

Answers to QUIZ 46 – Football

1	Sir Matt Busby	11	Highbury
2	Brighton and Hove Albion	12	Leicester City
3	Golden goal	13	Ibrox
4	Barcelona	14	Turin
5	Three	15	Sven-Göran Eriksson
6	Derby	16	Everton
7	Bobby Moore	17	*Abide with Me*
8	Blue	18	Cristiano Ronaldo
9	Goalpost	19	Tottenham Hotspur
10	1986	20	Yellow

1   Which duo had a 1986 hit with *Edge of Heaven*?

2   Which animal is known as a moose in the USA?

3   Who wrote the 1847 novel *Wuthering Heights*?

4   Which London Underground line is coloured red on maps?

5   What is the fifth sign of the zodiac?

6   What is the official language of the Canadian province of Quebec?

7   In the nursery rhyme *Mary, Mary, Quite Contrary*, what colour are the bells in her garden?

8   What name is given to an official population count?

9   What is the nickname of Sheffield Wednesday FC?

10 What is proverbially said to be as good as a feast?

11 Which port is the largest coastal city in Belgium?

12 Which Staffordshire university is situated near Stoke-on-Trent?

13 What is the only English town to appear in the title of a Shakespeare play?

14 In the children's series *Roobarb and Custard*, what kind of animal was Roobarb?

15 Which drink is associated with California's Napa Valley?

16 Which flaky white cheese is produced in North Yorkshire?

17 Which actress starred in the *Nanny McPhee* films?

18 In the nursery rhyme, which stoat-like animal goes "pop"?

19 What kind of boat has twin parallel hulls?

20 What is the name of London's famous botanical gardens?

Easy

Medium

Hard

Answers to QUIZ 47 – Pot Luck

1	Singapore Sling	11	Kebab
2	John McEnroe	12	Carp
3	Japan	13	Sigourney Weaver
4	*Episodes*	14	Kemp
5	Jericho	15	Garfield
6	Caribbean Sea	16	Siam
7	Gambit	17	Kent
8	Jess	18	Jilly Cooper
9	FTSE	19	Kiln
10	Loadsamoney	20	King's

1 Who, in Greek mythology, were the older gods who preceded the Olympians?

2 Which chemical element is named after the Roman god of communication?

3 What was the name of the Roman goddess of the hunt?

4 Which Norse god was Thor's father?

5 Who was the Greek goddess of love...?

6 ...and who was her Roman counterpart?

7 What did Prometheus steal from the gods?

8 What flower is named after a mythical, self-absorbed youth?

9 Who was the Roman sun god?

10 Which lost continent of legend is said to have sunk below the sea?

11 What is the alternative name for Jupiter, the supreme god of the Romans?

12 What, in Greek mythology, was a female spirit that tormented evil-doers?

13 Which Gorgon's name is also used for a jellyfish?

14 Which three-pronged spear is traditionally carried by Neptune?

15 Where in the Mediterranean was home to the Minotaur?

16 Which god of property boundaries gave his name to a station at the end of the line?

17 Who was the Roman god of love?

18 What is the name of the resting place for the souls of slain heroes in Norse mythology?

19 What was the name of Jason's ship, in Greek mythology?

20 After which Anglo-Saxon god was Wednesday named?

Answers to QUIZ 48 – Television

1	Summer Bay	11	*Game of Thrones*
2	Bob Holness	12	Teddy
3	Tom Hiddleston	13	Jim
4	Gromit	14	Damian Lewis
5	Michelle Dockery	15	*The Sopranos*
6	Natasha Kaplinksy	16	Chris Noth
7	*The Muppet Show*	17	*Casualty*
8	Baroness Karren Brady	18	Kojak
9	Comic Relief	19	Hugh Laurie
10	Monty Don	20	Carol Vorderman

1   What is the world's fastest land animal?

2   What is the name of the commemorative pillar near Pudding Lane in London?

3   What is the science of moral principles?

4   Which puppet fox has the catchphrase "Boom! Boom!"?

5   Where in the body is the hippocampus?

6   What name is given to a sporting event consisting of a series of boat or yacht races?

7   Who was the goddess of the dawn in Roman mythology?

8   In which city is Beverly Hills?

9   Maraschino liqueur is made from which fruit?

10 Which group sang *Lonely This Christmas* in 1974?

11 What is the capital city of Estonia?

12 What volcanic rock forms the Giant's Causeway in Northern Ireland?

13 What is Cockney rhyming slang for "hair"?

14 Which old tax-collecting government department changed its name in 2005?

15 Who was the mid-5th-century king of the Huns?

16 What is the name of Homer Simpson's mother in the *The Simpsons*?

17 What is the "season of mists and mellow fruitfulness", according to Keats?

18 Who composed the music for *Star Wars*?

19 In which county is Crewe?

20 Leghorn is a breed of what animal?

Answers to QUIZ 49 – Pot Luck

1	Wham!	11	Ostend
2	Elk	12	Keele
3	Emily Brontë	13	Windsor
4	Central	14	Dog
5	Leo	15	Wine
6	French	16	Wensleydale
7	Silver	17	Dame Emma Thompson
8	Census	18	Weasel
9	The Owls	19	Catamaran
10	Enough	20	Kew

QUIZ 52 – Royalty

1 Which Royal House opposed the House of York in the Wars of the Roses?

2 What was the name of 18 French kings?

3 Elizabeth Woodville married which king?

4 Who was king of England during WWII?

5 Which 11th-century English king was nicknamed "the Unready"?

6 What is the name of the royal residence in Norfolk?

7 Who was Queen Victoria's consort?

8 Which king of England was defeated at the Battle of Hastings?

9 What was George I's native language?

10 Which castle built for Edward I is situated on the south-eastern shore of Anglesey?

11 What was the name of the ruling dynasty of Scotland from 1371 to 1714?

12 Which king signed the *Magna Carta*?

13 Who was Queen of England from 1558 to 1603?

14 In which royal residence can you view Queen Mary's dolls' house?

15 Which English king, according to legend, burned the cakes?

16 In which city were the remains of Richard III found in 2012?

17 Mary of Teck was the wife of which British monarch?

18 What was the family nickname of both Edward VII and George VI?

19 In which year did Edward VIII abdicate?

20 What was the name of Henry VIII's first wife?

Answers to QUIZ 50 – Mythology

1	Titans	11	Jove
2	Mercury	12	Fury
3	Diana	13	Medusa
4	Odin	14	Trident
5	Aphrodite	15	Crete
6	Venus	16	Terminus
7	Fire	17	Cupid
8	Narcissus	18	Valhalla
9	Sol	19	*Argo*
10	Atlantis	20	Woden

QUIZ 53 – Pot Luck

1 Cathay is an old name for which country?

2 What kind of rays cause skin to go brown in the sun?

3 What is the Latin name of the prayer Hail Mary, set to music by many composers?

4 Which 2002 romcom starred Nia Vardalos and John Corbett?

5 Which city hosted the 2018 Winter Olympics?

6 How is actor Nicolas Coppola better known?

7 What cake is traditionally eaten during the Easter period in the UK?

8 Which city is the capital of the Tyrol?

9 Which bird is the emblem of the RSPB?

10 Who composed the piece known as the *Minute Waltz* (1847)?

11 What school is associated with a collar, a crop and the wall game?

12 Who Is the Greek goddess of victory?

13 What are the announcements in church of a forthcoming wedding called?

14 Which group had a hit in 1985 with *Road to Nowhere*?

15 What is the name of Tokyo's financial index?

16 Which classic weepie starred Ali MacGraw and Ryan O'Neal?

17 What was the nickname of revolutionary Ernesto Guevara?

18 What term is given to a spindle that joins two wheels?

19 Which iconic fashion doll was launched in 1959?

20 In which county is Robin Hood's Bay?

Easy

Medium

Hard

Answers to QUIZ 51 – Pot Luck

1	Cheetah	11	Tallinn
2	Monument	12	Basalt
3	Ethics	13	Barnet Fair
4	Basil Brush	14	Inland Revenue (to HM Revenue and Customs)
5	In the brain	15	Attila
6	Regatta	16	Mona
7	Aurora	17	Autumn
8	Los Angeles	18	John Williams
9	Cherry	19	Cheshire
10	Mud	20	Chicken

1 Yellowfin is a species of which fish?

2 What is the real name of TV's Keith Lemon?

3 Which Dutch town is famous for its cheese which usually has a yellow coating?

4 Princess Jasmine is a character in which 1992 Disney film?

5 In Formula 1, what does a single yellow flag warn a driver to do?

6 Which insect transmits the disease yellow fever?

7 Which is the largest of the Canary Islands?

8 Which buttercup-like flower has greater and lesser varieties?

9 Which US state is also known as the "Yellowhammer State"?

10 Meadowlark Lemon (1932-2015) was a professional player in which sport?

11 The yellow jersey is worn by the leader of which sporting event?

12 Which group sang *Tie a Yellow Ribbon Round the Ole Oak Tree* in 1973?

13 Which fictional sleuth has a secretary called Miss Lemon?

14 In which US state is Yellowstone National Park mainly situated?

15 How many points are awarded for potting the yellow ball in the game of snooker?

16 Who played Saffron in the TV series *Absolutely Fabulous*?

17 The Beatles released *Yellow Submarine* as a double A-sided single with which other song?

18 Which fish of the plaice family has a lemon variety?

19 Which actor starred in the 2004 film *Lemony Snicket's A Series of Unfortunate Events*?

20 In which area of London is Canary Wharf?

---

1   Which word meaning "poet" is commonly applied to Shakespeare?

2   Dom Perignon is a brand of which drink?

3   Which branch of science deals with the elements and their compounds?

4   Which spectacular North American cascade divides Canada and the USA?

5   Which French fashion designer introduced the New Look in 1947?

6   Which two academic qualifications were replaced by the GCSE exam?

7   In which county is Hexham?

8   Which military force was founded by Trotsky?

9   Which nursery rhyme character had no food for her dog?

10 What style of bay window is also the name of an Oxford college?

11 Which adventure hero visited the *Kingdom of the Crystal Skull* in 2008?

12 What is the capital city of Morocco?

13 What is "eight" in Spanish?

14 An Orcadian is a resident of which group of islands?

15 Who was the original presenter of the UK version of *MasterChef*?

16 What name is given to scissors that leave a zigzag instead of a straight edge?

17 Which male singing voice falls between tenor and bass?

18 What imperial measure is just over half a litre?

19 Which small horse is slang for £25?

20 Which food item is associated with the town of Melton Mowbray?

Answers to QUIZ 53 – Pot Luck

1	China	11	Eton
2	Ultraviolet	12	Nike
3	*Ave Maria*	13	Banns
4	*My Big Fat Greek Wedding*	14	Talking Heads
5	Pyeongchang	15	Nikkei
6	Nicolas Cage	16	*Love Story*
7	Simnel cake	17	Che
8	Innsbruck	18	Axle
9	Avocet	19	Barbie®
10	Chopin	20	North Yorkshire

Easy

1 What is the capital city of Scotland?

2 Which canal, completed in 1822, links Inverness and Fort William?

3 What is the name of the old Roman barrier along the Scottish/English border?

4 Who is the patron saint of Scotland?

5 Carnoustie is a famous venue for which sport?

6 Which Shakespeare play is traditionally thought to bring bad luck to its actors?

7 Which city is also known as "the Granite City"?

8 What is the longest river in Scotland?

9 On which island is there a monastery founded by St Columba?

10 Which Celtic language is spoken in many parts of the Western Isles of Scotland?

11 Which Scottish village was the traditional destination for runaway couples?

Medium

12 Which 1983 film set in a Scottish village featured music by Mark Knopfler?

13 What name is given to a turnip in Scotland?

14 A sequel to which 1996 film set in Scotland was released in January 2017?

15 Which fabric pattern is particularly associated with Scotland?

16 What is the name of the largest island in the Firth of Clyde?

17 Up till 2008, which coin had a Scottish thistle with a crown on top on the reverse?

18 In which council region is St Andrews?

19 What is the name of the Scottish rugby team's home ground?

20 Which palace is situated just north of Perth?

Hard

1   What is the collective noun for a group of lions?

2   Who won the fourteenth series of *Strictly Come Dancing* in 2016?

3   Which German sports car manufacturer created the Carrera model?

4   What term is given to a case for holding arrows?

5   What is the sixth colour of the rainbow?

6   Which Formula 1 team signed Lewis Hamilton as a young driver in 2007?

7   What is the capital of Spain?

8   Which title was assumed by Oliver Cromwell in 1653?

9   What is the last letter of the Greek alphabet?

10 Who were "on the run" according to the title of the 1990 Robbie Coltrane film?

11 What are the two official languages of Sri Lanka?

12 Which liqueur was originally made by Carthusian monks?

13 Which group had a 1980 hit with *Baggy Trousers*?

14 Which National Theatre auditorium was named after the first actor to be made a life peer?

15 What name is given to a bird of prey's hooked claw?

16 Where is the Sea of Tranquility?

17 The word for which system of weights and measures can also refer to an empire?

18 Which vegetable has pearl and Spanish varieties?

19 Which 1990s interior design show was presented by Carol Smillie from 1996 to 2003?

20 Which musical instruction means "very quickly"?

Easy

Medium

Hard

Answers to QUIZ 55 – Pot Luck

1	Bard	11	Indiana Jones
2	Champagne	12	Rabat
3	Chemistry	13	Ocho
4	Niagara Falls	14	Orkney
5	Christian Dior	15	Loyd Grossman
6	CSE and GCE	16	Pinking shears
7	Northumberland	17	Baritone
8	Red Army	18	Pint
9	Old Mother Hubbard	19	Pony
10	Oriel	20	Pork pie

Easy

1 What is the tallest living mammal?

2 Which animal is known as "the ship of the desert"?

3 What name is given to a badger's burrow?

4 Is a carp a freshwater or sea fish?

5 What term is given to animals that eat food of both plant and animal origin?

6 Which bird shares its name with a chess piece?

7 What is a young hare called?

8 Which seabird is traditionally thought to bring bad luck to sailors?

9 The capybara is native to which continent?

10 Threshers and hammerheads are types of what?

11 What type of creature is a devil's coach-horse?

12 Which is the largest living land mammal?

13 Which bird has long-eared, snowy and barn species?

14 A copperhead is what type of creature?

Medium

15 What is the alternative name for the viper?

16 Which spotted cat, related to the leopard, is the largest big cat in the Americas?

17 Are polar bears found in the Arctic or Antarctic?

18 Which sea mammal has bottlenose, short-beaked and spinner species?

19 A drey is home to which animal?

20 Which insect lives in an organised colony known as a formicary?

Hard

Answers to QUIZ 56 – Scotland

1	Edinburgh	11	Gretna Green
2	Caledonian	12	*Local Hero*
3	Hadrian's Wall	13	Neep
4	St Andrew	14	*Trainspotting*
5	Golf	15	Tartan
6	*Macbeth*	16	Arran
7	Aberdeen	17	5p
8	Tay	18	Fife
9	Iona	19	Murrayfield
10	Gaelic	20	Scone

1 In which room in a church are the ceremonial robes housed?

2 Who succeeded James I (James VI of Scotland) as king of England, Ireland and Scotland?

3 What term is given to the introduction of a poem or play?

4 Who captained the 2012 European Ryder Cup team?

5 What did the Fairy Godmother use to create Cinderella's coach?

6 Which name represents "C" in the radio phonetic alphabet?

7 Who played Wonder Woman in the 1970s TV series?

8 What is the study of the mind called?

9 What is another name for ascorbic acid?

10 Which 15th-century Florentine politician and writer's name is synonymous with devious ambitiousness?

11 Which peninsula lies between the Mersey and Dee estuaries?

12 King Edward is a variety of which vegetable?

13 What branch of medicine is concerned with resistance to disease?

14 Who wrote the 1970 song *Big Yellow Taxi*?

15 Which group had a hit in 1995 with *Wonderwall*?

16 In which country is the ancient city of Petra?

17 What is the location of Kubla Khan's pleasure dome in Coleridge's famous poem?

18 Who starred in the 1990 film *Home Alone*?

19 What name was given to a rioting machine-wrecker of the early 19th century?

20 What is the term for the pointed front part of a ship's bow?

Easy

Medium

Hard

Answers to QUIZ 57 – Pot Luck

1	Pride	11	Tamil and Sinhalese
2	Ore Oduba	12	Chartreuse
3	Porsche	13	Madness
4	Quiver	14	Olivier
5	Indigo	15	Talon
6	McLaren	16	On the Moon
7	Madrid	17	Imperial
8	Lord Protector	18	Onion
9	Omega	19	*Changing Rooms*
10	Nuns	20	Prestissimo

Easy

1   What type of bicycle is designed for two riders?

2   Which car manufacturer has a rampant horse for its logo?

3   In the tyre pressure measure PSI, what does the "I" stand for?

4   Which group had a hit with *Car Wash* in 1976?

5   What term is given to the cheapest accommodation on a ship?

6   Which liquid is put into car batteries?

7   Gondolas are associated with which city?

8   Which classic car caper film was remade in 2003?

9   Who wrote the novel *Trainspotting*?

10 What is the French term applied to a two-door car with a sloping rear?

Medium

11 Who directed the 1951 thriller *Strangers on a Train*?

12 How many horses pull a troika?

13 Which US city has the only cable car system to still be operated manually?

14 Who was the Scottish inventor of the pneumatic bicycle tyre?

15 What three-masted ship was used by Spanish and Portuguese traders in the 15th and 16th centuries?

16 Which company launched a rocket with a car attached to it in February 2018?

17 Who wrote the novel *Three Men in a Boat*?

18 On which famous train did Dame Agatha Christie set one of her novels?

19 Which small car was designed by Sir Alec Issigonis?

20 Queen released *Bicycle Race* as a double A-side single with which other song?

Hard

1   What is the common name for the obverse of a coin?

2   Traditionally drunk at Christmas, what is the drink of yolk, beer and spirit?

3   What is the usual background colour of motorway signs?

4   What is held in a creel?

5   A blast furnace is mainly used to produce which metal?

6   Who won the Wimbledon men's singles title in 1975?

7   What is the principal religion of Iran?

8   Who wrote the 2001 novel *Life of Pi*?

9   Which town is the capital of the Isle of Man?

10 What nationality was psychologist Carl Jung?

11 The postcode prefix LS denotes which English city?

12 Which actor topped the charts in 1997 with *Men In Black*?

13 What machine is used for turning and shaping wood?

14 In which county is the beauty spot of Box Hill?

15 Which animal is said to be unable to change its spots?

16 Nichelle Nichols played which *Star Trek* lieutenant?

17 What, in law, is written defamation of character?

18 Which part of the body was Achilles' weakness?

19 On which London road would you find the Royal Courts of Justice?

20 Which group won *The X Factor* in 2011?

Easy

Medium

Hard

Answers to QUIZ 59 – Pot Luck

1	Vestry	11	Wirral
2	Charles I	12	Potato
3	Prologue	13	Immunology
4	José Maria Olazabal	14	Joni Mitchell
5	Pumpkin	15	Oasis
6	Charlie	16	Jordan
7	Lynda Carter	17	Xanadu
8	Psychology	18	Macaulay Culkin
9	Vitamin C	19	Luddite
10	Machiavelli	20	Prow

Easy

1 What did Jack plaster his head with after falling down the hill?

2 Where was the cow in the rhyme *Little Boy Blue*?

3 How many full bags of wool did the black sheep have?

4 Where was Doctor Foster when he stepped in a puddle?

5 What colour was Mary's lamb's fleece?

6 Was it Jack Sprat or his wife who could eat no lean?

7 Where was the queen eating bread and honey in *Sing a Song of Sixpence*?

8 What did Little Tommy Tucker have to sing for?

9 Where had the pussy cat been to see the Queen?

10 What did Little Jack Horner find in his Christmas pie?

Medium

11 In the rhyme *Hey Diddle Diddle*, what did the dish run away with?

12 Who was the third man in the tub with the butcher and the candlestick maker?

13 Who pulled the pussy out of the well after Little Johnny Green had put her in there?

14 Where did Bobby Shaftoe wear his silver buckles?

15 Who sat on a wall and had a great fall?

16 Which creature was climbing up the spout?

17 How much did Johnny earn a day in *Seesaw Margery Daw*?

18 Who took the kettle off after Polly put it on?

19 Which two creatures were fighting for the crown all around the town?

20 Who found Lucy Locket's pocket?

Hard

Answers to QUIZ 60 – Transport

1	Tandem	11	Sir Alfred Hitchcock
2	Ferrari	12	Three
3	Inch	13	San Francisco
4	Rose Royce	14	John Dunlop
5	Steerage	15	Galleon
6	Distilled water	16	SpaceX
7	Venice	17	Jerome K Jerome
8	*The Italian Job*	18	The *Orient Express*
9	Irvine Welsh	19	Mini
10	Coupé	20	*Fat Bottomed Girls*

1   The character of Mrs Robinson appears in which 1967 film?

2   How many lines are there on a stave of music?

3   What is the common name for a turf accountant?

4   Who had a hit in 1973 with *Paper Roses*?

5   What was the fabled city of gold sought by Spanish conquistadors?

6   A champagne bottle which has the capacity of two ordinary bottles is given what name?

7   What type of business is London's Lombard Street most associated with?

8   Which brand of yeast and vegetable extract takes its name from a French metal cooking pot?

9   *The Music of the Night* is a song from which musical?

10 Which adjective describes energy created by atomic fission?

11 What term was applied to lively, fashionable young women of the 1920s?

12 In what county is Stonehenge located?

13 What is the name of the Washington headquarters of the US armed forces?

14 What term is given to a flower that blooms year after year?

15 In which 1960s TV series did Patrick McGoohan play "Number Six"?

16 Which imperial length measurement is equivalent to three feet?

17 What was the Irish currency unit before the euro?

18 In which Scandinavian country is the city of Uppsala located?

19 The Tower of London is an example of which style of architecture?

20 What letter is furthest to the right on the bottom row on a standard keyboard?

Easy

Medium

Hard

Answers to QUIZ 61 – Pot Luck

1	Heads	11	Leeds
2	Eggnog	12	Will Smith
3	Blue	13	Lathe
4	Fish	14	Surrey
5	Iron	15	Leopard
6	Arthur Ashe	16	Uhura
7	Islam (Shia)	17	Libel
8	Yann Martel	18	His heel
9	Douglas	19	The Strand
10	Swiss	20	Little Mix

1   Which is the third planet from the Sun?

2   Who was Henry VIII's third wife?

3   Which is China's principal river and the third longest river in the world?

4   In a medley race, which is the third of the four swimming styles?

5   Which is Spain's third largest city?

6   The book and screenplay *The Third Man* was written by which English author?

7   Who won a third term as US President in 1940?

8   Which is the third largest of the Channel Islands?

9   Who wrote the third of the New Testament gospels?

10 Who starred in the 1977 film *Close Encounters of the Third Kind*?

11 What is the third-highest rank in the peerage?

12 Third place in an Olympic event is awarded which colour medal?

13 What is the third letter of the Greek alphabet?

14 What does the acronym U3A stand for?

15 What is Italy's third largest lake?

16 Which is the third novel in the *Lord of the Rings* series?

17 What is the third sign of the zodiac?

18 Which is the third largest of the Balearic Islands?

19 In the nativity story, which third Wise Man accompanied Caspar and Melchior?

20 Which is the third largest US state, by land area?

Answers to QUIZ 62 – Nursery Rhymes

1	Vinegar and brown paper	11	The spoon
2	In the corn	12	The baker
3	Three	13	Little Johnny Stout
4	Gloucester	14	At his knee
5	White as snow	15	Humpty Dumpty
6	His wife	16	Itsy Bitsy Spider
7	Parlour	17	A penny
8	His supper	18	Sukey
9	London	19	The lion and the unicorn
10	A plum	20	Kitty Fisher

1   Which prison reformer was depicted on the Bank of England £5 note from 2002 to 2017?

2   The island of Key West is in which US state?

3   What is the name of the marshy area of East Anglia?

4   Which living ingredient makes bread rise?

5   Michelangelo's statue of David is in which Italian city?

6   Which acid is found in milk?

7   Which animal has species called Bewick's, whooper and mute?

8   What is the name of the double-dot mark used to modify a vowel in German?

9   Who played President Bartlet in the TV series *The West Wing*?

10 The 2008 Olympic Games were held in which country?

11 A golden anniversary celebrates how many years of marriage?

12 Which actress starred in the 1990 film *Misery*?

13 What term is given to substances in the periodic table?

14 Who won the first series of *Pop Idol*?

15 What name was given to a woman doing farm work to support the war effort during WWII?

16 What is a whist competition or tournament called?

17 In which county is Folkestone?

18 What was the name of Henry VIII's elder daughter?

19 Which children's TV series featured a lion called Parsley and an owl called Sage?

20 Which prefix means "to a factor of one million"?

Answers to QUIZ 63 – Pot Luck

1	*The Graduate*	11	Flappers
2	Five	12	Wiltshire
3	A bookmaker	13	Pentagon
4	Marie Osmond	14	Perennial
5	El Dorado	15	*The Prisoner*
6	Magnum	16	Yard
7	Finance	17	The punt
8	Marmite®	18	Sweden
9	*The Phantom of the Opera*	19	Norman
10	Nuclear	20	M

Easy

1 Which planet is closest to the Sun?

2 "The Swan" is the common name for which constellation?

3 What term is given to an interstellar cloud of dust and gas?

4 Which heavenly body was "demoted" from planet status in 2006?

5 What phenomenon occurs when the Moon passes between the Sun and the Earth?

6 In which county is the Jodrell Bank Observatory?

7 What term is given to the second-brightest star in a constellation?

8 A shooting star can also be referred to as what one-word term?

9 What is the name of Earth's galaxy?

10 Which word for the universe is also the name of a garden flower?

Medium

11 What word means "bear" in major and minor constellations?

12 What is the point in the heavens opposite the zenith?

13 Which type of star emits regular bursts of radio waves?

14 What name is given to a field of extremely strong gravitational pull in space?

15 What is another name for the North Star or Pole Star?

16 Hale-Bopp is an example of which heavenly phenomenon?

17 The space telescope launched in 1990 was named after which astronomer?

18 Which constellation forms a W-shape in the sky?

19 What term is given to the small celestial bodies between the orbits of Mars and Jupiter?

20 Which constellation's name is Latin for "crab"?

Hard

Answers to QUIZ 64 – Third Place

1	Earth	11	Earl
2	Jane Seymour	12	Bronze
3	Yangtze	13	Gamma
4	Breaststroke	14	University of the Third Age
5	Valencia	15	Como
6	Graham Greene	16	*The Return of the King*
7	Franklin D Roosevelt	17	Gemini
8	Alderney	18	Ibiza
9	Luke	19	Balthazar
10	Richard Dreyfuss	20	California

1　How many days did it take to tour the world in the title of the Jules Verne novel?

2　What was the surname of the father and daughter who appeared in the film *On Golden Pond*?

3　What is the next highest prime number above 13?

4　What is the surname of the police chief in *The Simpsons*?

5　What is the name of the chapel at Windsor Castle?

6　What name is given to a group of eight musicians?

7　What is a young horse called?

8　In the Beatles song, what is the name of the meter maid?

9　What is the capital of Saudi Arabia?

10　Which nut is obtained from the hickory tree?

11　Who won Olympic gold medals in the decathlon in 1980 and 1984?

12　What is the trunk of the human body called?

13　"I've been alone with you inside my mind" is the opening lyric from which song?

14　In the context of education, where is the UEA located?

15　What condition does pluvius insurance cover?

16　Which city of South Wales is known locally as Abertawe?

17　Which condiment contains cauliflower, onion and gherkin, seasoned with mustard and turmeric?

18　Which fairy-tale character, locked in a tower by a witch, lets down her long golden hair?

19　What is used to make the soles of espadrilles?

20　Who co-starred with Tom Hanks in *Sleepless in Seattle*?

Answers to QUIZ 65 – Pot Luck

1	Elizabeth Fry	11	50
2	Florida	12	Kathy Bates
3	Fens	13	Elements
4	Yeast	14	Will Young
5	Florence	15	Land girl
6	Lactic	16	(Whist) Drive
7	Swan	17	Kent
8	Umlaut	18	Mary
9	Martin Sheen	19	*The Herbs*
10	China	20	Mega

Easy

Medium

Hard

ANSWERS ON PAGE 70

Easy

1   Which 2013-16 series, starring Jeremy Piven, followed the life of a famous retailer?

2   Who played the title role in the series *Foyle's War*?

3   Which Tolstoy novel was adapted for TV in 2016 and starred James Norton?

4   Which US series set in South Dakota starred Ian McShane as Al Swearengen?

5   Which 1970s costume drama, set in Eaton Square, was revived in 2010?

6   What is the name of the convent in *Call the Midwife*?

7   Which series was named after the home belonging to the Crawley family?

8   Jonathan Rhys Meyers starred as which monarch in the 2007-10 series *The Tudors*?

9   Who played Charles Ryder in the 1981 adaptation of *Brideshead Revisited*?

10 What was The Halcyon in the 2017 ITV drama series?

11 Which series was set in the fictional village of Aidensfield?

12 Which 1970s drama series about the Roman Empire starred Derek Jacobi in the title role?

13 Who originally played Robin of Loxley in the 1980s series *Robin of Sherwood*?

14 Damian Lewis played Major Richard Winters in which WWII drama series?

15 The BBC series *The Hollow Crown* are adaptations of which playwright?

Medium

16 Sir Mark Rylance played which historical figure in the series *Wolf Hall*?

17 Which drama series, revived in 2015, is based on the novels by Winston Graham?

18 What is the title of the Netflix drama series about Elizabeth II?

19 Who played Athos in the 2014 TV series *The Musketeers*?

20 Which *The X-Files* actress appeared in the BBC 2005 adaptation of *Bleak House*?

Hard

1 Which Pacific state dropped "Western" from its name in 1997?

2 Which jubilee did Queen Elizabeth II celebrate in February 2017?

3 What is the capital of Iraq?

4 What was the surname of Shakespeare's wife?

5 What term is given to prayer cushions for kneeling on?

6 What is four score and ten?

7 What name is given to copies of a book published at one time?

8 On the original version of the quiz show *Fifteen to One*, who asked the questions?

9 Which bread roll of Jewish origin is in the shape of a ring?

10 Which style of architecture is epitomised by Bath's Royal Crescent?

11 What is the main alcoholic ingredient of a Pink Lady cocktail?

12 Which Native American chief was the subject of a Longfellow poem?

13 Which spicy peanut sauce is a feature of Asian cuisine?

14 In which European country is the Black Forest?

15 Which light wood is much used in model-making?

16 Which theatre term indicates movement away from the audience?

17 What is the opposite of "yin" in Chinese philosophy?

18 The town of Dunstable is in which county?

19 What kind of bet puts money on a horse finishing in the first three places?

20 Which Somerset town, legendary burial place of King Arthur, is famous for its music festival?

Easy

Medium

Hard

Answers to QUIZ 67 – Pot Luck

1	80	11	Daley Thompson
2	Fonda (Henry and Jane)	12	Torso
3	17	13	*Hello* (Lionel Richie)
4	Wiggum	14	Norwich (University of East Anglia)
5	St George's	15	Rain
6	Octet	16	Swansea
7	Foal	17	Piccalilli
8	Rita	18	Rapunzel
9	Riyadh	19	Rope
10	Pecan	20	Meg Ryan

Easy

1   Which chemical element is also known as quicksilver?

2   Boz was a pen-name of which famous author?

3   What is the stage name of singer Alecia Moore?

4   Which African mammal is also known as the antbear?

5   How is the building at London's 30 St Mary Axe commonly known?

6   Pontoon, twenty-one and vingt-et-un are alternative names for which card game?

7   What is the official name for an Oscar?

8   Who is the comic-strip alter ego of Peter Parker?

9   Acton, Currer and Ellis Bell were the pen names of which sisters?

10 What plant is also known as the Michaelmas daisy?

11 What name was used by the unspeaking Marx brother whose birth name was Adolph?

12 The Granta is another name for which East Anglian river?

13 What is the Indian term for a vegetable also known as "ladies' fingers" and "okra"?

14 Which breed of dog is also known as the German shepherd?

Medium

15 How were Graeme Garden, Bill Oddie and Tim Brooke-Taylor collectively known?

16 In which city is Storkyrkan, officially named Sankt Nicolai kyrka?

17 Which musician's real name is Vincent Furnier?

18 What was the real name of writer George Orwell?

19 Which American wild cat is also known as a cougar or mountain lion?

20 Which British city has the nickname "Auld Reekie"?

Hard

Answers to QUIZ 68 – Television Costume Drama

1	Mr Selfridge	11	Heartbeat
2	Michael Kitchen	12	I, Claudius
3	War and Peace	13	Michael Praed
4	Deadwood	14	Band of Brothers
5	Upstairs, Downstairs	15	William Shakespeare
6	Nonnatus House	16	Thomas Cromwell
7	Downton Abbey	17	Poldark
8	Henry VIII	18	The Crown
9	Jeremy Irons	19	Tom Burke
10	A hotel	20	Gillian Anderson

1   Liverpool and Birkenhead are linked by which tunnel?

2   Which word means both a fencing sword and a thin metal sheet?

3   What was Elvis Presley's middle name?

4   Who played the title role in the 1970s children's TV series *Catweazle*?

5   Chilli was originally native to which country?

6   What name is given to an official with the power to evict people from their houses?

7   Who wrote the nonsense poem *The Hunting of the Snark*?

8   The *Back to the Future* films starred which actor as Marty McFly?

9   How many sheets of paper are there in a ream?

10   Ni is the chemical symbol for which element?

11   Which French president succeeded Jacques Chirac?

12   Which actor starred in the 1955 thriller *To Catch A Thief*?

13   What is the name of the game that Americans call tic-tac-toe?

14   In which year did Kate Bush have a no.1 hit with *Wuthering Heights*?

15   What does the letter "O" stand for in the phrase "SWOT analysis"?

16   Sauchiehall Street is in which city?

17   Which spoof soap included the character of Mrs Overall?

18   The remote and uninhabited interior of Australia is given what name?

19   What term is given for the standard score for each golf hole and for the entire course?

20   What type of animal is a Tamworth?

Easy

Medium

Hard

Answers to QUIZ 69 – Pot Luck

1	Samoa	11	Gin
2	Sapphire (65 years)	12	Hiawatha
3	Baghdad	13	Satay
4	Hathaway	14	Germany
5	Hassocks	15	Balsa
6	90	16	Upstage
7	Edition	17	Yang
8	William G Stewart	18	Bedfordshire
9	Bagel	19	Each-way
10	Georgian	20	Glastonbury

Easy

1 Which American national holiday is celebrated in late November?

2 The Up Helly Aa festival is held in which group of islands?

3 What name is given to the Hindu Festival of Lights?

4 The Eisteddfod festival takes place in which country?

5 What is the Jewish candelabrum traditionally used during Hanukkah?

6 Which Christian feast is celebrated on January 6?

7 ANZAC Day is marked by which two countries?

8 The Day of the Dead festival is celebrated in which country?

9 What religious festival is celebrated ten days before Yom Kippur?

10 St Patrick's Day is celebrated in which month?

11 Which Chinese Year started in February 2018?

12 In the Christian church, what is the period before Christmas called?

13 Which Scottish celebration takes place on January 25?

14 What is the Shrove Tuesday festival in New Orleans called...?

Medium

15 ...and what does its name mean in English?

16 What term is given to the seven days before Easter in the Christian church?

17 What name is All Hallows Eve more commonly known as?

18 At what age does a bar mitzvah usually take place?

19 Which Muslim festival marks the end of Ramadan?

20 Which saint's feast day is celebrated on December 26?

Hard

1   What was the first name of English composer Vaughan Williams?

2   Palaeontology is the study of which objects?

3   Which measurement of distance is the equivalent of 1.61 kilometres?

4   Who was Stan Laurel's comedy-film partner?

5   Which decade saw the imposition of the three-day week in the UK to conserve fuel supplies?

6   Daventry is in which county?

7   What is the official language of Brazil?

8   Which Indonesian holiday island lies off the eastern tip of Java?

9   According to the proverb, what comes before a fall?

10 Which critically panned 2003 film starred Ben Affleck and Jennifer Lopez?

11 What do the initials "REM" stand for in relation to sleep?

12 The musical *Chess* was written by Sir Tim Rice along with two members of which group?

13 What is the chief city of Majorca?

14 The character of Mrs Merton was created by which actress?

15 "The backbone of England" describes which range of hills?

16 Who wrote the book *The Snowman* (1987)?

17 What is the first name of TV's Grampa Simpson?

18 Which old entertainment company had a large gong as its company logo?

19 How many years of marriage are celebrated at a ruby wedding anniversary?

20 Merlot grapes produce what colour wine?

Easy

Medium

Hard

Answers to QUIZ 71 – Pot Luck

1	The Mersey Tunnel	11	Nicolas Sarkozy
2	Foil	12	Cary Grant
3	Aaron	13	Noughts and crosses
4	Geoffrey Bayldon	14	1978
5	Mexico	15	Opportunities
6	Bailiff	16	Glasgow
7	Lewis Carroll	17	*Acorn Antiques*
8	Michael J Fox	18	Outback
9	500	19	Par
10	Nickel	20	A pig

ANSWERS ON PAGE 76

Easy

1 Which Hogwarts Minister did Robert Hardy play in the films?

2 Who is Harry's corpulent cousin...?

3 ...and what are the names of that cousin's parents?

4 What is the name of Harry's owl?

5 Harry's wand is made from which wood?

6 What is Hermione's surname?

7 What did Harry get for Christmas in his first term at Hogwarts?

8 How many players are on each team in a game of Quidditch?

9 Professor McGonagall was played by which actress in the films?

10 What was "*Philosopher's*" changed to in the title of the US version of the first book?

11 What is the first name of Hogwarts headmaster Mr Dumbledore?

12 What is a person from a non-magical family called?

13 Where do students eat their dinner at Hogwarts?

14 What is the first name of Harry's creator?

15 What model was Harry's first broomstick?

16 The fourth book in the series has what subtitle?

17 Which English castle was used as Hogwarts in the films?

18 Which play, set 19 years later than the books, premiered in London in 2016?

19 The Leaky Cauldron is what type of building?

20 Who played Sirius Black in the films?

Answers to QUIZ 72 – Notable Occasions

1	Thanksgiving	11	Dog
2	The Shetland Islands	12	Advent
3	Diwali	13	Burns Night
4	Wales	14	Mardi Gras
5	Menorah	15	Fat Tuesday
6	Epiphany	16	Holy Week
7	Australia and New Zealand	17	Hallowe'en
8	Mexico	18	13
9	Jewish New Year	19	Eid
10	March (17th)	20	Stephen

1 What is the name of Goneril and Cordelia's sister in Shakespeare's *King Lear*?

2 What is a series of games that makes up part of a tennis match called?

3 Which US watercourse is nicknamed "Ol' Man River"?

4 What term is given to a military unit headed by a colonel?

5 *Casa di Giulietta* and its balcony are a feature of which Italian city?

6 For which 1985 James Bond film did Duran Duran provide the theme tune?

7 What term applies to someone who doesn't eat or use animal products?

8 In music, how should a piece marked "largo" be played?

9 Who is Betty's husband in *The Flintstones*?

10 Chocolate, ginger and pineapple are varieties of which culinary herb?

11 What is the Spanish title for a married woman?

12 By what name is the larva of a butterfly or moth known?

13 Who starred as Joy Adamson in the 1966 film *Born Free*?

14 In the Bible, who was the second son of Adam and Eve?

15 What is an ancient Celtic priest known as?

16 What sort of creature is a merganser?

17 Which group was fronted by Frankie Valli?

18 Warwickshire County Cricket Club has which ground as its home?

19 What is the name of the royal residence on the River Dee in Scotland?

20 What kind of musical instrument is a tom-tom?

Easy

Medium

Hard

---

1 What does DRS stand for?

2 What driver safety measure was introduced in 2018?

3 Former team owner Eddie Jordan became a presenter on which motoring series in 2016?

4 Which country hosted the first race of the 2018 season?

5 What is the governing body of Formula 1?

6 Which former driver turned commentator is famous for his pre-race grid walk?

7 Who became team principal of Mercedes in 2013?

8 Nico Rosberg represented Germany, but which country did his father Keke drive for?

9 What is the name of Red Bull's junior team?

10 Which European principality first hosted its street circuit Grand Prix in 1929?

11 Who won the World Championship every year from 2010 to 2013?

12 A green flag being shown indicates what to the drivers?

13 What relation was Ayrton Senna to former F1 driver Bruno Senna?

14 At which track has the British Grand Prix been held since 1987?

15 In the 2016 season who became the youngest ever winner of an F1 race...?

16 ...and what is his nationality?

17 Which car number is associated with Lewis Hamilton?

18 What nationality is former World Champion Fernando Alonso?

19 Which company has been the sole supplier of tyres to F1 since 2011?

20 The 2009 World Championship was won by which British driver?

Answers to QUIZ 74 – Harry Potter

1	Cornelius Fudge	11	Albus
2	Dudley Dursley	12	Muggle
3	Vernon and Petunia	13	The Great Hall
4	Hedwig	14	Joanne
5	Holly	15	Nimbus 2000
6	Granger	16	The Goblet of Fire
7	An invisibility cloak	17	Alnwick
8	Seven	18	Harry Potter and the Cursed Child
9	Dame Maggie Smith	19	A pub
10	Sorcerer's	20	Gary Oldman

1   The rear inner surface of the eye has what name?

2   What is the Spanish equivalent of champagne?

3   What is the name of the Californian river which flows into a desert of the same name?

4   Which of Disney's dwarfs is known for his shyness?

5   From which city does Neapolitan ice cream originate?

6   What was the title of the 1982 chart-topping single by Renée and Renato?

7   What name is given to one of the original inhabitants of Australia?

8   The 1988 Summer Olympics were staged in which Asian city?

9   In which National Park would you find Buckler's Hard and Lymington?

10 What is the US term for a curriculum vitae?

11 Which assembled group recorded the 1984 charity song *Do They Know It's Christmas*??

12 The name of which sheltering device is the Italian for "little shade"?

13 For what is the Victoria Cross awarded, as inscribed on the medal itself?

14 How many players are there in a rugby league team?

15 Which private was played by John Laurie in the original TV series of *Dad's Army*?

16 What number is represented by the Roman numerals IX?

17 Which salad is made from apple, celery, walnuts and mayonnaise?

18 What is the ancient citadel of Athens called?

19 In which country was the actor Richard Burton born?

20 Which Disney elephant learned to fly using his huge ears?

Easy

Medium

Hard

Answers to QUIZ 75 – Pot Luck

1	Regan	11	Señora
2	A set	12	Caterpillar
3	Mississippi	13	Virginia McKenna
4	Regiment	14	Abel
5	Verona	15	Druid
6	*A View to a Kill*	16	A duck
7	Vegan	17	The Four Seasons
8	Very slowly	18	Edgbaston
9	Barney (Rubble)	19	Balmoral
10	Mint	20	Drum

QUIZ 78 – Organisations

ANSWERS ON PAGE 80

1 Where was the Open University founded?

2 What are the initials of the UK professional doctors' organisation?

3 J Edgar Hoover once headed which crime-fighting agency?

4 Who was the General Secretary of the TUC from 1973 to 1984?

5 Wisley gardens in Surrey are owned by which organisation?

6 Who was appointed Managing Director of the International Monetary Fund in 2011?

7 Which conservation organisation has oak leaves as its symbol?

8 In which year was the United Nations formed?

9 What do the initials RAC stand for in a motoring context?

10 Which agency is responsible for World Heritage Sites?

11 Which branch of the Red Cross operates in Muslim countries?

12 The film *Calendar Girls* featured which organisation?

13 What name is given to a member of the Society of Friends?

14 What is the name of the British actors' union?

15 Which voluntary organisation features in the TV series *Saving Lives at Sea*?

16 "Nation shall speak peace unto nation" is the motto of which organisation?

17 What does the "T" of NATO stand for?

18 What is the symbol of the World Wide Fund for Nature?

19 The Lodge, Sandy, Bedfordshire is the headquarters of which conservation charity?

20 The General Synod is the governing body of which organisation?

Answers to QUIZ 76 – Formula 1

1	Drag Reduction System	11	Sebastian Vettel
2	Halo	12	Track clear
3	*Top Gear*	13	Uncle
4	Australia	14	Silverstone
5	FIA	15	Max Verstappen
6	Martin Brundle	16	Dutch
7	Toto Wolff	17	44
8	Finland	18	Spanish
9	Toro Rosso	19	Pirelli
10	Monaco	20	Jenson Button

1   What was the name of Stacey's best friend in the TV series *Gavin & Stacey*?

2   What is a seven-part ensemble called?

3   Grave, acute and circumflex are examples of what?

4   What is the main ingredient of tahini?

5   Which river flows through Worcester?

6   Who had a hit in 1978 with *Copacabana*?

7   Scottish warlord Robert MacGregor had what nickname?

8   Which meringue-based dessert was named after a Russian ballerina?

9   What category of road signs are triangular with a red border?

10   In song, what do you pack up in your old kit bag?

11   What term is used for an American pharmacy dispenser?

12   In which county is Leamington Spa?

13   Which Scottish city gives its name to a variety of fruit cake?

14   Wookey Hole in Somerset is famous for what natural features?

15   Which 2003 Christmas comedy starred Will Ferrell?

16   What term is given to the use of needles to relieve pain?

17   What is the young of the eel called?

18   The single postcode letter B is used for which English city?

19   Who wrote *A Room with a View* (1908)?

20   For what is London's Billingsgate Market famous?

Answers to QUIZ 77 – Pot Luck

1	Retina	11	Band Aid
2	Cava	12	Umbrella
3	Mojave	13	Valour
4	Bashful	14	13
5	Naples	15	Private Frazer
6	*Save Your Love*	16	Nine
7	Aborigine	17	Waldorf
8	Scoul	18	Acropolis
9	The New Forest	19	Wales
10	Résumé	20	Dumbo

QUIZ 80 – Video Games ANSWERS ON PAGE **82**

Easy

1   Which Nintendo® hedgehog is capable of running at tremendous speeds?

2   Which popular free-to-play location-based augmented reality game was released on July 6, 2016?

3   Who is the Nintendo® gorilla who was originally conceived as an enemy of Mario?

4   What is the name of the star of the *Tomb Raider* games...?

5   ...and who portrayed her on screen in 2001 and 2003?

6   In which 2011 game does play focus on the breaking and placing of blocks?

7   What is the title of the 2D table tennis sports game first released in 1972 as an arcade game?

8   Who is Mario's younger brother, often dressed in a green shirt?

9   Microsoft®'s gaming brand has what name?

10   What is the title of the falling-block matching puzzle game first released in 1984?

11   In which year did Nintendo® release the Wii™?

12   In which 1978 game does the player defend the world from aliens?

13   In which game does the player navigate a maze while avoiding ghosts and eating dots?

14   In which year was the Nintendo® Game Boy™ released in Europe?

15   Who starred in the 2010 film adaptation of *Prince of Persia: The Sands of Time*?

16   In which 1985 game does the player attempting to make deliveries from a bicycle along a suburban street?

17   Which popular warfare game was first released for Microsoft® Windows in 2003?

18   Released in 1981, which arcade video game involves directing amphibians to their homes?

19   Which 2012 animated film featured a game character who wanted to become a hero?

20   What is the name of the video gaming brand created and owned by Sony?

Medium

Hard

Answers to QUIZ 78 – Organisations

1	Milton Keynes	11	Red Crescent
2	BMA	12	The Women's Institute
3	FBI	13	Quaker
4	Len Murray	14	Equity
5	The Royal Horticultural Society	15	RNLI
6	Christine Lagarde	16	BBC
7	The National Trust	17	Treaty
8	1945	18	Giant panda
9	Royal Automobile Club	19	RSPB
10	UNESCO	20	The Church of England

1 Which French term means "in a group, all together"?

2 Which Welsh resort lies between Prestatyn and Colwyn Bay?

3 Collectively, what term is applied to geese on land?

4 *Rolling in the Deep* was a 2010 hit for which singer?

5 What is the name of the volcano which is the highest point of Japan?

6 What ingredients give a quiche Lorraine its flavour?

7 Which animated character lives on Mossy Bottom Farm?

8 In 1909, Louis Blériot became the first person to fly over which body of water?

9 What is the capital city of Lebanon?

10 What is the focal point of an earthquake?

11 Which is India's most sacred river?

12 Campanology is more commonly known by what name?

13 Which actor starred, alongside Paul McGann, in the 1987 film *Withnail & I*?

14 What is fermented to make the Japanese drink sake?

15 *Every Breath You Take* was a chart-topper for The Police in which year?

16 Which wide-angled lens used in photography has a curved front?

17 In linguistics, what is the name given to a describing word?

18 Which fortified wine takes its name from the Spanish town of Jerez?

19 Vince Clarke and Andy Bell formed which pop duo?

20 Which golfer won The Masters in 2017?

Answers to QUIZ 79 – Pot Luck

1	Nessa	11	Druggist
2	Septet	12	Warwickshire
3	Accents	13	Dundee
4	Sesame seeds	14	Caves
5	Severn	15	*Elf*
6	Barry Manilow	16	Acupuncture
7	Rob Roy	17	Elver
8	Pavlova	18	Birmingham
9	Warning signs	19	EM Forster
10	Your troubles	20	Fish

Easy

Medium

Hard

Easy

1 What is the highest mountain in Great Britain?

2 Which mountain was carved with the faces of four US presidents?

3 Table Mountain overlooks which city?

4 Which mountains form the backbone of South America?

5 France and Spain are divided by which range?

6 What is the name of the active volcano that stands above the Bay of Naples?

7 What is the second highest mountain in the world?

8 Who was with Sir Edmund Hillary when he reached the summit of Everest in 1953?

9 On which mountain is it said that Noah's Ark came to rest?

10 In which European country is Mount Olympus?

11 On which continent are the Atlas Mountains?

Medium

12 What term is given to a Scottish mountain that is over 3,000 feet high?

13 Which mountain range is known as "the backbone of Italy"?

14 The Columbia Icefield is in which range of mountains?

15 Where is Olympus Mons, the highest mountain in our Solar System?

16 Which continent is separated from Europe by the Ural mountains?

17 What is the highest mountain in England?

18 The longest mountain range in the world is beneath which ocean?

19 Where is Mauna Kea?

20 In which range would you find the highest 14 mountains in the world?

Hard

Answers to QUIZ 80 – Video Games

1	Sonic	11	2006
2	Pokémon™ Go	12	Space Invaders
3	Donkey Kong	13	Pac-Man™
4	Lara Croft	14	1990
5	Angelina Jolie	15	Jake Gyllenhaal
6	Minecraft	16	Paperboy
7	Pong	17	Call of Duty
8	Luigi	18	Frogger
9	Xbox	19	Wreck-it-Ralph
10	Tetris®	20	PlayStation®

1   What are Canterbury bells?

2   What is the everyday term for the tibia?

3   According to the song title, in which London square is a nightingale said to sing?

4   Who is Jack Worthing's alter ego in a famous Oscar Wilde comedy?

5   An Australian rugby union player is given the nickname of which marsupial?

6   On which continent would you find the country of Lesotho?

7   Which fairy-tale character pricked her finger on a spindle?

8   Which is the largest of Italy's lakes?

9   What is Latin for "and the rest"?

10 Which archaeological period followed the predominance of bronze?

11 Who starred in the film *Gandhi*?

12 What type of creature is a wrasse?

13 What is the title of dignity in Portugal and Brazil?

14 In ice hockey what shape is a puck?

15 Who founded the Boy Scouts?

16 Who had a 1984 hit with *I Feel For You*?

17 Of which Scottish island is Portree the largest town?

18 What is an irrational fear of open places called?

19 What nickname is given to the southern states of the USA?

20 From which biblical paradise were Adam and Eve expelled?

Easy

Medium

Hard

Answers to QUIZ 81 – Pot Luck

1	En masse	11	The Ganges
2	Rhyl	12	Bell-ringing
3	Gaggle	13	Richard E Grant
4	Adele	14	Rice
5	Fuji	15	1983
6	Cheese and bacon	16	Fisheye
7	Shaun the Sheep	17	Adjective
8	English Channel	18	Sherry
9	Beirut	19	Erasure
10	Epicentre	20	Sergio García

QUIZ 84 – The Romans

ANSWERS ON PAGE **86**

1 Which British queen and leader of the Iceni led a revolt against the Romans?

2 What is the name of the large ancient amphitheatre in Rome?

3 In which county is the Roman fort of Housesteads?

4 Which number is represented by "L" in Roman numerals?

5 Vulcan was the god of which element?

6 What name was given to the 15th of certain months in the Roman calendar?

7 The character of Maximus was played by which actor in the 2000 film *Gladiator*?

8 A Roman mansion was known by what general name?

9 What general name was given to the oar-propelled boat used by the ancient Romans?

10 What was the Roman name for the Iberian peninsula?

11 What decorative feature was often seen on the floors of Roman houses?

12 The Roman remains at Chedworth are in which county?

13 Who played the title role in the 1960 film *Spartacus*?

14 What was the Roman name for Ireland?

15 Who was emperor when fire destroyed half of Rome in AD 64?

16 Which poet wrote *Metamorphoses*?

17 In a Roman bathhouse was the *caldarium* a hot or cold bath?

18 What name was given to a square where business and political matters were discussed?

19 Which English city was called Deva in Roman times?

20 What title was given to Roman emperors?

Answers to QUIZ 82 – Mountains

1	Ben Nevis	11	Africa
2	Mount Rushmore	12	A Munro
3	Cape Town, South Africa	13	Apennines
4	The Andes	14	Rockies
5	The Pyrenees	15	Mars
6	Vesuvius	16	Asia
7	K2 (also called Mount Godwin-Austen)	17	Scafell Pike
8	Sherpa Tensing Norgay	18	Atlantic Ocean
9	Mount Ararat	19	Hawaii
10	Greece	20	The Himalayas

ANSWERS ON PAGE 87

1   How many players are there in a netball team?

2   What is the capital of Northern Ireland?

3   Which French word is used for a large creamy layered cake?

4   The Space Needle is a landmark in which US city?

5   How many pockets does a snooker table have?

6   What is the leader of a Cub pack called?

7   In *The Avengers* series of films who plays Tony Stark?

8   Which type of sweet is a rose-flavoured jelly coated with icing sugar?

9   What word is used to describe an inactive volcano?

10 In a military context, what does the "A" of SAS stand for?

11 What is the name of the New York stock exchange?

12 Which islands off Cornwall include St Mary's and St Martin's?

13 *Private Life* and *Slave to the Rhythm* were hits for which actress and singer?

14 What is the second book of the Old Testament?

15 What is the North American term for a saloon car?

16 The Bantu language is spoken on which continent?

17 Who duetted with Meat Loaf on the single *Dead Ringer for Love*?

18 Which word meaning "to strike noisily" is also the location of Ireland West Airport?

19 Which word follows *Titus* in the title of a Shakespeare play set in Rome?

20 Inhabitants of Manchester are known by what name?

Easy

Medium

Hard

Answers to QUIZ 83 – Pot Luck

1	Flowers	11	Sir Ben Kingsley
2	Shin bone	12	A fish
3	Berkeley	13	Dom
4	Ernest	14	Circular
5	Wallaby	15	Lord Robert Baden-Powell
6	Africa	16	Chaka Khan
7	Sleeping Beauty	17	Skye
8	Garda	18	Agoraphobia
9	*Et cetera*	19	Dixie
10	The Iron Age	20	The Garden of Eden

Easy

1   Which North Yorkshire fishing port is associated with Dracula?

2   Anna Sewell created which fictional horse?

3   Who wrote *The Mill on the Floss* (1860)?

4   Mr Bumble in *Oliver Twist* holds which parish position?

5   Who wrote the 1954 novel *Lucky Jim*?

6   Which character in *The Wind in the Willows* was obsessed with motor cars?

7   Alice's pet cat has what name in *Alice's Adventures in Wonderland* (1865)?

8   Who wrote *The Tenant of Wildfell Hall* (1848)?

9   What is the surname of Atticus, hero of *To Kill a Mockingbird* (1960)?

10   What is the title of the only novel written by Oscar Wilde?

11   Which American historical event provides the backdrop to *Gone with the Wind*?

12   Who is the main character in *The Pilgrim's Progress* (1678)?

13   What is the name of the youngest Bennet sister in Jane Austen's *Pride and Prejudice*?

14   How many steps are there in the title of the 1915 adventure book and film?

Medium

15   Who is the heroine of *Vanity Fair* (1847)?

16   In the Robert Louis Stevenson novel, what was the name of Henry Jekyll's alter ego?

17   Who wrote the novel *Ivanhoe* (1820)?

18   What is the first name of F Scott Fitzgerald's character Gatsby?

19   What was Jane Eyre's profession?

20   Who wrote the 1939 novel *The Grapes of Wrath*?

Hard

Answers to QUIZ 84 – The Romans

1	Boudicca	11	Mosaic
2	The Colosseum	12	Gloucestershire
3	Northumberland	13	Kirk Douglas
4	50	14	Hibernia
5	Fire	15	Nero
6	Ides	16	Ovid
7	Russell Crowe	17	Hot
8	Villa	18	A forum
9	Galley	19	Chester
10	Hispania	20	Caesar

QUIZ 87 – Pot Luck

ANSWERS ON PAGE 89

1 What is a baby deer called?

2 Who is the Irish pirate, Hook's sidekick, in *Peter Pan*?

3 The *Four Seasons* concertos were written by which composer?

4 Which fictional Gordon famously declared on film that "greed is good"?

5 How many players are in a cricket team?

6 What term describes a plant with a two-year life cycle?

7 Which river runs through Newcastle and Gateshead?

8 What type of creature is a taipan?

9 What does PAYE stand for?

10 Which US gangster was known as "Scarface"?

11 What is the art of knotting string to make decorative items?

12 In which pursuit was Gary Kasparov a World Champion?

13 What term is given to the art of clear diction and expressive speech?

14 *Wind Beneath My Wings* was a 1988 hit for which singer and actress?

15 What is the capital of Bulgaria?

16 What acronym is given to the catering organisation in the armed forces?

17 Which is the largest US state?

18 The outer bark of which tree is used for making bottle stoppers?

19 Who is the actor brother of Daniel, Stephen and William Baldwin?

20 Which type of constrictor snake is also the name of something worn around the neck?

Easy

Medium

Hard

Answers to QUIZ 85 – Pot Luck

1	Seven	11	Dow Jones
2	Belfast	12	Isles of Scilly
3	Gateau	13	Grace Jones
4	Seattle	14	Exodus
5	Six	15	Sedan
6	Akela	16	Africa
7	Robert Downey Jr	17	Cher
8	Turkish delight	18	Knock
9	Dormant	19	*Andronicus*
10	Air	20	Mancunians

Easy

1. What fictional substance is Superman's main weakness?

2. What is Wonder Woman's real name...?

3. ...and who played her in the 2017 film *Wonder Woman*?

4. Which Marvel character has the catchphrase, "Don't make me angry. You wouldn't like me when I'm angry"...?

5. ...and what is the name of his alter ego?

6. What is the name of the newspaper that Clark Kent/Superman works for?

7. In the 2014 film, *Guardians of the Galaxy*, which tree-like alien was voiced by Vin Diesel?

8. What is the name of the DC superhero whose main power is superhuman speed...?

9. ...and who plays him in the TV series that started in 2014?

10. Who played the title role in the 2017 film *Spider Man: Homecoming*?

Medium

11. The TV series *Legends of Tomorrow* features which time-travelling spaceship?

12. Which Marvel team debuted in their first comic in 1961?

13. Who plays the title role in Marvel's 2015 film *Ant-Man*?

14. Captain America usually carries which offensive and defensive item?

15. Which actor has starred as the hero in the 2011 film *Green Lantern* and 2016 film *Deadpool*?

16. What is the name of Ray Palmer's superhero?

17. Superman's adopted parents have which first names?

18. Who played Lois Lane in the TV series *Lois & Clark: The New Adventures of Superman*?

19. The character of Thermoman from planet Ultron featured in which sitcom?

20. Who plays Storm in the *X-Men* film series?

Hard

---

1   In which country was the 2010 Ryder Cup played?

2   Na is the symbol for which chemical element?

3   What is a more common name for the New World?

4   What is the white substance around an egg yolk?

5   Stubbornness is particularly associated with which animal?

6   Which Swiss city is the second-largest home of the United Nations?

7   Which creamy dessert is named after a famous English public school?

8   The films *Groundhog Day* and *Lost in Translation* both starred which actor?

9   Which Amsterdam football club shares its name with a hero of the Trojan War?

10 Tangier is a city in which country?

11 In which West Sussex city is there a Festival Theatre?

12 What do Americans call the numbers at the end of their address?

13 Which 1966 Sir Michael Caine film was remade with Jude Law in 2004?

14 Which part of speech adds information about an action?

15 What is Japanese horseradish also called?

16 In folklore, which astronomical phase is associated with the sighting of werewolves?

17 How many official languages are there in Switzerland?

18 Which German car maker has a four-ring trademark?

19 The Rose of Texas is what colour, according to the song?

20 Which Italian title is often applied to a distinguished conductor?

Easy

Medium

Hard

Answers to QUIZ 87 – Pot Luck

1	Fawn	11	Macramé
2	Smee	12	Chess
3	Vivaldi	13	Elocution
4	Gekko (in Wall Street)	14	Bette Midler
5	Eleven	15	Sofia
6	Biennial	16	NAAFI
7	Tyne	17	Alaska
8	Snake	18	Cork
9	Pay As You Earn	19	Alec
10	Al Capone	20	Boa

Easy

1   Peter Gabriel and Phil Collins were members of which band?

2   Which band, fronted by Rod Stewart, had a 1971 hit with *Stay with Me*?

3   The Pink Floyd classic *Money* is from which album?

4   Which *American Idol* finalist subsequently provided lead vocals for Queen?

5   Which group had a hit in 1972 with *Silver Machine*?

6   Which iconic frontman was born Farrokh Bulsara in 1946?

7   Dave Grohl of the Foo Fighters was previously the drummer for which influential 1990s band?

8   Ultravox and Thin Lizzy have both featured which musician?

9   The band Bon Jovi were formed in which US state, the title of their fourth album?

10 Who had hits in the 1970s with *School's Out* and *Elected*?

Medium

11 Which band had a 1967 hit with *Light My Fire*?

12 Which group won the Mercury Music Prize for their 2008 album *The Seldom Seen Kid*?

13 The Guns N' Roses cover of which Bond theme was a hit in 1991?

14 Which rock group sang *My Generation* in 1965?

15 *I Predict a Riot* and *Ruby* were hits for which group?

16 Which UK band had chart success with *Whole Lotta Love* in 1969?

17 Which group opened Live Aid in 1985?

18 *Gimme All Your Lovin'* was a 1983 hit for which US band?

19 Which 1975 Ken Russell film was based on an album by The Who?

20 In which city were the band Def Leppard formed?

Hard

Answers to QUIZ 88 – Superheroes

1	Kryptonite	11	*The Waverider*
2	Diana Prince	12	The Fantastic Four
3	Gal Gadot	13	Paul Rudd
4	The Hulk	14	His shield
5	Dr Bruce Banner	15	Ryan Reynolds
6	*The Daily Planet*	16	The Atom
7	Groot	17	Martha and Jonathan
8	The Flash	18	Teri Hatcher
9	Grant Gustin	19	*My Hero*
10	Tom Holland	20	Halle Berry

1   Goal attack and goal defence are positions in which sport?

2   Who co-starred with Morgan Freeman in *The Bucket List*?

3   Carisbrooke Castle is on which island?

4   What was the round space in which gladiators fought?

5   *Signorina* is the form of address to an unmarried woman in which language?

6   Which word links a religious painting with a symbol on a computer screen?

7   Who had a hit with *Silver Lady* in 1977?

8   Which fibrous silicate mineral was used as a fire-resistant material until it was found to be harmful?

9   In aviation, what function does the black box serve?

10 Which material is associated with the Highland region of Harris?

11 Who won the men's singles title at Wimbledon in 1987?

12 Which children's comic featured Desperate Dan and Korky the Cat?

13 By which initials are Royal Dutch Airlines known?

14 What term is given to treatment of a disease by the use of water?

15 Who is the first actress to play the lead role in the TV series *Doctor Who*?

16 In which island group is Kos?

17 Someone described as a brunette has what colour hair?

18 Arborio is a type of which food?

19 What was the Roman name for Britain?

20 On which day of the week do Muslims gather to pray together?

Easy
Medium
Hard

Answers to QUIZ 89 – Pot Luck

1	Wales	11	Chichester
2	Sodium	12	Zip code
3	The Americas	13	*Alfie*
4	Albumen	14	Adverb
5	Mule	15	Wasabi
6	Geneva	16	Full moon
7	Eton mess	17	Four
8	Bill Murray	18	Audi
9	Ajax	19	Yellow
10	Morocco	20	Maestro

Easy

1   What colour is the Northern line on London Underground maps?

2   Which character was Adam West famous for playing on TV?

3   Which long-running BBC drama series features the location of Albert Square?

4   In which body of water is Dogger Bank?

5   Norfolk, Suffolk and Cambridgeshire make up which region of England?

6   Which country co-hosted the 2002 FIFA World Cup with Japan?

7   *Gold Digger* was a 2005 hit for which rapper?

8   Which actor starred in the 1959 thriller *North by Northwest*?

9   What is the name of the US military academy in New York State?

10 The West Indies is surrounded by which sea?

11 Which is the nearest city and port to the New Forest?

12 Which castle is the seat of the Dukes of Northumberland?

13 *Stay Another Day* was a hit for which group in 1994?

14 What is the administrative capital of South Africa?

Medium

15 Which US state is nicknamed "The Mountain State"?

16 Who wrote the 1855 novel *North and South*?

17 What term refers to the area around the North Pole?

18 The longest pleasure pier in the world is found in which English town?

19 What is the capital of New South Wales?

20 In which London borough is the Globe Theatre?

Hard

Answers to QUIZ 90 – Rock Music

1	Genesis	11	The Doors
2	Faces	12	Elbow
3	*Dark Side of the Moon*	13	*Live and Let Die*
4	Adam Lambert	14	The Who
5	Hawkwind	15	Kaiser Chiefs
6	Freddie Mercury	16	Led Zeppelin
7	Nirvana	17	Status Quo
8	Midge Ure	18	ZZ Top
9	New Jersey	19	*Tommy*
10	Alice Cooper	20	Sheffield

1 The dingo is a wild dog from which country?

2 What was the name of the Titan in Greek mythology who held the world on his shoulders?

3 Which dance style was spelled out by an Ottawan hit of 1980?

4 What name is given to a Viking ship?

5 "Per ardua ad astra" is the motto of which of the services?

6 Which Devon town is famous for its carpets?

7 "The king of beasts" describes which animal, native to Africa?

8 Which Scottish football club shares its name with a playing card suit?

9 What is the name of the saxophone-playing member of TV's Simpson family?

10 What word precedes "Kush" to denote an Asian mountain range?

11 Ludlow Castle is an example of what type of architecture?

12 Which 1982 Roxy Music album shares a name with an island in Arthurian legend?

13 In which county is the town of Blandford Forum?

14 Who wrote the 1953 play *Waiting for Godot*?

15 A crocodile is the logo of which sports clothing company?

16 The invasion of which country began the First Gulf War in 1991?

17 What city in Colorado sounds like a large rock?

18 In the 1999 romcom *Notting Hill*, who played Hugh Grant's scruffy flatmate?

19 What is the capital city of Chile?

20 What was Brotherhood of Man's winning Eurovision entry in 1976?

Easy

Medium

Hard

Answers to QUIZ 91 – Pot Luck

1	Netball	11	Pat Cash
2	Jack Nicholson	12	*Dandy*
3	Isle of Wight	13	KLM
4	Arena	14	Hydrotherapy
5	Italian	15	Jodie Whittaker
6	Icon	16	Dodecanese
7	David Soul	17	Brown
8	Asbestos	18	Rice
9	Flight recorder	19	Britannia
10	Tweed	20	Friday

1 Which Disney film features the panther Bagheera?

2 What type of fish is Nemo in the 2003 film *Finding Nemo*?

3 Who voiced the character of Joy in the 2015 film *Inside Out*?

4 In which 1970 Disney film does the character Thomas O'Malley appear?

5 *Early Man* is a 2018 film produced by which studio?

6 In which 2009 film did a pensioner travel in a house lifted by balloons?

7 What is the name of the princess in the 1959 Disney film *Sleeping Beauty*?

8 The 2013 film *Frozen* is based on the story *The Snow Queen* by which author?

9 What was the title of the first feature-length film produced by Pixar?

10 What is the name of Disney's Little Mermaid?

11 Who voiced the title character in the 2018 film *Peter Rabbit*?

12 *Minions* (2015) is a spin-off from which series of films?

13 In which part-animated 2007 Disney film did Amy Adams play a princess who found herself in New York?

14 What was the title of the 2013 prequel to *Monsters Inc.*?

15 Who voiced the title character in the 2011 film *Puss in Boots...*?

16 ...and in which 2004 film did the character first appear?

17 Which 2002 film featured a woolly mammoth?

18 Who is Stitch's best friend in the 2002 Disney film?

19 What is the name of the hero of the *How to Train Your Dragon* series of films?

20 Which film features the song *Walking in the Air*?

Easy · **Medium** · **Hard**

Answers to QUIZ 92 – Points of the Compass

1	Black	11	Southampton
2	Batman	12	Alnwick
3	*EastEnders*	13	East 17
4	North Sea	14	Pretoria
5	East Anglia	15	West Virginia
6	South Korea	16	Elizabeth Gaskell
7	Kanye West	17	Arctic Circle
8	Cary Grant	18	Southend-on-Sea
9	West Point	19	Sydney
10	Caribbean	20	Southwark

1   What does QI stand for in the name of the TV panel game?

2   What term is given to a baby with five siblings of the same age?

3   Who was *Crying* at the top of the charts in 1980?

4   Which word meaning "having a jagged edge" comes from the Latin word for "saw"?

5   A yarmulke is a type of what item of clothing?

6   Which race is run over a distance of just over 13 miles?

7   Morocco has four Imperial cities: Fez, Meknes, Rabat and which other?

8   A Hawaiian garland of flowers is given what name?

9   What term is given to a brief film or TV role by a prominent actor?

10 Which 1989 Sir John Hurt film was about the Profumo affair?

11 Bet Gilroy is a former landlady of which fictional TV pub?

12 Which Irish castle has a famous stone that claims to confer the power of eloquent speech?

13 What are training shoes called in the US?

14 What was the name of Mark Hamill's character in the *Star Wars* films?

15 Jarvis Cocker fronted which 1990s group?

16 What is the nationality of opera singer Andrea Bocelli?

17 Which is the highest mountain in Wales?

18 The musical *We Will Rock You* features songs by which group?

19 Which river flows through Hereford?

20 Which kind of volcanic rock is used for exfoliating hard skin?

Easy

Medium

Hard

1. How many chambers are there in a human heart?
2. Which element has the chemical symbol Au?
3. What is Earth's closest star?
4. The first cloned mammal was given what name?
5. Which adjective relates to the kidneys?
6. Which physicist is known for his theory of relativity?
7. Hydroelectric generators are powered by what substance?
8. What is the coloured part of the eye?
9. What term is given to an instrument for measuring heights?
10. Diabetes is treated with which substance?
11. What is the chemical opposite of an acid?
12. When the sound barrier is broken what noise occurs?
13. Who was the first man on the moon?
14. What term is given to a scientist who specialises in plants?

15. German measles has what medical name?
16. What term is given to a six-sided plane figure?
17. Tinnitus affects which part of the body?
18. Which chemical is used to disinfect swimming pools?
19. What is the medical name for the windpipe?
20. What does the "I" stand for in the astronomical abbreviation ISS?

Answers to QUIZ 94 – Animated Films

1	*The Jungle Book*	11	James Corden
2	A clownfish	12	*Despicable Me*
3	Amy Poehler	13	*Enchanted*
4	*The Aristocats*	14	*Monsters University*
5	Aardman Animations	15	Antonio Banderas
6	*Up*	16	*Shrek 2*
7	Aurora	17	*Ice Age*
8	Hans Christian Andersen	18	Lilo
9	*Toy Story*	19	Hiccup
10	Ariel	20	*The Snowman*

1 About which fictional otter did Henry Williamson write?

2 Which Californian grape variety is used to make pinkish white wine?

3 Which imperial weight measure approximates to 28 grams?

4 Which Jamaican-American singer had hits in 2000 with *It Wasn't Me* and *Angel*?

5 What is the chemical symbol for phosphorus?

6 In which county is The Wrekin hill?

7 What term was given to early 1980s groups such as Duran Duran and Spandau Ballet?

8 Epping is on which London Underground line?

9 What was the first name of Jane Leeves' character in the TV series *Frasier*?

10 What is the term for the Asian dot of forehead colour?

11 LaGuardia airport serves which city?

12 Which style of music with a syncopated rhythm is associated with the composer Scott Joplin?

13 In which country is the Lada car made?

14 Which actor won an Oscar for his starring role in the 2008 film *Milk*?

15 Which TV choirmaster formed the Military Wives Choir?

16 A Chinese boat and unsolicited mail are linked by which word?

17 In which town in South Wales is the *Parc y Scarlets* rugby stadium?

18 Which popular girls' comic featured *The Four Marys*?

19 What was the stage name of Ian Kilmister of Motorhead?

20 Which UK Prime Minister said "A week is a long time in politics"?

Easy

Medium

Hard

Answers to QUIZ 95 – Pot Luck

1	Quite Interesting	11	Rovers Return
2	Sextuplet	12	Blarney
3	Don McLean	13	Sneakers
4	Serrated	14	Luke Skywalker
5	Skullcap	15	Pulp
6	Half-marathon	16	Italian
7	Marrakesh	17	Snowdon
8	A lei	18	Queen
9	Cameo	19	Wye
10	*Scandal*	20	Pumice

Easy

1   Arnold Palmer, Jack Nicklaus and which other golfer were known as "The Big Three"?

2   The long grass on a golf course is referred to by what name?

3   What colour jacket is awarded to the winner of The Masters tournament?

4   Virginia Water in Surrey is home to which famous golf course?

5   Which animal's limb is used to describe a hole that bends between the tee and the green?

6   "The Great White Shark" is a nickname of which Australian golfer?

7   Which peg is used to support a golf ball?

8   The 2016 Ryder Cup was won by which team?

9   Ailsa Craig is a hole on which Scottish course?

10 What term is given to an area of sand designed as a course obstacle?

11 In which country is the Celtic Manor course?

12 The clubhouse or pub on a golf course is referred to as which hole?

13 What is Tiger Woods' real first name?

Medium

14 What is a scratch golfer's handicap?

15 What is the lowest level of par given to a hole?

16 How is a shot described which a right-handed player pulls to the left, as opposed to a slice?

17 A seaside course is given what name?

18 In 2009 which US golfer came close to winning The Open at the age of 59?

19 What nationality is Ernie Els?

20 What is the name of the trophy presented to the winner of The Open tournament?

Hard

Answers to QUIZ 96 – Science

1	Four	11	Alkali
2	Gold	12	Sonic boom
3	The Sun	13	Neil Armstrong
4	Dolly (a sheep)	14	Botanist
5	Renal	15	Rubella
6	Albert Einstein	16	Hexagon
7	Water	17	The ears
8	The Iris	18	Chlorine
9	Altimeter	19	The trachea
10	Insulin	20	International

1   Which New York department store features in the film *Miracle on 34th Street*?

2   What, in tennis, is a service obstructed by the net?

3   The lychee is a fruit from which country?

4   Which child star sang *On the Good Ship Lollipop* in the 1934 film *Bright Eyes*?

5   What were the initials of the former Soviet secret service?

6   What are the leather shorts worn with braces popular with both men and boys in Bavaria called?

7   Which mid-Kent town has an "International" station?

8   In UK road signs, what does a red circle with a white horizontal bar forbid?

9   Who played Ronni Mitchell in *EastEnders?*

10 Geronimo was a member of which Native American tribe?

11 In which body of water are the Maldives?

12 Which small musical instrument did Larry Adler play?

13 What type of rock is associated with Blaenau Ffestiniog in North Wales?

14 "Adam's Ale" is a term for which liquid?

15 Who was the original host of the series *Room 101*?

16 Which district of south London is famous for its Common and Junction?

17 In which county is Shepton Mallet?

18 Who was Dudley Moore's 1960s comedy partner?

19 Proverbially, what does a stitch in time save?

20 In which country is Penang?

Easy

Medium

Hard

Answers to QUIZ 97 – Pot Luck

1	Tarka	11	New York
2	Zinfandel	12	Ragtime
3	An ounce	13	Russia
4	Shaggy	14	Sean Penn
5	P	15	Gareth Malone
6	Shropshire	16	Junk
7	New Romantics	17	Llanelli
8	The Central Line	18	*Bunty*
9	Daphne (Moon)	19	Lemmy
10	Bindi	20	Harold Wilson (Baron Wilson of Rievaulx)

QUIZ 100 – Horses

ANSWERS ON PAGE 102

Easy

1 What name is given to the occupation of a person who fits horseshoes?

2 What is the female parent of a horse called?

3 Bucephalus belonged to which leader?

4 Which joint on a horse is the equivalent of a human ankle?

5 What is the name for an old Russian or Ukrainian warrior, famed for his horsemanship?

6 The stirrup supports which part of the body when riding a horse?

7 What word describes a horse with a bay or chestnut coat dotted with grey and white?

8 What was the name of the Lone Ranger's horse?

9 The Clydesdale originates from which country?

10 Which creature of Greek mythology was half-human, half-horse?

Medium

11 Annual horse trials are held at which Lincolnshire stately home?

12 Young racehorses between 12 and 24 months old are given what name?

13 What was the name of the winning horse in the 2018 Grand National?

14 Which equestrian pace comes between walk and canter?

15 Doncaster has been the venue for which annual horse race since 1776?

16 Which word means "related to or connected with horses"?

17 What part of a bridle goes into the horse's mouth?

18 Black Bess belonged to which highwayman?

19 Which was the winged horse in Greek mythology that gave its name to a constellation?

20 Which Ford car is named after a wild horse?

Hard

Answers to QUIZ 98 – Golf

1	Gary Player	11	Wales
2	The rough	12	19th
3	Green	13	Eldrick
4	Wentworth	14	Zero
5	Dog-leg	15	Three
6	Greg Norman	16	Hook
7	Tee	17	Links
8	United States	18	Tom Watson
9	Turnberry	19	South African
10	Bunker	20	Claret jug

1   Who was "educated" in a 1950s radio series?

2   What is the unit of currency in Turkey?

3   The name of which small domestic fowl is also used to describe a weight in boxing?

4   Which French term describes a pervasive feeling of boredom and languor?

5   Who played the title role in the 2006 film *Marie Antoinette*?

6   November 2 marks which Catholic festival?

7   What four-letter term can describe both a bathing beach and an outdoor swimming pool?

8   Who sang the 1972 song *Walk on the Wild Side*?

9   The TV series *Downton Abbey* was created by which screenwriter?

10 What gymnastic apparatus has two rails, at different heights?

11 What name is given to a person who scavenges at low tide?

12 In the novel *Moby-Dick*, who is the captain of the Pequod?

13 In which US state do the Amish mainly live?

14 What name is given to the checkerboard diamond pattern often used on socks?

15 In the TV series *Last of the Summer Wine*, what was Nora's surname?

16 Who is Roald Dahl's fictional champion of the world?

17 Which Irish town gives its name to a famous illuminated book of Latin Gospels?

18 Which fruit shares its name with the official form of the Chinese language?

19 What is the stiff bristle on an ear of barley called?

20 Emmental cheese originates from which country?

Easy

Medium

Hard

Answers to QUIZ 99 – Pot Luck

1	Macy's	11	Indian Ocean
2	Let	12	Harmonica
3	China	13	Slate
4	Shirley Temple	14	Water
5	KGB	15	Nick Hancock
6	Lederhosen	16	Clapham
7	Ashford	17	Somerset
8	Entry	18	Peter Cook
9	Samantha Womack	19	Nine
10	Apache	20	Malaysia

1   On which Hawaiian island is Pearl Harbor situated?

2   Diamondback can refer to a terrapin and which other reptile?

3   The playing area in which sport is known as a diamond?

4   A pearl anniversary marks how many years of marriage?

5   Which actress starred in the 2003 film *Girl With a Pearl Earring...*?

6   ...and who wrote the 1999 novel on which it is based?

7   Diamonds are a form of which element?

8   Pearls are formed by which creature?

9   Are diamonds a major or minor suit in contract bridge?

10 Who wrote the opera *The Pearl Fishers*?

11 Who had hits with *Sweet Caroline* and *Love on the Rocks*?

12 Pearl is a birthstone for which month?

13 Who starred in the 2006 film *Blood Diamond*?

14 In which year did Queen Elizabeth II celebrate her diamond jubilee...?

15 ...and in which year did Queen Victoria celebrate the same jubilee?

16 Who had a 1977 hit with *Pearl's a Singer*?

17 In a Beatles song, who was "in the sky with diamonds"?

18 Who played James Bond in *Diamonds are Forever...*?

19 ...and who performed the theme song?

20 Who released a 1991 album entitled *Diamonds and Pearls*?

Answers to QUIZ 100 – Horses

1	Farrier	11	Burghley
2	Dam	12	Yearlings
3	Alexander the Great	13	Tiger Roll
4	Fetlock	14	Trot
5	Cossack	15	The St Leger
6	Foot	16	Equine
7	Roan	17	Bit
8	Silver	18	Dick Turpin
9	Scotland	19	Pegasus
10	Centaur	20	Mustang

1. Which aromatic spice is obtained from the shell of nutmegs?

2. Where is a cummerbund worn?

3. A marlin is what type of creature?

4. Which compound is added to toothpaste?

5. Which religion is associated with Krishna?

6. Who sang the theme song to the TV series *Dad's Army*?

7. Which area of Liverpool is home to the Grand National?

8. Jule Styne and Stephen Sondheim wrote which musical based on the true story of a famous striptease artist?

9. What is the name of Porky Pig's cartoon duck companion?

10. In the Middle Ages, what name was given to a person who studied the art and craft of turning base metals into gold?

11. Who starred in the TV series *Doctor Foster*?

12. Which city of New York State shares its name with the American bison?

13. What name is given to radioactive material produced by nuclear explosions?

14. The flowers of the laburnum tree are which colour?

15. Which overhead train system runs on one track?

16. How many players are there in a volleyball team?

17. What word denotes a Mexican state and a small breed of dog?

18. What term is given to a piece of leather used for sharpening razors?

19. The 1963 film *The Great Escape* starred which actor as "The Cooler King"?

20. Which strongly flavoured blue-veined cheese is named after a Cambridgeshire village?

Easy

Medium

Hard

Answers to QUIZ 101 – Pot Luck

1	Archie	11	Mudlark
2	Lira	12	Ahab
3	Bantam	13	Pennsylvania
4	Ennui	14	Argyle
5	Kirsten Dunst	15	Batty
6	All Souls' Day	16	Danny
7	Lido	17	Kells
8	Lou Reed	18	Mandarin
9	Julian Fellowes (Baron Fellowes of West Stafford)	19	Awn
10	Asymmetric or uneven bars	20	Switzerland

Easy

1 Where does the Ceremony of the Keys take place every night?

2 How many bronze lions are there in Trafalgar Square?

3 What is the name of the ferris wheel on the banks of the Thames, built to celebrate the millennium?

4 What exactly is Big Ben?

5 What is the official residence of the Prime Minister in London...?

6 ...and who lives at the next-door house one number higher?

7 Who was the architect of St Paul's Cathedral?

8 Which river crossing is "falling down" in a popular nursery rhyme?

9 Rotten Row is in which area of London?

10 In which famous building are coronations held?

11 By what name is the statue in the middle of Piccadilly Circus known?

12 What gift from the Norwegian people is placed in Trafalgar Square every year?

13 Which silent film star is immortalised by a statue in Leicester Square?

Medium

14 What is the name of the ceremony that takes place on the forecourt of Buckingham Palace?

15 The London Underground has what nickname?

16 What Egyptian obelisk stands on the Thames Embankment?

17 Battersea is in which borough?

18 In which year did London buses stop accepting cash fares?

19 Which Beatles album is named after a London street?

20 Which famous financial institution can be found on London's Threadneedle Street?

Hard

Answers to QUIZ 102 – Diamonds and Pearls

1	Oahu	11	Neil Diamond
2	Rattlesnake	12	June
3	Baseball	13	Leonardo DiCaprio
4	30	14	2012
5	Scarlett Johansson	15	1897
6	Tracy Chevalier	16	Elkie Brooks
7	Carbon	17	Lucy
8	Oyster	18	Sir Sean Connery
9	Minor	19	Dame Shirley Bassey
10	Bizet	20	Prince

1 Which English dynasty began with Henry VII and ended with Elizabeth I?

2 Lowestoft is in which county?

3 Which saint is celebrated on February 14?

4 *Coz I Luv You* was the first UK no.1 for which band?

5 What time of day does the adjective "crepuscular" refer to?

6 What was the river crossed by ferryman Charon in Greek mythology?

7 Cuthbert, Dibble and Grubb are firemen in which fictional town?

8 What name is given to the fleshy hanging part at the back of the soft palate?

9 What is conscription called in the USA?

10 What is the national language of Pakistan?

11 Who took over from John Nettles as Midsomer's Inspector Barnaby?

12 Which parasitic plant is associated with kissing at Christmas?

13 A macchiato is what type of drink?

14 What was the name of the central family in *The Godfather*?

15 What term is given to a touchdown in rugby?

16 What is a proviso or part of a sentence?

17 What was the Black Bottom, popular in the US in the 1920s?

18 Mount Ararat is in which country?

19 Which wedding anniversary is celebrated with china?

20 What is the main ingredient of guacamole?

Easy
Medium
Hard

Answers to QUIZ 103 – Pot Luck

1	Mace	11	Suranne Jones
2	Round the waist	12	Buffalo
3	Fish	13	Fallout
4	Fluoride	14	Yellow
5	Hinduism	15	Monorail
6	Bud Flanagan	16	Six
7	Aintree	17	Chihuahua
8	Gypsy	18	Strop
9	Daffy	19	Steve McQueen
10	Alchemist	20	Stilton

Easy

1 In which London borough is The Shard?

2 The CN tower is in which Canadian city?

3 Which Royal Palace is located in Edinburgh?

4 For which performing arts building is Sydney Harbour renowned?

5 Which palace on the River Thames is famous for its maze?

6 St Basil's Cathedral stands in which Russian square?

7 On which body of water is Urquhart Castle located?

8 What is Lancashire's highest landmark and tourist attraction?

9 The Notre-Dame cathedral in Paris is an example of which type of architecture?

10 Which Scottish castle is the main setting for Shakespeare's *Macbeth*?

Medium

11 In which Gulf state is the Burj Khalifa skyscraper?

12 The Hall of Mirrors is a famous gallery in which French palace?

13 In which year was Buckingham Palace first opened to the public?

14 The Lincoln Memorial is situated in which US city?

15 Which English cathedral was struck by lightning in July 1984?

16 What is the name of the 13th-century Moorish palace near Granada, Spain?

17 The Petronas Towers, one of the world's tallest buildings, are in which city?

18 Which famous building do Beefeaters guard?

19 The Duke of Wellington's tomb is in which London building?

20 In which Italian region is the Leaning Tower of Pisa?

Hard

Answers to QUIZ 104 – London

1	The Tower of London	11	Eros
2	Four	12	A Christmas tree
3	London Eye	13	Sir Charlie Chaplin
4	A bell	14	Changing of the Guard
5	10 Downing Street	15	The Tube
6	The Chancellor of the Exchequer	16	Cleopatra's Needle
7	Sir Christopher Wren	17	Wandsworth
8	London Bridge	18	2014
9	Hyde Park	19	*Abbey Road*
10	Westminster Abbey	20	Bank of England

QUIZ 107 – Pot Luck

ANSWERS ON PAGE **109**

1 Which day of the week is first alphabetically?

2 Which word means both a unit of measurement and the rhythm of a piece of poetry?

3 What were people encouraged to do for Victory in a WWII slogan?

4 Hugo Weaving played which wise elf in the *Lord of the Rings* series of films?

5 What is the radio operators' code word for the letter between tango and victor?

6 What is a broad ditch surrounding a castle called?

7 Crème de menthe liqueur has what flavour?

8 Which Atlantic colony gives its name to a type of shorts?

9 Who sang *99 Red Balloons* in 1984?

10 What type of substance induces insensitivity to pain?

11 What does the "D" of "CD" stand for?

12 What was there "under the Sun" in the title of a 1982 Poirot film?

13 The Lombardy poplar tree is native to which country?

14 What was the name of Su Pollard's character in the TV series *Hi-de-Hi!*?

15 What is the square root of 100?

16 Jessica Tandy co-starred with which actor in the film *Driving Miss Daisy*?

17 What is the official examination of a company's books called?

18 What archaic word for "letter" is used in the New Testament for St Paul's to the Thessalonians, for instance?

19 How many years are celebrated at a bicentenary?

20 How many carats are there in pure gold?

Easy

Medium

Hard

Answers to QUIZ 105 – Pot Luck

1	Tudor	11	Neil Dudgeon
2	Suffolk	12	Mistletoe
3	Valentine	13	Coffee
4	Slade	14	Corleone
5	Twilight	15	Try
6	Styx	16	Clause
7	Trumpton	17	Dance
8	Uvula	18	Turkey
9	Draft	19	20th
10	Urdu	20	Avocado

Easy

1. What is the London home of the Royal Ballet?

2. Which Irish dance shares its name with a device designed to hold a component during machining?

3. Which dance in triple time derives its name from the German word for "roll"?

4. What was the first name of early Hollywood choreographer Mr Berkeley?

5. *Let's Dance* was a hit for which singer in 1983?

6. Which English choreographer famously created a version of *Swan Lake* with male swans?

7. For which occasion was *Riverdance* originally created in 1994?

8. Which former ballerina joined the judging panel of *Strictly Come Dancing* in 2012?

9. In which traditional English form of dance are bell pads worn on the shins?

10. The 1970s pogo was associated with which form of music?

11. In which city is the Bolshoi ballet based?

12. Who choreographed the original Broadway production of *Chicago*?

13. In which country was Carlos Acosta born?

14. Which 2000 film starred Jamie Bell as a boy who wanted to dance?

15. Who choreographed the 1970s dance troupe Hot Gossip...?

16. ...and which singer did they back on the 1978 song *I Lost My Heart to a Starship Trooper*?

17. The bossa nova dance originates from which South American country?

18. Who was the original presenter of *Strictly Come Dancing: It Takes Two*?

19. In ballet, what is a dance for two people called?

20. Which "dance" was a hit for Terry Wogan in 1978?

Answers to QUIZ 106 – Famous Buildings

1	Southwark	11	Dubai
2	Toronto	12	Versailles
3	Holyrood	13	1993
4	Sydney Opera House	14	Washington DC
5	Hampton Court	15	York Minster
6	Red Square	16	Alhambra
7	Loch Ness	17	Kuala Lumpur
8	Blackpool Tower	18	Tower of London
9	Gothic	19	St Paul's Cathedral
10	Glamis	20	Tuscany

ANSWERS ON PAGE 111

1   The mystery of *The Body in the Library* was solved by which fictional sleuth?

2   Who starred in the 2008 film *The Duchess*?

3   Who played Queen Elizabeth I in the TV series *Blackadder II*?

4   Which US senator was notorious for his 1950s "witch-hunts"?

5   "Pulmonary" relates to which organs of the body?

6   Which actress co-starred with Tom Hanks in the 2017 film *The Post*?

7   Which five-line humorous verse is named after a place in Ireland?

8   The Archbishop of Canterbury's residence is in which London palace?

9   What name was given to Schubert's eighth symphony?

10   Which 1960s group was fronted by Reg Presley?

11   The Bernabéu football stadium is located in which city?

12   What type of vehicle is a Chinook?

13   What is the first name of the Bond villain Blofeld?

14   What word can refer to both a coat peg and a boxing punch?

15   *Open Arms* was a hit for which singer in 1996?

16   In which county is the racecourse of Market Rasen?

17   Which biblical character had a wife who was turned into a pillar of salt?

18   In 1908 who, along with Mills, founded a publishing company famous for romantic novels?

19   Who played Chandler in the TV series *Friends*?

20   What is the monetary unit of Denmark and Norway?

Easy

Medium

Hard

Answers to QUIZ 107 – Pot Luck

1	Friday	11	Disc
2	Metre	12	Evil
3	Dig	13	Italy
4	Elrond	14	Peggy
5	Uniform	15	Ten
6	Moat	16	Morgan Freeman
7	Peppermint	17	Audit
8	Bermuda	18	Epistle
9	Nena	19	200
10	Anaesthetic	20	24

Easy

1 Who took over as host of *The Late Late Show* on CBS in 2015?

2 Who won *The X Factor* in 2012?

3 Who wrote the children's story *James and the Giant Peach*?

4 Which TV presenter featured in his *Man Lab* and told *Toy Stories*?

5 Which word describes the reign of James I?

6 What household item is Sir James Dyson famous for making?

7 What was the name of Polly James' character in the TV series *The Liver Birds*?

8 In which film did Pierce Brosnan first appear as James Bond?

9 *Chaos and the Calm* is a 2015 album by which singer/songwriter?

10 Which Greek hero shares his name with the title of a novel by James Joyce?

11 In which country is James Clavell's novel *Shogun* set?

12 Who was the fourth US president?

Medium

13 Who played Lady Rose in the TV series *Downton Abbey*?

14 Who had a 2005 hit with *Goodbye My Lover*?

15 On which London thoroughfare is St James's Palace?

16 Which crime writer created the character of Adam Dalgliesh?

17 In the New Testament, James was the brother of which other apostle?

18 Who was UK Prime Minister from 1976 to 1979?

19 Which musical instrument is associated with Sir James Galway?

20 Who played Idi Amin's personal physician in the 2006 film *The Last King of Scotland*?

Hard

Answers to QUIZ 108 – Dance

1	Royal Opera House	11	Moscow
2	Jig	12	Bob Fosse
3	Waltz	13	Cuba
4	Busby	14	*Billy Elliot*
5	David Bowie	15	Arlene Phillips
6	Sir Matthew Bourne	16	Sarah Brightman
7	The Eurovision Song Contest	17	Brazil
8	Dame Darcey Bussell	18	Claudia Winkleman
9	Morris dancing	19	*Pas de deux*
10	Punk	20	*The Floral Dance*

1   The spicy soup mulligatawny originated in which country?

2   From whom do all Jews trace their ancestry?

3   Which clergyman created Thomas the Tank Engine?

4   Which date in spring is traditionally seen as a day on which to play pranks?

5   In which fairground game are wooden balls thrown at a dummy?

6   Who was comic-strip hero Dan Dare's arch-enemy?

7   What name is given to a narrow strip of land connecting two land areas?

8   Which UK Prime Minister was in office at the time of "Black Wednesday"?

9   Which Tolkien heroine did Liv Tyler play in the *Lord of the Rings* films?

10 What is one circuit of a track in a race called?

11 What term is given to a column made from a single stone?

12 Who wrote the 1969 autobiography *I Know Why the Caged Bird Sings*?

13 In the adage, what sort of hands does the devil find work for?

14 What is the first name of Woody Guthrie's folk-singer son?

15 English singer Alfie Boe (b.1973) is from which county?

16 What type of food is a bloomer?

17 Indicating an anonymous party in a US court case, what is the surname of "John"?

18 Which dessert has a French name meaning "froth"?

19 What word can mean a Turkish commander or a brand of cooker?

20 Which Christmas song features a "one-horse open sleigh"?

Easy

Medium

Hard

Answers to QUIZ 109 – Pot Luck

1	Miss Marple	11	Madrid
2	Keira Knightley	12	Helicopter
3	Miranda Richardson	13	Ernst
4	Joseph McCarthy	14	Hook
5	Lungs	15	Mariah Carey
6	Meryl Streep	16	Lincolnshire
7	Limerick	17	Lot
8	Lambeth	18	Boon
9	The *Unfinished*	19	Matthew Perry
10	The Troggs	20	Krone

Easy

1 What does AI stand for?

2 Which video hosting site was founded in 2005?

3 Google, Bing and Yahoo are what type of online resource?

4 Which social networking site doubled the length of posts which users could make in 2017?

5 Who was the co-founder of Apple, portrayed by Michael Fassbender in a 2015 film?

6 What do AR and VR stand for?

7 The three laws of robotics were invented by which sci-fi writer?

8 In what year was the iPad first released?

9 Mark Zuckerberg co-founded which social media site?

10 In what year was the World Wide Web invented?

Medium

11 The "Deep Blue" computer beat the reigning world champion in what game in 1996?

12 Which test was developed in 1950 to determine a machine's ability to exhibit behaviour indistinguishable from a human's?

13 What does GPS stand for?

14 Which cryptocurrency and worldwide payment system first came into existence in 2009?

15 Which machine located near Geneva was built to create and study the Higgs boson?

16 A pilotless aircraft operated by remote control is given what name?

17 For what does the acronym WYSIWYG stand in relation to electronic display?

18 Which computer programming language is named after the mathematician daughter of Lord Byron?

19 What name for a mechanical person comes from the Czech word for "forced labour"?

20 What does HTML stand for?

Hard

Answers to QUIZ 110 – James

1	James Corden	11	Japan
2	James Arthur	12	James Madison
3	Roald Dahl	13	Lily James
4	James May	14	James Blunt
5	Jacobean	15	Pall Mall
6	Vacuum cleaner	16	PD James (Baroness James of Holland Park)
7	Beryl	17	John
8	*GoldenEye*	18	James Callaghan (Baron Callaghan of Cardiff)
9	James Bay	19	Flute
10	Ulysses	20	James McAvoy

1   What is the name of the Scottish National Park region north-east of Loch Lomond?

2   Who composed the 19th-century piece *Air on a G String*?

3   What was the surname of US newspaper tycoon William Randolph (b.1863)?

4   What term is given to a pocket-watch chain?

5   What is a dotterel?

6   What is the firing mechanism in a car's engine called?

7   *Porgy and Bess* is a 1935 opera by which composer?

8   Which is the National Book Town of Wales?

9   From which country does the fandango dance originate?

10 What is a native of England, Wales or Scotland called?

11 Which island-based TV series starred Matthew Fox as a plane-crash survivor?

12 What name links an Israeli port with an orange?

13 Julia Roberts co-starred with which actor in the 1990 film *Pretty Woman*?

14 Which Lewis Carroll character gave a tea-party?

15 What was the name of Michael Crawford's character in *Some Mothers Do 'Ave 'Em*?

16 What is the main ingredient of paella?

17 Which independent country, once part of the British Raj, is formally known as the Union of Myanmar?

18 On which river does Düsseldorf stand?

19 Which town, on Romney Marsh, is the site of London Ashford Airport?

20 Who wrote *The Day of the Jackal* (1971)?

Easy

Medium

Hard

Answers to QUIZ 111 – Pot Luck

1	India	11	Monolith
2	Abraham	12	Maya Angelou
3	Reverend Wilbert Awdry	13	Idle
4	April 1	14	Arlo
5	Aunt Sally	15	Lancashire
6	The Mekon	16	A loaf of bread
7	Isthmus	17	Doe
8	Sir John Major	18	Mousse
9	Arwen	19	Aga
10	A lap	20	*Jingle Bells*

Easy

1 Which musical is set in Rydell High?

2 The musical *Our House* features hits from which band?

3 Which musical features Nathan Detroit and Sky Masterson?

4 Who wrote the music and lyrics for the musical *Matilda*?

5 In *The Sound of Music*, who is the eldest von Trapp daughter?

6 The song *If I Were a Rich Man* is from which musical?

7 Which 1996 film starred Antonio Banderas as Che?

8 Which musical was based on Shakespeare's *The Taming of the Shrew*?

9 Eliza Doolittle is the main character in which musical?

10 Who played Roxie Hart in the 2002 film *Chicago*?

11 Which 1999 musical set in Greece features Donna and her daughter Sophie?

12 John Travolta starred as Edna Turnblad in which 2007 film?

13 Which musical features the song *Tomorrow*?

14 *A Couple of Swells* featured in which 1948 Fred Astaire film?

Medium

15 What is the name of the 2015 musical about one of the Founding Fathers?

16 Which adjective describes the lion in *The Wizard of Oz*?

17 Who wrote the musical *Oliver!*?

18 Which musical by Andrew Lloyd Webber (Baron Lloyd-Webber) was based on a collection of poems by TS Eliot?

19 The 2017 talent show *Let it Shine* searched for the cast of a musical featuring songs by which band?

20 What is the name of the Sharks' rival gang in Leonard Bernstein's *West Side Story*?

Hard

Answers to QUIZ 112 – Technology

1	Artificial intelligence	11	Chess
2	YouTube™	12	Turing Test
3	Search engines	13	Global Positioning System
4	Twitter™	14	Bitcoin
5	Steve Jobs	15	The Large Hadron Collider
6	Augmented reality and virtual reality	16	Drone
7	Isaac Asimov	17	What you see is what you get
8	2010	18	Ada
9	Facebook™	19	Robot
10	1989	20	Hypertext Markup Language

1   Daryl Hannah played a mermaid in which 1984 film?

2   Which international agency aims to improve youngsters' health and education?

3   What nationality was the poet Dylan Thomas?

4   *Vienna* was a hit for which 1980s band?

5   Who starred as Derek Zoolander in the *Zoolander* films?

6   What term is given to the frilly collar associated with the Elizabethan and Jacobean periods?

7   What flower is worn as a symbol of remembrance up to the 11th November in the UK?

8   Who wrote the 1867 work *Das Kapital* (Volume 1)?

9   King Charles is a variety of which breed of dog?

10 What collective name is used for large-calibre guns used in land warfare?

11 What is the medical name for the breastbone?

12 In bookkeeping, what is an entry in an account of a sum owing?

13 The Golden Temple is in which holy city of the Punjab?

14 Which actor starred opposite Jennifer Lawrence in the 2012 film *Silver Linings Playbook*?

15 The herb rosemary usually has what colour flowers?

16 Who played Perry Mason on TV in the 1960s and 1970s?

17 The 1869 novel *Lorna Doone* was written by which author?

18 What was the nationality at birth of Olympic gymnast Nadia Comaneci?

19 Osaka is a city in which country?

20 What is the first name of Donald Trump's eldest daughter?

Easy

Medium

Hard

Answers to QUIZ 113 – Pot Luck

1	The Trossachs	11	*Lost*
2	Johann Sebastian Bach	12	Jaffa
3	Hearst	13	Richard Gere
4	Fob	14	The Mad Hatter
5	Bird	15	Frank Spencer
6	Ignition	16	Rice
7	George Gershwin	17	Burma
8	Hay-on-Wye	18	Rhine
9	Spain	19	Lydd
10	Briton	20	Frederick Forsyth

1 A mule is a cross between which two animals?

2 Who wrote the music and lyrics to the musical *Kinky Boots*?

3 What name is given to the traditional wooden shoe worn in the Netherlands?

4 *The Slipper and the Rose* is a film version of which fairy tale?

5 *Pump it Up* was a 1978 single for which group?

6 Which actor came to TV fame as Eddie Shoestring in 1979?

7 What is the wooden or metal form on which a shoe is fashioned or repaired?

8 In which English city was the retail chain Boots founded?

9 Which 2005 film starred Toni Collette and Cameron Diaz as sisters?

10 A Moscow mule cocktail contains which main alcoholic ingredient?

11 Which Italian bread is so named because the shape resembles a slipper?

12 What is the part of a shoe above the sole called?

13 What is the capital city of New Zealand?

14 Which strong shoe shares its name with a description of a regional accent?

15 *These Boots Are Made for Walkin'* was a hit for which singer in 1966?

16 In which county is the town of Shoeburyness?

17 What type of flower is a lady's slipper?

18 What are soft top-stitched leather shoes worn by Native Americans called?

19 In which English city is the Pump Room restaurant?

20 Who starred in the TV series *Crocodile Shoes*?

Answers to QUIZ 114 – Musicals

1	*Grease*	11	*Mamma Mia!*
2	Madness	12	*Hairspray*
3	*Guys and Dolls*	13	*Annie*
4	Tim Minchin	14	*Easter Parade*
5	Liesl	15	*Hamilton*
6	*Fiddler on the Roof*	16	Cowardly
7	*Evita*	17	Lionel Bart
8	*Kiss Me Kate*	18	*Cats*
9	*My Fair Lady*	19	Take That
10	Renée Zellweger	20	Jets

1. What kitchen measure equals ten millilitres?

2. What name is given to a ring-like coral reef?

3. The character of Wishee Washee appears in which pantomime?

4. Which group topped the UK singles chart with *Words* in 1996?

5. Which Alpine mountain range is located in north-east Italy?

6. What colours are on the flag of Argentina?

7. Who was the first person to win the jackpot on the UK's *Who Wants to Be a Millionaire*?

8. Which religion involves the quest for enlightenment?

9. What name is given to a loose Japanese robe with wide sleeves?

10. The sitcom *Goodnight Sweetheart* starred which actor?

11. Haematophobia is the fear of what?

12. Which Canadian singer/songwriter wrote *Both Sides Now*?

13. What is the unit of depth measurement equal to six feet?

14. Who won the Olympic gold medal in the men's long jump in 2012?

15. The 2005 novel *Never Let Me Go* was written by which author?

16. What is the national airline of Spain?

17. Who won a Best Actor Oscar for his role in the 2014 film *The Theory of Everything*?

18. What singing voice is highest for males and lowest for females?

19. What is the main international airport of Cyprus?

20. Kahlua and vodka are used to make which "Black" cocktail?

Answers to QUIZ 115 – Pot Luck

1	*Splash*	11	The sternum
2	UNICEF	12	Debit
3	Welsh	13	Amritsar
4	Ultravox	14	Bradley Cooper
5	Ben Stiller	15	Blue
6	Ruff	16	Raymond Burr
7	Poppy	17	RD Blackmore
8	Karl Marx	18	Romanian
9	Spaniel	19	Japan
10	Artillery	20	Ivanka

QUIZ 118 – Action Films

1 The 1997 film *Air Force One* starred which actor as the US President?

2 Which martial arts actor is best known for the *Rush Hour* series of films?

3 Which 2016 film featured a group of boys trying to find their way out of a labyrinth?

4 In the 1998 film *Armageddon*, what poses a threat to Earth?

5 Japan was the location for which 2003 Tom Cruise film?

6 By what nickname was Bond film producer Albert Broccoli known?

7 Which actor starred in the 1993 film *Last Action Hero*?

8 What was the subtitle of the second film in the *Pirates of the Caribbean* series?

9 Mike Myers created which spoof spy?

10 In the title of a 2009 film, which year saw John Cusack battling a series of global catastrophies?

11 Who played the original Mad Max?

12 Linda Hamilton played which character in the first two *Terminator* films?

13 What was the surname of Clint Eastwood's "Dirty Harry"?

14 Who was Sylvester Stallone's character in the 1982 film *First Blood*?

15 The African kingdom of Wakanda is the setting for which 2018 film?

16 Who directed the 2018 film *Ready Player One*?

17 Which actor starred in *The Bourne Ultimatum*?

18 In which year was *Raiders of the Lost Ark* released?

19 Bruce Willis plays which character in the *Die Hard* films?

20 What catastrophe occurs in the 1997 film *Dante's Peak*?

Easy

Medium

Hard

Answers to QUIZ 116 – Footwear

1 A (male) donkey and a (female) horse
2 Cyndi Lauper
3 Clog
4 *Cinderella*
5 Elvis Costello and the Attractions
6 Trevor Eve
7 Last
8 Nottingham
9 *In Her Shoes*
10 Vodka
11 Ciabatta
12 The upper
13 Wellington
14 Brogue
15 Nancy Sinatra
16 Essex
17 An orchid
18 Moccasins
19 Bath
20 Jimmy Nail

Easy

Medium

Hard

1   What is the name of the stately home at Woodstock near Oxford?

2   *Teenage Kicks* and *My Perfect Cousin* were hits for which band?

3   Who was the "Desert Fox" of WWII?

4   Which Welsh county has the longest border with England?

5   Peter Falk played which TV detective?

6   What colour is the drink Campari®?

7   Which language is spoken in Kuwait?

8   What word links a salt container with an underground room?

9   What is the unit of speed at sea?

10 The poem *To a Skylark* was written by which English Romantic poet of the early 19th century?

11 Which actress was Oscar-nominated for her starring role in the film *Changeling*?

12 Sir Christopher Cockerell designed which vehicle that rides on a cushion of air?

13 Which fruit has varieties including Gala and Granny Smith?

14 Who created the characters of Samuel Whiskers and Squirrel Nutkin?

15 Morticia and Gomez appeared in which TV and film series?

16 What is the lowest-ranking chess piece?

17 Cerulean is a shade of which colour?

18 Which tree's leaf is depicted on the Canadian flag?

19 What is the Spanish equivalent of "mister"?

20 What word can mean a doughnut and a native of Germany's capital city?

Answers to QUIZ 117 – Pot Luck

1	Dessertspoonful	11	Blood
2	Atoll	12	Joni Mitchell
3	*Aladdin*	13	Fathom
4	Boyzone	14	Greg Rutherford
5	Dolomites	15	Kazuo Ishiguro
6	Blue and white	16	Iberia
7	Judith Keppel	17	Eddie Redmayne
8	Buddhism	18	Alto
9	Kimono	19	Larnaca
10	Nicholas Lyndhurst	20	Black Russian

Easy

1   Which European city is home to NATO's HQ?

2   Transylvania is a region of which country?

3   Which is the largest of the Channel Islands?

4   On which river does the city of Cologne stand?

5   What sparkling wine is made in the Piedmont region of Italy?

6   In 1992 where were the Summer Olympic Games held?

7   Which body of water lies between Greece and Turkey?

8   What is the capital city of Iceland?

9   Which small European principality contains the district of Monte Carlo?

10   Which flower is most closely associated with the Netherlands?

Medium

11   Goulash is a traditional stew from which country?

12   Which European country saw the Solidarity movement in the early 1980s?

13   Graz and Linz are both located in which European country?

14   What is the official residence of the president of France?

15   With which country does Portugal share its only border?

16   In which German state is the city of Munich?

17   Which country lies between Estonia and Lithuania?

18   Which state within Rome contains St Peter's?

19   Europe's first Disney theme park was built near which city?

20   Which French city in Burgundy is famed for its mustard?

Hard

Answers to QUIZ 118 – Action Films

1	Harrison Ford	11	Mel Gibson
2	Jackie Chan	12	Sarah Connor
3	*The Maze Runner*	13	Callahan
4	Asteroid	14	Rambo
5	*The Last Samurai*	15	*Black Panther*
6	Cubby	16	Steven Spielberg
7	Arnold Schwarzenegger	17	Matt Damon
8	*Dead Man's Chest*	18	1981
9	Austin Powers	19	John McClane
10	2012	20	A volcanic eruption

1   Which 1987 thriller starred Glenn Close and Michael Douglas?

2   In which city is Tiananmen Square found?

3   What is the medical term for lockjaw?

4   What style of canoe is used by the Inuit?

5   *Ol' Man River* is a song from which musical?

6   In which English county is the Lake District?

7   Which actor starred in the 2017 film *American Made*?

8   The famous dandies Nash and Brummell shared which nickname?

9   Who was the lead singer of the Eurythmics?

10   What word describes a lifestyle devoted to pleasure-seeking?

11   In which county is Ventnor located?

12   What was the first name of legendary Russian ballerina Miss Pavlova?

13   The TV series *Ally McBeal* starred which actress in the title role?

14   Which small guitar has a name meaning "jumping flea"?

15   What was the title of the 1970s sitcom about a self-sufficient couple in suburbia?

16   What is the use of fragrant essential oils as a treatment in alternative medicine called?

17   Ancient writers Homer and Sophocles wrote in which language?

18   Which river flows through Stockport and Warrington?

19   Which Russian seaport shares its name with a heavenly being?

20   What colour are the flowers of the herb borage?

Answers to QUIZ 119 – Pot Luck

1	Blenheim Palace	11	Angelina Jolie
2	The Undertones	12	Hovercraft
3	(Erwin) Rommel	13	Apple
4	Powys	14	Beatrix Potter
5	Columbo	15	*The Addams Family*
6	Red	16	Pawn
7	Arabic	17	Blue
8	Cellar	18	Maple
9	Knot	19	Señor
10	Shelley	20	Berliner

QUIZ 122 – Money

1 In which year was the first polymer banknote issued by the Bank of England?

2 What term is given to an investment or insurance policy that pays a fixed sum of money at regular intervals?

3 What is the old term for money or food given to the poor?

4 In which year did the UK introduce decimalisation?

5 What is a person who studies the production and consumption of wealth called?

6 Which initials describe a bank's "hole in the wall"?

7 Which US institution acts as a central bank?

8 A "grand" refers to how many pounds?

9 What name is given to a person in charge of a society's funds?

10 On which day of the week is Maundy Money traditionally given?

11 Who appeared on the £5 note before Jane Austen?

12 Who became Chancellor of the Exchequer in July 2016?

13 In which year was the £1 coin introduced?

14 What do the letters ISA stand for in a UK financial context?

15 What name is given to a situation of increased prices and a fall in the value of money?

16 NatWest became part of which banking group in 2000?

17 Which famous New York thoroughfare is the US financial centre?

18 Which pre-decimal coin was commonly known as a tanner?

19 "My Word is My Bond" is the motto of which British institution?

20 Which decimal coin was last produced in 1984?

Answers to QUIZ 120 – Europe

1 Brussels
2 Romania
3 Jersey
4 Rhine
5 Asti
6 Barcelona
7 Aegean Sea
8 Reykjavik
9 Monaco
10 Tulip
11 Hungary
12 Poland
13 Austria
14 The Élysée Palace
15 Spain
16 Bavaria
17 Latvia
18 Vatican City
19 Paris
20 Dijon

1   Who wrote the award winning 1984 novel *Hotel du Lac*?

2   The 41st and 43rd US presidents of the USA shared which surname?

3   Which god is the Greek equivalent of Neptune?

4   Which is Britain's oldest cathedral?

5   What is the selection of small dishes served in a Spanish restaurant called?

6   What term is given to the widow of a peer who retains his property or title?

7   Which bulbous narrow-necked bottle is used in domestic wine-making?

8   Meg Ryan co-starred with which actor in the 1989 film *When Harry Met Sally*?

9   In which country was tennis champion Novak Djokovic born?

10   What was the name of Ross Kemp's character in *EastEnders*?

11   What term is given to the projecting part on a wheel?

12   Weymouth and Corfe Castle are found in which English county?

13   Which item, sometimes eaten for breakfast, contains pork, dried blood and suet?

14   Which ornamental fabric is a traditional hallmark of Nottingham?

15   The 2000 film *How the Grinch Stole Christmas* starred which actor?

16   Which French word is used for a funeral procession?

17   Which country is bordered by Bolivia and Paraguay to the north?

18   *Back to Black* was a 2006 album for which singer?

19   Which London street leads from Trafalgar Square to the Houses of Parliament?

20   Which 1984 sci-fi film was based on a Frank Herbert novel?

Easy

Medium

Hard

Answers to QUIZ 121 – Pot Luck

1	*Fatal Attraction*	11	Isle of Wight
2	Beijing	12	Anna
3	Tetanus	13	Calista Flockhart
4	Kayak	14	Ukulele
5	*Show Boat*	15	*The Good Life*
6	Cumbria	16	Aromatherapy
7	Tom Cruise	17	Greek
8	Beau	18	Mersey
9	Annie Lennox	19	Archangel
10	Hedonism	20	Blue

Easy

1   What flavouring is used in Earl Grey tea?

2   Which substance obtained from burning wood is used as a drawing stick?

3   Who created the character of Little Grey Rabbit?

4   Which group had a hit with *Grey Day* in 1981?

5   Pewter is an alloy of tin and which other metal?

6   Which actress played Lois Lane in the 2013 film *Man of Steel*?

7   The greyhound dog lends its name to a company specialising in long-distance travel using which vehicle?

8   In the title of the 1984 film, which fictional character was associated with the legend of Greystoke?

9   What two paint colours are mixed to make grey?

10 What was the name of Leslie Ash's character in the TV series *Men Behaving Badly*?

11 Who wrote the 2011 best-seller *Fifty Shades of Grey*?

12 Which cook and food writer wrote the 2010 autobiography *Toast*?

13 Whose debut novel was *Agnes Grey* (1847)?

Medium

14 What was the nickname of Jennifer Grey's character in the 1987 film *Dirty Dancing*?

15 Which hair colour can be described as "platinum"?

16 In greyhound racing, what colour does the dog in trap one wear?

17 Which fictional detective made great use of his "little grey cells"?

18 Who played hairdresser Truvy Jones in the 1989 film *Steel Magnolias*?

19 What title is given to a monk who is a member of an order founded by St Francis of Assisi?

20 Which South Yorkshire city is particularly associated with steel?

Hard

Answers to QUIZ 122 – Money

1	2016	11	Charles Darwin
2	An annuity	12	Philip Hammond
3	Alms	13	1983
4	1971	14	Individual Savings Account
5	An economist	15	Inflation
6	ATM	16	Royal Bank of Scotland
7	Federal Reserve	17	Wall Street
8	1000	18	Sixpence
9	Treasurer	19	The Stock Exchange
10	Thursday	20	1/2p

QUIZ 125 – Pot Luck

ANSWERS ON PAGE 127

1 How is the domestic cavy better known?

2 Which British painter (b.1922) was the grandson of Sigmund Freud?

3 From which fish is caviar obtained?

4 What type of creature is a howler?

5 Who were the founders of the city-state Tenochtitlan?

6 Which 1969 Ken Loach film centres around a boy and his pet bird?

7 Which region of France forms a peninsula between the Bay of Biscay and the English Channel?

8 *Rock the Casbah* was a 1982 single by which group?

9 Which famous piece of needlework shows the Norman Conquest?

10 Which hymn begins with the words "And did those feet in ancient time"?

11 Who was Bailey's partner in the famous American circus?

12 What was the name of Lynda Baron's character in *Open All Hours* and its sequel?

13 Who commanded China's Long March in the 1930s?

14 *Cider with Rosie* is an autobiographical novel by which author?

15 Which US state is known as the "Lone Star State"?

16 Which former US Secretary of State shared the Nobel Peace Prize in 1973?

17 Who recorded the 1976 album *Songs in the Key of Life*?

18 Acetylsalicylic acid is the scientific name for which common painkiller?

19 Which alloy is a mixture of copper and tin?

20 Which four letters indicate that a reply to a letter is required?

Answers to QUIZ 123 – Pot Luck

1	Anita Brookner	11	Cam
2	Bush	12	Dorset
3	Poseidon	13	Black pudding
4	Canterbury	14	Lace
5	Tapas	15	Jim Carrey
6	Dowager	16	Cortège
7	Demijohn	17	Argentina
8	Billy Crystal	18	Amy Winehouse
9	Serbia	19	Whitehall
10	Grant Mitchell	20	*Dune*

Easy

1. Which group had a hit in 2004 with *Somewhere Only We Know*?

2. Which song was the only UK no.1 hit for Babylon Zoo?

3. In which year was *Hold My Hand* a hit for Jess Glynne...?

4. ...and with whom did she feature the previous year on *Rather Be*?

5. What type of creature was seen in an advert for Cadbury's playing the drums to Phil Collins' *In The Air Tonight*?

6. In which decade did Snap! have a hit with *Rhythm is a Dancer*?

7. Ellie Goulding covered which Sir Elton John song in 2010?

8. Which group had a 1982 hit with *Living on the Ceiling*?

9. Which Rolling Stones song was used by Microsoft to advertise Windows® 95?

10. *The Impossible Dream* is a song from which 1964 musical?

11. What item of clothing did Lord David Dundas want to put on in 1977?

12. *The Final Countdown* was the only UK no.1 hit for which band?

Medium

13. Which song begins "Left a good job in the city, working for the man ev'ry night and day"?

14. The flight of which insect provided inspiration for a piece of music by Rimsky-Korsakov?

15. Who recorded 1992's *The Passenger*, minus Ricky Gardiner?

16. Dvorak's *New World Symphony* featured in a famous advert for which brand of sliced bread?

17. Who wrote Bonnie Tyler's hit *Total Eclipse of the Heart*?

18. In which year did Take That top the charts with *Shine*?

19. Which composer wrote *The Flower Duet*, used in a 1989 British Airways advert?

20. Which band had a 1989 hit with *I Want it All*?

Hard

Answers to QUIZ 124 – Shades of Grey

1	Bergamot	11	EL James
2	Charcoal	12	Nigel Slater
3	Alison Uttley	13	Anne Brontë
4	Madness	14	Baby
5	Lead	15	Blonde
6	Amy Adams	16	Red
7	Bus	17	Hercule Poirot
8	Tarzan	18	Dolly Parton
9	Black and white	19	Grey Friar
10	Deborah	20	Sheffield

1 What was the nickname of Wellington, who defeated Napoleon at Waterloo in 1815?

2 What is the collective name for plants of the heather family?

3 Who, in folklore, pulled a thorn from the paw of a lion?

4 In which European country would you find the city of Bilbao?

5 What is the common name of nitrous oxide?

6 In which city can you visit *HMS Victory*?

7 Which actor starred in the 1967 film *Half a Sixpence*?

8 What is the name of the *David Copperfield* character who optimistically expects that "something will turn up"?

9 Which town in south-east England is famed for its Ford car factory?

10 What word describes a building officially designated as historically or culturally significant?

11 Which Italian city is capital of the Lombardy region?

12 What is the study of the nature of God and religion?

13 What is the term for a fear of spiders?

14 *When a Man Loves a Woman* was a hit in 1966 for which singer?

15 The Pilgrim Fathers sailed from which port in 1620?

16 Mayonnaise combined with ketchup is the basis for which sauce?

17 What term is given to a male duck?

18 What was the name of Trevor Eve's character in the TV series *Waking the Dead*?

19 Cabbage belongs to which plant genus?

20 In which US state is the region of Death Valley?

Easy

Medium

Hard

Answers to QUIZ 125 – Pot Luck

1	A guinea pig	11	Barnum
2	Lucian Freud	12	Gladys Emmanuel
3	Sturgeon	13	Mao Zedong
4	Monkey	14	Laurie Lee
5	Aztecs	15	Texas
6	*Kes*	16	Henry Kissinger
7	Brittany	17	Stevie Wonder
8	The Clash	18	Aspirin
9	Bayeux Tapestry	19	Bronze
10	*Jerusalem*	20	RSVP

Easy

1. Which game used to be known as "housey housey"?
2. The highest hand in poker is what kind of flush?
3. Which chess piece can only move diagonally?
4. Which Algarve city has the same name as a card game?
5. What is the American name for the board-game draughts?
6. How many weapons are there in Cluedo®?
7. Which game is played on a board with 24 narrow triangles?
8. A board and pegs are traditionally used to keep score in which card game?
9. Which board game takes its name from the Latin for "I play"?
10. What colour are the history questions in Trivial Pursuit™?
11. What is the cheapest property on a standard Monopoly™ board?
12. Which card game shares its name with a type of bridge?

Medium

13. Squidgers are used in which indoor game?
14. Which children's card game traditionally includes Mr Bun the Baker?
15. In solo whist, what is a call of nine tricks?
16. What is the highest-ranking suit of cards in a game of bridge?
17. Which gambling game has a French name meaning "small wheel"?
18. The Pokémon™ Pikachu is what colour?
19. In which decade was Pictionary® first published?
20. In which game do players act out the titles of films, books etc?

Hard

Answers to QUIZ 126 – Music Used in Adverts

1	Keane	11	Jeans
2	*Spaceman*	12	Europe
3	2015	13	*Proud Mary*
4	Clean Bandit	14	Bumblebee
5	Gorilla	15	Iggy Pop
6	1990s	16	Hovis®
7	*Your Song*	17	Jim Steinman
8	Blancmange	18	2006
9	*Start Me Up*	19	Delibes
10	*Man of La Mancha*	20	Queen

ANSWERS ON PAGE 131

1   Who was the first woman to fly the Atlantic solo?

2   Which singer had a hit with *On a Night Like This* in 2000?

3   Which mound-building insect is also called the white ant?

4   What type of food is focaccia?

5   Which gas makes up about 21% of the earth's atmosphere?

6   Which actor starred as James Stevens in the 1993 film *The Remains of the Day*?

7   Who wrote *Lady Chatterley's Lover*?

8   On which English river is Evesham situated?

9   Which French word is applied to the design and making of clothes to customers' requirements?

10   What name is given to a vocal piece such as *Nessun Dorma*?

11   According to legend, which lady rode naked through the streets of Coventry?

12   Which international airport has the code MIA?

13   Which wealthy industrialist was portrayed by Leonardo DiCaprio in the 2004 film *The Aviator*?

14   Which 20th-century word was coined to describe promotional copy for a book or film?

15   How many "Tribes" took Frankie Goes to Hollywood to the top of the charts in 1984?

16   Which ocean lies to the east of South Africa?

17   What was the surname of Ralph Waldo, the American philosopher and poet?

18   In which county is Weston-super-Mare?

19   Which 1970s TV series starred John Thaw and Dennis Waterman?

20   What is the common name for the tympanum?

Easy

Medium

Hard

Answers to QUIZ 127 – Pot Luck

1	The Iron Duke	11	Milan
2	Erica	12	Theology
3	Androcles	13	Arachnophobia
4	Spain	14	Percy Sledge
5	Laughing gas	15	Plymouth
6	Portsmouth	16	Thousand Island dressing
7	Tommy Steele	17	Drake
8	Mr Micawber	18	Peter Boyd
9	Dagenham	19	*Brassica*
10	Listed	20	California

ANSWERS ON PAGE 132

Easy

1   Stephen Fry played a solicitor in which series set in the fictional town of Market Shipborough?

2   What was the first name of 1980s TV barrister Rumpole of the Bailey?

3   Which actress played Patty Hewes in the series *Damages*?

4   Which series starred Maxine Peake and Rupert Penry-Jones as barristers?

5   Who played the title role in the series *Judge John Deed*?

6   Who starred in the series *New Street Law*?

7   Which long-running US series that started in 1990 shows a crime from both the police and the court perspective...?

8   ...and in the British version, who played DS Ronnie Brooks?

9   Alicia Florrick is the title character in which series...?

10   ...and what is the title of the sequel series that began in 2017?

11   What was the name of William Shatner's character in the series *Boston Legal*?

12   In which series did Meghan Markle appear from 2011 to 2018?

13   In the ITV drama series *Eternal Law*, what type of beings were Zak and Thomas?

14   Which series featured a firm with partners Leland McKenzie and Douglas Brackman Jr?

Medium

15   Which actress starred in the sitcom *Is It Legal*?

16   What was the nickname of Andrew Lincoln's character in the 1990s series *This Life*?

17   Who played the title role in the 1980s series *Garrow's Law*?

18   Which actor starred in the series *The Irish RM*?

19   John Thaw played the title role in which 1990s series about a barrister?

20   Which former *Spooks* actress starred as a divorce lawyer in the 2018 series *The Split*?

Hard

Answers to QUIZ 128 – Games

1	Bingo	11	Old Kent Road
2	Royal flush	12	Pontoon
3	Bishop	13	Tiddlywinks
4	Faro	14	Happy Families
5	Checkers	15	Abundance
6	Six	16	Spades
7	Backgammon	17	Roulette
8	Cribbage	18	Yellow
9	Ludo	19	1980s
10	Yellow	20	Charades

1   "Clap along if you feel like a room without a roof", are lyrics from which 2013 song?

2   What is the name of the former county of west Wales, abolished in 1996, which had the chief town Carmarthen?

3   Who directed the 1972 film *Cabaret*?

4   Of the four chambers of the human heart, what are the two larger, lower chambers called?

5   In which temperature scale does water boil at 212°?

6   Which religion is presided over by the Pope?

7   Danny DeVito played dispatcher Louie in which US comedy series?

8   What is the most famous feature of St Mary and All Saints Parish Church in Chesterfield?

9   What colour is carmine?

10   What mixture of sand, gravel and pitch is used for roads and roofs?

11   The TV series *Desperate Housewives* was set in which fictional road?

12   Who was the Wimbledon women's singles champion in 1977?

13   What is the surname of the Sheridan character known for her word blunders?

14   What kind of establishment is "Bart's" in London?

15   The *Famous Five* series was written by which author?

16   In terms of business, what do the initials CBI stand for?

17   What is the name of the main body of the church where the congregation sit?

18   Traditionally, Béarnaise sauce is served with what main dish?

19   What name is given to the young of an elephant?

20   Who was the lead singer of The Boomtown Rats?

Easy

Medium

Hard

Answers to QUIZ 129 – Pot Luck

1	Amelia Earhart	11	Godiva
2	Kylie Minogue	12	Miami
3	Termite	13	Howard Hughes
4	Bread	14	Blurb
5	Oxygen	15	Two
6	Sir Anthony Hopkins	16	Indian
7	DH Lawrence	17	Emerson
8	Avon	18	Somerset
9	Couture	19	*The Sweeney*
10	Aria	20	The eardrum

Easy

1. PD James' 2011 novel *Death Comes to Pemberley* is a sequel to which classic novel?
2. The TV series *Smallville* follows the early life of which superhero?
3. Which musical is a backstory of *The Wizard of Oz*?
4. What was the title of the sequel to Walt Disney's *Fantasia*, released 59 years after the original?
5. *Young Hyacinth* was a 2016 one-off prequel to which TV series?
6. Which actor starred in the 2005 prequel *Batman Begins*?
7. What was the sequel to *Saturday Night Fever*, directed by Sylvester Stallone?
8. What was the title of the prequel to *Only Fools and Horses...*?
9. ...and what was the title of the sequel featuring Boycie and his family?
10. What was the sequel to the 1984 film *Romancing the Stone*?

Medium

11. *Young Sheldon* is a prequel to which sitcom?
12. *Tokyo Drift* was the 2006 sequel in which film franchise?
13. Who played Stephanie in the 1982 film *Grease 2*?
14. The 2009 novel *Return to the Hundred Acre Wood* featured which children's character?
15. In the Inspector Morse prequel *Endeavour*, who plays the title role...?
16. ...and who played James Hathaway in the sequel *Lewis*?
17. The TV series *Bates Motel* is a contemporary prequel to which classic film?
18. Who provided the voice of the Fairy Godmother in the 2004 film *Shrek 2*?
19. What is the title of the sequel to *Alice's Adventures in Wonderland*?
20. Who played the title role in the 2009 film *X-Men Origins: Wolverine*?

Hard

---

1 *Tiger Feet* was a 1974 hit for which group?

2 Which central Asian inland sea has been shrinking since the 1960s?

3 What imperial measurement unit is equal to 0.9144 metres?

4 Which gas has the chemical symbol H?

5 Which is Africa's largest venomous snake?

6 Which brass instrument shares its name with a wild flower and a plastic bead?

7 Gary Cooper and Grace Kelly starred in which classic 1952 western?

8 How many points win championship darts games?

9 Which tennis player won the tournament at Queen's in 2018?

10 Tinseltown refers to which part of Los Angeles?

11 Which language is spoken in Prague?

12 Which former county of north-west London was abolished in 1965?

13 Which car manufacturer produced the Silver Ghost?

14 Which river flows through Manchester?

15 Which adjective refers to the nose?

16 What French term denotes a thing done, or a decision already made?

17 In the songwriting duo Burt Bacharach and Hal David, who wrote the lyrics?

18 From which language did the Romance languages derive?

19 Which fruit has a morello variety?

20 In which county is High Wycombe?

Answers to QUIZ 131 – Pot Luck

1	*Happy* (Pharrell Williams)	11	Wisteria Lane
2	Dyfed	12	Virginia Wade
3	Bob Fosse	13	Malaprop
4	Ventricles (left and right)	14	Hospital
5	Fahrenheit	15	Enid Blyton
6	Catholicism	16	Confederation of British Industry
7	*Taxi*	17	Nave
8	Crooked spire	18	Steak
9	Red	19	Calf
10	Asphalt	20	Bob Geldof

1   The cake parkin is flavoured with which spice?

2   Eskimo Pie was the first type of which sweet treat?

3   What is the Italian word for "nougat"?

4   Which dessert is made with bread, jam and meringue?

5   What name is given to a sponge that has more than one colour?

6   From what are Pontefract cakes made?

7   What type of pastry is used to make a chocolate éclair?

8   What are the two main ingredients of a meringue?

9   At what time of year would a bûche de Noël be eaten?

10 Which nuts are used to make a macaroon?

11 Pectin is used in making what sweet item?

12 Which cocktail consists of white rum, sugar, lime juice, sparkling water and mint?

13 Gelato is what type of dessert?

14 Bakewell tart takes its name from a town in which county?

15 Which Scottish whisky liqueur, first produced in 1910, is sweetened with honey?

16 Tablet is a type of fudge from which country?

17 What cake is made of pink and yellow squares and covered in marzipan?

18 What name is given to the popular French dessert of upside-down apple pie?

19 Which type of bean is used as a substitute for chocolate?

20 An Eccles cake is a pastry filled with what?

Answers to QUIZ 132 – Prequels and Sequels

1	*Pride and Prejudice*	11	*The Big Bang Theory*
2	Superman	12	*Fast and Furious*
3	*Wicked*	13	Michelle Pfeiffer
4	*Fantasia 2000*	14	Winnie-the-Pooh
5	*Keeping Up Appearances*	15	Shaun Evans
6	Christian Bale	16	Laurence Fox
7	*Staying Alive*	17	*Psycho*
8	*Rock & Chips*	18	Jennifer Saunders
9	*The Green Green Grass*	19	*Alice Through the Looking Glass*
10	*The Jewel of the Nile*	20	Hugh Jackman

1 Which West Indian republic has Port-au-Prince as its capital?

2 Which soft metal has the symbol Cu?

3 In which Welsh city was the TV series *Torchwood* originally set?

4 Chevre cheese is made from the milk of which animal?

5 Who directed the 2013 version of *The Great Gatsby*?

6 Which expression is used after a good fencing hit?

7 Which first name is shared by architects Gehry and Lloyd Wright?

8 What type of animal has a grizzly variety?

9 In which county is Alderley Edge?

10 Which country won the Eurovision Song Contest three years in a row from 1992?

11 Which type of hardy cabbage has a curly variety?

12 Which Irish group's debut hit was *Runaway* in 1996?

13 Which river forms much of the boundary between Devon and Cornwall?

14 Philip K Dick's short story *We Can Remember it for You Wholesale* is the basis for which sci-fi film?

15 Which symbol is given to beaches meeting stringent environmental and safety standards?

16 What was the name of the secret base in *Thunderbirds*?

17 In which year did the 50p coin first come into circulation?

18 Which of the Great Lakes of North America is not in Canada?

19 Where in London is Speakers' Corner?

20 Who had a UK hit in 1975 with *Stand By Your Man*?

Easy

Medium

Hard

Answers to QUIZ 133 – Pot Luck

1	Mud	11	Czech
2	Aral	12	Middlesex
3	A yard	13	Rolls Royce
4	Hydrogen	14	Irwell
5	Mamba	15	Nasal
6	Bugle	16	*Fait accompli*
7	*High Noon*	17	Hal David
8	501	18	Latin
9	Marin Čilić	19	Cherry
10	Hollywood	20	Buckinghamshire

Easy

1 New York's Brooklyn Bridge connects Brooklyn to which other borough?

2 In which county is the Test cricket ground of Trent Bridge located?

3 What creature lived under the bridge in the tale of *The Three Billy Goats Gruff*?

4 Which area of Bristol is famous for its suspension bridge?

5 In which Italian city is the Ponte Vecchio?

6 Which footbridge across the Thames was briefly opened in 2000 then closed until 2002?

7 Which Scottish river, rising in the Trossachs, gives its name to a famous railway bridge?

8 Which football team plays its home games at Stamford Bridge?

9 The bridge at Kyle of Lochalsh links the Scottish mainland to which island?

10 The Golden Gate Bridge is in which American city?

11 Which Australian bridge is nicknamed "The Coathanger"?

12 In which county is Ironbridge Gorge?

13 The TV series *The Bridge*, first broadcast in 2011, is set in which two countries?

14 Where does the Oxford and Cambridge Boat Race start?

Medium

15 Which duo had a 1970 hit with *Bridge Over Troubled Water*?

16 Which walled market town on the north coast of Wales has a castle and a suspension bridge?

17 The Rialto Bridge is a famous landmark in which city?

18 What is the name of the bridge at the Dartford Crossing over the Thames?

19 Who co-starred with Meryl Streep in *The Bridges of Madison County*?

20 Who wrote the 1886 novel *The Mayor of Casterbridge*?

Hard

Answers to QUIZ 134 – Sweet Things

1	Ginger	11	Jam
2	Choc-ice	12	Mojito
3	Torrone	13	Ice-cream
4	Queen of Puddings	14	Derbyshire
5	Marble cake	15	Drambuie®
6	Liquorice	16	Scotland
7	Choux	17	Battenberg
8	Egg whites and sugar	18	Tarte tatin
9	Christmas	19	Carob
10	Almonds	20	Currants

ANSWERS ON PAGE 139

1   Who was Sooty and Sweep's panda friend in the 1960s TV puppet show?

2   In which body of water is Lundy Island?

3   "Love apple" was an old name for which food item?

4   What is the surname of the family in *The Darling Buds of May*?

5   Which actor starred in the 1990 film *Kindergarten Cop*?

6   Which sport has "lawn" and "real" versions?

7   How many finger holes are there in a tenpin bowling ball?

8   Which actor starred as Ryan Bingham in the 2009 film *Up in the Air*?

9   What term is given to a first coat of plaster applied to a wall?

10   What is the nickname for a native of Tyneside?

11   Who played Captain Salazar in the 2017 *Pirates of the Caribbean: Dead Men Tell No Tales* film?

12   What is the name given to the grounds or buildings of a college or university?

13   Split is a city in which European country?

14   Who wrote *The Hunchback of Notre-Dame* (1831)?

15   What is a male pig called?

16   Pernod® has what flavour?

17   What term is given to a mound of stones used as a memorial or landmark?

18   Who sang *Livin' La Vida Loca* in 1999?

19   The Tiber river runs through which European capital city?

20   Armando Iannucci co-wrote and directed which film released in 2017?

Easy

Medium

Hard

Answers to QUIZ 135 – Pot Luck

1	Haiti	11	Kale
2	Copper	12	The Corrs
3	Cardiff	13	Tamar
4	The goat	14	*Total Recall*
5	Baz Luhrmann	15	Blue flag
6	Touché	16	Tracy Island
7	Frank	17	1969
8	Bear	18	Lake Michigan
9	Cheshire	19	Hyde Park
10	Ireland	20	Tammy Wynette

Easy

1   Doric, Ionian and which other style make up the three orders of Greek architecture?

2   What shape is a gable?

3   On which part of a building would you find a cupola?

4   Which cathedral sits on Ludgate Hill?

5   For what purpose did Mughal Emperor Shah Jahan build the Taj Mahal?

6   What type of feature is a transom?

7   In which city is the Bird's Nest Olympic stadium?

8   Which Hungarian architect's surname did Ian Fleming borrow for a Bond villain?

9   Which French engineer designed the internal structure of the Statue of Liberty?

10   On which type of building might you find bartizans and a portcullis?

11   Of what material is the London Shard made?

12   Who designed the Millennium Dome?

13   What shape is a rotunda?

14   Of which surprising material is the dome of the Roman Pantheon constructed?

Medium

15   For what purpose is rock wool used in a building?

16   Which Glaswegian architect and designer created several Art Nouveau buildings in his home city?

17   What term is given to a small floor built between two main floors of a building?

18   In which New Zealand city is the Cardboard Cathedral, created after a 2011 earthquake?

19   Who designed London's Cenotaph?

20   What name is given to a sun-dried building brick?

Hard

Answers to QUIZ 136 – Bridges

1	Manhattan	11	Sydney Harbour Bridge
2	Nottinghamshire	12	Shropshire
3	Troll	13	Denmark and Sweden
4	Clifton	14	Putney Bridge
5	Florence	15	Simon and Garfunkel
6	The Millennium Bridge	16	Conwy
7	Forth	17	Venice
8	Chelsea FC	18	Queen Elizabeth II Bridge
9	Skye	19	Clint Eastwood
10	San Francisco	20	Thomas Hardy

1   Which gardening implement has Dutch and draw varieties?

2   *Hotel California* was a 1970s hit for which group?

3   Which French word means a very thin pancake?

4   What is the study of history through excavation?

5   Which citrus fruit takes its name from a Moroccan port?

6   Which Latin phrase means "for a specific purpose only"?

7   On *University Challenge,* which category of question is worth ten points?

8   In which county are the Lost Gardens of Heligan?

9   Peter Sellers played which military scientist in a 1964 Stanley Kubrick film?

10   What name is given to the area between about 23° north and south of the Equator?

11   What armoured vehicle was first used on the Somme in 1916?

12   Which London Underground line terminates at Elephant and Castle?

13   The agave plant is the source of which distilled Mexican spirit?

14   Which kind of state has a president rather than a monarch?

15   Which Beatles song includes the line "cos I don't care too much for money"?

16   What is the sign of BSI approval?

17   What name is given to a gathering of witches?

18   The TV series *Lovejoy* starred which actor in the title role?

19   How many lives is a cat said to have?

20   Which flower is the national emblem of Japan?

Answers to QUIZ 137 – Pot Luck

1	Soo		11	Javier Bardem
2	Bristol Channel		12	Campus
3	Tomato		13	Croatia
4	Larkin		14	Victor Hugo
5	Arnold Schwarzenegger		15	Boar
6	Tennis		16	Aniseed
7	Three		17	Cairn
8	George Clooney		18	Ricky Martin
9	Render		19	Rome
10	Geordie		20	*The Death of Stalin*

Easy

1   Which two summer months were named after Roman emperors?

2   What term is used to describe a year with 29 days in February?

3   Who starred as Ron Kovic in the 1989 film *Born on the Fourth of July*?

4   Who played Betty Draper in *Mad Men*?

5   What, according to TS Eliot, is "the cruellest month"?

6   What is the state capital of Maine, USA?

7   Who sang *January February* in 1982?

8   Who played Edina's mother in *Absolutely Fabulous*?

9   *June is Bustin' Out All Over* is a song from which musical?

10 Which song was the only UK no.1 single for The Four Seasons?

11 Which "mad" animal is associated with the month of March?

12 The Oktoberfest takes place in which European city?

13 Who recorded the 1971 song *Maggie May*?

14 March is named after which Roman god?

Medium

15 Which month represents a consonant in the radio phonetic alphabet?

16 Who played April in the TV series *Parks and Recreation*?

17 What month did Earth, Wind and Fire sing about in 1978?

18 What was *Red October* in the title of a 1990 film?

19 Who won the 2005 Best Actress Oscar for her role as June Carter Cash in *Walk the Line*?

20 In which year did Theresa May become UK Prime Minister?

Hard

Answers to QUIZ 138 – Architects and Architecture

1	Corinthian	11	Glass
2	Triangular	12	Richard Rogers (Baron Rogers of Riverside)
3	Roof	13	Round
4	St Paul's	14	Concrete
5	As a mausoleum for his favourite wife	15	Insulation
6	Window (or a crossbar above it)	16	Charles Rennie Mackintosh
7	Beijing	17	Mezzanine
8	Goldfinger	18	Christchurch
9	Gustav Eiffel	19	Sir Edwin Lutyens
10	Castle	20	Adobe

1   Which container port lies across the Thames Estuary from Gravesend?

2   How many crotchets are there in a semibreve?

3   *El Gordo* is the lottery in which country?

4   What is the device that controls an aircraft by instruments called?

5   Which film series starred Vanessa Hudgens and Zac Efron?

6   What title is given to the wife of an earl?

7   In which city is the Crucible, home of the world snooker tournament?

8   What was the first name of epic film director Mr B DeMille?

9   What colour is the ribbon on the Victoria Cross?

10   Who topped the charts in the 1970s with *How Can I Be Sure* and *Daydreamer*?

11   What is the reading system of raised type for blind people?

12   The active volcano Cotopaxi Is In which range of mountains?

13   Which racecourse has an annual meeting called "Glorious"?

14   What are male hares called?

15   What is the title of Fleetwood Mac's eleventh album, released in 1977?

16   Chatsworth House is the ancestral home of which duke?

17   An MOT is required for cars over what age?

18   Which US city hosted the 1996 Summer Olympics?

19   In 1875 what did Captain Matthew Webb become the first person to do?

20   In which county is Frome?

Easy

Medium

Hard

Answers to QUIZ 139 – Pot Luck

1	Hoe	11	Tank
2	Eagles	12	The Bakerloo line
3	Crêpe	13	Tequila
4	Archaeology	14	A republic
5	Tangerine	15	*Can't Buy Me Love*
6	Ad hoc	16	Kitemark
7	Starter question	17	Coven
8	Cornwall	18	Ian McShane
9	Dr Strangelove	19	Nine
10	The Tropics	20	Chrysanthemum

Easy

1   What is the capital of Italy...?

2   ...and in which administrative region does it lie?

3   On which island is the Blue Grotto?

4   Which almond-flavoured liqueur is used to flavour tiramisu?

5   *The Birth of Venus* is a 15th-century work by which Italian artist?

6   Who was the leader of Italy at the outbreak of WWII?

7   What do Italians call the city of Florence?

8   *Nove* is the Italian word for which number?

9   What is the Italian name for squid?

10 An Italian autostrada has what British equivalent?

11 What was the Italian currency unit until 2002?

12 Which island lies at the "toe" of Italy?

13 Basil, oil, Parmesan and pine nuts are the usual ingredients of which green sauce?

14 Which Italian city is the centre of the fashion industry?

Medium

15 Which 19th-century Italian patriot shares his name with a currant biscuit?

16 In which Italian region is Chianti produced?

17 Frittata is an Italian version of which dish?

18 The Testarossa is a model of which Italian car?

19 Which small Italian dumplings are made from semolina or potato?

20 The name of which Italian opera house translates as "The Staircase"?

Hard

Answers to QUIZ 140 – Months

1	July and August	11	Hare
2	Leap year	12	Munich
3	Tom Cruise	13	Sir Rod Stewart
4	January Jones	14	Mars
5	April	15	November
6	Augusta	16	Aubrey Plaza
7	Barbara Dickson	17	September
8	Dame June Whitfield	18	A submarine
9	*Carousel*	19	Reese Witherspoon
10	*December 1963 (Oh, What a Night)*	20	2016

1   Which town is indicated by a postcode prefix of KT?

2   Which London church is the British Catholic Church's headquarters?

3   What is the name given to the crime of deliberately setting fire to property?

4   Heriot-Watt University is in which city?

5   Which canine breed is named from the Welsh for "dwarf dog"?

6   In 2018, which TV series won the Best Drama Series BAFTA?

7   What is the art of growing miniature trees in pots?

8   In which city is Arthur's Seat?

9   What is the birth sign of someone born on New Year's Day?

10   Who starred as a psychologist in the film *The Sixth Sense*?

11   In music, what note is written on the middle line of the treble clef?

12   What is the common name of the Gravelly Hill interchange on the M6?

13   In which county is Beaulieu Motor Museum?

14   Which French dish consists of chicken cooked in red wine?

15   In which body part is the conjunctiva located?

16   Who had a hit in 1986 with *Sledgehammer*?

17   What word is applied to both a synthetic fibre used in knitwear and a type of paint?

18   From which country does Lego® originate?

19   Keswick is located on the northern shore of which lake?

20   What name is given to a lawyer who pleads a case in an English court?

Answers to QUIZ 141 – Pot Luck

1	Tilbury	11	Braille
2	Four	12	The Andes
3	Spain	13	Goodwood
4	Autopilot	14	Bucks
5	*High School Musical*	15	*Rumours*
6	Countess	16	Duke of Devonshire
7	Sheffield	17	Three years
8	Cecil	18	Atlanta
9	Purple	19	Swim the English Channel
10	David Cassidy	20	Somerset

1 Which ship transported the Pilgrim Fathers to America?

2 What slab of rock was discovered in 1799 and enabled the deciphering of Egyptian hieroglyphics?

3 Which volcanic Indonesian island erupted catastrophically in 1883?

4 What was the former name of the Indian city of Chennai?

5 Which Australian state was formerly known as Van Diemen's Land?

6 What was the name given to an Australasian expeditionary soldier during WWI?

7 What was the given name of the Russian tsar known as "the Terrible"?

8 To which Roman conspirator were Julius Caesar's last words supposedly spoken?

9 Which Texas mission was famously defended by Davy Crockett and others in 1836?

10 Which people were conquered by Hernán Cortés?

11 After which Vietnamese statesman is Saigon now named?

12 Which US Civil War battle gave its name to a famous speech made in November 1863?

13 Which former structure in Germany was erected in 1961?

14 Which African country's southern part seceded in 2011?

15 The Enigma Code was cracked at which Buckinghamshire site?

16 Which Norwegian explorer was the first man to reach the South Pole?

17 What was the name given to the part of the Roman Empire now called France?

18 During which conflict did the Gallipoli campaign take place?

19 Which international news agency was founded in London in 1851?

20 On which South Atlantic island did Napoleon die?

Answers to QUIZ 142 – Italy

1	Rome	11	Lira
2	Lazio	12	Sicily
3	Capri	13	Pesto
4	Amaretto	14	Milan
5	Botticelli	15	Garibaldi
6	Benito Mussolini	16	Tuscany
7	Firenze	17	Omelette
8	Nine	18	Ferrari
9	Calamari	19	Gnocchi
10	Motorway	20	La Scala

1   What is the capital of the Bahamas?

2   The Commonwealth Games took place in which British city in 2002?

3   What is the chicken filled with in the dish Chicken Kiev?

4   What was the name of the receptionist in the TV series *The Office*?

5   Which former prison was located in San Francisco Bay?

6   The winter resort of Zermatt is in which country?

7   What was the title of the England World Cup Squad's no.1 hit in 1970?

8   Which poet wrote *A Shropshire Lad*?

9   In which country was actress Salma Hayek born?

10   Which wild cat has varieties including Bengal, Siberian and Sumatran?

11   What type of entertainment is associated with Sadler's Wells?

12   What is the name of Bill Sikes' girlfriend in *Oliver Twist*?

13   Who were Cromwell's Civil War supporters?

14   What is the art of stuffing animals for preservation called?

15   The Italian-inspired village of Portmeirion is in which country?

16   Which bone connects the shoulder to the elbow?

17   Who composed the 1829 opera *William Tell*?

18   What was John Wayne's real name?

19   What is a repository of public and historical records called?

20   In which forest is Robin Hood said to have lived?

Easy

Medium

Hard

Answers to QUIZ 143 – Pot Luck

1	Kingston-upon-Thames	11	B
2	Westminster Cathedral	12	Spaghetti Junction
3	Arson	13	Hampshire
4	Edinburgh	14	Coq au vin
5	Corgi	15	Eye
6	*Peaky Blinders*	16	Peter Gabriel
7	Bonsai	17	Acrylic
8	Edinburgh	18	Denmark
9	Capricorn	19	Derwent Water
10	Bruce Willis	20	Barrister

Easy

1   Who was the original host of the game show *Sale of the Century*?

2   Who replaced Fern Britton as a regular co-presenter of *This Morning*?

3   Main presenters of which series have included Percy Thrower and Toby Buckland?

4   Which *Coast* presenter also presented *A History of Celtic Britain*?

5   Which gameshow was presented by Les Dawson from 1984 to 1990?

6   Who presented all the main series of *Big Brother* when it was on Channel 4?

7   Angus Deayton presented which panel show from 1990 to 2002?

8   Who was the BBC commentator for the Eurovision Song Contest from 1980 to 2008?

9   Alan Titchmarsh presented behind-the-scenes series for Channel 5 in 2017 and 2018 about which organisation?

10 Who became the host of *Fifteen to One* in 2014?

11 Which game show did Jim Bowen host in the 1980s and 1990s?

12 Craig Charles presented which engineering competition from 1998 to 2004?

13 Who was the original presenter of *Blind Date*?

Medium

14 Who is Phil Spencer's regular property programme co-presenter?

15 Which BBC breakfast presenter took part in the 2016 series of *Strictly Come Dancing*?

16 Ruth Langsford married which other presenter in 2010?

17 In which city was Lorraine Kelly born?

18 Who was the 1983-88 female co-host of *Good Morning Britain*?

19 What is the name of Kirsty Gallacher's famous sporting father?

20 What is the name of the series that the three former *Top Gear* hosts went on to present in 2016?

Hard

Answers to QUIZ 144 – World History

1	*Mayflower*	11	Ho Chi Minh
2	The Rosetta Stone	12	Gettysburg
3	Krakatoa	13	Berlin Wall
4	Madras	14	Sudan
5	Tasmania	15	Bletchley Park
6	Anzac	16	Roald Amundsen
7	Ivan	17	Gaul
8	Brutus	18	WWI
9	The Alamo	19	Reuters
10	The Aztecs	20	St Helena

1 In which TV series and film did the character of Huggy Bear appear?

2 What compound is removed during the process of desalinisation?

3 Which university in Birmingham was founded in 1966?

4 Which actor starred as CS Lewis in the 1993 film *Shadowlands*?

5 In which country is the mountainous plateau of the Massif Central?

6 *I'm in the Mood for Dancing* was a 1979 hit for which group of Irish sisters?

7 Which mythical Greek poet entered the underworld to secure release of his wife Eurydice?

8 Which fishing town in Angus is famous for its smoked haddock, known as "smokies"?

9 Grappa is a strong brandy from which country?

10 Which road tunnel is located near the Thames Barrier?

11 Who was the original host of the quiz programme *Mastermind*?

12 Which "Cross" in London refers to the junction of Strand, Whitehall and Cockspur Street?

13 What name is given to an ordained minister ranking next below a priest?

14 Oboes are part of which section of an orchestra?

15 Who preceded Justin Welby as Archbishop of Canterbury?

16 What is a novella?

17 Who was Arnold Ridley's character in *Dad's Army*?

18 What name is given to the distance across a circle, through its centre?

19 American writer Samuel Langhorne Clemens adopted which pen-name?

20 Which fictional city is associated with Batman?

Easy

Medium

Hard

Answers to QUIZ 145 – Pot Luck

1	Nassau	11	Dance
2	Manchester	12	Nancy
3	Garlic butter	13	Roundheads
4	Dawn	14	Taxidermy
5	Alcatraz	15	Wales
6	Switzerland	16	Humerus
7	*Back Home*	17	Rossini
8	AE Housman	18	Marion Morrison
9	Mexico	19	Archive
10	Tiger	20	Sherwood

Easy

1 What term is given to an actor's unscripted lines?

2 Which of Shakespeare's plays features the character of Shylock?

3 What is the final run-through of a play before it is performed?

4 Which allergy is also the title of a play by Sir Noël Coward?

5 In theatrical terms, what do the initials ASM stand for?

6 Who wrote the play *Blood Brothers*?

7 What nationality was the playwright Henrik Ibsen?

8 Which pantomime character frees a genie from a lamp?

9 Where in a theatre would you find the wings?

10 How many people speak during a monologue?

Medium

11 Which playwright wrote *Barefoot in the Park* (1963)?

12 Who wrote the long-running play *The Mousetrap*?

13 What is the name of the thoroughfare in the heart of New York's theatreland?

14 Who wrote the 1954 two one-act plays collectively called *Separate Tables*?

15 What name is given to a film or theatre wardrobe assistant?

16 The play *Toad of Toad Hall* was based on which classic 1908 book?

17 What term is given to a public performance of a play before its official opening?

18 In which area of London is the National Theatre?

19 Which English playwright is famously associated with Scarborough?

20 What name is given to the actors' place of rest in a theatre?

Hard

Answers to QUIZ 146 – Television Presenters

1	Nicholas Parsons	11	*Bullseye*
2	Holly Willoughby	12	*Robot Wars*
3	*Gardeners' World*	13	Cilla Black
4	Neil Oliver	14	Kirstie Allsopp
5	*Blankety Blank*	15	Naga Munchetty
6	Davina McCall	16	Eamonn Holmes
7	*Have I Got News For You*	17	Glasgow
8	Sir Terry Wogan	18	Anne Diamond
9	The National Trust	19	Bernard Gallacher
10	Sandi Toksvig	20	*The Grand Tour*

1 What three colours make up the German flag?

2 On which New York thoroughfare is the Empire State Building?

3 What was the call sign of Val Kilmer's character in the 1986 film *Top Gun*?

4 Which genus of plants includes onions, leeks and garlic?

5 In which county is the town of Biggleswade?

6 Who played Maria in the 1965 film *The Sound of Music*?

7 Which nostalgic TV series took its name from a late 1950s Buddy Holly hit?

8 In Formula 1, what does a red flag mean?

9 What is the secreting structure in a plant or animal such as the thyroid called?

10 What is the Buddhist and Hindu concept of reaping what you sow?

11 The 2009 film *A Single Man* starred which actor?

12 Zucchini is the American term for which vegetable?

13 Who is Roo's mother in the *Winnie-the-Pooh* books?

14 What is the main ingredient of marshmallow?

15 What is a shorter term for adipose tissue?

16 Which classic song was the 1975 Christmas no.1?

17 In Cockney rhyming slang, what phrase is used to refer to a suit?

18 What is the first name of Ms Yousafzai, co-recipient of the 2014 Nobel Peace Prize?

19 The song *Memory* is from which musical?

20 Vienna is the capital of which European country?

Easy

Medium

Hard

Answers to QUIZ 147 – Pot Luck

1	*Starsky and Hutch*	11	Magnus Magnusson
2	Salt	12	Charing
3	Aston	13	Deacon
4	Sir Anthony Hopkins	14	Woodwind
5	France	15	Rowan Williams
6	The Nolan Sisters	16	A short novel
7	Orpheus	17	Private Godfrey
8	Arbroath	18	The diameter
9	Italy	19	Mark Twain
10	Blackwall	20	Gotham

Easy

1 Who wrote the novel *What Katy Did* (1872)?

2 Who had a 2013 hit single with *Roar*?

3 In which film did Kate Winslet play Rose DeWitt Bukater?

4 Who did Katie Derham partner in the 2015 series of *Strictly Come Dancing*...?

5 ...and which series of annual classical concerts is she associated with as a presenter?

6 Kate Ford took over the role of which *Coronation Street* character in 2002?

7 Whose first single in 2003 was *The Closest Thing to Crazy*?

8 Which former *Springwatch* presenter was a presenter on *Top Gear* in the late 1990s?

9 In 2002 who became the first female winner of *Big Brother*?

10 In which English town was model Kate Moss born?

11 Which author created the character of Jackson Brodie, played on TV by Jason Isaacs?

12 2005's *Suddenly I See* won which singer/songwriter an Ivor Novello award?

13 Kate Hudson is the daughter of which famous actress?

14 Who presented the first three series of *The X Factor*?

Medium

15 What is the name of Kate Mara's actress sister?

16 Which singer recorded *Running Up That Hill* in 1985?

17 Who won the 2015 series of *Celebrity Big Brother*...?

18 ...and who was the runner-up?

19 At which university did Prince William and Kate Middleton meet?

20 What is the first name of Mary-Kate Olsen's twin sister?

Hard

Answers to QUIZ 148 – Theatre

1	Ad-libs	11	Neil Simon
2	*The Merchant of Venice*	12	Dame Agatha Christie
3	Dress rehearsal	13	Broadway
4	*Hay Fever*	14	Sir Terence Rattigan
5	Assistant stage manager	15	Dresser
6	Willy Russell	16	*The Wind in the Willows*
7	Norwegian	17	Preview
8	Aladdin	18	The South Bank
9	Either side of the stage	19	Sir Alan Ayckbourn
10	One	20	The green room

1   What name is given to a female donkey?

2   Who was the 39th President of the USA?

3   Who is the heroine of Pasternak's novel *Doctor Zhivago*?

4   The M1 motorway opened in which year?

5   Which French-speaking city in Belgium was the birthplace of writer Georges Simenon and tennis-player Justine Henin?

6   Which British athlete won a second successive Olympic gold medal in the skeleton in 2018?

7   In bingo, which number is traditionally called "Snakes Alive"?

8   What sort of animal is a Cheviot?

9   Who was the two-faced Roman god of doors?

10 What is the term for a follower of Guru Nanak?

11 What is the southernmost province of mainland Spain?

12 What name is given to a follower of St Ignatius Loyola?

13 Which plant is also known as "Adam's Needle"?

14 Ewan McGregor starred with which actress in *A Life Less Ordinary*?

15 What type of drink is amontillado?

16 Who was Rachel's biblical sister?

17 Which South Kensington museum opened in 1857?

18 Who was Poet Laureate from 1968 to 1972?

19 Which fashion designer co-presented the TV series *The Clothes Show* in the 1980s?

20 What is the currency unit of Nepal?

Answers to QUIZ 149 – Pot Luck

1	Black, yellow and red	11	Colin Firth
2	Fifth Avenue	12	Courgette
3	Iceman	13	Kanga
4	*Allium*	14	Sugar
5	Bedfordshire	15	Fat
6	Dame Julie Andrews	16	*Bohemian Rhapsody*
7	*Heartbeat*	17	Whistle and flute
8	The session has been stopped	18	Malala
9	A gland	19	*Cats*
10	Karma	20	Austria

Easy

1   Which 1990s series starred Richard Griffiths as a policeman running a restaurant?

2   Who created the series *Line of Duty*?

3   Which novelist created the characters of Dalziel and Pascoe?

4   Who played Sarah Linden in the US remake of the Danish series *The Killing*?

5   Which US series featured brothers Don and Charlie, an FBI agent and a mathematician?

6   In which 1980s detective series did Pierce Brosnan play the lead role?

7   Which US series starred Michael Emerson as billionaire Harold Finch?

8   Which fictional detective's cases included *The Dead of Jericho* and *The Daughters of Cain*?

9   Who starred in the 1980s series *The Chinese Detective*?

10   In which series did Geraldine Somerville play DS Penhaligon?

Medium

11   What is the name of the lead character in the series *Orange is the New Black*?

12   Who played Detective Jimmy McNulty in the series *The Wire*?

13   Which series starred Anna Carteret as Inspector Kate Longton?

14   In which town is the Welsh series *Hinterland* set?

15   What was the title of the US version of *Broadchurch*?

16   Who starred in the 1970s and 80s TV series *Quincy M.E.*?

17   In which series did Detective John Munch first appear?

18   Who played Hastings to David Suchet's Hercule Poirot between 1989 and 2003?

19   Who created the series *Happy Valley*?

20   Who played Jack Malone in the series *Without a Trace*?

Hard

Answers to QUIZ 150 – Kate

1	Susan Coolidge	11	Kate Atkinson
2	Katy Perry	12	KT Tunstall
3	*Titanic*	13	Goldie Hawn
4	Anton du Beke	14	Kate Thornton
5	The Proms	15	Rooney Mara
6	Tracy Barlow	16	Kate Bush
7	Katie Melua	17	Katie Price
8	Kate Humble	18	Katie Hopkins
9	Kate Lawler	19	St Andrews
10	Croydon	20	Ashley

QUIZ 153 – Pot Luck

ANSWERS ON PAGE 155

1   The mazurka is a dance from which country?

2   Which 2007 film about a serial killer starred Jake Gyllenhaal?

3   What is the name of the imaginary kingdom in Anthony Hope's *The Prisoner of Zenda* (1894)?

4   Which Old Testament character was known for his patience?

5   Singer Robyn Fenty is better known by what stage name?

6   Who was the men's Wimbledon singles champion in 2002?

7   In computing, what does RTF stand for in relation to file types?

8   Port Said is in which country?

9   Which British general in the Crimean War gave his name to a style of sleeve?

10 Zoroastrianism is associated with which ancient kingdom?

11 Who invented the cat's eye?

12 Which Italian dessert consists of egg yolks, Marsala and sugar?

13 Who wrote the 2004 novel *My Sister's Keeper*?

14 Skye is separated from the mainland by which body of water?

15 Which flower part consists of an anther and a filament?

16 Which is Australia's largest lake?

17 Who won a National Television Award for her portrayal of Cilla Black in *Cilla*?

18 What was the name of EW Hornung's "gentleman burglar"?

19 According to Greek mythology, who was the first woman?

20 Which now obsolete profession, made famous by Chaucer, involved the selling of papal indulgences?

Answers to QUIZ 151 – Pot Luck

1	Jenny	11	Cadiz
2	Jimmy Carter	12	Jesuit
3	Lara	13	Yucca
4	1959	14	Cameron Diaz
5	Liège	15	Sherry
6	Lizzy Yarnold	16	Leah
7	55	17	Science
8	Sheep	18	Cecil Day-Lewis
9	Janus	19	Jeff Banks
10	Sikh	20	Rupee

1   In which sport do women compete for the Solheim Cup?

2   In which version of hockey would you use a bladeless stick called a caman?

3   What colour is the outermost ring on an archery target?

4   In which year did the boxing match known as "The Rumble in the Jungle" take place?

5   House, sweeping and tee are terms in which sport?

6   Who won the 2017 World Rally Championship?

7   How many gold medals did gymnast Max Whitlock win at the 2016 Rio Summer Olympics?

8   Minnesota Vikings and Detroit Lions are professional teams in which sport?

9   Spa motor racing circuit is in which country?

10 Over what distance is an Olympic steeplechase?

11 Eddy Merckx was a professional in which sport?

12 What is the highest possible score in a game of tenpin bowling?

13 What term is given to a score of three under par in golf?

14 Who captained the England women's Ashes team in 2017?

15 How many times did Stephen Hendry win the World Snooker Championship?

16 What is the name of the cricket test match ground in Brisbane?

17 Which sport other than tennis is played at the All England Club in Wimbledon?

18 How many wickets did Jim Laker take in the 1956 cricket test match against Australia?

19 Which equestrian discipline is known by the French word for "training"?

20 Which was the first club in English football to be awarded a goal by VAR (Video Assistant Referee) technology?

Answers to QUIZ 152 – Television Crime Drama

1	*Pie in the Sky*	11	Piper Chapman
2	Jed Mercurio	12	Dominic West
3	Reginald Hill	13	*Juliet Bravo*
4	Mireille Enos	14	Aberystwyth
5	*Numb3rs*	15	*Gracepoint*
6	*Remington Steele*	16	Jack Klugman
7	*Person of Interest*	17	*Homicide: Life on the Street*
8	Inspector Morse	18	Hugh Fraser
9	David Yip	19	Sally Wainwright
10	*Cracker*	20	Anthony LaPaglia

1   Which comedian starred in the 1926 silent film *The General*?

2   Who was awarded the Nobel Prize in Literature in 2017?

3   In which New York borough is JFK airport?

4   What type of animal is a Mexican hairless?

5   Which singer released her debut single *Stone Cold Sober* in 2009?

6   In the Old Testament, who is the older brother of Moses?

7   Which actress starred in the 2007 film *The Brave One*?

8   What nickname was given to the 16th-century Spanish painter Domenikos Theotokopoulos?

9   Which US state is nicknamed "Old Line State"?

10 On which date is St Swithin's Day?

11 Which novelist created Doctor Finlay?

12 The Mönch and the Jungfrau form a trio along with which Swiss mountain?

13 What is the name of the Italian Grand Prix circuit near Milan, built in 1922?

14 Which Swedish pop group formed as Festfolk in 1970?

15 What Latin phrase means "with hindsight"?

16 What is October's birthstone?

17 Which long-running BBC current affairs programme launched in 1953?

18 Which Egyptian sky-god has the head of a falcon?

19 Who was the UK Prime Minister from 1908 to 1916?

20 The term "viva voce" would be applied to what type of exam?

Answers to QUIZ 153 – Pot Luck

1	Poland	11	Percy Shaw
2	*Zodiac*	12	Zabaglione
3	Ruritania	13	Jodi Picoult
4	Job	14	Sound of Sleat
5	Rihanna	15	Stamen
6	Lleyton Hewitt	16	Lake Eyre
7	Rich text format	17	Sheridan Smith
8	Egypt	18	Raffles
9	Raglan	19	Pandora
10	Persia	20	Pardoner

Easy

1. Who was the keyboard player in the Communards, and is now a minister and TV presenter?

2. *A Groovy Kind of Love* by Phil Collins featured in which 1988 film?

3. Who had a 1985 hit with *Move Closer*?

4. Who played harmonica on the Eurythmics hit *There Must Be an Angel (Playing with My Heart)*?

5. From which Album was A-Ha's *The Sun Always Shines on TV* taken?

6. Who partnered Neil Tennant in The Pet Shop Boys?

7. *Rock Me Amadeus* was a 1986 hit for which singer?

8. What were the first names of music producers Stock, Aitken and Waterman?

9. Who is the lead singer with T'Pau?

10. What was Kylie Minogue's first hit single in Australia?

Medium

11. What was the title of U2's debut album?

12. Which group did Enya belong to before going solo?

13. Who duetted with Marc Almond on 1989's *Something's Gotten Hold of My Heart*?

14. Who was the lead singer with The Housemartins?

15. Eddy Grant's *I Don't Wanna Dance* topped the charts in which year?

16. Which girl group had a hit in 1988 with *Nathan Jones*?

17. Who topped the UK singles chart in 1982 with *Goody Two Shoes*?

18. On which date did the first Live Aid concert take place?

19. Which male singer featured on Cherelle's *Saturday Love* in 1985?

20. Which comedian released the 1981 single *Ullo John, Got a New Motor*?

Hard

Answers to QUIZ 154 – Sport

1	Golf	11	Cycling
2	Shinty	12	300
3	White	13	Albatross
4	1974	14	Heather Knight
5	Curling	15	Seven
6	Sebastien Ogier	16	The Gabba
7	Two	17	Croquet
8	American football	18	19
9	Belgium	19	Dressage
10	3000m	20	Leicester City

1. Which tan-coloured breed of horse has a white mane and tail?

2. Who was the wife of Zeus in Greek mythology?

3. What was the name of Patrick Swayze's character in the 1987 film *Dirty Dancing*?

4. Les Paul is associated with the development of which musical instrument?

5. In which National Park are Loweswater and Wasdale Head?

6. By what name is singer Paul Hewson better known?

7. In Arthurian legend, who was the son of Lancelot?

8. Who directed the 2016 film *I, Daniel Blake*?

9. Which river of Switzerland and France flows into the Mediterranean?

10. In which year did the first Red Nose Day take place?

11. Which genus of plants includes the buttercup?

12. Who invented the flying shuttle, used In weaving?

13. In which country was philanthropist Andrew Carnegie born?

14. Who composed the operetta *The Merry Widow* (1905)?

15. In biology, which taxonomic rank comes above family and below class?

16. Which organisation awards the Dickin Medal?

17. At which golf course was the 2013 Open Championship held?

18. What is the French word for "butterfly"?

19. Which Tuscan port is the location of the Italian Naval Academy?

20. What term is given to a vein of metal ore found in rock?

Easy

Medium

Hard

Answers to QUIZ 155 – Pot Luck

1	Buster Keaton	11	AJ Cronin
2	Kazuo Ishiguro	12	Eiger
3	Queens	13	Monza
4	A dog	14	ABBA
5	Paloma Faith	15	*A posteriori*
6	Aaron	16	Opal
7	Jodie Foster	17	*Panorama*
8	El Greco	18	Horus
9	Maryland	19	Herbert Asquith (First Earl of Oxford and Asquith)
10	July 15	20	An oral exam

Easy

1 How many sides are there on an icosahedron?

2 Which gas is the main constituent of natural gas?

3 In which constellation is Betelgeuse?

4 Where in the body is the talus bone located?

5 Which American chemist is credited with the discovery of nylon?

6 What is the alternative name for potassium nitrate, a substance used in preserving meat?

7 In which year was Halley's Comet last seen from Earth?

8 *Lepidoptera* is an order of which insects?

9 Which semiconductor allows current to flow in only one direction round a circuit?

10 Which chemical element has the symbol F?

Medium

11 Which scientist developed the anti-polio vaccine?

12 What is the SI unit of illumination?

13 Who was the first American in space?

14 Which is the largest of Saturn's moons?

15 Which element has the atomic number 2?

16 Who invented the Analytical Engine (c.1833)?

17 How is riboflavin more commonly known?

18 What was the name of the spacecraft that carried the Philae lander?

19 What is the chemical symbol for platinum?

20 Which word describes angles adding up to 180 degrees?

Hard

Easy

1   In what year was the Dangerous Dogs Act implemented in the UK?

2   Which of these cartoon dogs was created first: Scooby Doo or Snoopy?

3   Into how many breed groups does the Kennel Club of Great Britain divide dogs?

4   Which breed of working dog is most associated with the Western Alps?

5   To which biological family do domestic dogs belong?

6   Which Wallace and Gromit animation featured a robot dog?

7   How many teeth does the average adult dog have?

8   From which country does the Akita breed originate?

9   In Charles Dickens' *Oliver Twist*, what was the name and breed of Bill Sikes' dog?

10 Where on a dog would you find the carpal pad?

11 In the *Ren and Stimpy Show*, what breed of dog is Ren?

12 In which year did Pudsey the dog win *Britain's Got Talent*?

13 Which dog gave its name to the 2003 European Space Agency Mars Lander?

14 Which desert creature is the smallest member of the dog family?

Medium

15 What is the name of the mythological three-headed dog that guarded the entrance to Hades?

16 What was the original location of Battersea Dogs & Cats Home?

17 Which breed of dog was originally bred for hauling freight?

18 The withers are the highest part of what on a dog?

19 The Lhasa Apso breed originates from which Himalayan region?

20 In which sport do teams of four dogs compete in relay over a course of hurdles to release a tennis ball?

Hard

Answers to QUIZ 158 – Science

1	20	11	Jonas Salk
2	Methane	12	Lux
3	Orion	13	Alan Shepard (1961)
4	Ankle	14	Titan
5	Wallace Carothers	15	Helium
6	Saltpetre	16	Charles Babbage
7	1986	17	Vitamin B2
8	Moths and butterflies	18	*Rosetta*
9	Diode	19	Pt
10	Fluorine	20	Supplementary

ANSWERS ON PAGE **163**

1   What word describes the legal rights of the owner of land adjoining a river?

2   The maneki-neko is a Japanese figurine depicting which creature?

3   Frank Matcham was famous for designing what types of building?

4   What term describes having a lack of or reduction of pigmentation but normal eye colouring?

5   What does NGO stand for?

6   Which set of principles aims to maximise the greatest happiness of the greatest number?

7   Which is the top taxonomic classification?

8   The Commonwealth of Nations has its headquarters in which London building?

9   In 1932 a mass trespass happened at which Derbyshire location?

10 What do the letters PP stand for when seen on a plastic item?

11 In which children's TV series of the 1970s did Aswad's Brinsley Forde appear?

12 Which actress co-starred with Tom Cruise in the 1986 film *Top Gun*?

13 Thoron is a radioisotope of which gas?

14 The Hetch Hetchy Valley is in which US National Park?

15 How is Rapa Nui also known?

16 In which city is the Radcliffe Observatory?

17 Who wrote the 1859 philosophical work *On Liberty*?

18 What do the initials CHP mean in the context of energy?

19 Which role did Madonna play in the 1989 film *Dick Tracy*?

20 Which South Asian country's government is guided by the measure of the Gross National Happiness Index?

Easy

Medium

Hard

Answers to QUIZ 159 – Pot Luck

1	Kappa	11	*Rush*
2	Schiphol	12	Satchmo
3	Yarborough	13	Simon Pegg
4	Frank Whittle	14	Ruth
5	*In extremis*	15	Taiwan
6	Salisbury	16	Wolf
7	Imago	17	John Donne
8	On the side of a ship	18	St Jude
9	Inch	19	Jorja Smith
10	Judy Garland	20	Imperfect

Easy

1 What is the term for a love of anything new or novelty?

2 Which term is often used to describe a fear of clowns?

3 What is the term for someone who is attracted to foreigners?

4 What the term for a fear of flying?

5 Pogonophobia is a fear of what?

6 What is the term for someone who loves wine?

7 What is calligynephobia a fear of?

8 Stigmatophilia is a love for what?

9 What is the term for someone who loves cheese?

10 Ailurophilia is a love of what?

11 Hydrophobia is another name for which disease?

12 What is acrophobia a fear of?

13 What is the term for a fear of writing?

14 Dendrophilia is a love of what?

Medium

15 What is the term for an irrational fear of dogs?

16 What is the term for a fear of fire?

17 A thalassophile is someone who loves what?

18 What is triskaidekaphobia a fear of?

19 What is the term for someone who loves to work?

20 What is a hippophobe scared of?

Hard

Answers to QUIZ 160 – Dogs

1	1991	11	Chihuahua
2	Snoopy (1950)	12	2012
3	Seven	13	Beagle
4	St Bernard	14	Fennec fox
5	*Canidae*	15	Cerberus
6	*A Close Shave*	16	Holloway, North London
7	42	17	Alaskan malamute
8	Japan	18	The shoulders
9	Bullseye, the bull terrier	19	Tibet
10	On the back of each foreleg	20	Flyball

1   Which historian presented the 1969 TV series *Civilisation*?

2   The Yas Marina Formula 1 circuit is in which country?

3   In which year did Nick Berry have a hit with *Every Loser Wins*?

4   Which word means "created by people or caused by human activity"?

5   In which year did the Peak District become a National Park?

6   What do the initials NODA stand for in relation to the performing arts?

7   Which ancient Egyptian city on the Nile is now called Luxor?

8   What prefix indicates 10^{12}?

9   Which animal has the Latin name *Rattus rattus*?

10 In a trade context, what does the "E" of OPEC stand for?

11 Which character in the TV series *Lost* was named after an English philosopher and physician?

12 Which is the most northerly of the inhabited Shetland Islands?

13 Which gem is July's birthstone?

14 Which 1980s drama series starring Larry Lamb featured the crew and passengers of a North Sea ferry?

15 Which band had a UK 1982 top ten hit with *Strange Little Girl*?

16 What is the chemical symbol for methane?

17 Who wrote the 1830 poem *Mariana*?

18 Which is the oldest university in Scandinavia?

19 What is the main alcoholic ingredient of a planter's punch?

20 Which major supermarket business was founded by Sir Jack Cohen?

Answers to QUIZ 161 – Pot Luck

1	Riparian	11	*Here come the Double Deckers*
2	Cat	12	Kelly McGillis
3	Theatres	13	Radon
4	Leucistic	14	Yosemite
5	Non-governmental organisation	15	Easter Island
6	Utilitarianism	16	Oxford
7	Kingdom	17	John Stuart Mill
8	Marlborough House	18	Combined heat and power
9	Kinder Scout	19	Breathless Mahoney
10	Polypropylene	20	Bhutan

Easy

1 Who composed *The Flying Dutchman* (1840)?

2 Which German composer of four symphonies died in 1897?

3 From which instrument's A note does an orchestra tune up?

4 Which 1930s choral work by Carl Orff is based on 13th-century poems?

5 What type of musical composition, associated with Bach, uses counterpoint?

6 Who was the composer of the ballet *Billy the Kid* (1938)?

7 The character of Mimi features in which opera by Puccini?

8 What is the title of John Cage's 1952 "silent" work?

9 The bassoon is a member of which woodwind family?

10 What is the title of Beethoven's only opera?

11 Who was the Russian composer of *Prince Igor* (1890)?

12 What sort of instrument is a marimba?

Medium

13 Which composer's rivalry with Mozart was the subject of the film *Amadeus*?

14 What tree extract is used for treating violin bows?

15 Which 18th-century Austrian composer wrote 108 symphonies?

16 What term is given to a group of sharps and flats at the beginning of a music score?

17 What nationality was composer Frederick Delius?

18 How should a piece of music marked "doloroso" be played?

19 What is a short musical composition, usually for piano, designed as an exercise called?

20 What do the initials "DS" stand for on a musical score?

Hard

ANSWERS ON PAGE **167**

1   Who played Carson in the TV series *Downton Abbey*?

2   What ion-containing substance is found in batteries?

3   Which former British coin was worth two shillings?

4   Which ex-Spice Girl had a solo hit with *Not Such an Innocent Girl*?

5   Which Old Testament prophet was swallowed by a great fish?

6   How many grams are there in a kilogram?

7   Of which South American country is Montevideo the capital?

8   Which Ibsen play centres on the character of Helen Alving?

9   What is the title of the 1983 film directed by and starring Barbra Streisand?

10   Who composed the song *White Christmas*?

11   What name is given to the group of islands within the West Indies which includes St Lucia and Dominica?

12   What is the official language of Cambodia?

13   Ikebana is the Japanese art of what?

14   On which river does Brecon stand?

15   What fruit is also known as a Chinese gooseberry?

16   What do the letters ERNIE stand for in the Premium Bond number picker?

17   Where in the UK are the mountains known as the Cuillins?

18   Which character tells the first of Chaucer's *Canterbury Tales*?

19   Which 18th-century naturalist lived at Selborne in Hampshire?

20   What nickname was given to Edward I of England on account of his unusual height?

Answers to QUIZ 163 – Pot Luck

1	Kenneth Clark (Baron Clark)	11	John Locke
2	United Arab Emirates (Abu Dhabi)	12	Unst
3	1986	13	Ruby
4	Anthropogenic	14	*Triangle*
5	1951	15	The Stranglers
6	National Operatic and Dramatic Association	16	CH_4
7	Thebes	17	Alfred, Lord Tennyson
8	Tera	18	Uppsala
9	Black rat	19	Rum
10	Exporting	20	Tesco

1   Which was the first novel to feature the character of Jack Reacher?

2   Who wrote the 1994 novel *Captain Corelli's Mandolin*?

3   What is the name of the police sergeant in Wilkie Collins' *The Moonstone* (1868)?

4   Which Irish poet wrote *The Lake Isle of Innisfree*?

5   Who created the character of Tudor lawyer Matthew Shardlake?

6   What was in Winston Smith's Room 101, in a classic novel of 1949?

7   Who was the Roman author of the *Aeneid*?

8   What monster is lurking under the waves in the Book of Job in the Bible?

9   In 1668, who was appointed the first official Poet Laureate?

10 Which actor's autobiography was entitled *The Moon's a Balloon* (1972)?

11 What was the dog's name in the *Famous Five* children's books?

12 Who wrote the 2003 novel *We Need to Talk About Kevin*?

13 What was the real name of the novelist who was published under the name of George Eliot?

14 The TV series *Wire in the Blood* was based on the books by which author?

15 Which Swedish detective was created by Henning Mankell?

16 What kind of animal was Grip, Barnaby Rudge's pet?

17 What is the first part of Dante's *The Divine Comedy*?

18 Who wrote the poem *The Ballad of East and West* (1889)?

19 Which author created Paddington Bear?

20 Who is the Soviet spymaster in John le Carré's Smiley novels?

Answers to QUIZ 164 – Classical Music

1	Richard Wagner	11	Alexander Borodin
2	Johannes Brahms	12	Percussion (xylophone)
3	Oboe	13	Antonio Salieri
4	*Carmina Burana*	14	Rosin
5	Fugue	15	Franz Joseph Haydn
6	Aaron Copland	16	Key signature
7	*La bohème*	17	English
8	4'33"	18	Plaintively
9	Oboe	19	Étude
10	*Fidelio*	20	Dal segno (from the sign)

1   Which actress starred in the 1987 comedy film *Overboard*?

2   Which girl's name comes from the Greek word for "peace"?

3   In the Old Testament, which priest was teacher to the prophet Samuel?

4   Which part of the body is affected by Ménière's disease?

5   Which figure of Greek mythology was said to be the mother of Helen of Troy?

6   Ferdinand, King of Navarre, is the main character in which of Shakespeare's plays?

7   Which European city is nicknamed "La Serenissima"?

8   What Jane Austen novel features Jane Fairfax and a vicar named Elton?

9   Sword lilies are another name for which tall garden flowers?

10   Which Japanese city is famed for its beef?

11   Which Formula 1 team was featured in a 2017 documentary film?

12   What is the method of printing from a stone or metal plate?

13   Which famous bell can be seen at Lloyd's of London?

14   *Bitter Sweet Symphony* was a 1997 hit for which group?

15   Which rope is attached to the top of a mast?

16   Which *Torchwood* actor went on to appear as Malcolm Merlyn in the TV series *Arrow*?

17   In which National Park is Malham Tarn?

18   What is a complete circle in a fingerprint called?

19   In which country is the city of Shiraz?

20   Seymour and Audrey are the lead characters in which 1982 musical?

Easy
Medium
Hard

Answers to QUIZ 165 – Pot Luck

1	Jim Carter	11	Windward Islands
2	Electrolyte	12	Khmer
3	Florin	13	Flower arranging
4	Victoria Beckham	14	Usk
5	Jonah	15	Kiwi fruit
6	1000	16	Electronic Random Number Indicator Equipment
7	Uruguay	17	Isle of Skye
8	*Ghosts*	18	Knight
9	*Yentl*	19	Gilbert White
10	Irving Berlin	20	Longshanks

Easy

1 Which country, whose seat of government is La Paz, is named after "El Libertador"?

2 How many years had Nelson Mandela spent in captivity when he was released in 1990?

3 Which city replaced Samarkand as capital of Uzbekistan in 1930?

4 Founded in 1636, which is America's oldest university?

5 Which inlet of the Tasman Sea is the site of Captain James Cook's landing in Australia?

6 In which year did Tony Blair become UK Prime Minister?

7 Which country was once ruled by the Duvaliers?

8 Which ancient North African city was the enemy of Rome in the Punic Wars?

9 On which date did Apollo 11 land on the moon?

10 In which year did the American Civil War start?

Medium

11 Who commanded the British East India Company at the Battle of Plassey in 1757?

12 Which port is the capital of the United Arab Emirates?

13 Texas was part of which North American country until 1836?

14 In which year did Martin Luther King deliver his "I have a dream" speech?

15 What was the capital of New Zealand until 1865?

16 Which Russian leader died on January 21, 1924?

17 Who became the world's first "test tube baby" in 1978?

18 Which empire ended when the Ottoman Empire conquered Constantinople in 1453?

19 Which great pharaoh had Abu Simbel constructed?

20 In which year was Pakistan established as a country?

Hard

Answers to QUIZ 166 – Literature

1	*Killing Floor*	11	Timmy
2	Louis de Bernières	12	Lionel Shriver
3	Sergeant Cuff	13	Mary Ann Evans
4	WB Yeats	14	Val McDermid
5	CJ Sansom	15	Kurt Wallander
6	Rats	16	Raven
7	Virgil	17	*Inferno*
8	Leviathan	18	Rudyard Kipling
9	John Dryden	19	Michael Bond
10	David Niven	20	Karla

1   Which city is home to the Burrell Art Collection?

2   How is the plant *Hedera helix* better known?

3   Which band recorded the 1997 hit *Your Woman*?

4   Which rugby position is also known as "stand-off" or "outside half"?

5   What is the Russian coin equivalent to 100th of a rouble?

6   In which Belgian town is the Menin Gate war memorial?

7   What does a numismatist collect?

8   Which very hot, spicy curry originates from the Indian region of Goa?

9   Who wrote *Silas Marner* (1861)?

10 In chess, what term is given to a checkmate in the fewest number of moves?

11 In which country was shoe designer Jimmy Choo born?

12 Which US university is situated at New Haven, Connecticut?

13 Who invented the Spinning Jenny, patented in 1770?

14 What title does the wife of a Marquis use?

15 Which is the second god of the Hindu trinity?

16 On which London street is Madame Tussauds located?

17 Which famous train crosses Australia north to south?

18 In which month is the US remembrance holiday of Memorial Day?

19 Trowbridge is the administrative centre of which county?

20 What is the national fruit of India?

Easy

Medium

Hard

Answers to QUIZ 167 – Pot Luck

1	Goldie Hawn	11	Williams
2	Irene	12	Lithography
3	Eli	13	Lutine Bell
4	Inner ear	14	The Verve
5	Leda	15	Mainstay
6	*Love's Labours Lost*	16	John Barrowman
7	Venice	17	Yorkshire Dales
8	*Emma*	18	Whorl
9	Gladioli	19	Iran
10	Kobe	20	*Little Shop of Horrors*

1 Which English-born American poet wrote *Funeral Blues* in the late 1930s?

2 Which organisation is reponsible for commemorative blue plaques on buildings in England?

3 The mineral Blue John is found in which English National Park?

4 Which TV series starred Caroline Quentin as DCI Janine Lewis?

5 In which year was ELO's *Out of the Blue* album released?

6 In which county does the Bluebell railway run?

7 Who won the Best Actress Oscar for the 2013 film *Blue Jasmine*?

8 Which US state is known as "the Bluegrass State"?

9 Who wrote the 1952 play *The Deep Blue Sea*?

10 What sort of animal is a blue-faced Leicester?

11 What was the name of the craft in which Donald Campbell set speed records?

12 In which Australian state are the Blue Mountains?

13 What was the title of the Moody Blues' first UK chart-topper?

14 Which actor starred as Michael Felgate in the 1999 film *Mickey Blue Eyes*?

15 Which blue characters were created by the Belgian comics artist Peyo?

16 What type of food is blue vinney?

17 Who played WPC Shirley Trewlove in the TV series *Endeavour*?

18 What badge is worn by members of the Order of the Garter?

19 Who co-starred with Ryan Gosling in the 2010 film *Blue Valentine*?

20 What type of animal is a Kerry Blue?

Answers to QUIZ 168 – World History

1	Bolivia (Simón Bolivar)	11	Robert Clive
2	27	12	Abu Dhabi
3	Tashkent	13	Mexico
4	Harvard	14	1963
5	Botany Bay	15	Auckland
6	1997	16	Lenin
7	Haiti	17	Louise Brown
8	Carthage	18	Byzantine Empire
9	July 21, 1969	19	Rameses II
10	1861	20	1947

ANSWERS ON PAGE 173

1   Who won the Wimbledon Ladies' Singles title in 2017?

2   What is actor David Tennant's real surname?

3   Who was the star of the 1980s TV series *The Equalizer*?

4   In which US state is Cape Canaveral?

5   Who is the mother of Uranus in Greek mythology?

6   Which former boyband member had a 2016 solo no.1 with *Pillowtalk*?

7   What Italian herb liqueur is named after a 19th-century war hero?

8   Who played the witch in the 2014 film *Into the Woods*?

9   What was the scene of the first pitched battle of the English Civil War, fought in 1642?

10   Which Red Sea Israeli resort is adjacent to the Jordanian port of Aqaba?

11   To what class of mollusc do slugs, snails, cowries and whelks belong?

12   Which US poet wrote the *Leaves of Grass* collection?

13   What type of rock is marble?

14   The Kuga is a make of car by which manufacturer?

15   Which river flows through Melbourne?

16   From which country does mariachi music originate?

17   Which actor starred as Dr Chris Kelvin in the 2002 film *Solaris*?

18   What mixture of opium and alcohol was commonly prescribed for ailments during Victorian times?

19   Who released the 1980 album *Double Fantasy*?

20   Which Irish county north of Kilkenny was formerly known as Queen's?

Easy

Medium

Hard

Answers to QUIZ 169 – Pot Luck

1	Glasgow	11	Malaysia
2	Ivy	12	Yale
3	White Town	13	James Hargreaves
4	Fly-half	14	Marchioness
5	Kopek	15	Vishnu
6	Ypres	16	Marylebone Road
7	Coins	17	The Ghan
8	Vindaloo	18	May
9	George Eliot	19	Wiltshire
10	Fool's mate	20	Mango

1. How is the fruit *Rubus idaeus* more commonly known?
2. What term is given to a mixture of root vegetables used as a base for stew or sauce?
3. What is a chanterelle?
4. Asparagus is a member of which plant family?
5. What is a *jus*?
6. Jarlsberg cheese comes from which country?
7. Which cocktail is made from gin, Cointreau® and lemon juice?
8. Prunes are wrapped with what to make devils on horseback?
9. What is a mangelwurzel?
10. What is the name of the Cornish pie where fish heads show through the pastry crust?
11. The red wine Barolo is from which country?
12. Anjou and Bartlett are types of which fruit?
13. Used in Indian cooking, what is a brinjal called in the UK?
14. If an aperitif is something that precedes a meal, what term is given to something that follows it?
15. The botanical name for which spice is *Zingiber officinale*?
16. What fruit is a hybrid of a tangerine and a grapefruit?
17. Which type of beer takes its name from the German word for "store"?
18. How is the garbanzo bean better known?
19. Which English cheese is coated with nettles?
20. Orange pekoe is a variety of which drink?

Answers to QUIZ 170 – Blue

1. WH Auden
2. English Heritage
3. Peak District
4. *Blue Murder*
5. 1977
6. East Sussex
7. Cate Blanchett
8. Kentucky
9. Sir Terence Rattigan
10. A sheep
11. *Bluebird*
12. New South Wales
13. *Go Now*
14. Hugh Grant
15. Smurfs
16. Cheese
17. Dakota Blue Richards
18. Blue riband
19. Michelle Williams
20. A dog (terrier)

QUIZ 173 – Pot Luck

ANSWERS ON PAGE 175

1   Who played the title role in the 2008 film *The Incredible Hulk*?

2   What is the substance in wheat that makes dough elastic?

3   What is the capital city of Belarus?

4   Which author wrote *Five Children and It* (1902)?

5   Who directed the classic 1927 film *Metropolis*?

6   Which fine-quality coffee is named after a port in Yemen?

7   Who was the mythological father of Heracles?

8   Libreville is the capital city of which African nation?

9   The 1973 film and recent TV series *Westworld* are based on a novel by which writer?

10 Stratfield Saye is the stately home of which duke?

11 What prefix indicates 10^{-6}?

12 Who was Formula 1 World Champion In 1975, 1977 and 1984?

13 What were the first names of the two "Princes in the Tower"?

14 Which call is worth more than spades in bridge?

15 What type of creature is a flying fox?

16 Which river runs through Knaresborough?

17 What was the title of Matt Cardle's 2010 chart-topping single?

18 What was the name of the caravel on which Columbus sailed back to Spain in 1492?

19 Whom did Jamie Murray partner to win the 2017 Wimbledon Mixed Doubles title?

20 "Tar Heel" is the nickname of which US state?

Answers to QUIZ 171 – Pot Luck

1	Garbiñe Muguruza	11	Gastropoda
2	McDonald	12	Walt Whitman
3	Edward Woodward	13	Metamorphic
4	Florida	14	Ford
5	Gaia	15	Yarra
6	Zayn	16	Mexico
7	Galliano	17	George Clooney
8	Meryl Streep	18	Laudanum
9	Edgehill	19	John Lennon and Yoko Ono
10	Eilat	20	Laois

ANSWERS ON PAGE **176**

1   Watling Street is an example of what type of thoroughfare?

2   Which London street was the home of poet Elizabeth Barrett?

3   Which WWI French general gave his name to a Parisian avenue leading from the Arc de Triomphe?

4   Between which two US states did Route 66 run?

5   In which city is the shopping destination of Grafton Street?

6   The Via Dolorosa is in which city?

7   What is the name of the zigzag road in San Francisco which features eight hairpin bends?

8   Who designed The Circus in Bath?

9   In which English city are there alleyways known as the Lanes?

10 The famous Abbey Road pedestrian crossing is close to the junction with which other thoroughfare?

11 Which Roman street begins at the bottom of the Spanish Steps?

12 On which London thoroughfare is the Apollo theatre?

13 Who was "walking with my feet ten feet off of Beale" in a 1991 song?

14 Barcelona's La Rambla connects Plaça de Catalunya with which landmark?

15 In which borough of New York is the Bowery?

16 In which city is the shopping destination of Buchanan Street?

17 What are the names of the covered walkways in the four main streets in the city of Chester?

18 Kärntner Strasse is in which European city?

19 In which arrondissement of Paris is the Champs-Élysées?

20 What type of business is associated with London's Jermyn Street?

Answers to QUIZ 172 – Food and Drink

1	Raspberry	11	Italy
2	Mirepoix	12	Pear
3	Mushroom	13	Aubergine
4	Lily	14	A digestif
5	A gravy or extract	15	Ginger
6	Norway	16	Tangelo
7	White lady	17	Lager
8	Bacon	18	Chickpea
9	A root vegetable	19	Yarg
10	Stargazy pie	20	Tea

ANSWERS ON PAGE **177**

1   The argan tree is native to which continent?

2   In which region of France was the Cabernet Sauvignon black wine grape originally grown?

3   What is the currency unit used in Kabul?

4   In which German city is the car manufacturer BMW based?

5   Which Lutyens-designed stately home near Dartmoor was the last castle to be built in England?

6   What is the drink lassi mostly made from?

7   Who, in Shakespeare's play, became king of Scotland after the death of Macbeth?

8   Which Irish port is at the mouth of the River Lee?

9   In which southern French town did Van Gogh famously paint his bedroom?

10   What is the name of the girl detective in the novels by Carolyn Keene?

11   Which island is known as Kerkyra in Greek?

12   In *The Lord of the Rings*, what sort of spirit inhabits trees?

13   Who won the Best Actress Oscar for her performance in the 1960 film *Two Women*?

14   In which state is the easternmost point of the 48 contiguous United States?

15   What name was taken by former Lord Chancellor Quintin Hogg when he became a Lord?

16   Which American silent-film star was famous for scenes involving hanging from clocks?

17   The spice cardamom is a member of which family?

18   What is New Zealand's highest mountain?

19   What was an allemande, popular in Germany in the 16th century?

20   Which poet wrote the 1818 poem *Endymion*?

Answers to QUIZ 173 – Pot Luck

1	Edward Norton	11	Micro
2	Gluten	12	Niki Lauda
3	Minsk	13	Edward and Richard
4	Edith Nesbit	14	No trumps
5	Fritz Lang	15	Fruit bat
6	Mocha	16	Nidd
7	Zeus	17	*When We Collide*
8	Gabon	18	*Nina*
9	Michael Crichton	19	Martina Hingis
10	Duke of Wellington	20	North Carolina

Easy

1   Who played Izzie in the series *Grey's Anatomy*?

2   Who won the BBC Overseas Sports Personality of the Year in 2017 for a record fourth time?

3   In the series *Mad Men*, what was the name of the advertising agency?

4   Who played companion Martha Jones in *Doctor Who*?

5   Which *Pirates of the Caribbean* actor played Miles in the series *This Life*?

6   What are the two colours of a standard *Blue Peter* badge?

7   Which actress co-starred with Alexander Armstrong in the series *Life Begins*?

8   Which actor narrated *The Wombles* in the early 1970s?

9   Which 1960s western series featured the Cartwright family?

10 Vicky Pattison rose to fame on which show?

11 Who was the first questionmaster on the quiz *Eggheads*?

12 Paul Nicholas starred as Vince Pinner in which sitcom?

13 Which Dame Esther Rantzen series launched the career of singer Sheena Easton?

14 Who played Robert Catesby in the 2017 mini-series *Gunpowder*?

15 Keith Barron starred in which 1980s sitcom about a holiday in Spain?

16 Who created the animated series *Family Guy*?

17 Which actress played Sable Colby in the original series of *Dynasty*?

18 Who was the cafe owner in *Last of the Summer Wine*, played by Jane Freeman?

19 A car called KITT featured in which series?

20 Who starred as Bernard Black in the series *Black Books*?

Medium

Hard

Answers to QUIZ 174 – Famous Roads

1	Roman road	11	Via Condotti
2	Wimpole	12	Shaftesbury Avenue
3	Foch	13	Marc Cohn (*Walking in Memphis*)
4	California and Illinois	14	Columbus Monument
5	Dublin	15	Manhattan
6	Jerusalem	16	Glasgow
7	Lombard Street	17	The Rows
8	John Wood the Elder	18	Vienna
9	Brighton	19	Eighth
10	Grove End Road	20	Tailoring

1   The Etruscans were an ancient race living in part of which modern country?

2   In which Irish county is the small seaside town of Bray, located south of Dublin?

3   What is a calabash?

4   Which RAF rank is equivalent to vice admiral or lieutenant general?

5   What, according to Irish author Edna O'Brien, is "a wicked month"?

6   Whom did Sienna Miller portray in the 2006 film *Factory Girl*?

7   What was the first name of the 19th-century French artist Delacroix?

8   In 2011, which country became Africa's largest, by area?

9   What is the title of the Verdi opera commissioned for the opening of the Suez Canal?

10   Camembert cheese originates from which area of France?

11   What was the real name of the prolific 20th-century author Jean Plaidy?

12   The Lancaster WWII bomber was manufactured by which company?

13   Who wrote the 1982 play *Noises Off*?

14   What device records underwater distance?

15   What was the surname of the American inventor of the safety razor?

16   The fictional band The Majestics featured in which 1987 TV series?

17   What is the two-word term given to the point of entry of the optic nerve?

18   On which day of the week does the Christian feast day Ascension always occur?

19   What is the name given to a model that depicts a scene using three-dimensional figures, often in miniature?

20   Which Portuguese town was famed for religious visions in 1917?

Answers to QUIZ 175 – Pot Luck

1	Africa	11	Corfu
2	Bordeaux	12	An Ent
3	Afghani	13	Sophia Loren
4	Munich	14	Maine
5	Castle Drogo	15	Lord Hailsham
6	Yoghurt	16	Harold Lloyd
7	Malcolm	17	Ginger
8	Cork	18	Aoraki/Mount Cook
9	Arles	19	A dance
10	Nancy Drew	20	John Keats

1 The source of the River Thames is in which county?

2 On which river does the German shipbuilding port of Bremen stand?

3 What is the English name of the town that sits at the mouth of the River Teifi?

4 Which island is surrounded by the East, Harlem and Hudson rivers?

5 Which Spanish river flows through the Rioja wine-growing region?

6 The Three Gorges dam spans which river?

7 On which north-east river does Stockton stand?

8 In which country are the rivers Adige and Arno?

9 The West Sussex town of Lancing stands on which river?

10 On which river is the Mosul Dam?

11 Which is the longest river in Europe...?

12 ...and which is the second-longest European river?

13 What is the name of the Cumbrian river that flows into the Solway Firth?

14 Which river flows through Hamburg?

15 What is the name of the river on St David's peninsula in Wales?

16 Which seaside resort of northern Cornwall lies at the mouth of the River Neet?

17 On which river are Africa's Victoria Falls?

18 On which river did Chesley Sullenberger famously land a plane in 2009?

19 Which is the longest river in the Iberian Peninsula?

20 In which district of West Sussex, named after its river, is Littlehampton?

Easy

Medium

Hard

Answers to QUIZ 176 – Television

1	Katherine Heigl	11	Dermot Murnaghan
2	Roger Federer	12	*Just Good Friends*
3	Sterling Cooper & Partners	13	*The Big Time*
4	Freema Agyeman	14	Kit Harington
5	Jack Davenport	15	*Duty Free*
6	Blue and white	16	Seth MacFarlane
7	Caroline Quentin	17	Stephanie Beacham
8	Bernard Cribbins	18	Ivy
9	*Bonanza*	19	*Knight Rider*
10	*Geordie Shore*	20	Dylan Moran

1   By what name is grape sugar more usually called?

2   Which English essayist, along with his sister Mary, wrote *Tales from Shakespeare* (1807)?

3   What is an Indian place of retreat called?

4   In which country was the 19th-century explorer Mungo Park born?

5   In the 1966 film *The Good, the Bad and the Ugly*, who played Tuco?

6   Which Moroccan city was devastated by an earthquake in 1960?

7   Who wrote the novel *The Call of the Wild* (1903)?

8   Which English constitutional settlement was passed in 1689?

9   Which is the largest city in the US state of New Hampshire?

10 Who was the Greek goddess of war and wisdom?

11 The clothing retailer Gap was founded in which US city in 1969?

12 What is the meaning of the Latin phrase *ipso jure*?

13 To what creatures does the term "passerine" apply?

14 Which 1960s Cockney singer was backed by the Bruvvers?

15 The 1959 novel *The Tin Drum* was written by which author?

16 Which Northern Irish county has a county town of the same name on the shores of Lough Neagh?

17 What is the title of the 1987 film about the life of singer Ritchie Valens?

18 Which show involving puppets won the Best Musical at the 2004 Tony awards?

19 The investigations of unit AC-12 feature in which TV police drama?

20 Which member of Take That had solo hits with *Child* and *Clementine*?

Answers to QUIZ 177 – Pot Luck

1	Italy	11	Eleanor Hibbert
2	Wicklow	12	Avro
3	A tree, or its fruit (a gourd)	13	Michael Frayn
4	Air Marshal	14	Echograms
5	August	15	Gillette
6	Edie Sedgwick	16	*Tutti Frutti*
7	Eugène	17	Blind spot
8	Algeria	18	Thursday
9	*Aida*	19	Diorama
10	Normandy	20	Fatima

ANSWERS ON PAGE 182

Easy

1 A cricket umpire raises his index finger above his head to indicate what?

2 Arsène Wenger was manager of Arsenal FC between which years?

3 The ITTF is the governing body of which sport?

4 Korfball originated in which country?

5 Where did the Italian national rugby team play their home Six Nations games from 2000 to 2011?

6 The winners of both the men's and women's 2017 World Squash Championships were from which country?

7 Which English game, similar to cricket, has the "wicket" at head or shoulder height?

8 In which indoor game might you be a "tweener" or a "cranker"?

9 Which football club plays its home games at Home Park?

10 "Gridiron" is another term for which sport?

Medium

11 Beach volleyball became an official Olympic sport in which year?

12 What sport is played at Cowdray Park?

13 Which golf club hosted the 2016 Open Championship?

14 Which was the only grand slam tennis title that Pete Sampras did not win?

15 Who won the 2017 World Championship Snooker title?

16 In which decade did BBC Radio's *Test Match Special* begin?

17 What is the nickname of Chicago's NBA basketball team?

18 Who was the 2016 winning Ryder Cup team captain?

19 In which country was the FIFA Women's World Cup held in 2015?

20 Which future monarch took part in the Wimbledon tennis championships in 1926?

Hard

Answers to QUIZ 178 – Rivers

1	Gloucestershire	11	Volga
2	Weser	12	Danube
3	Cardigan	13	Eden
4	Manhattan Island, NY	14	Elbe
5	Ebro	15	Alun
6	Yangtze	16	Bude
7	Tees	17	Zambezi
8	Italy	18	Hudson River
9	Adur	19	Tagus
10	Tigris	20	Arun

QUIZ 181 – Pot Luck

ANSWERS ON PAGE 183

1   Which town is the adminstrative centre of Angus, in Scotland?

2   In which city was the 20th-century artist and sculptor Joan Miró born?

3   Who wrote the 1978 novel *The Human Factor*?

4   Which purplish colour derives its name from a northern Italian location?

5   In which Lake District town was the first pencil made?

6   In which month are the feast days of saints Bernadette and Anselm?

7   The surname of which Texas rancher is used to descibe an unbranded animal and an unorthodox person?

8   Who was the first chief executive of Channel 4?

9   What is the main flavour of a ganache?

10 What type of firearm would originally have been carried by a fusilier?

11 The people of which ancient civilisation lived in the area now covered by Yucatan, Belize and northern Guatemala?

12 Which Texan city stands on the Rio Grande opposite Juárez, Mexico?

13 Which Belgian town was the scene of the first major WWI battle?

14 Who was the subject of the 1964 *Carry On* film?

15 What was the first name of the engineer who invented the Moog synthesizer?

16 Charlotte Dujardin rode which horse to double gold at the London 2012 Olympics?

17 What was the name of the fairy queen referred to in Shakespeare's *Romeo and Juliet*?

18 Which US drama starring Peter Krause was set in a funeral home?

19 What is the scientific study of solid inorganic substances?

20 Which musical term means "jokingly", or "in a playful manner"?

Answers to QUIZ 179 – Pot Luck

1	Dextrose	11	San Francisco
2	Charles Lamb	12	"By operation of law"
3	Ashram	13	Birds
4	Scotland	14	Joe Brown
5	Eli Wallach	15	Günter Grass
6	Agadir	16	Antrim
7	Jack London	17	*La Bamba*
8	Bill of Rights	18	*Avenue Q*
9	Manchester	19	*Line of Duty*
10	Athena	20	Mark Owen

1   What is the main ingredient of the dish sauerkraut?

2   How many constituent states does Germany have?

3   Which river flows through Heidelberg?

4   How is the *Schwarzwald* known in English?

5   Who preceded Angela Merkel as Chancellor of Germany?

6   The Berlin Wall was torn down in which year?

7   What is the English translation of *Rathaus*?

8   Which 18th-century monument in Berlin was built on the orders of Prussian king Frederick William II?

9   Germany shares a border with the Netherlands, Czechia (Czech Republic), Luxembourg, France, Belgium, Switzerland and which three other countries?

10 What is Germany's highest mountain?

11 In German, what is the name of Germany?

12 What form of entertainment is associated with Bayreuth?

13 Which German city is called Aix-la-Chapelle in French?

14 "The cradle of the automobile" is a name given to which city?

15 Which 20th-century art movement was founded in the city of Weimar?

16 Pumpernickel bread is made from what type of flour?

17 What is the largest lake on German territory?

18 What German word is used to describe the experience of joy from learning of the misfortune of others?

19 Germany is bordered by which two seas?

20 What is the largest city on the Rhine?

Answers to QUIZ 180 – Ball Sports

1	The batsman is out	11	1996
2	1996-2018	12	Polo
3	Table tennis	13	Royal Troon
4	The Netherlands	14	French Open
5	Stadio Flaminio	15	Mark Selby
6	Egypt	16	1950s
7	Stoolball	17	Bulls
8	Tenpin bowling	18	Davis Love III
9	Plymouth Argyle	19	Canada
10	American Football	20	George VI

1   Which Italian river flows into the sea at Ostia?

2   Who played the title role in the 1966 film *Our Man Flint*?

3   Which Arab capital city was known as Philadelphia during Roman times?

4   Who wrote the 1919 novel *The Moon and Sixpence*?

5   Which musical features the song *Getting to Know You*?

6   In which London thoroughfare is Drapers' Hall?

7   Angola was formerly a colony of which European country?

8   What is the largest natural lake in Wales?

9   Which Scottish town on the River Leven shares its name with an Egyptian city?

10 *Portrait of my Love* was which British singer's 1960 debut?

11 Who co-founded Microsoft® along with Bill Gates?

12 Who won an Oscar for composing the score of the 1957 film *Bridge Over the River Kwai*?

13 Which relative of a US President took a major role in organising the 1773 Boston Tea Party?

14 Which word means "representing different Christian churches"?

15 In mythology, which maiden was loved by Eros?

16 Which US state lies north of Missouri, south of Minnesota, east of Nebraska and west of Illinois?

17 In the sitcom *Drop the Dead Donkey*, who played Dave Charnley?

18 Which Spanish poet and dramatist (b.1898) was killed in the Spanish Civil War?

19 Which boxer (b.1921) only lost once in his first 123 bouts?

20 The location of Dingley Dell features in which Charles Dickens novel?

Easy

Medium

Hard

Answers to QUIZ 181 – Pot Luck

1	Forfar	11	Maya
2	Barcelona	12	El Paso
3	Graham Greene	13	Mons
4	Magenta	14	Cleo
5	Keswick	15	Robert (Moog)
6	April	16	Valegro
7	Maverick	17	Mab
8	Sir Jeremy Isaacs	18	*Six Feet Under*
9	Chocolate	19	Mineralogy
10	Musket	20	Scherzando

1   What is the name of the Earth's lowest layer of atmosphere?

2   Mount Fuji is situated on which island?

3   Which is the world's smallest ocean?

4   What two-word phrase is given to the upper limit of population that an area can support?

5   A caldera is found in which natural feature?

6   The Earth's crust and the upper part of the mantle are collectively described by what term?

7   What are the vast lowland plains of Argentina called?

8   What does a feature described as "fluviatile" relate to?

9   What term is given to the study of seasonal timings of events such as flowering and migration?

10   What is an area of rock underneath the ground which absorbs and holds water called?

11   The swampy coniferous forest region of Siberia is given what name?

12   Angel Falls, the world's highest waterfall, is in which country?

13   Which is the deepest lake in the world...?

14   ...and which is the world's largest lake?

15   What type of rock is formed from compacted deposits of material in air, ice or water?

16   In relation to the atmosphere, what does "ppm" stand for?

17   Which Malaysian city's name means "muddy estuary"?

18   Which is the largest natural lake in England?

19   What term is given to the proportion of sunlight that is reflected from a surface?

20   The most southerly point of Ireland is marked by which rock?

Answers to QUIZ 182 – Germany

1	Cabbage	11	Deutschland
2	16	12	Opera
3	Neckar	13	Aachen
4	Black Forest	14	Stuttgart
5	Gerhard Schröder	15	Bauhaus
6	1989	16	Rye
7	Town hall	17	Lake Constance
8	Brandenburg Gate	18	Schadenfreude
9	Denmark, Poland and Austria	19	North Sea and Baltic Sea
10	Zugspitze	20	Cologne

Easy

Medium

Hard

1   Actor Chevy Chase was given what first name at birth?

2   In which city might you travel on a traghetto?

3   What was the surname of brothers Auguste and Louis, the French motion-picture pioneers?

4   Which fruit with a stone has the Latin name *Prunus domestica*?

5   Which old currency unit was worth £1.05?

6   What is a leave of absence from a boarding school?

7   What is Homer Simpson's favourite brand of beer?

8   The East Sussex house of Bateman's belonged to which author?

9   Which bank launched the UK's first credit card?

10 Which US state is nicknamed "Buckeye"?

11 Of which rock are Dartmoor's tors formed?

12 Which animal's name derives from the ancient Greek for "river horse"?

13 What was the first chart-topper for The Rubettes?

14 Which castle near Grantham is the seat of the Duke of Rutland?

15 What name is given to a steak cut between two ribs?

16 The 2017 TV series *SS-GB* was based on a book by which author?

17 What type of creature is a lamprey?

18 Who directed the 1965 film *Doctor Zhivago*?

19 Who won the 1969 Nobel Prize in Literature?

20 Who starred as Ann Darrow in the 2005 version of *King Kong*?

Easy

Medium

Hard

Answers to QUIZ 183 – Pot Luck

1	Tiber	11	Paul Allen
2	James Coburn	12	Malcolm Arnold
3	Amman	13	Samuel Adams
4	W Somerset Maugham	14	Ecumenical
5	*The King and I*	15	Psyche
6	Throgmorton Street	16	Iowa
7	Portugal	17	Neil Pearson
8	Bala	18	Federico García Lorca
9	Alexandria	19	Sugar Ray Robinson
10	Matt Monro	20	*The Pickwick Papers*

Easy

1   *Brighton Beach Memoirs* (1982) and *Biloxi Blues* (1984) are semi-autobiograpical works by which playwright?

2   Which British author wrote the play *The Second Mrs Tanqueray* (1893)?

3   The play *Festen* (2004) is based on a film in which language?

4   What are the names of the two main characters in *Waiting for Godot*?

5   In the 1945 JB Priestly play *An Inspector Calls*, what is the name of the inspector?

6   What is the title of the Sir Tom Stoppard play about two minor characters from Shakespeare's *Hamlet*?

7   What nationality was playwright Dario Fo?

8   Who wrote the Greek tragedy *Antigone*?

9   In the 1959 play *Billy Liar*, what was Billy's surname?

10 Who wrote *Art* (1994)?

Medium

11 Which 1996 play features sisters Teresa, Mary and Catherine gathered for the funeral of their mother Vi?

12 Which play with a script by Jack Thorne won the Laurence Olivier award for Best New Play in 2017?

13 Who wrote *Murder in the Cathedral* (1935)?

14 Which playwright was awarded the Nobel Prize in Literature in 2005?

15 Which Sir Terence Rattigan play deals with the events following the theft of a five-shilling postal order?

16 Who wrote the 1960s works *After the Fall* and *The Price*?

17 John Osborne's 1956 play *Look Back in Anger* premiered at which London theatre?

18 What nationality was playwright Edward Albee?

19 What was the name of William Shakespeare's mother?

20 Who wrote *The Seagull* (1895)?

Hard

Answers to QUIZ 184 – Planet Earth

1	Troposphere	11	Taiga
2	Honshu	12	Venezuela
3	Arctic Ocean	13	Lake Baikal (Russia)
4	Carrying capacity	14	Caspian Sea
5	A volcano	15	Sedimentary
6	Lithosphere	16	Parts per million
7	Pampas	17	Kuala Lumpur
8	Rivers	18	Windermere
9	Phenology	19	Albedo
10	Aquifer	20	Fastnet

1 Which bridge in the north-east of England is the world's first tilting bridge?

2 Which company was granted the first registered trademark in 1876?

3 Who flew from Newfoundland to Clifden in Ireland in 1919?

4 What was the first name of KFC founder Colonel Sanders?

5 A mash tun is used in making which drink?

6 Which bid in solo whist declares a hand that will win no tricks?

7 Which former *The X Factor* contestant won 2009's *Dancing on Ice*?

8 In which year did the Bahrain Formula 1 Grand Prix become a night race?

9 When does a noctilucent cloud appear?

10 In which country is Murlough Nature Reserve?

11 What does "gsm" stand for in relation to paper and card?

12 The Home Insurance Building in Chicago became the world's first what in 1885?

13 The International or European Article Number is a standard for what identification?

14 Which stately home on Anglesey contains a mural painted by Rex Whistler?

15 In which decade were the Blackpool Illuminations first lit?

16 Which inventor filed 1093 patents in his lifetime?

17 Who wrote *The Shell Seekers* (1987) and *September* (1990)?

18 Which medal was awarded to Tenzing Norgay?

19 What was Greta Garbo's real surname?

20 Who directed the 2015 film *The Martian*?

Easy

Medium

Hard

Answers to QUIZ 185 – Pot Luck

1	Cornelius	11	Granite
2	Venice	12	Hippopotamus
3	Lumière	13	*Sugar Baby Love*
4	Plum	14	Belvoir
5	Guinea	15	Entrecôte
6	*Exeat*	16	Len Deighton
7	Duff	17	Fish
8	Rudyard Kipling	18	Sir David Lean
9	Barclays	19	Samuel Beckett
10	Ohio	20	Naomi Watts

Easy

1 Which famous girls' school near Brighton was founded by the Lawrence sisters in 1885?

2 The TV series *Glee* was set mainly in which fictional school?

3 The London School of Economics and Political Science was founded in 1875 by members of which society?

4 Which is the world's oldest university museum?

5 What does ROSLA stand for in an academic context?

6 Which English university was founded in 1209?

7 The 1940s novels about St Clare's boarding school were written by which author?

8 What was the title of the 1970s *Please Sir!* spin-off series?

9 LLB after a name indicates that the person has graduated in what subject?

10 What is the literal English translation of the German word *Kindergarten*?

Medium

11 Which two-word Latin phrase is used to describe the university or college of a former student?

12 What is the name of the university based in Middlesbrough?

13 In which year did polytechnics in the UK become universities?

14 At which fictional school did Mr McGuffey, Mrs McClusky and Mr Bronson teach?

15 Which youth achievement award scheme was introduced in 1956 for boys and in 1958 for girls?

16 Estyn is the Welsh equivalent of which English body?

17 Which independent Berkshire boarding school was founded in 1440?

18 What do the initials UCAS stand for?

19 Which world-renowned educationist born in Italy in 1870 gives her name to a "Method" of early education?

20 In which year were GCSE exams introduced?

Hard

Answers to QUIZ 186 – Plays and Playwrights

1	Neil Simon	11	*The Memory of Water* (Shelagh Stephenson)
2	Arthur Wing Pinero	12	*Harry Potter and the Cursed Child*
3	Danish	13	TS Eliot
4	Vladimir and Estragon	14	Harold Pinter
5	Inspector Goole	15	*The Winslow Boy*
6	*Rosencrantz and Guildenstern Are Dead*	16	Arthur Miller
7	Italian	17	The Royal Court
8	Sophocles	18	American
9	Fisher	19	Mary Arden
10	Yazmina Reza	20	Anton Chekhov

ANSWERS ON PAGE **191**

1   Who was the proverbially wealthy king of ancient Lydia?

2   Who presented Radio 4's *Desert Island Discs* from 1988 until 2006?

3   What was the name of the hotel in Stephen King's *The Shining* (1977)?

4   Which part of a church is named from the Latin word for "ship"?

5   Which country won the Eurovision Song Contest in 2014?

6   In Norse mythology, what was the home of the gods?

7   Which town in south-east Switzerland hosted the 1928 Winter Olympics?

8   In which Derbyshire town are the Heights of Abraham?

9   Which single did Wings release as a double A side with *Mull of Kintyre*?

10   Who wrote the 1970 best-selling novel *Love Story*?

11   Kampala is the capital of which African nation?

12   The Wraith is a model from which luxury car manufacturer?

13   Which island is linked politically with Antigua?

14   What is the more common name for the linden tree?

15   Which is the westernmost of the Balearic Islands?

16   Which pale yellow variety of crystalline quartz resembles topaz?

17   Richmond is the capital of which US state?

18   What is the more common name for urticaria?

19   What is the ancient language of the Hindu scriptures?

20   In which country did the word "bungalow" originate?

Answers to QUIZ 187 – Pot Luck

1	Gateshead Millennium bridge	11	Grams per square metre
2	Bass Brewery	12	Skyscraper
3	Alcock and Brown	13	Barcode
4	Harland	14	Plas Newydd
5	Whisky	15	1870s (1879)
6	Misère	16	Thomas Edison
7	Ray Quinn	17	Rosamunde Pilcher
8	2014	18	George Medal
9	At night	19	Gustafsson
10	Northern Ireland	20	Sir Ridley Scott

Easy

1   Who played James Bond in the 1989 film *Licence to Kill*?

2   What was the profession of the real James Bond who lent his name to the fictional spy?

3   In which of the James Bond films did the Aston Martin DB5 first appear?

4   What was the first name of James Bond's wife, to whom he was briefly married in *On Her Majesty's Secret Service*?

5   In which 1983 Bond film did Maud Adams co-star with Sir Roger Moore?

6   Which of the Bond films shares its title with Ian Fleming's Jamaican estate?

7   Which character did Jack Lord play in *Dr No* (1962)?

8   In which of the Ian Fleming novels is Vivienne Michel the central character?

9   In which year did Sir Sean Connery star in *Never Say Never Again*?

10 In how many films did Bernard Lee play the character of "M"?

11 Who played Kara Milovy in the 1987 film *The Living Daylights*?

12 Which was the first novel to be published featuring James Bond?

13 The theme tune to which James Bond film was sung by Matt Monro?

Medium

14 Who played Blofeld in the 2015 film *Spectre*?

15 In which James Bond film is there a character called Dr Christmas Jones?

16 What is the name of the industrialist in *Moonraker*?

17 In which film did Teri Hatcher play Paris Carver?

18 In which country was Bond actor George Lazenby born?

19 Daniel Craig first played Bond on film in which year?

20 Max Zorin is the villain in which film?

Hard

Answers to QUIZ 188 – Education

1	Roedean	11	*Alma mater*
2	William McKinley High	12	Teesside
3	The Fabian Society	13	1992
4	Ashmolean (Oxford)	14	Grange Hill
5	Raising of School Leaving Age	15	Duke of Edinburgh's Award
6	Cambridge	16	Ofsted
7	Enid Blyton	17	Eton College
8	*The Fenn Street Gang*	18	Universities and Colleges Admissions Service
9	Law	19	Maria Montessori
10	Garden for the children	20	1988

QUIZ 191 – Pot Luck

ANSWERS ON PAGE **193**

1   Who was the oldest man in the Bible?

2   In which country is the ski resort of Klosters?

3   Which US state is known as the "Sunflower State"?

4   In which 1975 film did Warren Beatty play a hairdresser?

5   What is the name of the character in *Macbeth* whose title is Thane of Lochaber?

6   What was the title of Spandau Ballet's first single?

7   Prawle Point is the most southerly tip of which English county?

8   How many tusks does a warthog have?

9   Carson City is the capital of which US state?

10 What is the name of the cavity containing the eyeball?

11 Which ballet features the supernatural women called the Wilis?

12 In South Africa, what is a *kraal*?

13 Which actor starred in the 2007 film *Fred Claus*?

14 Which group had a no.1 in 1971 with *Chirpy Chirpy Cheep Cheep*?

15 In mythology, what kind of animal was slain by Hercules as the first of his Twelve Labours?

16 Which is the second largest of the Orkney Islands?

17 What term is given to a crucifix set at the entrance to the chancel of a church?

18 Who wrote the 1951 novel *My Cousin Rachel*?

19 Who played Belle in the 2017 live film version of *Beauty and the Beast*?

20 In which sport are the LA Lakers a professional team?

Easy

Medium

Hard

Answers to QUIZ 189 – Pot Luck

1	Croesus	11	Uganda
2	Sue Lawley	12	Rolls-Royce
3	Overlook Hotel	13	Barbuda
4	Nave	14	The lime
5	Austria	15	Ibiza
6	Asgard	16	Citrine
7	St Moritz	17	Virginia
8	Matlock Bath	18	Nettle-rash
9	*Girls' School*	19	Sanskrit
10	Erich Segal	20	India

1   In which National Park is the Snake Pass?

2   Which two actors co-starred in the 1969 film *Easy Rider*?

3   Who wrote the novel *Jurassic Park*?

4   In the rhyme *Ride a Cock Horse*, in which county would the rider be at the end of the journey?

5   The Simon Park Orchestra had a 1973 hit with *Eye Level*, the theme to which detective series?

6   Who directed the 1985 western *Pale Rider*?

7   The Formula 1 street circuit of Albert Park is in which country?

8   Which group had a 1989 no.1 record with *Ride on Time*?

9   At which tourist attraction in the UK is the roller coaster ride Colossus located?

10 Who starred in the original series of *Knight Rider*?

11 In which year of the 19th century was the Great Exhibition held in Hyde Park?

12 The 1991 album *Joyride* was recorded by which duo?

13 Which Scottish National Park was established in 2003?

14 The teenage spy character of Alex Rider was created by which author?

15 In which county is the racecourse of Fontwell Park?

16 In which year was *Riders on the Storm* a hit for the Doors?

17 The station of Holland Park is on which London Underground line?

18 What was the first name of novelist H Rider Haggard?

19 Fratton Park is the home ground of which football team?

20 Which American duo issued a cover of the Beatles' *Ticket to Ride* in 1969?

Easy

Medium

Hard

Answers to QUIZ 190 – James Bond

1	Timothy Dalton	11	Maryam d'Abo
2	Ornithologist	12	*Casino Royale* (1953)
3	*Goldfinger*	13	*From Russia with Love*
4	Tracy	14	Christoph Waltz
5	*Octopussy*	15	*The World is Not Enough*
6	*GoldenEye*	16	Hugo Drax
7	Felix Leiter	17	*Tomorrow Never Dies*
8	*The Spy Who Loved Me*	18	Australia
9	1983	19	2006
10	11	20	*A View to a Kill*

ANSWERS ON PAGE 195

1   Which US measuring unit is equivalent to eight fluid ounces or 16 tablespoons?

2   In the Battle of Bosworth Field which English king was killed?

3   Which historic Belgian city lies between Brussels and Bruges?

4   What is another name for china clay?

5   Which state of north-west Borneo became a Commonwealth member in 1984?

6   *I Can See Clearly Now* was a hit for which singer in 1972?

7   Who wrote the novel *Cold Comfort Farm*?

8   What is the name of the road bridge over the Firth of Forth opened in August 2017?

9   What was the name of the Pet Shop Boys' second chart-topper in 1987?

10 Which physics unit of matter shares its name with a soft cheese?

11 "Kernow" is the local name of which English county?

12 Who was the first woman in space?

13 What is added to icing sugar to make royal icing?

14 Atahualpa was the last leader of which empire?

15 Who was King Edward I's first queen?

16 What is the fifth book of the Old Testament?

17 In the 2016 Summer Olympics, which British track cyclist won his sixth Olympic gold medal?

18 What is the French equivalent of an Oscar?

19 What is the dome-shaped sheet of muscle that separates the chest from the abdomen called?

20 ET is the international vehicle registration for which country?

Easy

Medium

Hard

Answers to QUIZ 191 – Pot Luck

1	Methuselah	11	*Giselle*
2	Switzerland	12	Enclosed village
3	Kansas	13	Vince Vaughn
4	*Shampoo*	14	Middle of the Road
5	Banquo	15	Lion
6	*To Cut a Long Story Short*	16	Hoy
7	Devon	17	Rood
8	Four	18	Dame Daphne du Maurier
9	Nevada	19	Emma Watson
10	Orbit	20	Basketball

1 In which city in Shaanxi Province can China's famous terracotta warriors be seen?

2 What is a yawl?

3 Which German word describes the defining mood of a particular period of history?

4 What was the subtitle of the 2016 film in the X-Men franchise?

5 Yorktown was the site of the last major battle in which war?

6 The zapateado is a dance from which country?

7 What is the phonetic alphabet code word for the letter X?

8 Captain John Yossarian is the main character in which 1961 novel?

9 Which outdoor pursuit involves rolling in a transparent sphere?

10 Which line on a graph is usually marked as the x-axis, the horizontal or vertical?

11 Yerevan is the capital city of which country?

12 Which US writer married Zelda Sayre in 1920?

13 What is the chemical symbol for xenon?

14 In which National Park is Yes Tor?

15 What type of food is ziti?

16 From which country does the language Xhosa originate?

17 In which year was *YMCA* a hit for the Village People?

18 Which country has the zloty as its currency?

19 Who played the title role in the TV series *Xena: Warrior Princess*?

20 In which county is the river Yare?

Answers to QUIZ 192 – Park and Ride

1	Peak District	11	1851
2	Peter Fonda and Dennis Hopper	12	Roxette
3	Michael Crichton	13	Cairngorms
4	Oxfordshire (Banbury Cross)	14	Anthony Horowitz
5	*Van Der Valk*	15	West Sussex
6	Clint Eastwood	16	1971
7	Australia (Melbourne)	17	Central Line
8	Black Box	18	Henry
9	Thorpe Park	19	Portsmouth FC
10	David Hasselhoff	20	The Carpenters

1   The town of Duffel is in which EU country?

2   What was Japan's imperial capital until 1868?

3   Which band released an album called *The Works* in 1984?

4   The song *Good Morning Starshine* is from which musical?

5   Which volcano overlooks the city of Catania?

6   Which classic London double-decker bus, with an open platform at the rear, was launched in 1954?

7   Who wrote *The Little Paris Kitchen* cook book?

8   Which philosopher wrote *Leviathan* (1651)?

9   What slang term for England comes from a Hindi word for "foreign country"?

10 A hairstyle known as a tonsure would be sported by what type of person?

11 What is an alternative name for the snow leopard?

12 Which town, situated between Yeovil and Warminster, has a well-known racecourse?

13 The quarter-mile long building at Chatham was used to make which material?

14 Which river of South Wales flows through Pontypridd?

15 A feature of Edinburgh castle, what is "Mons Meg"?

16 Who directed the 1970s films *Mean Streets* and *Taxi Driver*?

17 In relation to nuclear power plants, what does the "W" of PWR stand for?

18 What nationality is a person from Tobruk?

19 Which seaside resort on the south coast has an airport at Hurn?

20 What is the piece of metal on a ship to which ropes are attached?

Answers to QUIZ 193 – Pot Luck

1	Cup	11	Cornwall
2	Richard III	12	Valentina Tereshkova
3	Ghent	13	Egg white
4	Kaolin	14	Inca
5	Brunei	15	Eleanor
6	Johnny Nash	16	Deuteronomy
7	Stella Gibbons	17	Jason Kenny
8	Queensferry Crossing	18	César
9	*It's a Sin*	19	Diaphragm
10	Quark	20	Egypt

1 What is the name of Julia Roberts' older brother, also an actor?

2 *Grandpa's Great Escape* is a children's novel by which comedian?

3 Which Knight of the Round Table was the nephew of King Arthur?

4 In the TV series *Brothers & Sisters*, which actress played Sally Field's daughter Kitty?

5 Who was the mother of Henry VIII?

6 In Greek mythology, who killed her two sons by husband Jason?

7 Which father and son of the same name developed the furnace manufacture of pig iron?

8 Artist Bernardo Bellotto was the nephew of which famous Italian artist?

9 Who was the youngest of Chekhov's *Three Sisters*?

10 Which singer was the father of actress Carrie Fisher?

11 What is the surname of *Cold Comfort Farm* character Aunt Ada?

12 What was the name of Charles Darwin's grandfather, a founding member of the Lunar Society?

13 In the Gilbert and Sullivan operetta, who was the son of the Mikado?

14 Which Mitford sister became the Duchess of Devonshire?

15 Which father and son appeared on TV as *The Hungry Sailors*?

16 Who was the father of Paris and Hector, in Homer's *Iliad*?

17 Which daughter of a famous poet is often regarded as the first computer programmer?

18 *Son of My Father* was a 1972 hit for which group?

19 Which village in West Yorkshire was the home of the Brontë sisters?

20 In 2005 which Hollywood actor named his son Kal-El?

Answers to QUIZ 194 – XYZ

1	Xi'an	11	Armenia
2	A fishing boat	12	F Scott Fitzgerald
3	*Zeitgeist*	13	Xe
4	*Apocalypse*	14	Dartmoor
5	American War of Independence	15	Pasta
6	Spain	16	South Africa
7	X-ray	17	1978
8	*Catch-22*	18	Poland
9	Zorbing	19	Lucy Lawless
10	Horizontal	20	Norfolk

1   What was the name of the werewolf son in *The Munsters*?

2   The Bedlington terrier is named after a town in which county?

3   What is the alcoholic ingredient in a screwdriver cocktail?

4   How many pence was the old English groat worth?

5   Which venue hosted the shooting events at the 2012 London Olympics?

6   Which actress co-wrote and starred in *Bridesmaids*?

7   What forms the tectonic boundary between the Pacific Plate and the North American Plate?

8   Which North Yorkshire river near Richmond is a tributary of the Ure?

9   PitmanScript is a version of what type of system?

10 Which US state is nicknamed "the Diamond State"?

11 What is the Saudi Arabian currency unit?

12 On which hill does Jerusalem stand?

13 The Carnegie Medal is awarded in which area of literature?

14 The Cornish village of Gweek, near Helston, has a sanctuary for which type of animal?

15 Which saxophonist was nicknamed "Bird", a shortened form of "Yardbird"?

16 Who wrote the 1854 poem *The Charge of the Light Brigade*?

17 The Grace Gates form the entrance to which sports ground?

18 Which actor provided the voice of Kipper in the animated TV series?

19 How is the fictional law enforcer John Reid better known?

20 What is the capital of Macedonia?

Easy

Medium

Hard

Answers to QUIZ 195 – Pot Luck

1	Belgium	11	Ounce
2	Kyoto	12	Wincanton
3	Queen	13	Rope
4	*Hair*	14	Taff
5	Etna	15	Cannon
6	Routemaster	16	Martin Scorsese
7	Rachel Khoo	17	Water
8	Thomas Hobbes	18	Libyan
9	Blighty	19	Bournemouth
10	A monk	20	A cleat

Easy

1. In which year was Lady Jane Grey briefly Queen of England?
2. Who was Britain's first Prime Minister?
3. Who was the mother of Richard the Lionheart and King John?
4. The 1890s Klondike gold rush took place in which Canadian territory?
5. Which stamp succeeded the Penny Black?
6. The Suez Canal was nationalised by which Egyptian president?
7. Who was Queen of the Netherlands from 1980 to 2013?
8. Which Russian leader was born Vladimir Ilyich Ulyanov?
9. Who was the second president of the USA?
10. Josiah Wedgwood gave which Italian name to his Stoke-on-Trent pottery works?

Medium

11. In which Greater Manchester town was the Co-operative movement born?
12. Which monarchs jointly took over the British throne in 1689?
13. Crowned in 800, who was the first Holy Roman Emperor?
14. What was the former name of the Democratic Republic of the Congo?
15. Who formed the Society of Friends?
16. Lloyd's of London began in what type of institution?
17. In which country was Florence Nightingale born?
18. The horse Copenhagen belonged to which military figure?
19. Which architect introduced the Palladian style into England?
20. What was the Roman name for the city of York?

Hard

Answers to QUIZ 196 – Famous Relatives

1	Eric	11	Doom
2	David Walliams	12	Erasmus Darwin
3	Gawain	13	Nanki-Poo
4	Calista Flockhart	14	Deborah
5	Elizabeth of York	15	Dick and James Strawbridge
6	Medea	16	Priam
7	Abraham Darby	17	Ada Lovelace (daughter of Byron)
8	Canaletto	18	Chicory Tip
9	Irina	19	Haworth
10	Eddie Fisher	20	Nicolas Cage

1   Who co-starred with Nick Nolte in the 1991 film *The Prince of Tides*?

2   What is the capital of Liechtenstein?

3   Which early Irish saint is a patron of mariners and seafarers?

4   Who sang the theme song to the 1981 Bond film *For Your Eyes Only*?

5   Who wrote the 1818 poem *Isabella, or the Pot of Basil*?

6   What type of food is Monterey Jack?

7   St Piran's flag is flown by which county?

8   What nationality was László Bíró, inventor of the ballpoint pen?

9   Which instrument was associated with jazz musician Humphrey Lyttelton?

10 Which Midlands cathedral city was badly damaged in WWII?

11 Scott Bakula starred as Sam Beckett in which 1989-93 sci-fi series?

12 What type of animal is a Suffolk Punch?

13 Which playwright wrote *The Iceman Cometh* (1939)?

14 Who had a 1982 hit with *Happy Talk*?

15 David Cornwell is the real name of which novelist?

16 What is the name of Ilchester's river?

17 Which Belgian seaport is linked by canal with Bruges?

18 In Greek mythology, who was the daughter of Agamemnon and Clytemnestra?

19 Which plant fibre is obtained from agave?

20 The Sidlaw Hills are near which Scottish city?

Easy

Medium

Hard

1. Who presented the prime-time edition of *Are You Smarter than a 10 Year Old* from 2007 to 2010?

2. Which of the Eggheads won the World Quizzing Championship in 2017 for the sixth time...?

3. ...and who was the first winner of *Make Me an Egghead* in 2008, who went on to join the quiz team?

4. The 2013-14 quiz *Pressure Pad* was hosted by which actor?

5. What is the title of the *Mastermind* theme tune?

6. Who hosted *Every Second Counts* from 1986 to 1993?

7. How many contestants started each episode of *The Weakest Link*?

8. In which 2003 quiz co-hosted by Carol Vorderman did contestants each pay £1,000 to take part?

9. Which quiz programme aired as a regular series for the first time in 1970 with David Vine as host?

10. Who was the original host of *The Krypton Factor*?

11. In which year did *The Chase* first air...?

12. ...and which "Chaser" went on to host *Britain's Brightest Family*?

13. The 2017 play *Quiz* centres around an incident on which prime-time show?

14. Who hosted the first series of *The People Versus*?

15. *Sale of the Century* was originally produced by which TV company?

16. What was the name of the computer which competed on the US show *Jeopardy!* in 2011?

17. Which 2014-15 quiz split contestants into different teams in each round depending on their "Yes" or "No" answer to a question?

18. Who was the original presenter of *Going for Gold*?

19. In which sitcom did a team from Scumbag College take part in *University Challenge*?

20. What is the name of the daytime quiz hosted by Warwick Davis where contestants aim to complete lists?

Answers to QUIZ 198 – History

1	1553	11	Rochdale
2	Robert Walpole (First Earl of Orford)	12	William III and Mary II
3	Eleanor of Aquitaine	13	Charlemagne
4	Yukon	14	Zaire
5	Penny Red	15	George Fox
6	Gamal Nasser	16	Coffee shop
7	Beatrix	17	Italy
8	Lenin	18	Duke of Wellington
9	John Adams	19	Inigo Jones
10	Etruria	20	Eboracum

1   Which band had 1980s hits with *Hard to Say I'm Sorry* and *Hard Habit to Break*?

2   What is the county town of Ireland's County Meath?

3   Ottawa is located in which Canadian province?

4   Polish and Czech are members of which family of languages?

5   Who was *King of the Road* at the top of the UK charts in 1965?

6   Which BBC arts series was launched in 1975?

7   Mary, Queen of Scots was executed in which castle?

8   Which record label did Jerry Dammers found in 1979?

9   In the USA, what term is used for any swampy area in Louisiana?

10 Who is the chief officer of the Royal Household?

11 Which Berkshire village was the destination for an annual CND march in the late 1950s and early 1960s?

12 The garden flower, the antirrhinum, has which common name?

13 In the 1952 children's novel *Charlotte's Web*, what is the name of the young girl?

14 What is Switzerland's largest city?

15 In the 2009 film *Julie & Julia*, which actress co-starred with Meryl Streep in a title role?

16 Which girl's name is also the botanical name for the laurel bush?

17 Who played Goldfinger in the 1964 Bond film of the same name?

18 The Guildhall School of Music and Drama is situated in which City of London arts complex?

19 Which Moroccan city is said to have the world's oldest university?

20 What was the name of the one-eyed woman in the cartoon series *Futurama*?

Easy

Medium

Hard

Answers to QUIZ 199 – Pot Luck

1	Barbra Streisand	11	*Quantum Leap*
2	Vaduz	12	Horse
3	Brendan	13	Eugene O'Neill
4	Sheena Easton	14	Captain Sensible
5	John Keats	15	John le Carré
6	Cheese	16	Yeo
7	Cornwall	17	Zeebrugge
8	Hungarian	18	Electra
9	Trumpet	19	Istle
10	Coventry	20	Dundee

Easy

1   In which year were the UK charts first compiled...?

2   ...and what was the first UK no.1 single?

3   Which 1950s musician was known as "The Man with the Golden Trumpet"?

4   *Secret Love* featured in which 1953 film musical?

5   Who sang the theme song to *Three Coins in the Fountain*?

6   In which year did Connie Francis top the UK charts with *Who's Sorry Now*?

7   Who had a 1955 hit with the title song from the musical *Rose Marie*?

8   *Mary's Boy Child* was a 1957 hit for which singer?

9   Tony Bennett had a 1955 hit with which song from the musical *Kismet*?

10   Which singer was known as "The Girl with the Giggle in Her Voice?"

11   In which year did Elvis Presley have his first UK no.1?

Medium

12   What instrument was Winifred Atwell famous for playing?

13   *Thank Heaven for Little Girls* is a song from which musical?

14   Which British singer topped the charts in 1959 with *What Do You Want*?

15   Which Buddy Holly hit was the last single released in his lifetime?

16   Who had a hit with *Dream Lover* in 1959?

17   Which 1950s singer went on to play Teen Angel in the 1978 film *Grease*?

18   *This Ole House* was a 1954 hit for which singer?

19   Who was the older of the two Everly brothers?

20   Who had a 1956 no.1 UK hit with *Memories are Made of This*?

Hard

Answers to QUIZ 200 – Television Quizzes

1	Noel Edmonds	11	2009
2	Kevin Ashman	12	Anne Hegerty
3	Barry Simmons	13	*Who Wants to Be a Millionaire?*
4	John Barrowman	14	Kirsty Young
5	*Approaching Menace*	15	Anglia
6	Paul Daniels	16	Watson
7	Nine	17	*Two Tribes*
8	*Grand Slam*	18	Henry Kelly
9	*A Question of Sport*	19	*The Young Ones*
10	Gordon Burns	20	*Tenable*

ANSWERS ON PAGE 205

1 Which singer's 2011 debut single *Swagger Jagger* went straight to no.1?

2 What is the imaginary dukedom in which Shakespeare's *Twelfth Night* is set?

3 What honorary title is given to a retired professor?

4 Which island lies just north of Scotland's Isle of Arran?

5 What is the most famous feature of the Sagarmatha National Park?

6 In 1989, who became a principal dancer for The Royal Ballet at the age of 20?

7 What is the first name of Kramer in the TV series *Seinfeld*?

8 Which brothers formed the group Sparks?

9 The 2008 film *Ghost Town* starred which comedian?

10 Which taxonomic classification is immediate below "family"?

11 The anchor hallmark is applied to silver made in which British city?

12 The ABC Islands of the Lesser Antilles consist of Bonaire, Curaçao and which other territory of the Kingdom of the Netherlands?

13 Which 1995 film was based on the children's book *The Sheep-Pig*?

14 Who was Edward II's queen consort?

15 The accordion is a member of which family of musical instruments?

16 In 1955, which product was the first to be advertised on ITV?

17 Which actor starred in the 1983 film *WarGames*?

18 Who wrote the 1996 novel *Popcorn*?

19 Which famous Roman statesman and orator died in 43 BC?

20 In 1923, which Irish poet was awarded the Nobel Prize in Literature?

Easy

Medium

Hard

Answers to QUIZ 201 – Pot Luck

1	Chicago	11	Aldermaston
2	Navan	12	Snapdragon
3	Ontario	13	Fern
4	Slavonic	14	Zürich
5	Roger Miller	15	Amy Adams
6	*Arena*	16	Daphne
7	Fotheringhay	17	Gert Fröbe
8	2-Tone	18	Barbican
9	Bayou	19	Fez (founded 859)
10	Lord Chamberlain	20	Leela

1. In which year was *Thelma & Louise* released in the cinema?

2. Who starred alongside Ben Affleck in *Gone Girl*?

3. What was the name of Sting's character in the 1979 film *Quadrophenia*?

4. Rachel Weisz won an Oscar for which 2005 film?

5. Which actor starred in the 1939 film *Goodbye, Mr Chips*?

6. In *2001: A Space Odyssey*, what was the name of the computer?

7. Which 1973 film starring Steve McQueen was set on Devil's Island?

8. Who starred in the 1951 film *The Great Caruso*?

9. Which comedian played Flash Harry in the 2007 version of *St Trinians*?

10. For which film did Denzel Washington receive his second Oscar?

11. In the 1963 film *The Pink Panther*, to what did the title refer?

12. What was the surname of silent-film "It" girl Clara?

13. For which 1981 film did Warren Beatty win the Best Director Oscar?

14. In 1993, which actor starred in the film *Six Degrees of Separation*?

15. What was the subtitle of the 1984 *Star Trek III* film?

16. Which actress starred as Maggie in the 1958 film *Cat on a Hot Tin Roof*?

17. Who directed the 1986 film *Stand By Me*?

18. In the 1998 film *Shakespeare in Love*, who played the title role?

19. For which 1996 film did Frances McDormand win the Best Actress Oscar?

20. Who played Huggy Bear in the 2004 film *Starsky & Hutch*?

ANSWERS ON PAGE 207

1   Through which mountains does the St Gotthard Pass run?

2   Cape Cod and Martha's Vineyard are in which US state?

3   Whose tenth album *X* was released in 2007?

4   Which letter of the Greek alphabet precedes iota?

5   What land measure is equivalent to 4840 square yards?

6   What nationality was sociologist Ulrich Beck (b.1944)?

7   Who created the *Mr Men*?

8   What is the name of the Isle of Man's main airport?

9   James IV of Scotland was killed at which 1513 battle?

10   In which European city is Wencelas Square?

11   In a standard pack of cards, what are the queens pictured holding?

12   Which actor played the *Nightmare on Elm Street* character Freddy Krueger?

13   The ancient city of Palmyra is in which present-day country?

14   Which Arabian cargo ship is distinguished by its lateen sail?

15   The Mappa Mundi is housed in which city's cathedral?

16   What term is used for members of the Egyptian Orthodox Church?

17   Richard O'Brien was the original host of which game show, revived in 2017?

18   Who played Arthur to Colin Morgan's Merlin in the TV series of that name?

19   Which is the first letter of the Hebrew alphabet?

20   In Abrahamic religions, what are angelic beings of the second order called?

Easy

Medium

Hard

Answers to QUIZ 203 – Pot Luck

1	Cher Lloyd	11	Birmingham
2	Illyria	12	Aruba
3	Emeritus	13	*Babe*
4	Bute	14	Isabella (of France)
5	Mount Everest	15	Reed organ
6	Dame Darcey Bussell	16	Gibbs SR toothpaste
7	Cosmo	17	Matthew Broderick
8	Ron and Russell Mael	18	Ben Elton
9	Ricky Gervais	19	Cicero
10	Genus	20	WB Yeats

Easy

1   In which novel does the diary of Marian Halcombe appear?

2   Which 1953 Marilyn Monroe film is based on a fictional diary by Anita Loos?

3   Which actor's diaries formed the basis for the TV film *Fantabulosa!*?

4   The first instalment of whose diaries was entitled *Prelude to Power 1994-97*?

5   In which 1897 novel does Jonathan Harker's diary describe his encounters with a vampire?

6   Which actor and traveller's diaries give an insider's view of the Monty Python team?

7   Who wrote in his diary about the "excruciating dialogue" he had to speak in *Star Wars*?

8   Published by her father in 1947, who wrote *The Diary of a Young Girl*?

9   Which thriller author wrote three volumes of his *A Prison Diary*, entitled *Hell, Purgatory* and *Heaven*?

10 Based on her own diaries, who wrote the WWI memoir *Testament of Youth*?

11 Which British queen's journals totalled 122 volumes?

12 Whose fictional comic diary is loosely based on *Pride and Prejudice*?

13 Who commits *thoughtcrime* by writing "DOWN WITH BIG BROTHER" in his diary?

Medium

14 Jeff Kinney created which fictional US schoolboy's diaries?

15 Whose 1906 *Country Diary* was a publishing sensation in the late 1970s and early 1980s?

16 Which 1949 novel was narrated through the journal of Cassandra Mortmain?

17 Which long-running radio series began in 1948 and featured the journals of a doctor's wife?

18 In *Harry Potter and the Chamber of Secrets*, whose diary plays a crucial role?

19 Which politician's diaries unlocked the secrets of Baroness Margaret Thatcher's government?

20 Which revolutionary documented his youthful travels in *The Motorcycle Diaries*?

Hard

Answers to QUIZ 204 – Films

1	1991	11	A diamond
2	Rosamund Pike	12	Bow
3	Ace Face	13	*Reds*
4	*The Constant Gardener*	14	Will Smith
5	Robert Donat	15	*The Search for Spock*
6	Hal (9000)	16	Elizabeth Taylor
7	*Papillon*	17	Rob Reiner
8	Mario Lanza	18	Joseph Fiennes
9	Russell Brand	19	*Fargo*
10	*Training Day*	20	Snoop Dogg

1 How are the musicians Roland Orzabal and Curt Smith as a duo known?

2 Who won the men's 800m Olympic gold medal in 2012 and 2016?

3 Who played Mrs Coulter in the 2007 film *The Golden Compass*?

4 *The Government Inspector* (1836) was written by which Russian author?

5 Which author lived at Chawton House in Hampshire?

6 What is the capital of Slovenia?

7 Which Italian port is the capital of the Apulia region?

8 Which famous drink is made in Charente, France?

9 In which 1960s children's series did the puppet Troy Tempest appear?

10 Which Roman emperor made Christianity a state religion?

11 Where in London was the US Embassy located from 1960 to 2018?

12 Which sea is between Poland and Sweden?

13 Which Latin term means "from the beginning"?

14 *New Rules* was a 2017 single by which artist?

15 What was Calder Hall the first UK example of?

16 What was the pen-name of Edith Pargeter, author of the Brother Cadfael mysteries?

17 How was the old comedy team Moe, Larry and Curly collectively known?

18 In which year was the driving test introduced in the UK?

19 Who founded the Tamla Motown record label?

20 What is the common name of the herb genus *Satureja*, which has summer and winter varieties?

Easy

Medium

Hard

Answers to QUIZ 205 – Pot Luck

1	Alps	11	A flower
2	Massachusetts	12	Robert Englund
3	Kylie Minogue	13	Syria
4	Theta	14	Dhow
5	Acre	15	Hereford
6	German	16	Copts
7	Roger Hargreaves	17	*The Crystal Maze*
8	Ronaldsway	18	Bradley James
9	Flodden	19	Aleph
10	Prague	20	Cherubim

1 Who played Inspector Clouseau in the 2006 version of *The Pink Panther*?

2 Which 1980s band covered the 1955 hit *Cherry Pink and Apple Blossom White*?

3 What type of fruit is a Pink Lady?

4 Which character is played by Jada Pinkett Smith in *The Matrix* series of films?

5 Which opera features the character Lieutenant Pinkerton?

6 Which guitarist replaced Syd Barrett in Pink Floyd in 1968?

7 In which decade was the *Financial Times* first printed on pink paper?

8 Which finger is referred to as a pinkie?

9 The winner of which national cycle race is awarded a pink jersey?

10 In business, what is a "pink slip"?

11 Which actress starred in the 1986 film *Pretty in Pink*?

12 What type of creatures are the title characters in the animated TV series *Pinky and the Brain*?

13 Who wrote the 1984 song *Pink Cadillac...*?

14 ...and who had a hit with it in 1988?

15 The flower known as the common pink belongs to which plant genus?

16 Which children's author created the character of Mr Pink-Whistle?

17 Which fashion designer popularised shocking pink?

18 What was Pink's first UK solo no.1 hit...?

19 ...and on which 2001 no.1 record did she sing?

20 What gives a Pink Lady cocktail its pink colour?

Answers to QUIZ 206 – Diaries

1	*The Woman in White* (Wilkie Collins)	11	Queen Victoria
2	*Gentlemen Prefer Blondes*	12	*Bridget Jones's Diary*
3	Kenneth Williams	13	Winston Smith (in *Nineteen Eighty-Four*)
4	Alastair Campbell	14	*Diary of a Wimpy Kid*
5	*Dracula*	15	An Edwardian Lady (Edith Holden)
6	Michael Palin	16	*I Capture the Castle* (Dodie Smith)
7	Sir Alec Guinness	17	*Mrs Dale's Diary*
8	Anne Frank	18	Tom Riddle
9	Jeffrey Archer	19	Alan Clark
10	Vera Brittain	20	Che Guevara

1   Which decade saw the first FA cup final take place at the original Wembley Stadium?

2   The 1990s TV series *Peak Practice* was set in which county?

3   The title of which Samuel Butler novel is an anagram of "nowhere"?

4   Which singer had a cameo role in the first episode of the seventh series of *Game of Thrones*?

5   Which children's show featured a scientist called Dr Bunsen Honeydew?

6   What is the largest city on the Baja California peninsula in Mexico?

7   On which continent are the Carpathian Mountains located?

8   Which Portuguese explorer led the first expedition to circumnavigate the world?

9   Who was Neville Chamberlain's predecessor as Prime Minister?

10 In which 2001 film did siblings Jake and Maggie Gyllenhaal appear as brother and sister?

11 Which opera was the inspiration for the musical *Rent*?

12 In the RAF, what rank is below wing commander but above flight lieutenant?

13 Which language is spoken in the western Pyrenees?

14 Which element has the atomic number 8?

15 Who sang the theme tune to the Bond film *Spectre*?

16 London's Mount Pleasant is the location for which museum?

17 Which Greek saint gave his name to the alphabet now used in Russia and certain eastern European countries?

18 Who was Biggles' cousin in the books by WE Johns?

19 What is the other name of Rome's Leonardo da Vinci airport?

20 Which girl group had a hit with *Hole in the Head* in 2003?

Easy
Medium
Hard

Answers to QUIZ 207 – Pot Luck

1	Tears for Fears	11	Grosvenor Square
2	David Rudisha	12	Baltic
3	Nicole Kidman	13	*Ab initio*
4	Nikolai Gogol	14	Dua Lipa
5	Jane Austen	15	Nuclear power station
6	Ljubljana	16	Ellis Peters
7	Bari	17	The Three Stooges
8	Cognac	18	1935
9	*Stingray*	19	Berry Gordy Jr
10	Constantine	20	Savory

Easy

1 Which medal did the GB women's curling team win at the 2014 Winter Games?

2 In which year were the Winter Games held in Lillehammer?

3 Who won the 800m gold medal at the 1980 Summer Games?

4 In which year did Canada first host the Winter Games?

5 Which British rower wrote the 2004 book *Four Men in a Boat* about the 2000 Olympics?

6 How many Olympic medals did swimmer Michael Phelps win in total?

7 What was the title of the official sound track to the opening ceremony of the 2012 London Summer Games...?

8 ...and who directed the ceremony?

9 Which boxer won a bronze medal at the 1996 Olympics in the featherweight division?

10 Which was the first South American country to host the Summer Games?

Medium

11 Which country won the most medals at the 2018 Winter Games?

12 The 1981 film *Chariots of Fire* features the Summer Games of which year?

13 At the 2008 Summer Games, in which administrative region of China were the equestrian events held?

14 What was the last year in which the Summer and Winter games were held in the same year?

15 Which gold-medal winning Paralympian took part in the 2017 series of *Strictly Come Dancing*?

16 Athletes from which country won the women's 100m gold medal in 2008, 2012 and 2016?

17 Which Japanese city hosted the 1998 Winter Games?

18 In which year were the first Summer Games held, following the formation of the International Olympic Committee?

19 Which country always leads the parade of participants at the Summer Games?

20 Who was the first British athlete to win Olympic gold in a throwing event?

Hard

Answers to QUIZ 208 – Pink

1 Steve Martin
2 Modern Romance
3 Apple
4 Niobe
5 *Madama Butterfly* (Puccini)
6 David Gilmour
7 1890s (1893)
8 Little finger
9 Giro d'Italia
10 Notice of redundancy
11 Molly Ringwald
12 Mice
13 Bruce Springsteen
14 Natalie Cole
15 *Dianthus*
16 Enid Blyton
17 Elsa Schiaparelli
18 *Just Like a Pill*
19 *Lady Marmalade*
20 Grenadine

QUIZ 211 – Pot Luck

ANSWERS ON PAGE 213

1   Who was David Walliams' co-star in the 2015 Agatha Christie series *Partners in Crime*?

2   Which Irish county lies north of Roscommon and east of Mayo?

3   Who was the oldest of the Marx Brothers?

4   For which 2015 film did Leonardo di Caprio win the Best Actor Oscar?

5   In which year did the Crimean War start?

6   Barbados is in which Caribbean island group?

7   Who writes the *Jack Reacher* series of books?

8   Which bay on the Isle of Wight is famous for its coloured sand?

9   Which Greek god of the arts lends his name to many theatres?

10 What type of rock is granite?

11 *Sonnets from the Portuguese* is a collection by which Victorian poetess?

12 Who shared the 2001 Nobel Peace Prize with the organisation that he led at the time?

13 Who designed the Crystal Palace for the 19th-century Great Exhibition?

14 In which sitcom did Christopher Biggins play a character nicknamed Lukewarm?

15 In which year was North Sea oil discovered?

16 Which river runs through Newton Abbot, Devon?

17 What type of construction is the Humber Bridge?

18 In which Danish port was Hans Christian Andersen born?

19 Which Greek mathematician wrote *The Elements*?

20 Singer Tom Jones had which original surname?

Easy

Medium

Hard

Answers to QUIZ 209 – Pot Luck

1	1920s	11	*La bohème*
2	Derbyshire	12	Squadron leader
3	*Erewhon*	13	Basque
4	Ed Sheeran	14	Oxygen
5	*The Muppet Show*	15	Sam Smith
6	Tijuana	16	The Postal Museum
7	Europe	17	Cyril
8	Ferdinand Magellan	18	Algy
9	Stanley Baldwin (First Earl Baldwin of Bewdley)	19	Fiumicino
10	*Donnie Darko*	20	Sugababes

1 What word describes marine life that lives in the upper waters of the open sea?

2 The adult of which large sea creature was caught on camera for the first time in 2004?

3 How many legs does a lobster have?

4 What is a female dolphin called?

5 What type of fish has a variety known as "sockeye"?

6 How is a member of the *Hippocampus* genus commonly known?

7 The name "krill" comes from the word for "young fish" in which language?

8 A loggerhead is a species of which sea creature?

9 Which is the largest living fish?

10 What common name is given to both the manatee and dugong?

11 Humboldt penguins are found in the wild on which continent?

12 "Sild" is the name given to the young of which species of fish?

13 Which edible mollusc is also called the sea-ear?

14 What name is given to a group of whales?

15 What type of invertebrate is the source of mother-of-pearl?

16 Sea otters are found in which ocean?

17 The male of which type of crab has an enlarged claw, waved for courtship and territorial display?

18 What is the common name for the group of fish which have their eyes on top of their heads?

19 The "coral" is another name for which part of a shellfish?

20 Octopuses and squid belong to which class of molluscs?

Answers to QUIZ 210 – The Olympic Games

1	Bronze	11	Norway (39)
2	1994	12	1924
3	Steve Ovett	13	Hong Kong
4	1988 (Calgary)	14	1992
5	Tim Foster	15	Jonnie Peacock
6	28	16	Jamaica
7	*Isles of Wonder*	17	Nagano
8	Danny Boyle	18	1896
9	Floyd Mayweather	19	Greece
10	Brazil (2016)	20	Tessa Sanderson

1   What name was given to the cavalry troopers of Oliver Cromwell?

2   *Eye of the Tiger* was from the soundtrack of which film?

3   Wolfsbane is the alternative name of which wild flower?

4   Which major Indian language is written in the Devanagari script?

5   What is the title of the opera by Verdi set in ancient Jerusalem about a Babylonian king?

6   Which Prime Minister succeeded Sir Winston Churchill in 1945?

7   At Salt Lake City in 2002, in which sport did Great Britain win their one gold medal?

8   Which actress starred in the 2003 film *How To Lose a Guy in 10 Days*?

9   Which mythological queen of Troy was the wife of Priam?

10   Which old British coin, legal tender until 1960, was worth one quarter of a penny?

11   *The Piper at the Gates of Dawn* was the first album by which band?

12   Which Kansas city was founded in 1872 as a frontier town?

13   How is Kehlsteinhaus, Berchtesgaden better known in English?

14   Lydford Gorge is in which National Park?

15   To which Irish county does Achill Island belong?

16   Ulan Bator is the capital of which country?

17   Which month is named in honour of a major Roman goddess?

18   Which actor starred as Jack Stanton in the 1998 film *Primary Colors*?

19   *Feels Like I'm in Love* was a 1980 hit for which singer?

20   The Mariinsky Theatre is located in which Russian city?

Easy
Medium
Hard

Answers to QUIZ 211 – Pot Luck

1	Jessica Raine	11	Elizabeth Barrett Browning
2	Sligo	12	Kofi Annan (United Nations)
3	Chico	13	Sir Joseph Paxton
4	*The Revenant*	14	*Porridge*
5	1853	15	1966
6	Windward Islands (within Lesser Antilles)	16	Teign
7	Lee Child	17	Cable suspension
8	Alum Bay	18	Odense
9	Apollo	19	Euclid
10	Igneous	20	Woodward

1 Who wrote the children's novel *Emil and the Detectives* (1929)?

2 Who received the 1921 Nobel Prize in Physics?

3 Who did Albert, Duke of York marry in 1923 at Westminster Abbey?

4 Which UK political party formed in 1925?

5 Howard Carter discovered the tomb of Tutankhamen in 1922 under the employment of which Earl?

6 To what did the LNER company rename the *Special Scotch Express* in 1924?

7 By what name was the Republic of Ireland known from 1921 to 1937?

8 Which style of décor first became popular in the 1920s, as seen in London's Eltham Palace?

9 To what did the Equal Franchise Act of 1928 lower the female voting age?

10 Who became Prime Minister of Italy in October 1922?

11 In which month did the General Strike of 1926 occur?

12 Which European long-distance car race was first run in 1923?

13 The Tennessee Scopes trial which took place in 1925 was dramatised in which 1960 film?

14 Which English composer was appointed Master of the King's Musick in 1924?

15 Which 1920s UK Prime Minister was born in what is now Canada?

16 In which year did women become full members of Oxford University?

17 Which mountaineer (d.1924) is reported to have said "Because it's there" in response to a question about why he wanted to climb Everest?

18 The UK 1923 Intoxicating Liquor Act prohibited the sale of alcohol to people under what age?

19 In which year did the Wall Street Crash happen?

20 In 1925 Cyril Brownlie was playing rugby for which country when he became the first person to be sent off in an international match?

Answers to QUIZ 212 – Sea Creatures

1	Pelagic	11	South America
2	Giant squid	12	Herring
3	Ten	13	Ormer (or abalone)
4	Cow	14	Pod
5	Salmon	15	Molluscs
6	Seahorse	16	Pacific
7	Norwegian	17	Fiddler crab
8	Turtle	18	Flatfish
9	Whale shark	19	Roe
10	Sea cow	20	*Cephalopoda*

ANSWERS ON PAGE **217**

1 How old was John Keats when he died?

2 In which year was the Bradwell nuclear power station decommissioned?

3 Which George Michael solo song had "90" added to the title to distinguish it from a Wham! song title?

4 What name is given to surgical tongs?

5 Who sang *I Talk to the Trees* in the 1969 film *Paint Your Wagon*?

6 Which former county town in the Clyde Valley is home of the William Wallace Heritage Trust?

7 In James Joyce's *Ulysses*, what is the surname of Leopold and Molly?

8 What sits on a dolly in a television studio?

9 What was the title of Cher's 1998 no.1 hit?

10 What is a cross-like emblem used in ancient Egypt as the symbol of life?

11 Buddy Holly was born in which Texas city?

12 In which Oxfordshire town is the Williams Formula 1 team based?

13 What was an old French five-centime piece called?

14 What was Coco Chanel's real first name?

15 Haiti and the Dominican Republic make up which island?

16 Which adjective describes the family of languages which includes Hebrew and Arabic?

17 During what event would you see Baily's beads?

18 Which Skye castle is the ancestral home of the clan MacLeod?

19 *Sheezus* was a 2014 album by which singer?

20 What was the name of Captain Scott's ship on his first voyage to Antarctica?

Easy

Medium

Hard

Answers to QUIZ 213 – Pot Luck

1	Ironsides	11	Pink Floyd
2	*Rocky III*	12	Dodge City
3	Aconite	13	Eagle's Nest (Hitler's retreat)
4	Hindi	14	Dartmoor
5	*Nabucco*	15	Mayo
6	Clement Attlee (First Earl Attlee)	16	Mongolia
7	Curling	17	June (Juno)
8	Kate Hudson	18	John Travolta
9	Hecuba	19	Kelly Marie
10	Farthing	20	St Petersburg

Easy

1 Who appeared as Tall Karen in the 2009 series *Monday Monday*?

2 Which author created the character of Thursday Next?

3 Who wrote *Manic Monday*, a hit for the Bangles?

4 Which TV series features Simon Bird as Adam Goodman?

5 Who was The Saturdays member Frankie Bridge paired with when she took part in *Strictly Come Dancing* in 2014?

6 Actress Tuesday Weld was given which first name at birth?

7 Which actor starred in the 1940 film *His Girl Friday*?

8 The Rolling Stones' *Ruby Tuesday* was released as a B side to which song in 1967?

9 Who wrote the 1908 novel *The Man who was Thursday*?

10 Which composer wrote the music and lyrics to *Sunday in the Park with George* (1984)?

11 Who played Wednesday in the 1991 film *The Addams Family*?

12 Which US TV show is known as *SNL*?

Medium

13 *Saturday Night and Sunday Morning* was a 1958 novel by which author...?

14 ...and who played Arthur Seaton in the 1960 film version?

15 The 2013 novels *Tuesday's Gone* and *Waiting for Wednesday* were published under the name of which author?

16 In which year did Blondie have a hit with *Sunday Girl*?

17 What was the real name of the dancer with the Happy Mondays, known as "Bez"?

18 Who wrote the 1954 novel *Sweet Thursday*?

19 *Tell Me on a Sunday* features music by Andrew Lloyd Webber (Baron Lloyd-Webber) and words by which lyricist?

20 Who sang the 1994 hit *Saturday Night*?

Hard

---

1   Which African republic has Dakar as its capital?

2   What is the name of Rome's ancient seaport?

3   The song *Send in the Clowns* was written by which composer?

4   Which actor co-starred with Audrey Hepburn in the 1953 film *Roman Holiday*?

5   Which carol did Bing Crosby and David Bowie record together?

6   Which shrub, also known as the wattle, is the source of gum arabic?

7   In which southern Swedish town are the *Wallander* novels set?

8   The name of which coarse woollen fabric is now used to describe any inferior substance?

9   Who is the haughty young woman in Dickens' *Great Expectations*?

10 Which Australian actor starred in *Oklahoma!* at London's National Theatre in 1998?

11 To which bird family does the puffin belong?

12 Which German astrologer was the subject of a drama by Goethe?

13 In 2015, who replaced the Foo Fighters to headline at the Glastonbury music festival?

14 Which fragrant oil comes from the damask rose?

15 Who co-starred with Martin Shaw in the TV series *The Professionals*?

16 Which is the longest railway line in the world?

17 Which 11th-century Spanish hero was the subject of a 1961 Charlton Heston film?

18 Adolphe Sax, inventor of the saxophone, had which nationality?

19 Which Egyptian god was the father of Horus?

20 Of which mammal is the aardwolf a species?

Easy

Medium

Hard

Answers to QUIZ 215 – Pot Luck

1	25	11	Lubbock
2	2002	12	Didcot
3	*Freedom*	13	Sou
4	Forceps	14	Gabrielle
5	Clint Eastwood	15	Hispaniola
6	Lanark	16	Semitic
7	Bloom	17	Solar eclipse
8	A camera	18	Dunvegan Castle
9	*Believe*	19	Lily Allen
10	Ankh	20	*Discovery*

Easy

1 For what purpose is a mixture of size applied to a sheet of paper?

2 Which cotton-like substance obtained from the fibrous cover of seeds is usually used to stuff soft toys?

3 What shade is the paint colour gamboge?

4 What general term is given to the components used to make jewellery, such as clasps and rings?

5 In encaustic art, how are colours transferred to the surface of an item?

6 What does the letter "H" indicate on a pencil?

7 The tile cutters used in making mosaics are given what name?

8 What term is given to opaque watercolour paint?

9 Lampwork is a technique to create items from what material?

10 In which craft are "fat quarters" used?

11 What is the hand tool called a brayer used for?

12 For what would an artist use a rigger brush?

13 Which Japanese craft translates as "folding paper"?

14 What term is given to a type of knitting where all the rows are knitted in plain stitch?

Medium

15 NAFAS is the association of clubs for which artistic pursuit?

16 In which craft would lazy daisy stitch be used?

17 What term is given to the threads passed across the warp on a weaving loom?

18 "Cloisonné" is a style of design where wire outlines are filled in with which material?

19 The name of which papercraft is derived from the French verb for "to cut"?

20 What name is given to the craft of burning designs on wood surfaces with a heated tool or flame?

Hard

Answers to QUIZ 216 – Days

1	Miranda Hart	11	Christina Ricci
2	Jasper Fforde	12	*Saturday Night Live*
3	Prince	13	Alan Sillitoe
4	*Friday Night Dinner*	14	Albert Finney
5	Kevin Clifton	15	Nicci French
6	Susan	16	1979
7	Cary Grant	17	Mark Berry
8	*Let's Spend the Night Together*	18	John Steinbeck
9	GK Chesterton	19	Don Black
10	Stephen Sondheim	20	Whigfield

1 Hylda Baker and Arthur Mullard recorded a spoof version of which 1978 song?

2 Which soft fruits are a cross between blackberries and raspberries?

3 What term is used for an inhabitant of Louisiana of French descent?

4 Which company started out as the California Perfume Company?

5 The 2004 film *Man on Fire* starred which actor as John Creasy?

6 What may be classified according to the Dewey Decimal System?

7 What is a gourami?

8 What is the capital of the Balearic island of Minorca?

9 *The Outsider* is the 2013 autobiography of which tennis player?

10 Which prehistoric flying reptile's name means "winged finger"?

11 What man-made feature can be seen at Foxton in Leicestershire?

12 Octavia Hill was one of the founders of which UK organisation?

13 Which old prison on London's South Bank was destroyed during the Gordon Riots of 1780?

14 What is Uruguay's unit of currency?

15 Which female novelist's debut was *White Teeth* in 2000?

16 LPL is the code for which UK airport?

17 What material represents the 13th wedding anniversary?

18 Which Beatle had a hit in 1972 with *Back Off Boogaloo*?

19 Who was Katharine Hepburn's co-star in the 1942 film *Woman of the Year*?

20 What legal phrase means "based on the first impression"?

Answers to QUIZ 217 – Pot Luck

1	Senegal	11	Auk
2	Ostia	12	Johann Faust
3	Stephen Sondheim	13	Florence and the Machine
4	Gregory Peck	14	Attar
5	*Little Drummer Boy*	15	Lewis Collins
6	Acacia	16	Trans-Siberian Railway
7	Ystad	17	El Cid
8	Shoddy	18	Belgian
9	Estella	19	Osiris
10	Hugh Jackman	20	Hyena

ANSWERS ON PAGE 222

Easy

1 The Fitzwilliam Museum is in which city?

2 Which river flows through Barnstaple?

3 Which hills straddle the English/Scottish border?

4 The Romans named which town Corinium?

5 What is the side of salted pork called, traditionally given to long-married couples in Dunmow, Essex?

6 Which English king was killed while hunting in the New Forest?

7 The village of Tolpuddle is in which county?

8 Which English Civil War battle took place near York in 1644?

9 Which Kent castle has been home to both the Astor family and the Boleyn family?

10 Knowsley is a district of which city?

Medium

11 Which cheese is associated with the town of Hawes?

12 Which shipping area lies between Dover and Portland?

13 William Wordsworth lived in which cottage in Grasmere?

14 What is the name of the lighthouse on Plymouth Hoe?

15 Which railway runs between Alton and Alresford in Hampshire?

16 The National Memorial Arboretum is in which county?

17 In which town was the TV series *Last of the Summer Wine* filmed?

18 Which Hertfordshire town was designated a New Town in 1946?

19 Which port on the south side of the Humber is managed jointly with Grimsby?

20 Which was the UK's City of Culture for 2017?

Hard

Answers to QUIZ 218 – Arts and Crafts

1	To seal it	11	Spreading ink
2	Kapok	12	Painting thin lines
3	Yellow	13	Origami
4	Findings	14	Garter stitch
5	By burning or fusing	15	Flower arranging
6	Hard	16	Embroidery
7	Nippers	17	Weft
8	Gouache	18	Enamel
9	Glass	19	Découpage
10	Quilting	20	Pyrography

1   Which actor starred as *Walker, Texas Ranger*?

2   Which group had a hit in 1976 with *Mississippi*?

3   What thick Scottish soup is made from smoked haddock, potato and onion?

4   A cete is a group of which type of animal?

5   Which part of a church lies at right angles to the nave?

6   Which Spanish town is associated with St Teresa?

7   In which US city is the Rock and Roll Hall of Fame?

8   Which island state is linked by a causeway to the Malay Peninsula?

9   What term is given to an assembly of cathedral canons?

10   Which river flows through Ludlow?

11   Which of the Savoy Operas is subtitled *The Peer and the Peri*?

12   On which body of water is the island of Inchmurrin?

13   In which TV series did Ricky Gervais play a retirement home worker?

14   What is the 18th letter of the Greek alphabet?

15   Who published the 1610 scientific pamphlet *The Starry Messenger*?

16   Which transport company started in Hibbing, Minnesota in 1914?

17   What word links a small flat-bottomed boat and a marine food fish?

18   In the 1994 film *Clear and Present Danger*, who starred as Jack Ryan?

19   What is the translation of the Japanese word "sudoku"?

20   What are sold at Tattersalls December Sales?

Answers to QUIZ 219 – Pot Luck

1	*You're the One That I Want*	11	Canal locks
2	Tayberries	12	The National Trust
3	Cajun	13	The Clink
4	Avon	14	Peso
5	Denzel Washington	15	Zadie Smith
6	Library books	16	Liverpool John Lennon
7	A fish	17	Lace
8	Mahón	18	Ringo Starr (Sir Richard Starkey)
9	Jimmy Connors	19	Spencer Tracy
10	Pterodactyl	20	*Prima facie*

Easy

1   What is the SI unit of electrical force?

2   With which area of physics is Michael Faraday most associated?

3   In relation to power, what does the PV stand for in "solar PV"?

4   What is measured in becquerels?

5   How many laws of motion are attributed to Newton?

6   What is the turning effect of force on an object called?

7   What name is given to the device on which a lever turns?

8   What unit is used to measure temperature on an absolute scale?

9   By which process are electrical or magnetic properties transferred from one circuit or body to another without physical contact?

10 Which German physicist (b.1858) is considered to be the founder of quantum theory?

11 What is the science of bodies in motion?

12 In which year did British scientist Peter W Higgs share the Nobel Prize in physics?

13 What are wire coils used in electrical circuits called?

14 In the term "CMB radiation", what does "CMB" stand for?

15 The Nobel Prize in Chemistry in 1908 was won by which physicist?

16 Which of the four laws of thermodynamics states that energy cannot be created or destroyed?

17 What is the SI unit of electric current?

18 What was the first name of the inventor of the Fahrenheit temperature scale?

19 Who wrote the 2008 book *Physics of the Impossible*?

20 How is the European Organisation for Nuclear Research better known?

Medium

Hard

Answers to QUIZ 220 – England

1	Cambridge	11	Wensleydale
2	Taw	12	Wight
3	Cheviots	13	Dove Cottage
4	Circencester	14	Smeaton's Tower
5	Flitch	15	The Watercress Line
6	William II (Rufus)	16	Staffordshire
7	Dorset	17	Holmfirth
8	Marston Moor	18	Stevenage
9	Hever	19	Immingham
10	Liverpool	20	Hull

QUIZ 223 – Pot Luck

1 Which lake constitutes the lowest point in Australia?

2 Which Egyptian city is located at the first cataract on the Nile?

3 The 1995 film *While You Were Sleeping* starred which actress?

4 What is the meaning of the word "germane"?

5 Who headed the late 1960s, early 1970s pop group the Family Stone?

6 Which was Britain's first Area of Outstanding Natural Beauty?

7 Who directed the 1960 film *La Dolce Vita*?

8 In poker, what is a run in sequence of five cards in the same suit?

9 What name links a series of mountain ranges on the Swiss-French border and an island of the Inner Hebrides?

10 Who was runner-up on *The X Factor* in 2009?

11 The *Helliconia* trilogy was written by which British sci-fi author?

12 Who is the Hindu creator of the Universe?

13 In carpentry, what is the piece of wood inserted into a mortise called?

14 Which old Roman road ran from Rome to Brindisi, via Capua?

15 What term is given to a male ferret?

16 *Drop Dead Gorgeous* was a 1997 hit for which band?

17 Which flag is flown by the British Merchant Navy?

18 What adjective refers to Cambridge University?

19 "Cinderella Man" was the nickname of which American boxer?

20 What was the former name of the National Theatre's Dorfman auditorium?

Easy

Medium

Hard

Answers to QUIZ 221 – Pot Luck

1	Chuck Norris	11	*Iolanthe*
2	Pussycat	12	Loch Lomond
3	Cullen skink	13	*Derek*
4	Badger	14	Sigma
5	Transept	15	Galileo Galilei
6	Avila	16	Greyhound Lines Inc
7	Cleveland, Ohio	17	Dory
8	Singapore	18	Harrison Ford
9	Chapter	19	Single number
10	Teme	20	Racehorses

ANSWERS ON PAGE **226**

Easy

1   What is another name for the cross of St Andrew?

2   Who wrote the 1742 novel *The History of the Adventures of Joseph Andrews*?

3   How old was Andy Murray when he was granted a knighthood?

4   Who succeeded Andrew Jackson as US President?

5   Who was the female star of the 1966 Hitchcock thriller *Torn Curtain*?

6   The 2001 novel *Looking for Andrew McCarthy* was written by which author?

7   Who had a top 5 hit in 1978 with *Never Let Her Slip Away*?

8   In which year did Sir Andrew Motion become Poet Laureate?

9   Which British singer recorded the 1971 song *Andy Warhol*?

10 Who was Andy Hamilton's co-writer on the TV series *Outnumbered*?

Medium

11 Which long-running TV series featured the character of Andy Sipowicz?

12 Which newspaper did presenter Andrew Neil edit from 1983 to 1994?

13 How were singers LaVerne, Maxene and Patricia collectively known?

14 Which retired sportsman won the first Australian series of *I'm a Celebrity...Get Me Out of Here!*?

15 Who presented the 2009 TV series *The Making of Modern Britain*?

16 Who played Andy Dufresne in the 1994 film *The Shawshank Redemption*?

17 Which Grand Slam title did Andy Roddick win in 2003?

18 Andy Fairweather-Low was a founder and lead singer of which 1960s band?

19 Which actor played Tommy in the 2010 film *Never Let Me Go*?

20 For what type of book is Andrew Morton best known?

Hard

Answers to QUIZ 222 – Physics

1	Volt	11	Kinetics
2	Electromagnetism	12	2013
3	Photovoltaic	13	Resistors
4	Radioactivity	14	Cosmic Microwave Background
5	Three	15	Sir Ernest Rutherford
6	Torque	16	First
7	Fulcrum	17	Ampere
8	Kelvin	18	Daniel
9	Induction	19	Michio Kaku
10	Max Planck	20	CERN

1 Which country is situated between Togo and Côte d'Ivoire?

2 Who had a Top Ten UK single in 1959 with *Beyond the Sea*?

3 The Royal Armouries Museum can be found in which city?

4 The 1994 Italian film *Il Postino* featured which poet as a central character?

5 What name was given to the group of three destiny-shaping goddesses of Greek mythology?

6 Who was the author of the poem *Childe Harold's Pilgrimage* (1812-18)?

7 What was found buried at Sutton Hoo in 1939?

8 What is the medical term for the bone of the upper jaw?

9 Which law of thermodynamics states that heat flows from hot to cold until equilibrium is reached?

10 What name is shared by twelve popes, three from the 20th century?

11 The TV series *Parents of the Band* starred which actor and singer?

12 What title is below an earl in the aristocratic hierarchy?

13 How many books are there in the Torah?

14 In the shipping forecast, which sea area neighbours Dogger and Fisher?

15 What branch of linguistics is concerned with the meanings of words?

16 Which port is Turkey's third-largest city?

17 In which stage musical do the audience get involved by reversing polarity?

18 Who directed and starred in the 2008 film *Gran Torino*?

19 What was the original name of an order to suppress news for reasons of national security?

20 What is the county town of Rutland?

Answers to QUIZ 223 – Pot Luck

1	Eyre	11	Brian Aldiss
2	Aswan	12	Brahma
3	Sandra Bullock	13	Tenon
4	Relevant	14	The Appian Way
5	Sly	15	Hob
6	Gower Peninsula	16	Republica
7	Federico Fellini	17	Red Ensign
8	Straight flush	18	Cantabrigian
9	Jura	19	James J Braddock
10	Olly Murs	20	Cottesloe

Easy

1. Who wrote the 1950 novel *The Grass Is Singing*?

2. Which Italian author created the character of Inspector Montalbano?

3. Which series of novels includes *At Lady Molly's* and *Hearing Secret Harmonies*?

4. Which poet (b.1788) had the first names George Gordon?

5. Which sorceress in Homer's *Odyssey* turned men into pigs?

6. What is the first name of Miss Varden in Dickens' *Barnaby Rudge*?

7. Who is the author of the *Eragon* series of novels?

8. In which year was Mary Shelley's *Frankenstein* first published?

9. Which 1911 Edith Wharton novel is set in the fictitious town of Starkfield, Massachusetts?

10. Which French cathedral city in Picardy is featured in Sebastian Faulks' novel *Birdsong*?

11. What is the name of the girl who joins Tom in the undersea world in *The Water-Babies* (1863)?

Medium

12. Who wrote *Memoirs of an Aesthete* (1948)?

13. Which writer (b.1883) created the character of Gregor Samsa?

14. Which Dutch Renaissance humanist and Catholic priest wrote *The Praise of Folly*?

15. What do the initials JB stand for in the name of the author JB Priestley?

16. Who wrote *The Shape of Things to Come* (1933)?

17. How many sonnets is Shakespeare known to have written?

18. Who is the Greek Muse of epic poetry?

Hard

19. Which French author wrote *Le Grand Meaulnes* (1913)?

20. *The Watsons*, published in 1871, is an unfinished novel by which author?

Answers to QUIZ 224 – Andrew

1	Saltire	11	*NYPD Blue*
2	Henry Fielding	12	*The Sunday Times*
3	29	13	The Andrews Sisters
4	Martin Van Buren	14	Andrew "Freddie" Flintoff
5	Dame Julie Andrews	15	Andrew Marr
6	Jenny Colgan	16	Tim Robbins
7	Andrew Gold	17	US Open
8	1999	18	Amen Corner
9	David Bowie	19	Andrew Garfield
10	Guy Jenkin	20	Biographies

ANSWERS ON PAGE 229

1   What is a more common word for prestidigitation?

2   Who is the eventual husband of Helena in Shakespeare's *All's Well That Ends Well*?

3   What was the real name of the WWI pilot nicknamed "The Red Baron"?

4   On which continent would you find the Drakensberg Mountains?

5   Who is the voice of Viper in the *Kung Fu Panda* films?

6   With which actress did David Essex record *True Love Ways* in 1994?

7   Which word for a colour is derived from the Persian for "dust"?

8   Which shipping forecast area off Northern Ireland is east of Rockall?

9   In which decade did the British Museum open?

10 Which girl's name means "bee" in Greek?

11 Who was the mythical king of Mycenae, killed by his wife and/or her lover?

12 Who was the heroine of Verdi's *Il Trovatore*?

13 Baharat spice is used in what style of cuisine?

14 What does the Mohs scale measure?

15 What is the capital of the Indian state of Karnataka?

16 In which weather phenomenon do warm and cold air collide?

17 For which 1938 film did Bette Davis win an Oscar?

18 In which constellation is the Boomerang, or Bow Tie nebula?

19 What is the name of Jersey's parliament?

20 Which 2015 film starred Tina Fey and Amy Poehler?

Easy

Medium

Hard

Answers to QUIZ 225 – Pot Luck

1	Ghana	11	Jimmy Nail
2	Bobby Darin	12	Viscount
3	Leeds	13	Five (Pentateuch)
4	Pablo Neruda	14	German Bight
5	The Fates	15	Semantics
6	Lord Byron	16	Izmir
7	A Saxon ship	17	*Return to the Forbidden Planet*
8	Maxilla	18	Clint Eastwood
9	Second	19	D-Notice
10	Pius	20	Oakham

1   Who played the bass guitar on Midge Ure's 1986 no.1 *If I Was*?

2   The Carpenters' hit *Calling Occupants of Interplanetary Craft* was originally recorded by which Canadian group?

3   What was the original name of singer Billy Ocean?

4   Which band backed Desmond Dekker?

5   *Attention* was a 2017 hit for which singer?

6   In which Irish county did Clannad form?

7   Who directed the Pet Shop Boys' video to *It's A Sin*?

8   What was the debut single by The Wanted?

9   In which year did Bono receive an honorary knighthood?

10   How is Adam Richard Wiles better known?

11   Which female singer featured on the Communards' 1986 hit *Don't Leave Me This Way*?

12   Pectoralz and Starfish are previous names for which band?

13   Which *Fame Academy* winner had a 2003 hit with *Maybe That's What it Takes*?

14   *Black Ice* was a 2008 album by which rock group?

15   Which country won the Eurovision Song Contest in 1985 with *Let It Swing*?

16   Who had her first UK no.1 single in 1997 with *All I Wanna Do*?

17   Ed Sheeran's *Castle on the Hill* was written about which town?

18   What was the name of Yazz's backing band on *The Only Way is Up*?

19   Who sang the 1960s hit *Catch the Wind*?

20   In which year did Beyoncé have a hit with *Halo*?

Answers to QUIZ 226 – Literature

1	Doris Lessing	11	Ellie
2	Andrea Camilleri	12	Harold Acton
3	*A Dance to the Music of Time*	13	Franz Kafka
4	Lord Byron	14	Erasmus
5	Circe	15	John Boynton
6	Dolly	16	HG Wells
7	Christopher Paolini	17	154
8	1818	18	Calliope
9	*Ethan Frome*	19	Alain-Fournier
10	Amiens	20	Jane Austen

ANSWERS ON PAGE 231

1   The tea clipper *Cutty Sark* was named after a character in which poem?

2   What type of weather is associated with cumulonimbus clouds?

3   Which lake forms the north-eastern border of Nigeria?

4   What is a sparable?

5   From which country does the Korat cat originate?

6   In which southern French town was the artist Toulouse-Lautrec born?

7   Which ancient Roman noblewoman was mother to emperor Tiberius?

8   What is the second highest peak in Scotland?

9   Which inflammable liquid is distilled from coal-tar?

10 Who topped the charts in 1976 with the song *No Charge*?

11 Which canal connects the North Sea with the Baltic Sea?

12 In which year was the first British Bank Holiday granted?

13 Which is the largest island of French Polynesia?

14 How is trinitrotoluene more commonly known?

15 Who wrote the novel *PS I Love You*, later filmed starring Hilary Swank?

16 What is a carbonnade?

17 In which 1990s US comedy-drama series did Adam Ant make a cameo appearance?

18 Which Toledo landmark was the scene of a Spanish Civil War siege?

19 How many symphonies did the composer Mahler complete?

20 Which Cambridge college was founded in 1441?

Easy

Medium

Hard

Answers to QUIZ 227 – Pot Luck

1	Conjuring tricks	11	Agamemnon
2	Bertram	12	Leonora
3	Manfred von Richthofen	13	Middle Eastern
4	Africa	14	Mineral hardness
5	Lucy Liu	15	Bengaluru (or Bangalore)
6	Catherine Zeta-Jones	16	Occluded front
7	Khaki	17	*Jezebel*
8	Malin	18	Centaurus
9	1750s (1759)	19	States
10	Melissa	20	*Sisters*

1   In which year was the National Trust founded?

2   What is the name of the ancient Roman province in what is now Romania?

3   Who was the last emperor of Russia?

4   Who was the botanist on Cook's 1768-71 expedition?

5   Which historic city was the old imperial capital of Vietnam?

6   Which Oxford college was founded in 1509?

7   Roland Berrill and Dr Lancelot Ware formed which society in 1946?

8   Who was crowned King of England as a result of the Battle of Towton?

9   Which ancient kingdom of Asia Minor, now Anatolia, had Sardis as its capital?

10 In which year did Hawaii become the 50th US state?

11 Of which country was Bernardo O'Higgins an independence leader?

12 Which seafood dish is named after the 11th month of the French revolutionary calendar?

13 Which Far Eastern former Portuguese colony was handed over to China in 1999?

14 Who ruled Scotland from 1124 to 1153?

15 Which Egyptian pharaoh was the father of Rameses II?

16 St Angela Merici founded which order of nuns at Brescia in 1535?

17 Which architect designed the Brighton Pavilion and Marble Arch?

18 Who was the king of Belgium from 1934 to 1951?

19 Which Roman emperor was Hadrian's predecessor?

20 China was ruled from 206 BC to AD 220 by which dynasty?

Answers to QUIZ 228 – Pop Music

1	Mark King	11	Sarah-Jane Morris
2	Klaatu	12	Coldplay
3	Leslie Charles	13	Alex Parks
4	Aces	14	AC/DC
5	Charlie Puth	15	Norway
6	Donegal	16	Dannii Minogue
7	Derek Jarman	17	Framlingham
8	All Time Low	18	The Plastic Population
9	2007	19	Donovan
10	Calvin Harris	20	2009

ANSWERS ON PAGE 233

1   Which orchestral instrument is descended from the shawm?

2   What does an irenologist study?

3   A zucchetto is an ecclesiastical skullcap named after which vegetable?

4   What term describes marine life that lives on the sea bed?

5   Battle Creek, Michigan houses the headquarters of which US company?

6   What was the name of the garden in Athens where Aristotle taught philosophy?

7   What is the currency unit of Panama?

8   *Zombie* was a 2014 hit for which singer/songwriter?

9   In which year did London's Tower Bridge come into operation?

10   Who wrote *The Swiss Family Robinson*?

11   What is the capital of Tatarstan, part of Russia?

12   Which two scientists confirmed the role of DNA in inheritance in 1952?

13   In which indoor game can the opposing player be forced to be "in zugzwang"?

14   Who wrote *The Beggar's Opera* (1728)?

15   In which Staffordshire town was Samuel Johnson born in 1709?

16   In which city is the Potala Palace?

17   Who wrote the satirical play *Volpone*?

18   What is the last book of the Old Testament?

19   Where would you find a frog on a horse?

20   Which mountain range is located at the meeting point of Russia, China, Mongolia and Kazakhstan?

Easy

Medium

Hard

Answers to QUIZ 229 – Pot Luck

1	*Tam O'Shanter*	11	Kiel
2	Thunderstorms	12	1871
3	Chad	13	Tahiti
4	Headless nail	14	TNT
5	Thailand	15	Cecelia Ahern
6	Albi	16	Beef stew
7	Livia	17	*Northern Exposure*
8	Ben Macdui	18	Alcázar
9	Naphtha	19	Nine
10	JJ Barrie	20	King's

Easy

1   Which is the brightest star in the constellation Aquila?

2   What does a lithologist study?

3   In 1995 Eileen Collins became the first woman to pilot which vehicle?

4   Which part of the body is affected by Addison's disease?

5   *Sciurus vulgaris* is the Latin name for which animal?

6   Which gas used in welding is produced from calcium carbide and water?

7   What Greek letter is the scientific symbol for wavelength?

8   How many joules are there in a calorie?

9   What is the common name for the disease variola?

10 What is the second stomach of a ruminant called?

11 What term is given to an abnormally slow heart rate?

12 At which Italian university was Galileo the chair of mathematics from 1592 to 1610?

13 Which is the middle of the eye's three layers?

14 What element has the atomic number 12?

Medium

15 "Parsec" is a measurement used in which branch of science?

16 What bodily tissue is composed of cells called chondrocytes?

17 X-rays were discovered by which German physicist?

18 Which institution published Sir Isaac Newton's *Principia* in 1687?

19 What are "KW Sagittarii" and "KY Cygni"?

20 What does the body lack in the condition hypoxia?

Hard

Answers to QUIZ 230 – History

1	1895	11	Chile
2	Dacia	12	Lobster Thermidor
3	Nicholas II	13	Macao (or Macau)
4	Sir Joseph Banks	14	David I
5	Hué	15	Seti I
6	Brasenose	16	Ursulines
7	Mensa	17	John Nash
8	Edward IV	18	Leopold III
9	Lydia	19	Trajan
10	1959	20	Han

1   What is the branch of philosophy that deals with the nature of being?

2   Who invented the pendulum clock?

3   The Darién Gap interrupts which road?

4   To what does the word "margaric" relate?

5   Which group released a 1979 album entitled *Spirits Having Flown*?

6   "Apple of Grenada" is an old name for which fruit?

7   Which early computer language was named after a French mathematician?

8   Who wrote the 2003 book *The Lunar Men*?

9   Who directed the 1981 film *Gallipoli*?

10 Who was world chess champion from 1975 to 1985?

11 Glen Prosen, Schönemann and Cascade Delight are varieties of which fruit?

12 Haddington Hill is the highest point in Buckinghamshire of which range of hills?

13 Which philosopher wrote the *Discourse on Method* in 1637?

14 What is the state flower of New York?

15 Which capital city is situated on the Chao Phraya River?

16 What is dupion?

17 Which British 10,000m runner competed at every Summer Olympics from 2000 to 2016?

18 Hector Hugh Munro wrote under what pseudonym?

19 What are Bernard Silver and Norman Woodland credited with inventing?

20 What is the standard monetary unit of Malaysia?

Answers to QUIZ 231 – Pot Luck

1	Oboe	11	Kazan
2	Peace	12	Alfred Hershey and Martha Chase
3	Small gourd	13	Chess
4	Benthic	14	John Gay
5	Kellogg's	15	Lichfield
6	Lyceum	16	Lhasa
7	Balboa	17	Ben Jonson
8	Jamie T	18	Malachi
9	1894	19	On the sole of its hoof
10	Johann Wyss	20	Altai Mountains

1   Which African nation's flag features two tribal spears, a staff and a shield?

2   Which Caribbean country's flag has a parrot as its centrepiece?

3   Which country's flag contains 13 horizontal stripes?

4   Which two countries' flags feature a depiction of yin and yang?

5   How many flags feature a single colour background with a flat circle of colour?

6   On which country's flag is there a map of itself?

7   Which country's flag features three green diamonds as its centrepiece?

8   What term is given to someone who studies flags?

9   Which country's flag is known as "the Flag of the Five Escutcheons"?

10   "The Sun and Stripes" is the nickname of which country's flag?

11   Which country's flag features a coat of arms containing a golden eagle devouring a rattle snake?

12   The largest religious monument in the world is depicted on the flag of which country?

13   On which country's flag would you find a Raggiana bird-of-paradise?

14   Which country's flag is known as "the Broken Trident"?

15   Which South American country's flag carries its national motto in full?

16   How many flags feature the Union Jack?

17   Which is the only country not to have a quadrilateral flag?

18   The flags of which two South American countries feature "the Sun of May"?

19   Which African country's flag is light blue with a central white star?

20   Which country's flag was a single colour between 1977 and 2011?

Answers to QUIZ 232 – Science

1	Altair	11	Bradycardia
2	Rocks	12	Padua
3	Space shuttle	13	Uvea
4	Adrenal glands	14	Magnesium
5	Red squirrel	15	Astronomy
6	Acetylene	16	Cartilage
7	Lambda	17	Wilhelm Röntgen
8	4184	18	The Royal Society
9	Smallpox	19	Stars (supergiants)
10	Reticulum	20	Oxygen

1　What is the number of Shakespeare's sonnet that begins "Shall I compare thee to a summer's day?"?

2　Iqique and Cuzco are cities on which of the world's continents?

3　What is the county town of Ireland's County Kildare?

4　*Cyanistes caeruleus* is the Latin name for which common garden bird?

5　In mythology, what is the collective name for Clotho, Lachesis and Atropos?

6　Which Christian festival is held on August 6?

7　Achluophobia is a fear of what?

8　Who wrote *The Ballad of Peckham Rye*?

9　Which jockey won the Prix de l'Arc de Triomphe in three successive years, from 1996 to 1998?

10　Sir Robert Peel was born in which Greater Manchester town?

11　In 1294, Celestine V was the first pope to do what?

12　In what make of plane did Alcock and Brown make their historic flight across the Atlantic?

13　Macquarie Harbour is in which Australian state?

14　Who was Aaron's sister in the Old Testament?

15　How is American singer Peter Hernandez better known?

16　Which former coal-mining town is the administrative centre of Blaenau Gwent?

17　What word describes a chemical reaction that releases energy?

18　In which area of the arts was Rudolf Laban famous?

19　What is another name for the areca palm seed?

20　Which striped animal is native to the Democratic Republic of the Congo?

Answers to QUIZ 233 – Pot Luck

1	Ontology	11	Raspberry
2	Christiaan Huygens	12	Chilterns
3	Pan-American Highway	13	René Descartes
4	Pearl	14	Rose
5	Bee Gees	15	Bangkok
6	Pomegranate	16	Silk fabric
7	Pascal	17	Jo Pavey
8	Jenny Uglow	18	Saki
9	Peter Weir	19	Barcode
10	Anatoly Karpov	20	Ringgit

Easy

1 In marine terms, what does RIB stand for?

2 Who was the first man to sail solo around the world...?

3 ...and who was the first man to sail solo around the world non-stop?

4 Who captained *HMS Beagle* during Charles Darwin's first expedition voyage to the South Americas?

5 What was the name of the UK's first nuclear submarine?

6 How many standard miles are in a nautical mile?

7 What is the highest rank in the Royal Navy?

8 What flag is used to recall all personnel to a ship that is about to go to sea?

9 What are the ropes and lines that support a ship's mast called?

10 Following the 2016 Games, which country had won the most Olympic gold medals for sailing since the sport was introduced?

11 Where did Captain James Cook meet his death?

Medium

12 Sir Ernest Shackleton travelled on which ship during his 1908 Antarctic expedition?

13 What is the name of the knot used to form a fixed eye at the end of a rope?

14 What was the name of the UK's first aircraft carrier?

15 Who was the captain of the *Titanic*?

16 What is the upper edge of the hull, or top timber on the rail round the outer edge of the deck known as?

17 What is a windlass?

18 Who was the first woman to sail solo, non-stop and unassisted around the world?

19 In which year was the wreck of Henry VIII's flagship the *Mary Rose* raised?

20 The 470 and 49er are classes in which Olympic sailing category?

Hard

Answers to QUIZ 234 – Flags

1	Eswatini (or Swaziland)	11	Mexico
2	Dominica	12	Cambodia (Angkor Wat)
3	United States	13	Papua New Guinea
4	Mongolia & South Korea	14	Barbados
5	Three (Bangladesh, Japan and Palau)	15	Brazil (*Ordem e Progresso*)
6	Cyprus	16	Five (Australia, Fiji, New Zealand, Tuvalu and UK)
7	St Vincent and the Grenadines	17	Nepal
8	Vexillologist	18	Argentina and Uruguay
9	Portugal	19	Somalia
10	Uruguay	20	Libya (green)

1. What is the name of the Hindu goddess who is the destroyer of evil forces?

2. What term is given to the statistical and sociological study of elections?

3. *Hernando's Hideaway* is a song from which musical?

4. What term is given to the oldest geological era?

5. In which branch of science did Benjamin Thompson, Count Rumford, specialise?

6. Which Old Testament book follows Ezekiel?

7. Where was the US Open golf tournament played in 2017?

8. Which tree has the Latin name *Prunus spinosa*?

9. Who wrote the 1889 book *Darwinism: An Exposition of the Theory of Natural Selection, with Some of its Applications*?

10. In which building is the Society of Antiquaries of London based?

11. *Fallen Empires* is a 2011 album by which band?

12. What name was given to the policy of non-violent resistance adopted by Mahatma Ghandi?

13. On which Caribbean island is the city of Cienfuegos?

14. Which taxonomic classification is immediately below "kingdom"?

15. With whom did Émile Gagnan invent the aqualung?

16. In which country is the Alqueva Dam?

17. Which UK ship, along with the *USS Niagara*, laid the first transatlantic cable in 1858?

18. From what is the caulking material oakum made?

19. What term is given to a round prison in which all cells are visible from the centre point?

20. What is the most northerly point of mainland Britain?

Easy

Medium

Hard

Answers to QUIZ 235 – Pot Luck

1	18	11	Abdicate or resign
2	South America	12	Vickers Vimy
3	Naas	13	Tasmania
4	Blue tit	14	Miriam
5	The Fates	15	Bruno Mars
6	Transfiguration	16	Ebbw Vale
7	Darkness	17	Exothermic
8	Dame Muriel Spark	18	Dance
9	Olivier Peslier	19	Betel nut
10	Bury	20	Okapi

1. Which Henry Fonda 1946 western takes its name from a folk song of the gold rush?

2. In which 2016 film does Jeff Bridges play a Texas Ranger trying to solve a string of bank robberies?

3. What was the name of James Dean's character in the 1955 film *East of Eden*?

4. The 2015 film *Focus* starred which actor as Nicky?

5. Which 1972 Hitchcock film is set in and around London's Covent Garden?

6. Who played the title character in the 1980 film *Flash Gordon*?

7. In the 2010 film *How to Train Your Dragon*, what is the name of the dragon befriended by Hiccup?

8. Who won the Best Actress Oscar for the 1994 film *Blue Sky*?

9. What was Marilyn Monroe's last film?

10. Who stars as Tris Prior in the *Divergent* series of films?

11. What was the name of Billy Zane's character in the 1997 film *Titanic*?

12. The 2007 film *There Will Be Blood* is based on which Upton Sinclair novel?

13. What is the name of the human-controlled underground city in the *Matrix* films?

14. For which film did Sally Field win her first Best Actress Oscar?

15. Which actress played the title role in the 2014 film *Effie Gray*?

16. Which famous scream was believed to have been used for the first time in the 1951 film *Distant Drums*?

17. *I Got Rhythm* and *'S Wonderful* are songs from which 1951 musical film?

18. Which 1988 film received four Oscars including Best Picture?

19. In the 2003 film *Love, Actually*, which actor played the US President?

20. Which 1982 Steve Martin film was in black and white and included scenes from classic films?

Answers to QUIZ 236 – Sailing

1	Rigid-hulled Inflatable boat	11	Hawaii
2	Joshua Slocum (1895-98)	12	*Nimrod*
3	Sir Robin Knox-Johnston	13	Bowline
4	Robert Fitzroy	14	*Ark Royal* (1955)
5	*Dreadnought*	15	Edward John Smith
6	1.1508 miles	16	Gunwale
7	Admiral of the Fleet	17	A winch used to raise heavy weights on board
8	Blue Peter	18	Kay Cottee (1988)
9	Shrouds	19	1982
10	Great Britain	20	Dinghy

ANSWERS ON PAGE 241

1   Which German city of the Ruhr is the site of the Krupp steelworks?

2   Who wrote the tale *Jack the Dullard*?

3   Which indigenous people of Borneo were once called "Sea Dayaks"?

4   Which theory explains the universe in terms of force or energy?

5   In Greek myth, who was the lover of Hippolytus?

6   Which figure of the French Revolution was assassinated in his bathtub by Charlotte Corday?

7   Who wrote the 1773 play *The Barber of Seville*?

8   From which country does the ornamental box called an "inro" originate?

9   In the TV series *Friends*, what was the name of Joey's agent?

10 Which is the only Central American country with English as an official language?

11 Which knitting technique shares its name with a medieval style of marquetry?

12 Daikon is a variety of which vegetable?

13 Who directed the 1954 film *On the Waterfront*?

14 Which monastic peninsula of northern Greece forbids entry to women?

15 What is the main island and capital of the Maldives?

16 Of what sort of unaccompanied part-songs were Gabrieli, Monteverdi and Palestrina among the classic composers?

17 What is schalstein?

18 Who was crowned King of Scotland on March 25, 1306?

19 Which large grey Australian crane is the emblem of Queensland?

20 What is the surname of Sir Jacob, the British sculptor whose piece *Rima* is displayed in Hyde Park?

Answers to QUIZ 237 – Pot Luck

1	Kali	11	Snow Patrol
2	Psephology	12	Satyagraha
3	*The Pajama Game*	13	Cuba
4	Pre-Cambrian	14	Phylum
5	Physics	15	Jacques Cousteau
6	Daniel	16	Portugal
7	Erin Hills, Wisconsin	17	*HMS Agamemnon*
8	Blackthorn	18	Rope
9	Alfred Russell Wallace	19	Panopticon
10	Burlington House	20	Dunnet Head

1 How many toes does a rhea have on each foot?

2 Which bird is the national bird of the Bahamas?

3 *Erithacus rubecula* is the Latin name for which European garden bird?

4 A tercel is a male of what type of bird?

5 "Mother Carey's Chicken" is an old name for which bird?

6 Which bird was reintroduced to Scotland's Black Isle in the late 1980s and early 1990s?

7 Wood grouse is an alternative name for which bird?

8 Which bird of prey has the Latin name *Bubo bubo*?

9 Gentoo and macaroni are species of which bird?

10 Which British summer visitor of the rail family is famously secretive, often only located by its distinctive rasping call?

11 What colour eggs do dunnocks lay?

12 In which decade was the collared dove introduced to Britain?

13 The call of the yellowhammer is often described as resembling which phrase?

14 Which bird of the finch family has a distinctive beak used to extract seeds from conifer cones?

15 Which bird sanctuary off the coast of North Berwick is home to thousands of seabirds?

16 Which family of birds have earned the nickname "butcher bird" due to their habit of storing prey on thorns or barbed wire?

17 What name is given to the tail of a peacock?

18 The condor is a member of which family?

19 What name is given to a puffin chick?

20 Where does a goldeneye duck build its nest?

Answers to QUIZ 238 – Film

1	*My Darling Clementine*	11	Cal Hockley
2	*Hell or High Water*	12	*Oil!*
3	Cal (Caleb Trask)	13	Zion
4	Will Smith	14	*Norma Rae* (1979)
5	*Frenzy*	15	Dakota Fanning
6	Sam J Jones	16	The "Wilhelm Scream"
7	Toothless	17	*An American in Paris*
8	Jessica Lange	18	*Rain Man*
9	*The Misfits*	19	Billy Bob Thornton
10	Shailene Woodley	20	*Dead Men Don't Wear Plaid*

ANSWERS ON PAGE **243**

1   What was the name of the Australian Prime Minister who mysteriously vanished in 1967?

2   A "Lett" was a former name of a citizen of which country?

3   What is the title of the 1864 poem by Alfred, Lord Tennyson about a fisherman turned merchant sailor?

4   By what name is singer Michael Barratt (b.1948) better known?

5   An indri is a species of which animal?

6   Who was the first aviator to fly over the South Pole?

7   Who featured on Ariana Grande's top 10 hit *Side to Side*?

8   Which river runs through St Petersburg?

9   *The Outsider* and *The Plague* are 1940s novels by which French writer?

10 What is a fichu?

11 Who played the title role in the 1960s TV series *I Dream of Jeannie*?

12 In which country is the Amboseli National Park?

13 Which communication precipitated the Franco-Prussian War in 1870?

14 What does "Caer" mean in a Welsh place name?

15 Which football team won the FIFA World Cup in 1934?

16 *Extreme Ways*, used as a theme in the *Bourne* films, is by which musician?

17 Which term describes a species of plant that has its male and female reproductive organs on separate plants?

18 *The River Fragments* are musings by which ancient philosopher?

19 Which British airport was originally known as Abbotsinch?

20 Which cathedral has the longest uninterrupted vaulted ceiling in England?

Easy

Medium

Hard

Answers to QUIZ 239 – Pot Luck

1	Essen	11	Intarsia
2	Hans Christian Andersen	12	Radish
3	Iban	13	Elia Kazan
4	Dynamism	14	Athos
5	Phaedra	15	Malé
6	Jean-Paul Marat	16	Madrigals
7	Pierre Beaumarchais	17	Metamorphic rock
8	Japan	18	Robert the Bruce
9	Estelle	19	Brolga
10	Belize	20	Epstein

1   Which rugby Premiership team play their home games at Kingsholm?

2   What was the name of the winning horse in the 2016 Epsom Derby?

3   Where did the Tour de France start in 2017?

4   Battledore was a forerunner of which indoor sport?

5   Who won the PDC World Darts Championship in 2015 and 2016?

6   How high is a basketball hoop from the ground?

7   Who was the inaugural Formula E champion?

8   In which year were medals first presented at the Olympic Games?

9   What is the German term for cross-country skiing?

10 In which sport do teams compete for the Stanley Cup trophy?

11 Which retired snooker player appeared at Glastonbury in 2016 as a DJ?

12 Which golfer won the 2003 Open in his first appearance in a major championship?

13 In 1962, who became World Heavyweight Boxing champion on beating Floyd Patterson?

14 Who won the Golden Boot at the 2006 FIFA World Cup?

15 Which TV presenter represented Wales at the 1990 Commonwealth Games in gymnastics?

16 Which area of London was home to England's first golf and hockey clubs and the oldest rugby club?

17 In which winter sport is Evgeni Plushenko a former World and Olympic champion?

18 In which event did Anita Wlodarczyk win Olympic gold medals in 2012 and 2016?

19 Who was the first player to reach 10,000 test runs?

20 Who formally started the 2018 London Marathon?

Answers to QUIZ 240 – Birds

1	Three	11	Greenish-blue
2	Flamingo	12	1950s
3	Robin	13	"A little bit of bread and no cheese"
4	Hawk	14	Crossbill
5	Storm petrel	15	Bass Rock
6	Red kite	16	Shrikes
7	Capercaillie	17	Train
8	Eagle owl	18	Vultures
9	Penguin	19	Puffling
10	Corncrake	20	In a tree

QUIZ 243 – Pot Luck

ANSWERS ON PAGE **245**

1   Who was the father of David in the Old Testament?

2   Which rare bear is native to British Columbia?

3   In 1982, which was the 500th single to top the UK charts?

4   Alf Wight was the real name of which English writer?

5   What other name is given to the white poplar tree?

6   The kinetoscope was an early form of which device?

7   Who was appointed Director of the Royal Ballet in July 2012?

8   People named in the Griffin Book are barred from entering what type of establishment?

9   Which Scottish engineer improved the condensation process of the steam engine designed by Thomas Newcomen?

10 In which decade was Harrow public school founded?

11 Which artist wrote the 1979 quest book *Masquerade*?

12 On which Greek island was Odysseus said to have been born?

13 Which actor starred in the title role in the 2016 remake of *Ben-Hur*?

14 What word describes a thermodynamic reaction that takes place without loss of heat or cold?

15 Who was the Austrian composer of *Lulu* (1935)?

16 What name is given to a person who cuts, polishes and engraves stones, especially precious stones?

17 The Palaeogene period occurred during which geological era?

18 What is notable about a sentence decribed as "sesquipedalian"?

19 In which Kent country house was Vita Sackville-West born in 1892?

20 Who was the founder of the Christian Science movement?

Answers to QUIZ 241 – Pot Luck

1	Harold Holt	11	Barbara Eden
2	Latvia	12	Kenya
3	*Enoch Arden*	13	Ems Telegram
4	Shakin' Stevens	14	Fort
5	Lemur	15	Italy
6	Richard Byrd (in 1929)	16	Moby
7	Nicki Minaj	17	Dioecious
8	Neva	18	Heraclitus
9	Albert Camus	19	Glasgow
10	Shawl	20	Exeter

1   In which US state is John Wayne Airport?

2   Who wrote the 2005 book *Marley & Me*?

3   Who played John Ross Ewing in the 2012 version of *Dallas*?

4   1960s singer Johnny Kidd was backed by which group?

5   Which Venetian explorer discovered Newfoundland?

6   Sir John Chilcot conducted a seven-year enquiry into which event, the results of which were published in 2016?

7   Which 1924 tale of the building of a railroad was John Ford's first full-scale western?

8   Who wrote the 1995 book *Longitude* about clockmaker John Harrison?

9   The character of John Doggett appeared in which TV series?

10 Which old county town lies sixteen miles south of John o' Groats?

11 Poet John Donne (b.1572) became dean at which building in 1621?

12 Who directed the 1999 film *Being John Malkovich*?

13 What was the real name of the Oliver Twist character known as "the Artful Dodger"?

14 Who played the title role in the 2014 film *John Wick* and its 2017 sequel?

15 John Ridd is the central male character in which 1869 novel?

16 With which player did John McEnroe win over 50 men's doubles titles, including four Wimbledon and three US Open titles?

17 What was the first name of John Nettles' character in the TV series *The Liver Birds*?

18 John Travolta starred in which 2007 biker film?

19 What title did John Prescott adopt when he took his seat in the House of Lords?

20 John of Gaunt (b.1340) was the son of which English king?

Answers to QUIZ 242 – Sport

1	Gloucester	11	Steve Davis
2	Harzand	12	Ben Curtis
3	Düsseldorf	13	Sonny Liston
4	Badminton	14	Miroslav Klose
5	Gary Anderson	15	Gabby Logan
6	Ten feet	16	Blackheath
7	Nelson Piquet Jr	17	Figure skating
8	1904 (St Louis Olympics)	18	Hammer
9	*Langlauf*	19	Sunil Gavaskar
10	Ice hockey	20	Queen Elizabeth II

1 Who played Marcus in the 2002 film *About a Boy*?

2 In the Old Testament, who was Methuselah's father?

3 Which Keats poem begins: "A thing of beauty is a joy forever"?

4 In which country is the city of Eger, famed for its castle and wines?

5 What vitamin-rich tropical fruit is also known as Barbados cherry and seriz?

6 What was the real surname of singer Marc Bolan?

7 What is the capital city of Mozambique?

8 In the TV series *The Wire*, who played Detective Lester Freamon?

9 Who wrote the song *Feeling Good*, famously covered by Michael Bublé?

10 Who wrote *Goodbye, Mr Chips* (1934)?

11 Which Greek character was punished by constant thirst?

12 A friand is what type of food?

13 Who released the 2017 album entitled *Piano Portraits*?

14 What part of Malaysia was known as Prince of Wales Island until 1867?

15 Iran ruled which sheikhdom from 1602 to 1783?

16 Who starred as Tilly Dunnage in the 2015 film *The Dressmaker*?

17 Which tennis player won the World ATP finals in November 2017 in his first appearance in the competition?

18 In heraldry, what type of symbol is a pheon?

19 In what does a mercer deal?

20 What was Arthur Wynne credited with inventing in 1913?

Answers to QUIZ 243 – Pot Luck

1	Jesse	11	Kit Williams
2	Kermode bear	12	Ithaca
3	*A Little Peace* (Nicole)	13	Jack Huston
4	James Herriot	14	Adiabatic
5	Abele	15	Alban Berg
6	Film camera	16	Lapidary
7	Kevin O'Hare	17	Cenozoic
8	Casinos	18	It uses long words
9	James Watt	19	Knole
10	1570s (1571)	20	Mary Baker Eddy

1 Which actor played Arnold Vinick in *The West Wing*?

2 Who won *The X Factor* in 2014?

3 Which broadcaster and writer appeared in the first *Celebrity MasterChef* in 2006, losing in the final to Matt Dawson?

4 In the 1990s sitcom *The Upper Hand,* who played Charlie Burrows?

5 Who created the drama series *Cold Feet*?

6 Which English actress played Margaery Tyrell in *Game of Thrones*?

7 Joseph Fiennes starred as FBI agent Mark Benford in which sci-fi TV series of 2009-10?

8 Whom did Michael Dorn play in *Star Trek: The Next Generation*?

9 The first panel on which musical programme included Alma Cogan and Susan Stranks?

10 Billy Crystal played which character in *Soap*?

11 Who began her acting career as Flick Scully in *Neighbours*?

12 Which TV family in the 1960s and 70s lived at 518 Crestview Drive, Beverly Hills?

13 What was the name of *The A-Team* character nicknamed BA?

14 In *Camberwick Green*, what was the name of the baker?

15 Who won the first series of *Fame Academy* and topped the charts with *Stop Living The Lie*?

16 Which 1989-95 series featured Dr Sheila Sabatini and Dr Jonathan Haslam?

17 How is cartoon character Dr. Robert Underdunk Terwilliger Jr better known?

18 What was the name of Penelope Pitstop's car in *Wacky Races*?

19 Who played Caroline Fairchild in the 1980s comedy series *Executive Stress*?

20 In 2016 which TV presenter and comedian released an album entitled *Upon a Different Shore*?

Answers to QUIZ 244 – John

1	California	11	St Paul's Cathedral
2	John Grogan	12	Spike Jonze
3	Josh Henderson	13	"Jack" (John) Dawkins
4	The Pirates	14	Keanu Reeves
5	John Cabot	15	*Lorna Doone*
6	The Iraq War	16	Peter Fleming
7	*The Iron Horse*	17	Paul
8	Dava Sobel	18	*Wild Hogs*
9	*The X-Files*	19	Baron Prescott of Kingston-upon-Hull
10	Wick	20	Edward III

1   What was the name of the last King of Italy?

2   In 1994, *Second Coming* was the second album by which band?

3   What is the meaning of "cupidity"?

4   Which north-east Indian state has Patna as its capital?

5   Who was the second person to run a mile in under four minutes?

6   How are Rose McDowall and Jill Bryson known musically?

7   In which African country is the Dallol volcano?

8   What famous landmark can be seen at Lake Havasu in Arizona?

9   In mythology, which princess was rescued from a sea-monster by Perseus?

10 Which Scottish football team plays at Gayfield Park?

11 *"Nullius in verba"* is the motto of which institution?

12 Which city was founded by Pizarro in 1535?

13 Who directed the 1944 film *Arsenic and Old Lace*?

14 On which 1995 hit did Michael Jackson duet with his sister Janet?

15 Who wrote the *Doctor Dolittle* novels?

16 The liqueur prunelle originates from which country?

17 Which Roman philosopher and dramatist died in AD 65?

18 What chemical compound is the base of common alcohol?

19 Traps and skeets are involved in which sport?

20 Which is the "Gem State" of the USA?

Answers to QUIZ 245 – Pot Luck

1	Nicholas Hoult	11	Tantalus
2	Enoch	12	A small (almond) cake
3	*Endymion*	13	Rick Wakeman
4	Hungary	14	Pinang
5	Acerola	15	Bahrain
6	Feld	16	Kate Winslet
7	Maputo	17	Grigor Dimitrov
8	Clarke Peters	18	Arrow
9	Anthony Newley and Leslie Bricusse	19	Fabric and cloth
10	James Hilton	20	The first modern crossword

1   Who was the first Prime Minister of Australia?

2   On what day does Brazil celebrate its Independence Day?

3   What is the official residence of the French Prime Minister?

4   Jacinda Ardern was elected prime minister of which country in October 2017?

5   Who was Hillary Clinton's running mate in the 2016 US presidential election?

6   In 1982, who succeeded Leonid Brezhnev as leader of the USSR?

7   Who was the Vice-President of the United States from 1969 to 1973?

8   Former Israeli prime ministers Olmert and Barak share which first name?

9   Who was Foreign Secretary in the 1945-51 Labour government?

10 How is the Naval Support Facility Thurmont in Maryland better known?

11 Which Russian leader had the nickname "Koba"?

12 Who founded the Fianna Fáil political party in the Republic of Ireland?

13 Which was the first country to give women the vote?

14 Iceland is generally considered to have the world's oldest parliament, dating from what year?

15 What is the name of the official Canberra home of Australia's Prime Minister?

16 In 1864, which two states went to war with Denmark?

17 What name is used for the lower chamber of the Russian parliament?

18 Who was US president from 1909 to 1913?

19 In which year was Germany first unified?

20 Shinzō Abe became Prime Minister of which country in 2012?

Answers to QUIZ 246 – Television

1	Alan Alda	11	Holly Valance
2	Ben Haenow	12	The Clampetts (*Beverly Hillbillies*)
3	Hardeep Singh Kohli	13	Bosco Baracus
4	Joe McGann	14	Mickey Murphy
5	Mike Bullen	15	David Sneddon
6	Natalie Dormer	16	*Surgical Spirit*
7	*FlashForward*	17	Sideshow Bob (in *The Simpsons*)
8	Worf	18	The Compact Pussycat
9	*Juke Box Jury*	19	Dame Penelope Keith
10	Jodie Dallas	20	Alexander Armstrong

QUIZ 249 – Pot Luck

ANSWERS ON PAGE 1

1   Of which small West African country is Lomé the capital?

2   In which year was tennis originally introduced as an Olympic sport?

3   Which French composer wrote *Daphnis et Chloë* (1912)?

4   Which is the longest river that is entirely in Switzerland?

5   The album *Roll With the Punches* was released in 2017 by which musician?

6   Which Tudor house in Derbyshire is referred to in a rhyme as "more glass than wall"?

7   What is measured by the gray SI unit?

8   Who was the Prime Minister of the UK from 1902 to 1905?

9   *Can't Feel My Face* was a 2015 hit for which band?

10 Who is the Roman god of the underworld?

11 *The Adventures of Roderick Random* (1748) was a novel by which author?

12 Which geological period followed the Jurassic Period?

13 Sheffield takes its name from which river?

14 Which Spanish region was united with Castile in 1479?

15 The *Cassini* probe explored which planet?

16 Which Old Testament book follows Joel?

17 What is the currency unit of Paraguay?

18 Which philosopher wrote *The Social Contract* in 1762?

19 In the sitcom *Waiting for God*, what was the name of the retirement home?

20 What is the name of Iago's wife in Shakespeare's *Othello*?

Easy
Medium
Hard

Answers to QUIZ 247 – Pot Luck

1	Umberto II	11	The Royal Society
2	The Stone Roses	12	Lima
3	Greed	13	Frank Capra
4	Bihar	14	*Scream*
5	John Landy	15	Hugh Lofting
6	Strawberry Switchblade	16	France
7	Ethiopia	17	Seneca
8	London Bridge	18	Ethyl
9	Andromeda	19	Clay pigeon shooting
10	Arbroath	20	Idaho

Easy

1. The German state of Rhineland-Palatinate has which city as its capital?

2. Which French-speaking Belgian city is known as Luik in Flemish?

3. Which lake near Naples was said by Virgil to be the entrance to the underworld?

4. Almada is a city in which country?

5. Between 1278 and 1993, which state was governed by the French head of state and the Spanish Bishop of Urgell?

6. *Ha en bra dag*! is Swedish for which common phrase?

7. In which European city could you visit the royal palace of Belvedere?

8. What is the chief town of County Clare?

9. In which country do 100 stotinki make up one lev?

10. Which avenue runs east from the Brandenburg Gate?

11. Until the French Revolution, which city in Provence was Papal property?

12. Which shipping forecast area, taking its name from a Norwegian island, abuts the Norwegian Sea?

13. Keflavik Airport is in which country?

Medium

14. In 1996, which Venice opera house was destroyed by fire?

15. Which Irish river flows into the Atlantic near Waterford?

16. Which Roman historian wrote a history of Rome entitled *Ab Urbe Condita*?

17. In which European capital city is the Jablonowski Palace?

18. Which channel separates Sicily from Italy?

19. In which year was the first European Cup Final played?

20. Who wrote the 1879 book *Travels with a Donkey in the Cévennes*, following a tour of Europe?

Hard

Answers to QUIZ 248 – World Politics

1	Edmund Barton	11	Joseph Stalin
2	September 7	12	Éamon de Valera
3	Hôtel Matignon	13	New Zealand (1893)
4	New Zealand	14	930
5	Tim Kaine	15	The Lodge
6	Yuri Andropov	16	Austria and Prussia
7	Spiro Agnew	17	Duma
8	Ehud	18	William Taft
9	Ernest Bevin	19	1871
10	Camp David	20	Japan

1   In which 2015 film does Tom Hardy play both Ronnie and Reggie Kray?

2   Which US state has Baton Rouge as its capital?

3   The Aswan Dam was originally built in 1902 to control the flood of which river?

4   Which French philosopher is famous for his remark, "I think, therefore I am"?

5   The 1964 comedy film *A Shot in the Dark* featured which fictional inspector?

6   Laxey on the Isle of Man is famous for which large industrial structure?

7   Which country disappeared when the Berlin Wall came down?

8   *The Cat in the Hat* (1957) was written by which American author?

9   Which TV crime-fighting duo's first names were Christine and Mary Beth?

10   What is the mark signifying the soft pronunciation of the letter "c" in French?

11   Anne Sullivan first became teacher to which famous pupil in 1887?

12   Which sense is related to the olfactory organs?

13   What is the name of Winnie-the-Pooh's donkey friend?

14   In Washington DC, what does the "DC" stand for?

15   *Up the Junction* was a 1979 hit for which group?

16   What name is given to the assembly of cardinals for the election of a pope?

17   Which river flows through Leeds?

18   A caber-tossing competition would appear at what type of event?

19   Which is the USA's 49th state?

20   What name is given to a male honey-bee?

Answers to QUIZ 499 – Pot Luck

1	Darrin and Samantha Stevens (*Bewitched*)	11	RKO
2	Tyramine	12	Margery Allingham
3	*Scenes from Childhood*	13	The Seekers
4	Goombay Dance Band	14	Draco
5	USA	15	Silvery white
6	Quarks	16	Pat Eddery
7	Manfred Mann	17	Kate Mara
8	Burghley House	18	Wayne Fontana
9	Zebra	19	Harrow
10	Sir Arthur Quiller-Couch	20	John Fowles

1. What type of creature is Beatrix Potter's Jeremy Fisher?

2. What is the name of the gentleman who accepts the wager in *Around the World in Eighty Days* (1873)?

3. Who wrote the 1993 book *Bravo Two Zero*?

4. Inspector Rebus was created by which writer?

5. Who was appointed Poet Laureate in 2009?

6. Which vegetable disturbs the sleep of the princess in the Hans Christian Andersen tale?

7. Who wrote *The Murders in the Rue Morgue* (1841)?

8. In *The Jungle Book* by Rudyard Kipling, what sort of animal is Shere Khan?

9. How much are the Bells of St Martins owed in the rhyme *Oranges and Lemons*?

10. Who wrote the 1859 novel *A Tale of Two Cities*?

11. The characters of Lisbeth Salander and Mikael Blomkvist were created by which author?

12. Which fictional detective was supposedly killed at Reichenbach Falls in Switzerland?

13. Who wrote *To Kill a Mockingbird* (1960)?

14. Which Roald Dahl story features Sophie and her large companion?

15. "I'll tell thee everything I can: there's little to relate" is sung by which Lewis Carroll character?

16. What is the name of TS Eliot's *Mystery Cat*?

17. Whose autobiography was entitled *The Long Walk to Freedom*?

18. *The Handmaid's Tale* is a 1985 novel by which author?

19. Which novel was the subject of an obscenity trial in 1960?

20. Who wrote the 1819 poem *Ode to a Nightingale*?

Answers to QUIZ 500 – Science

1	Mesozoic	11	Speed of light
2	See in the dark	12	Charles Darwin
3	Pythagoras (Venus)	13	Enrico Fermi
4	Edwin	14	Pascal
5	Computed Axial Tomography	15	2061
6	Collagen	16	Escape velocity
7	Peta	17	Poliomyelitis
8	Astronomy	18	Brass
9	B₁ (thiamin)	19	Ceres
10	Solar plexus	20	Myology

1 Who co-starred with Jim Carrey in *Eternal Sunshine of the Spotless Mind*?

2 What name is given to pieces of grain husk separated from flour after milling?

3 What is Sachertorte?

4 In the TV series *Life on Mars*, which actor played Sam Tyler?

5 Which group had hits in the 1980s with *System Addict* and *Rain or Shine*?

6 Conwy and Harlech are famous for what type of building?

7 What is the name of the process by which a plant makes it own food?

8 Which former empire gives its name to a low upholstered seat without back or arms?

9 In the 2007 TV talent contest *Any Dream Will Do*, who won the part of Joseph?

10 What was Calliope in Greek mythology?

11 Which city is the administrative centre of Scotland's Highland council area?

12 Which pack of cards, used for fortune telling, includes the Hierophant and the High Priestess?

13 On which London avenue is the Savoy Hotel situated?

14 In which European capital city would you find the Spanish Steps?

15 Who starred as Sweeney Todd in the 2007 film of the same name?

16 In which county is Rickmansworth?

17 Which dramatist wrote *The Birthday Party* (1957) and *The Caretaker* (1960)?

18 The WWII warden service was denoted by what initials?

19 Which shipping line operated the *QE2*?

20 The "clean and jerk" movement is used in which sports discipline?

Answers to QUIZ 251 – Pot Luck

1	*Legend*	11	Helen Keller
2	Louisiana	12	Smell
3	The Nile	13	Eeyore
4	René Descartes	14	District of Columbia
5	Inspector Clouseau	15	Squeeze
6	Water wheel	16	A conclave
7	East Germany	17	Aire
8	Dr Seuss	18	Highland Games
9	Cagney and Lacey	19	Alaska
10	Cedilla	20	Drone

1 For which 1998 film did Steven Spielberg win the Best Director award?

2 Which actress won an award for her role in the 1997 film *L.A. Confidential*?

3 The theme to *Skyfall* won the Best Song award for which singer?

4 Which 1939 film of a classic novel won eight Oscars, including Best Picture and Best Director?

5 Who won her first Best Actress award for *The Accused*?

6 Which 1981 film won four Oscars, prompting its writer to proclaim "The British are Coming" in his acceptance speech?

7 What was the title of the 1977 Oscar-winning film starring Diane Keaton?

8 Which 2016 musical film received 14 nominations, winning six of the categories?

9 Who won the Best Supporting Actress award for the 2017 film *I, Tonya*, on her first Oscar nomination?

10 *Dances with Wolves* (1990) won the Best Director award for which of its actors?

11 Which two-time winner of the Best Actress award in the 1970s went on to become a Labour MP from 1992-2015?

12 Who won an award for his role as Dudley Moore's butler in the 1981 film *Arthur*?

13 Who won the Best Actor award for his role in *The Godfather* but refused to attend the awards ceremony?

14 Jennifer Hudson, winner of an award for the 2006 film *Dreamgirls*, first came to fame on which talent show?

15 Who won the Best Actor Oscar for his portrayal of Sir Winston Churchill in the 2017 film *The Darkest Hour*?

16 How many Best Actress Oscars did Katharine Hepburn win?

17 Which Tom Hanks film won the Best Picture in 1994?

18 Which long-awaited 2017 sci-fi sequel won Oscars for Best Achievement in Cinematography and Best Achievement in Visual Effects?

19 Who won his second Best Actor award for the 2007 *There Will Be Blood*?

20 Which 2005 Wallace and Gromit full-length film won the Best Animated Feature award?

Answers to QUIZ 252 – Literature

1	A frog	11	Stieg Larsson
2	Phileas Fogg	12	Sherlock Holmes
3	Andy McNab	13	Harper Lee
4	Ian Rankin	14	*The BFG*
5	Carol Ann Duffy	15	The White Knight
6	A pea	16	Macavity
7	Edgar Allan Poe	17	Nelson Mandela
8	A tiger	18	Margaret Atwood
9	Five farthings	19	*Lady Chatterley's Lover*
10	Charles Dickens	20	John Keats

1   Who won the 2010 Wimbledon men's singles championship?

2   What is Miss Marple's first name?

3   What was the home planet of the aliens in the classic novel *The War of the Worlds*?

4   The Isle of Wight's "Needles" are formed of which substance?

5   What was the nickname of Robbie Coltrane's character in the TV series *Cracker*?

6   Dry ice, often used in stage shows, is a solid form of which gas?

7   Which actress starred in the 1991 film *Sleeping With the Enemy*?

8   Jacqueline du Pré played which instrument?

9   Which desert is found in the north of Chile?

10 What is the capital and chief port of the Philippines?

11 A craniologist studies what part of the body?

12 What title is given to a university official or the head of a cathedral chapter?

13 Who wrote *The Last Juror* (2004)?

14 *Swear it Again* was the 1999 debut no.1 hit for which boy band?

15 Which Latin phrase means "Let the buyer beware"?

16 Which plant's flowers are used to flavour beer?

17 The flag of the Soviet Union showed which two symbols?

18 Who had hits with *Rhinestone Cowboy* and *Wichita Lineman*?

19 What name is given to the ancient frame of beads used for counting?

20 Lady Penelope and her chauffeur Parker appeared in which children's TV series?

Easy

Medium

Hard

Answers to QUIZ 253 – Pot Luck

1	Kate Winslet	11	Inverness
2	Bran	12	Tarot
3	Chocolate cake	13	Strand
4	John Simm	14	Rome
5	Five Star	15	Johnny Depp
6	Castles	16	Hertfordshire
7	Photosynthesis	17	Harold Pinter
8	Ottoman	18	ARP
9	Lee Mead	19	Cunard
10	A Muse (of epic poetry)	20	Weightlifting

Easy

1   What is an electrically charged atom called?

2   What explosive substance consists of a mixture of saltpetre, sulphur and charcoal?

3   Loss of memory has what medical term?

4   Which unit is used to measure the intensity of noise?

5   What name is given to the science of studying the stars?

6   A Surrey town gives its name to which medicinal crystals?

7   Which 3-D image is produced by laser beams?

8   Which acids combine to form proteins?

9   What is the science of the use of technology in aircraft?

10 The symbol B represents which chemical element?

11 Charcoal is a form of which element?

12 What term is given to a positive electrode?

13 A neutral pH is given which number on the pH scale?

14 What is the main artery carrying blood away from the heart?

Medium

15 The scientific names of species are in which language?

16 What does the symbol ∞ represent?

17 Of what is anthropology the study?

18 What name is given to a piece of glass that resolves light into separate colours?

19 In our solar system, what is the second-largest planet?

20 What was the surname of Edmond, the astronomer who predicted the return of a comet?

Hard

Answers to QUIZ 254 – Oscar Winners

1	*Saving Private Ryan*	11	Glenda Jackson
2	Kim Basinger	12	Sir John Gielgud
3	Adele	13	Marlon Brando
4	*Gone with the Wind*	14	*American Idol*
5	Jodie Foster	15	Gary Oldman
6	*Chariots of Fire*	16	Four
7	*Annie Hall*	17	*Forrest Gump*
8	*La La Land*	18	*Blade Runner 2049*
9	Allison Janney	19	Sir Daniel Day-Lewis
10	Kevin Costner	20	*Curse of the Were-Rabbit*

1   Nile Rodgers was a founding member of which disco funk band?

2   What was the first name of David Schwimmer's character in *Friends*?

3   Which epic 1959 film won the Best Picture Oscar?

4   In the Old Testament, what was the name of the Philistine giant slain by David?

5   What is the surname of the family in *Peter Pan*?

6   Salt Lake City is the capital of which US state?

7   Who had hits in 2003 with *Cry Me a River* and *Rock Your Body*?

8   Human nails are made of which protein?

9   The city of Aleppo is in which country?

10   What is a ten-cent coin called in the USA?

11   Which nursery-rhyme girl ate curds and whey?

12   Astigmatism is a condition affecting which part of the body?

13   What is the western extremity of mainland England?

14   According to legend, what was the name of the site of King Arthur's court?

15   What is the basic unit of currency in Jordan and Bahrain?

16   What, according to the proverb, does he do "who pays the piper"?

17   Which small silvery fish are the fry of herring and sprat?

18   The *Inspector Morse* stories were written by which author?

19   How many sides has a heptagon?

20   Which Michigan port is famous for car manufacturing?

Easy

Medium

Hard

Answers to QUIZ 255 – Pot Luck

1	Rafael Nadal	11	The skull
2	Jane	12	Dean
3	Mars	13	John Grisham
4	Chalk	14	Westlife
5	Fitz	15	*Caveat emptor*
6	Carbon dioxide	16	Hop
7	Julia Roberts	17	Hammer and sickle
8	Cello	18	Glen Campbell
9	Atacama	19	Abacus
10	Manila	20	*Thunderbirds*

Easy

1   What do the initials lbw mean to a cricketer?

2   What is the longest that a test match can last?

3   Which radio cricket commentator was known as "Johnners"?

4   What does the abbreviation "st" stand for?

5   The "Home of Cricket" is the name given to which ground?

6   The Brian Statham End and the James Anderson End are found at which Test venue?

7   Which former cricketer became a team captain on *A Question of Sport* in 2008?

8   What name is given to a batsman who bats higher up the order than normal towards the end of a day's play?

9   Who stepped down as England cricket captain in 2017 after leading England for 59 Test matches?

10 Sir Donald Bradman played for which country?

11 Which shorter form of cricket that lasts only a few hours was first played in 2003?

12 If a batsman is "out for a duck", how many runs has he or she scored?

13 Which fielding position is situated just behind the batsman?

14 On which panel game did David Gower appear as a team captain from 1995 to 2003?

15 The outer surface of a cricket ball is made from what material?

16 What umpire's decision is indicated by holding the arms out horizontally on either side of the body?

17 Which team play their home matches at the County Cricket Ground in Chelmsford?

18 Who captained the England women's team from 2006 to 2016?

19 Sir Vivian Richards played for which national side?

20 What colour-related name is cricketing clothing known by?

Medium

Hard

Answers to QUIZ 256 – Science

1	Ion	11	Carbon
2	Gunpowder	12	Anode
3	Amnesia	13	Seven
4	Decibel (or bel)	14	Aorta
5	Astronomy	15	Latin
6	Epsom salts	16	Infinity
7	Hologram	17	Mankind
8	Amino acids	18	Prism
9	Avionics	19	Saturn
10	Boron	20	Halley

1   Who fronted the group Dire Straits?

2   Paul Potts was the first winner of which series?

3   Which river river joins the Severn near Chepstow?

4   Who is Pinocchio's "official conscience"?

5   The forsythia plant produces what colour flowers?

6   Which Beatle was the first narrator for the TV version of *Thomas the Tank Engine*?

7   What do Americans call the boot of a car?

8   What term of address is used for an unmarried Spanish woman?

9   Red, blue and yellow make up which group of colours?

10 In which London building is the Lord Mayor's Banquet held?

11 What is the name of the punctuation mark formed by two vertical dots?

12 Which legendary markswoman was a member of Buffalo Bill's Wild West Show?

13 *Too Much Too Young* was a 1979 EP by which band?

14 Who took over from Sue Lawley as presenter of Radio 4's *Desert Island Discs*?

15 Robert Galbraith is a pen-name for which famous author?

16 What was an ancient Greek warship with three banks of oars called?

17 Which 2005 Wes Craven thriller is set on a plane?

18 What body of water lies between Britain and Ireland?

19 In which football stadium is one of the stands known as the Kop?

20 Who starred as James Bond in *Moonraker* (1979)?

Easy

Medium

Hard

Answers to QUIZ 257 – Pot Luck

1	Chic	11	Little Miss Muffet
2	Ross	12	The eye
3	*Ben-Hur*	13	Land's End
4	Goliath	14	Camelot
5	Darling	15	Dinar
6	Utah	16	Calls the tune
7	Justin Timberlake	17	Whitebait
8	Keratin	18	Colin Dexter
9	Syria	19	Seven
10	Dime	20	Detroit

1 Who starred as himself in *The Fresh Prince of Bel-Air*?

2 Which series features two physicists who work at Caltech?

3 In which series did Hollywood star Chris Pratt play Andy Dwyer?

4 The phrase "jumping the shark" originated as a result of which series?

5 The fictional show *Tool Time* featured in which series starring Tim Allen?

6 Who was "*in the Middle*" in the title of a 2000s series?

7 What was the name of the coffee shop in *Friends*?

8 Which late 1970s sitcom featured the Tates and the Campbells?

9 In the series *M*A*S*H*, what did the letters stand for?

10 What was the name of Jerry's female sidekick in *Seinfeld*?

11 The sitcom *Frasier* was a spin-off from which series?

12 Who created and starred in *Curb Your Enthusiasm*?

13 Which 1964-72 series starred Elizabeth Montgomery as Samantha, daughter of Endora?

14 In *Roseanne*, what was the family's surname?

15 Who played Dick Van Dyke's wife in *The Dick Van Dyke Show* and later starred in her own show?

16 In the series *30 Rock*, which comedienne and actress played Liz Lemon?

17 Who was the eldest sister in *The Brady Bunch*?

18 In which 2000s series did Neil Patrick Harris play Barney Stinson?

19 Who is Scratchy's cartoon "co-star" in *The Simpsons*?

20 Who was Lucy in the 1950s series *I Love Lucy*?

Answers to QUIZ 258 – Cricket

1	Leg before wicket	11	Twenty20
2	Five days	12	None
3	Brian Johnston	13	Wicketkeeper
4	Stumped	14	*They Think It's All Over*
5	Lord's	15	Leather
6	Old Trafford	16	Wide
7	Phil Tufnell	17	Essex
8	Nightwatchman	18	Charlotte Edwards
9	Alastair Cook	19	The West Indies
10	Australia	20	Whites

1   The song *You'll Never Walk Alone* is from which musical?

2   Which group had hits in 1985 with *Alive and Kicking* and *Don't You (Forget About Me)*?

3   Which plant's leaves yield a reddish-orange pigment used as a hair dye?

4   *Borgen* was a TV drama about the prime minister of which country?

5   Who wrote the 2009 novel *Wolf Hall*?

6   Which New Testament apostle took his name from the Greek for "rock"?

7   In which English city is Lime Street railway station?

8   Which Peak District river flows through the Chatsworth estate?

9   The Friendly Islands is the former name of which Pacific group?

10 By what name is the fixed annual allowance to cover a monarch's household known?

11 Which successful play and 2011 film is based on a Michael Morpurgo story?

12 The character of Alan Partridge was created by which comedian?

13 *Downtown* was a 1964 hit for which singer?

14 What is the term for a Formula 1 motor race?

15 What is the American term for grilling?

16 In which Swiss city are the headquarters of the Red Cross?

17 Meryl Streep and Anne Hathaway starred in which 2006 film about the fashion industry?

18 What relation to you is your uncle's son?

19 Japan has which unit of currency?

20 What sort of creature is a lory?

Answers to QUIZ 259 – Pot Luck

1	Mark Knopfler	11	Colon
2	*Britain's Got Talent*	12	Annie Oakley
3	Wye	13	Specials
4	Jiminy Cricket	14	Kirsty Young
5	Yellow	15	JK Rowling
6	Ringo Starr (Sir Richard Starkey)	16	Trireme
7	The trunk	17	*Red Eye*
8	Señorita	18	Irish Sea
9	Primary colours	19	Anfield
10	Guildhall	20	Sir Roger Moore

Easy

1   Which 18th-century British admiral suffered mutiny while captaining *The Bounty*?

2   General Eisenhower was given what nickname?

3   Which empire did Catherine the Great rule?

4   Which 8th-century earthworks separated Mercia and Powys?

5   In the old Soviet Union, what was the name given to a political prison or a forced labour camp?

6   Who was the brother of aviation pioneer Orville Wright?

7   Sir Francis Drake attacked which Spanish port in 1587?

8   What name was given to the start of the Allied invasion of Europe in WWII?

9   Wyatt Earp's friend Holliday had what nickname?

10 In the Wars of the Roses, what colour was Lancaster's rose?

11 What was the name of Thor Heyerdahl's craft used for his 1947 Pacific expedition?

12 Which English historian was known as "the Venerable"?

13 In 1215, which bill of rights was signed at Runnymede?

Medium

14 The British Legion was founded by which earl?

15 Which politician was leader of the movement to abolish the slave trade?

16 Which Carthaginian general took elephants across the Alps?

17 Who led the Peasants' Revolt?

18 Mary I of England married which king of Spain in 1554?

19 Which New South Wales location was the site of the first penal colony in Australia?

20 On which part of Scotland's Western Isles was a famous collection of medieval chess pieces found?

Hard

Answers to QUIZ 260 – US Sitcoms

1	Will Smith	11	*Cheers*
2	*The Big Bang Theory*	12	Larry David
3	*Parks and Recreation*	13	*Bewitched*
4	*Happy Days*	14	Conner
5	*Home Improvement*	15	Mary Tyler Moore
6	Malcolm	16	Tina Fey
7	Central Perk	17	Marcia
8	*Soap*	18	*How I Met Your Mother*
9	Mobile Army Surgical Hospital	19	Itchy
10	Elaine	20	Lucille Ball

1   What is the Fahrenheit equivalent of 0° Celsius?

2   In which year did The Buggles have a hit with *Video Killed the Radio Star*?

3   The game of *Mornington Crescent* features on which radio show?

4   Which character in *Dad's Army* had the catchphrase "Don't panic"?

5   A game of netball is made up of four quarters each lasting what length of time?

6   What would a Native American refer to as a papoose?

7   Which word can describe both a piece of wood and a group of directors?

8   In *Alice's Adventures In Wonderland*, which creature smokes a hookah?

9   In various novels by PG Wodehouse, what sort of animal is the Empress of Blandings?

10 Which building holds the US gold reserves?

11 What, according to the proverb, does every cloud have?

12 In *The Simpsons*, which character drives the school bus?

13 St Helier is the capital of which Channel Island?

14 Which US Beat Generation author wrote the 1957 novel *On the Road*?

15 What part of the body is commonly called the voice box?

16 Of which drink is lapsang souchong a variety?

17 Which pigment is responsible for tanning of the skin?

18 In which county is the town of Budleigh Salterton?

19 Which country was formerly joined with Slovakia?

20 Which star sign comes between Virgo and Scorpio?

Answers to QUIZ 261 – Pot Luck

1	Carousel	11	War Horse
2	Simple Minds	12	Steve Coogan
3	Henna	13	Petula Clark
4	Denmark	14	Grand Prix
5	Dame Hilary Mantel	15	Broiling
6	Peter	16	Geneva
7	Liverpool	17	The Devil Wears Prada
8	Derwent	18	Cousin
9	Tonga	19	Yen
10	The Civil List	20	A bird

Easy

1. A putting green surrounds which sporting target?
2. Which actress starred in the 1990 film *Green Card*?
3. Who wrote the novel *Anne of Green Gables*?
4. Which children's programme is set in Greendale?
5. Which Teletubby is green?
6. The talent show *Opportunity Knocks* originally had which host?
7. Which long, green-skinned fruit is proverbially "cool"?
8. A greenshank is what type of creature?
9. Which green gemstone is a variety of the mineral beryl?
10. Greenland is a territory belonging to which European country?

Medium

11. Which Somerset town is also the name of a green leafy vegetable?
12. From which US state did the dessert of Key Lime Pie originate?
13. Which actor starred with Mark Benton in the TV series *City Lights*?
14. In the Edward Lear poem *The Owl and the Pussycat*, what specific colour is the boat?
15. What term is given to an area of open land around a British city?
16. A Florentine pizza features which green vegetable?
17. Who played Rachel Green in the TV series *Friends*?
18. Which Shakespearean character describes jealousy as "the green-eyed monster"?
19. Spring greens are young leaves from which vegetable?
20. "Greenback" is US slang for which banknote?

Hard

Answers to QUIZ 262 –History

1	William Bligh	11	*Kon-Tiki*
2	Ike	12	Bede
3	The Russian Empire	13	The *Magna Carta*
4	Offa's Dyke	14	Earl Haig
5	Gulag	15	William Wilberforce
6	Wilbur	16	Hannibal
7	Cadiz	17	Wat Tyler
8	D-Day	18	Philip II
9	Doc	19	Botany Bay
10	Red	20	Lewis

1 By what other name is wild marjoram known?

2 Which creature frightened Little Miss Muffet?

3 Who directed the 2005 film *Brokeback Mountain*?

4 In what do lugworms live?

5 Which square in New York is a focal point for New Year's Eve celebrations?

6 What is the call given by a bugle or drum to awaken troops?

7 In *A Midsummer Night's Dream*, what is the name of the character loved by Lysander and Demetrius?

8 What is the German term of address equivalent to "Mr"?

9 Which cocktail is made from champagne and chilled stout?

10 *Upside Down* was a hit for which singer in 1980?

11 Who were William the Conqueror's people, who invaded Britain in 1066?

12 Which wide London road runs between Admiralty Arch and Buckingham Palace?

13 In *The Adventures of Priscilla, Queen of the Desert* (1994), who or what is Priscilla?

14 Which actor played Tim Canterbury in *The Office*?

15 Clove hitch, running bowline and Hunter's bend are types of what?

16 What was the surname of the brothers who made up the Bee Gees?

17 Proverbially, what is a change as good as?

18 Who created the character Emma Harte, heroine of *A Woman Of Substance*?

19 The name of which sporting discipline is often abbreviated to Super-G?

20 At the border of which two countries is the peak known as the Matterhorn?

Easy
Medium
Hard

Answers to QUIZ 263 – Pot Luck

1	32°	11	A silver lining
2	1979	12	Otto
3	*I'm Sorry I Haven't a Clue*	13	Jersey
4	Corporal Jones	14	Jack Kerouac
5	15 minutes	15	Larynx
6	A baby	16	Tea
7	Board	17	Melanin
8	The caterpillar	18	Devon
9	A pig	19	Czechia (Czech Republic)
10	Fort Knox	20	Libra

1   The poet and painter Dante Rossetti (b.1828) had what middle name?

2   What nationality was artist Édouard Manet?

3   With with Italian city was Tintoretto associated?

4   In which area of the arts was Clarice Cliff famous?

5   Who painted *The Hay Wain* (1821)?

6   What term was given to the period in the 14th-16th centuries when there was a new interest in the arts in Europe?

7   In which country was photographer Annie Leibovitz born?

8   Which artist was noted for his 1960s paintings of soup cans?

9   In which Cornish town is the Barbara Hepworth Museum and Sculpture Garden?

10 Which artist painted two series of studies of sunflowers in the 1880s?

11 René Lalique was famous for working in what medium?

12 In 1871, which US artist famously painted a picture of his mother?

13 What was the birth name of photographer Lord Snowdon?

14 A branch of which art gallery is located at Albert Dock in Liverpool?

15 Which British artist was noted for his paintings of swimming pools?

16 In which London location is the National Gallery?

17 Which artist and sculptor, famous for his statue of David, worked on the design of the dome of St Peter's in Vatican City?

18 What does the abbreviation YBA, coined in the 1990s, stand for?

19 In which area of the arts is Anish Kapoor famous?

20 Which artist gave his name to a shade of brown and a beard?

Answers to QUIZ 264 – Green

1	Golf hole	11	Chard
2	Andie MacDowell	12	Florida
3	Lucy Maud Montgomery	13	Robson Green
4	*Postman Pat*	14	Pea-green
5	Dipsy	15	Green belt
6	Hughie Green	16	Spinach
7	Cucumber	17	Jennifer Aniston
8	Bird	18	Iago (*Othello*)
9	Emerald	19	Cabbage
10	Denmark	20	Dollar

Easy

Medium

Hard

ANSWERS ON PAGE **269**

1   What name is given to the River Thames at Oxford?

2   "Drink sangria in the park, And then later, When it gets dark, we go home" is a lyric from which song?

3   Which British actor plays Dr Watson to Robert Downey Jr's Sherlock Holmes?

4   According to the popular verse, Tuesday's child is what?

5   In which county is Sandwich golf course?

6   Which town in Germany, near Dresden, is famous for porcelain?

7   By what two-word title was Benito Mussolini known?

8   What canine breed is also known as a sausage dog?

9   Which actor starred as Will in the 2002 film *About a Boy*?

10 In Indian cuisine, what is the term for clarified butter?

11 What is the correct form of address to a duke?

12 What is meant by the Latin phrase *Veni, vidi, vici*?

13 Basra is in which country?

14 In which county is the racing circuit of Castle Combe?

15 What is the name of the heroine in *Gone With the Wind*?

16 A word for the land of sleep also means which gesture of agreement?

17 Which French word translates as a friendly understanding between states?

18 In what type of building are hops traditionally dried?

19 Which channel has been broadcasting since 1955?

20 Who had a 1986 hit with *A Different Corner*?

Easy

Medium

Hard

Answers to QUIZ 265 – Pot Luck

1	Oregano	11	The Normans
2	Spider	12	The Mall
3	Ang Lee	13	A bus
4	Sand or mud	14	Martin Freeman
5	Times Square	15	Knots
6	Reveille	16	Gibb
7	Hermia	17	A rest
8	Herr	18	Barbara Taylor Bradford
9	Black velvet	19	Super giant slalom
10	Diana Ross	20	Switzerland/Italy

Easy

1   What Latin word is used to classify musical works in order of publication?

2   The composer Mendelssohn had what first name?

3   What is the instrumental prelude to an opera or play called?

4   How many pedals does a grand piano have?

5   Which West Yorkshire city hosts an annual International Piano Competition?

6   Who composed the *Peer Gynt* suite (1875)?

7   What device marks time for musicians by giving a regular tick?

8   At which venue has the London Symphony Orchestra been resident since 1982?

9   Which orchestral instruments are also known as timpani?

10 In Rossini's *The Barber of Seville*, what is the name of the title character?

11 What term is given to the words of an opera?

12 *The Well-Tempered Clavier* was written by which composer?

13 Which wind instrument is also the name for a champagne glass?

14 What nationality was Mozart?

Medium

15 What is a group of nine musicians called?

16 The *Enigma Variations*, from which *Nimrod* is often played on state occasions, were written by which composer?

17 What was Beethoven's first name?

18 A famous Manchester orchestra and the German city where Handel was born are linked by what name?

19 Which musical term means "very loud"?

20 What is the title of the 1887 Verdi opera based on a Shakespeare tragedy?

Hard

Answers to QUIZ 266 – The Arts

1	Gabriel	11	Glass
2	French	12	James Whistler
3	Venice	13	Antony Armstrong-Jones
4	Ceramics	14	Tate
5	John Constable	15	David Hockney
6	Renaissance	16	Trafalgar Square
7	USA	17	Michelangelo
8	Andy Warhol	18	Young British Artists
9	St Ives	19	Sculpture
10	Vincent Van Gogh	20	Sir Anthony Van Dyck

1 Matt Smith was the eleventh actor to take on the starring role in which TV series?

2 What is a person summoned for compulsory state military service called?

3 Which group topped the charts in 2006 with *I Don't Feel Like Dancin'*?

4 In which war was the comedy series M*A*S*H set?

5 *Little Lies* was a hit for which group in 1987?

6 Which Russian goldsmith was famous for his jewelled Easter eggs?

7 What name is given to a small barrel usually containing less than ten gallons?

8 Which exercise system is known by the surname of the German physical fitness specialist who devised it?

9 Stacey in *Gavin & Stacey* was played by which actress?

10 Where is the famous Greek oracle site?

11 Which Chinese dish has a name that means "mixed pieces"?

12 The 2016 film *Inferno* is based on which author's book of the same name?

13 Which term is used for the peaceful region at the centre of a hurricane?

14 Which Arabian Nights character says "Open, Sesame!"?

15 Of which English county is Ipswich the county town?

16 What unit of weight of silk yarn describes the fineness of hosiery?

17 *The Listeners* (1912) was written by which poet?

18 What was the former name of Beijing?

19 Which car manufacturer's logo is two overlapping Rs?

20 "Shanks's pony" is a term for which mode of transport?

Answers to QUIZ 267 – Pot Luck

1	Isis	11	Your Grace
2	*Perfect Day* (Lou Reed)	12	I came, I saw, I conquered
3	Jude Law	13	Iraq
4	Full of grace	14	Wiltshire
5	Kent	15	Scarlett O'Hara
6	Meissen	16	Nod
7	Il Duce	17	Entente
8	Dachshund	18	Oast house
9	Hugh Grant	19	ITV
10	Ghee	20	George Michael

Easy

1   How many parts make up an insect's body?

2   Which large white seabird's name is also used to describe a greedy person?

3   A John Dory is what type of creature?

4   What is another name for the insect known as an emmet?

5   The male of which primate might be called a "silverback"?

6   A young beaver is given what name?

7   What type of creature is an orb weaver?

8   What term is used to decribe collectively the animal life of a particular area?

9   Pecorino cheese is made from the milk of which animal?

10 What name is given to the larva of a frog?

11 What are male rabbits called?

12 A Labrador is what type of dog?

13 The largest beetle is named after which Biblical character?

14 A salmon lays what colour eggs?

Medium

15 Which animal has Arabian and Bactrian species?

16 What is the term for an animal that re-chews food brought back from a first stomach?

17 Common, pygmy and water are species of which small British mammal?

18 What type of creature would be found in an apiary?

19 The Komodo dragon is the world's largest species of what animal?

20 What is a male swan called?

Hard

Answers to QUIZ 268 – Classical Music

1	*Opus*	11	Libretto
2	Felix	12	Johann Sebastian Bach
3	Overture	13	Flute
4	Three	14	Austrian
5	Leeds	15	Nonet
6	Edvard Grieg	16	Sir Edward Elgar
7	Metronome	17	Ludwig
8	Barbican	18	Hallé
9	Kettledrums	19	Fortissimo
10	Figaro	20	*Otello*

1   What type of creature is an oryx?

2   *Free* was a hit for which singer in 1976?

3   What is the first name of Timothy Spall's actor son?

4   *Mr Tambourine Man* was written by which singer/songwriter?

5   What is the milky liquid obtained from the rubber tree called?

6   In which city is the Louvre art gallery?

7   What is the largest island in the Greek Dodecanese group?

8   Which country hosted the FIFA World Cup in 2010?

9   Who wrote "She walks in beauty, like the night"?

10 In which English county is Maidenhead?

11 What is a small piece of tortilla topped with cheese called?

12 What term is given to an administrative division of Switzerland?

13 The RHS Chelsea Flower Show is held in the grounds of which building?

14 What was the name of Lily Munster's husband in TV's *The Munsters*?

15 What baked round of batter is traditionally eaten with roast beef?

16 In which series of disciplines did Jessica Ennis-Hill win Olympic gold?

17 Sherrie and Drew are the lead characters in which 2012 film featuring 1980s music?

18 What is the area under the pastoral care of a bishop, also known as a see, called?

19 The Sellafield site in Cumbria was previously known by what name?

20 What is the French word for Christmas?

Easy

Medium

Hard

Answers to QUIZ 269 – Pot Luck

1	*Doctor Who*	11	Chop suey
2	Conscript	12	Dan Brown
3	Scissor Sisters	13	The eye
4	Korean War	14	Ali Baba
5	Fleetwood Mac	15	Suffolk
6	Fabergé	16	Denier
7	Keg	17	Walter de la Mare
8	Pilates	18	Peking
9	Joanna Page	19	Rolls-Royce
10	Delphi	20	Walking

Easy

1 Which vegetable did Mark Twain describe as "a cabbage with a college education"?

2 Which vegetable gives pasta verde its green colour?

3 From which country did the vegetable stew ratatouille originate?

4 Which vegetable is associated with Wales?

5 What is the common name for *Allium cepa*, a plant with a large edible bulb?

6 Which vegetable's name is often used to mean "an incentive"?

7 Which vegetable features heavily in Thanksgiving meals in the USA?

8 Into the stalk of which small vegetable might you cut a cross before cooking it?

9 On which vegetable are silk, husks and kernels found?

10 How have tempura vegetables been cooked?

11 Which vegetables are proverbially identical when in their outer casing?

12 Where would you find samphire?

13 Which vegetable's name translates as "earth-apple" in French?

14 What is another name for the yam?

Medium

15 What name is given to the pieces of raw vegetable often served with dips?

16 Butternut is a variety of which fruit that is commonly used as a vegetable?

17 Which usually dark red vegetable also has golden and candy varieties?

18 Pak choi, also known as bok choy, originates from which country?

19 What name is given to a small cucumber that has been preserved in vinegar?

20 Which variety of celery has a large root that is used as a vegetable?

Hard

Answers to QUIZ 270 – Animal World

1	Three (head, thorax and abdomen)	11	Bucks
2	Gannet	12	Retriever
3	Fish	13	Goliath
4	Ant	14	Orange (light to dark)
5	Gorilla	15	Camel
6	A kit	16	Ruminant
7	Spider	17	Shrew
8	Fauna	18	Bee
9	Sheep	19	Lizard
10	Tadpole	20	Cob

1 Which traffic light follows green?

2 Austin is the capital of which US state?

3 What name was given to a member of the Royalist army during the English Civil War?

4 Which British group sang *Wild Thing* in 1966?

5 A Pomeranian is what type of creature?

6 Which type of pasta is shaped like seashells?

7 Which flower, also called the Lent lily, is an emblem of Wales?

8 Newbury is situated in which English county?

9 Whose backing group were The Mechanics?

10 How many Marx Brothers were there?

11 Which Swedish tennis player won eleven Grand Slam titles between 1974 and 1981?

12 Which comedian was famous for wearing a fez?

13 Alberta and Quebec are provinces of which country?

14 What term is given to the boundary of a circle?

15 What is the Spanish name for cold vegetable soup?

16 *Reggatta de Blanc* was a 1979 album by which band?

17 In which classic sitcom did Connie Booth play the part of Polly?

18 Moorfields hospital in London specialises in which part of the body?

19 What is the name of the former head of MI5 who, in July 2001, received permission to publish a book of memoirs?

20 Eva Peron was the First Lady of which country?

Answers to QUIZ 271 – Pot Luck

1	Antelope	11	Nacho
2	Deniece Williams	12	Canton
3	Rafe	13	Royal Hospital
4	Bob Dylan	14	Herman
5	Latex	15	Yorkshire Pudding
6	Paris	16	Heptathlon
7	Rhodes	17	*Rock of Ages*
8	South Africa	18	Diocese
9	Lord Byron	19	Windscale
10	Berkshire	20	*Noël*

ANSWERS ON PAGE 276

Easy

1 What term is given to a substance that speeds up a chemical reaction?

2 What type of substance is calcium carbonate?

3 What term is used to describe matter that is non-reactive?

4 Brimstone is an old name for which element?

5 Which Swedish chemist invented dynamite?

6 Pb is the symbol for which metal?

7 Which laboratory heat source was named after a German chemist?

8 What type of substance turns litmus paper red?

9 What is the branch of chemistry that is concerned with compounds of carbon?

10 Rust has what chemical name?

11 What is the smallest fundamental unit of a chemical compound?

12 What term is given to a metallic compound containing two or more elements?

13 Which process turns a liquid into vapour?

14 Which common compound has the formula NH_3?

Medium

15 What is the chemical symbol for iodine?

16 Which element, atomic number 88, was discovered by Marie and Pierre Curie in 1898?

17 Helium, neon, argon, krypton, xenon and radon are collectively known as what?

18 What type of glass tube is used to measure or transfer liquids?

19 The chemical symbol for silver is derived from which word, still used in heraldry?

20 Which term, also used in a weather context, is given to a solid substance separated out from gas or water?

Hard

Answers to QUIZ 272 – Vegetables

1	Cauliflower	11	Peas
2	Spinach	12	On the coast
3	France	13	Potato (*pomme de terre*)
4	Leek	14	Sweet potato
5	Onion	15	Crudités
6	Carrot	16	Squash
7	Pumpkin	17	Beetroot
8	Brussels sprout	18	China
9	Sweetcorn	19	Gherkin
10	Deep-fried	20	Celeriac

1   What type of resort links Bath and Cheltenham?

2   Who had a hit with the theme from the 1976 film *A Star is Born*?

3   In which 1976 horror film did Gregory Peck and Lee Remick play adoptive parents?

4   On which island was the TV series *Bergerac* set?

5   Which French emperor was defeated at Waterloo?

6   Which is the longest river in Ireland?

7   In 2017, who replaced Mary Berry as a judge on *The Great British Bake Off*?

8   What is a baby hedgehog called?

9   In which Devon city did Sir Francis Drake famously play bowls?

10 What is a co-driver in a car rally called?

11 Which US president succeeded Richard Nixon?

12 A verger called Alice featured in which sitcom?

13 What is the county town of Cumbria?

14 What is the term given to the spouse of a reigning monarch?

15 In which country is Copacabana Beach?

16 What is the term for speed and rhythm in music?

17 The French game of pétanque has what other name?

18 In Morse Code which letter is represented by three dots?

19 What is a circular tower built for coastal defence called?

20 Which ferry terminal is situated on an island off Anglesey?

Answers to QUIZ 273 – Pot Luck

1	Amber	11	Björn Borg
2	Texas	12	Tommy Cooper
3	Cavalier	13	Canada
4	The Troggs	14	Circumference
5	A dog	15	Gazpacho
6	Conchiglie	16	The Police
7	Daffodil	17	*Fawlty Towers*
8	Berkshire	18	Eye
9	Mike (Rutherford)	19	Stella Rimington
10	Five	20	Argentina

Easy

1   What is the French word for "castle"?

2   Which Scottish castle hosts an annual Military Tattoo in August?

3   In which county is Herstmonceux Castle?

4   Kronborg Castle is immortalised as Elsinore in which of Shakespeare's plays?

5   What is the central structure of the Tower of London known as?

6   What is the typical castle entrance called, characterised by lowerable wooden decks on chains?

7   *Schloss* is the word for "castle" in which language?

8   Castle Black is the location of the Night's Watch in which TV series?

9   Which royal ceremony took place at Caernarfon Castle in 1969?

10 Peel Castle is situated on which island?

11 Robert Dudley was granted Kenilworth Castle by which queen?

12 Bamburgh Castle lies on the coast of which county?

13 Castel Gandolfo is the summer residence of which church leader?

Medium

14 The London office building opened in 2001 to provide space for Members of Parliament and their staff was named after which part of a castle?

15 Tintagel Castle in Cornwall is associated with which legendary figure?

16 Which European castle was the subject of a 1970s wartime TV series?

17 Bolsover Castle and Dover Castle are in the care of which organisation?

18 Which castle near Maidstone has a name that suggests it should be located further north?

19 Castle Stalker is in which country?

20 The local authority of which county council has the address "The Castle, Winchester"?

Hard

Answers to QUIZ 274 – Chemistry

1	Catalyst	11	Molecule
2	Chalk	12	Alloy
3	Inert	13	Evaporation
4	Sulphur	14	Ammonia
5	Alfred Nobel	15	I
6	Lead	16	Radium
7	Bunsen burner	17	Noble gases
8	Acid	18	Pipette
9	Organic chemistry	19	Argent (Ag)
10	Iron oxide	20	Precipitate

1   What name is given to a native of Oxford?

2   Which group's first hit was *Seven Seas of Rhye*?

3   "All the leaves are brown and the sky is grey" are the opening words to which song?

4   What is the main ingredient of borscht?

5   *Not Waving but Drowning* was written by which poet?

6   What sort of food is Bel Paese?

7   What is a share of a company's profit paid to a shareholder called?

8   What colour is muscovado sugar?

9   What was the surname of the *My Family* clan?

10   Which film featured Ronan Keating's song *When You Say Nothing At All*?

11   In which part of the body is the sciatic nerve?

12   Who is the long-running presenter of *Flog It!*?

13   *Orinoco Flow* was which singer's debut solo hit in 1988?

14   Which French Riviera resort shares its name with a variety of biscuit?

15   What weight is equivalent to 14 pounds?

16   Who played the title role in the 1991 film *Robin Hood: Prince of Thieves*?

17   Which English racecourse lends its name to a betting card game?

18   Of which country is Bern the capital?

19   What is an alternative name for maize?

20   What is the term for a fence made from stakes?

Easy

Medium

Hard

Answers to QUIZ 275 – Pot Luck

1	Spa	11	Gerald Ford
2	Barbra Streisand	12	*The Vicar of Dibley*
3	*The Omen*	13	Carlisle
4	Jersey	14	Consort
5	Napoleon	15	Brazil
6	Shannon	16	Tempo
7	Prue Leith	17	Boules
8	Hoglet	18	S
9	Plymouth	19	Martello
10	Navigator	20	Holyhead

Easy

1   What type of food is baklava?

2   How many countries share a border with Greece?

3   With what is retsina flavoured?

4   What ancient temple on the Athenian Acropolis is dedicated to the goddess Athena?

5   Which white, crumbly cheese must be produced in Greece by law to keep its name?

6   Taramasalata is what colour?

7   What Greek letter is used in English to mean "the most dominant of a group"?

8   Before the euro, what was the currency of Greece?

9   What is the largest Greek island?

10 Is Greece ahead of or behind GMT?

11 In mythology, the Minotaur had the head of which animal?

12 What Greek city that lies along the Nedon River is renowned for its eponymous olives?

13 What is the largest lake in Greece?

14 The Greek flag has which two colours?

Medium

15 What name is given to the group composed of seven principal islands including Corfu?

16 What Greek goddess shares her name with a popular sportswear company?

17 How many letters are in the Greek alphabet?

18 Which dairy product forms the basis of tzatziki?

19 In what year did Greece join the EU?

20 What Greek dish is usually based on aubergine, tomato and minced meat?

Hard

Answers to QUIZ 276 – Castles

1	Château	11	Elizabeth I
2	Edinburgh Castle	12	Northumberland
3	East Sussex	13	The Pope
4	Hamlet	14	Portcullis (House)
5	The White Tower	15	King Arthur
6	Drawbridge	16	Colditz
7	German	17	English Heritage
8	Game of Thrones	18	Leeds Castle
9	Investiture of the Prince of Wales	19	Scotland
10	Isle of Man	20	Hampshire

1   Who topped the charts in 1979 with *I Will Survive*?

2   Who starred alongside Bruce Willis in the TV series *Moonlighting*?

3   In which position did Peter Shilton play football for England?

4   What is the order of knights in the *Star Wars* films?

5   Which Roman landmark was made famous by the film *Three Coins in the Fountain*?

6   Which 1940 Disney cartoon film had a soundtrack of classical music?

7   Which port and resort is Israel's southernmost city?

8   In a packet of Salt 'n' Shake crisps, what colour is the salt sachet?

9   *One Day in Your Life* was a 1981 hit for which singer?

10   Which Greek letter can also be a very small amount?

11   Which large water lily was sacred in ancient Egypt?

12   What is the name of the region in the "heel" of Italy?

13   Is the town of Tenby in North Wales or South Wales?

14   Which kind of TV signal has been replaced by digital?

15   What cereal is used in making American whiskey?

16   Which holiday company is famous for its Redcoats?

17   In relation to crops and food, what do the initials GM stand for?

18   During which Apollo flight did the famous "Houston we have a problem" statement occur?

19   What colour is sulphur?

20   When Simple Simon was going to the fair in the nursery rhyme, whom did he meet?

Easy

Medium

Hard

Answers to QUIZ 277 – Pot Luck

1	Oxonian	11	Leg
2	Queen	12	Paul Martin
3	*California Dreamin'*	13	Enya
4	Beetroot	14	Nice
5	Stevie Smith	15	Stone
6	Cheese	16	Kevin Costner
7	Dividend	17	Newmarket
8	Brown	18	Switzerland
9	Harper	19	Corn
10	*Notting Hill*	20	Palisade

1   Which president appears on the front of the US one-dollar bill?

2   What word follows "pound" in the official currency of the UK?

3   What is made available in a rights issue?

4   How is a teller more usually referred to in a bank?

5   Who was Chancellor of the Exchequer for ten years before becoming Prime Minister in 2007?

6   Children traditionally save money in a container resembling which animal?

7   What is the state of having been declared legally financially insolvent?

8   Known as NS&I, which organisation administers Premium Bonds?

9   What two-word term is given to a commercial treaty between two or more nations?

10   In which Scottish city was Clydesdale Bank formed in 1838?

11   Automatic enrolment in what type of financial scheme started in the UK in 2012?

12   What, from 1979 to 1999, was the precursor to the euro?

13   In which year did the National Lottery begin in the UK?

14   Which old UK coin was equivalent to 12.5 pence?

15   What is the currency unit of Sweden?

16   Where a person has an IVA with their creditors, for what does the "V" stand?

17   A "monkey" refers to what sum of money?

18   What was Spain's currency before it adopted the euro?

19   The introduction of TESSAs in 1991 was intended to encourage what?

20   What term describes a building society that is owned by its customers?

Answers to QUIZ 278 – Greece

1	A dessert pastry	11	Bull
2	Six	12	Kalamata
3	Pine resin	13	Lake Trichonida
4	The Parthenon	14	Blue and white
5	Feta	15	Ionian Islands
6	Pink	16	Nike
7	Alpha	17	24
8	Drachma	18	Yoghurt
9	Crete	19	1981
10	Ahead	20	Moussaka

1   Which religion has the Star of David as its symbol?

2   What name is given to the collective states of Connecticut, Maine, Massachusetts, New Hampshire, Rhode Island and Vermont?

3   Which ancient Greek city was known for its austere lifestyle?

4   Who starred in the 1969 film *The Prime of Miss Jean Brodie*?

5   *Speed of Sound* was a hit for which band in 2005?

6   Who was Labour Minister of Health from 1945 to 1951?

7   Who played the Swedish detective Kurt Wallander in the English TV version?

8   Gorilla, gibbon and orang-utan are varieties of which type of creature?

9   Which novel features the pirate Ben Gunn?

10   Who is the central character in the Disney film *The Lion King*?

11   What proverbially, cannot be made without breaking eggs?

12   Hungarian escapologist Erik Weisz is better known by which name?

13   Which river flows through Washington DC?

14   Selhurst Park is the home ground of which football club?

15   The Bluewater shopping centre is in which county?

16   A domesticated polecat has what name?

17   What is the semicircular recess at the eastern end of a church called?

18   Which champagne cocktail is made with peach?

19   Which pantomime features a boy who trades his cow on the way to market?

20   In which county is Basingstoke?

Easy

Medium

Hard

Answers to QUIZ 279 – Pot Luck

1	Gloria Gaynor	11	Lotus
2	Cybill Shepherd	12	Apulia
3	Goalkeeper	13	South Wales
4	Jedi	14	Analogue
5	Trevi Fountain	15	Rye
6	*Fantasia*	16	Butlin's
7	Eilat	17	Genetically modified
8	Blue	18	Apollo 13
9	Michael Jackson	19	Yellow
10	Iota	20	Pieman

1   Whoopi Goldberg starred as a singing nun in which 1992 film?

2   The 1985 film *Witness* featured which religious sect?

3   In which animated film did Mel Gibson provide the voice of a rooster called Rocky?

4   Who received his first Oscar nomination for his role in the 1977 film *Saturday Night Fever*?

5   Which Disney film features the song *Breaking Free*?

6   1998's *Lock, Stock and Two Smoking Barrels* saw which former footballer make his screen debut?

7   Who played Queen Victoria in the 2017 film *Victoria and Abdul*?

8   Which actor starred as "Bandit" in the 1977 film *Smokey and the Bandit*?

9   In the 1975 film *Jaws*, what was the name of the fictional island?

10 Which early US film studio was famous for its "Kops"?

11 Which 1976 film shot Sylvester Stallone to fame?

12 Jack Black provided the voice of Po in which 2008 animated film?

13 Which 1991 comedy film was about a band trying to bring soul music to Dublin?

14 Who directed the 2009 film *Avatar*?

15 In the 1974 James Bond film *The Man with the Golden Gun*, what is the name of the villain?

16 Which actress co-starred with Richard Gere in *An Officer and a Gentleman*?

17 The 2010 film *Tangled* is based on which fairy-tale character?

18 Who plays Black Widow in the *Avengers* series of films?

19 What was the name of the lioness in the film *Born Free*?

20 Which Spanish-born actress starred in the 2008 film *Vicky Cristina Barcelona*?

Answers to QUIZ 280 – Money

1	George Washington	11	Occupational pensions
2	Sterling	12	ECU (European Currency Unit)
3	Shares	13	1994
4	Cashier	14	Half-crown
5	Gordon Brown	15	Krona
6	Pig	16	Voluntary
7	Bankruptcy	17	£500
8	National Savings and Investments	18	Peseta
9	Trade agreement	19	Saving
10	Glasgow	20	Mutual

1. Who had a hit in 1974 with *The Air That I Breathe?*
2. What is the profession of the title character in the *Ace Ventura* films?
3. In a legal arrangement, which Latin term indicates a formal warning?
4. Which pop group topped the charts in 1998 with *Heartbeat/Tragedy?*
5. How many points is the blue ball worth in snooker?
6. Which people built Machu Picchu?
7. Which southern English county is divided into West and East?
8. What name is given to a Mexican cattle-farm manager or worker?
9. The Grand National horse race is run in which month?
10. Which actress played the title character in the 1989 film *Shirley Valentine?*
11. What word of naval origin describes diluted rum?
12. What name is given to a Japanese poem of seventeen syllables?
13. The state of Western Australia has which capital city?
14. Coulsdon and Purley are in which London borough?
15. Who played Tucker Jenkins in *Grange Hill* and its spin-off *Tucker's Luck?*
16. What are the saddlebags of a bicycle or motorcycle called?
17. How is an adult ovine female more commonly known?
18. What is written after a title to indicate that the author is unknown?
19. Which lake lies between Kenya, Tanzania and Uganda?
20. Guy Garvey is the frontman of which British group?

Answers to QUIZ 281 – Pot Luck

1	Judaism	11	An omelette
2	New England	12	Harry Houdini
3	Sparta	13	Potomac
4	Dame Maggie Smith	14	Crystal Palace
5	Coldplay	15	Kent
6	Aneurin Bevan	16	Ferret
7	Sir Kenneth Branagh	17	Apse
8	Ape	18	Bellini
9	*Treasure Island*	19	*Jack and the Beanstalk*
10	Simba	20	Hampshire

QUIZ 284 – Paper

ANSWERS ON PAGE 286

Easy

1   From what material is paper usually made?

2   Which father and daughter starred in the 1973 film *Paper Moon*?

3   What item is ignited by lighting a touchpaper?

4   In which 1906 novel by Edith Nesbit do the title characters observe a paper chase take place through a tunnel?

5   What term is given to the paper on which music is written?

6   *Paper Plane* was a 1972 single by which rock group?

7   Where would you find an endpaper?

8   What term is given to wallpaper that has a raised velvety surface?

9   Who wrote the 1966 song *Paperback Writer*?

10 In which country was papyrus used as an early writing material?

11 Which Scottish company, named after a historic country of the Highlands, is famous for its paperweights?

12 Rice paper is used in what activity?

13 Which US author wrote the 1888 novella *The Aspern Papers*?

14 Which two animals traditionally give their names to a paper chase?

15 A paperclip featured as the default Microsoft® Office Assistant character in software by which company?

16 What is indicated in the description of a company as a "paper tiger"?

17 What name is given to the collapsible Eastern light made of paper?

18 A paper napkin is also known by what name of French origin?

19 What was the name of the paper company in the original series of *The Office*?

20 How many quires of paper make up a ream?

Answers to QUIZ 282 – Films

1	*Sister Act*	11	*Rocky*
2	Amish	12	*Kung Fu Panda*
3	*Chicken Run*	13	*The Commitments*
4	John Travolta	14	James Cameron
5	*High School Musical*	15	Scaramanga
6	Vinnie Jones	16	Debra Winger
7	Dame Judi Dench	17	Rapunzel
8	Burt Reynolds	18	Scarlett Johansson
9	Amity	19	Elsa
10	Keystone	20	Penélope Cruz

1   Which actor played the title role in the 2000 film *Get Carter*?

2   In which Welsh city is the district called Tiger Bay?

3   Which spin-off from the original series of *Dallas* was set in a Californian cul-de-sac?

4   Tirana is the capital city of which country?

5   What two colours feature on a barber's pole?

6   Which footballer claimed the "Golden Boot" for finishing as the top scorer at the 2002 FIFA World Cup?

7   What was the forename of the character played by Lisa Kudrow in *Friends*?

8   The town of Bideford is in which county?

9   What is the name of the sauce made from melted butter, egg yolks and vinegar?

10 Which musical direction means "with brisk movement"?

11 Who produced the first pair of jeans in 1850?

12 In which body of water is the Isle of Man?

13 Which singer had hits in the 1990s with *Killer* and *Kiss from a Rose*?

14 The Mountbatten family home in Hampshire has what name?

15 What is the general name for a large blood vessel leading from the heart?

16 In the French comic strip, who is the best friend of Obelix?

17 What, in Greek mythology, is a river or spring nymph called?

18 From which London station did the first Eurostar service originally depart?

19 How many inches are there in two yards?

20 Which letter is furthest left on the bottom line of a standard keyboard?

Easy

Medium

Hard

Answers to QUIZ 283 – Pot Luck

1	The Hollies	11	Grog
2	Pet detective	12	Haiku
3	*Caveat*	13	Perth
4	Steps	14	Croydon
5	Five	15	Todd Carty
6	The Incas	16	Panniers
7	Sussex	17	Ewe
8	Ranchero	18	Anon
9	April	19	Lake Victoria
10	Pauline Collins	20	Elbow

Easy

1   What was the name of the 1944-45 battle also known as the Ardennes Offensive?

2   Who directed and starred in the 1941 film *Citizen Kane*?

3   The "Speedee Service System" was introduced in 1948 by which fast food company?

4   What do the initials VJ stand for in VJ Day, celebrated in 1945?

5   Who wrote the novel *Double Indemnity* (1943)?

6   First broadcast in 1946, which long-running radio programme's presenters include Jenni Murray and Jane Garvey?

7   Which US president was in office from 1945 to 1953?

8   The 1942 battle of Midway took place in which body of water?

9   Which medical organisation was founded in the UK in 1948?

10 Which was the only historic bridge in the Italian city of Florence that was not destroyed in 1944?

11 Sir Winston Churchill succeeded Neville Chamberlain as UK Prime Minister in which year?

12 In which country was Placido Domingo born in 1947?

13 Popular during this decade, what was the "jitterbug"?

Medium

14 Which 1948 film of a Shakespeare play won four Oscars, including Best Actor for Sir Laurence Olivier?

15 Where were the Summer Olympic Games held in 1948?

16 Which form of transport became fully owned by the state in the UK in 1948?

17 In which year did Queen Elizabeth II marry the Duke of Edinburgh?

18 The 1949 film *The Third Man* was set in which city?

19 What retail restriction began in the UK in January 1940?

20 To what did the Local Defence Volunteer Force change its name in 1941?

Hard

Answers to QUIZ 284 – Paper

1	Wood pulp	11	Caithness Glass
2	Ryan and Tatum O'Neal	12	Cooking
3	Firework (or gunpowder)	13	Henry James
4	*The Railway Children*	14	Hare and hounds
5	Manuscript paper	15	Microsoft
6	Status Quo	16	It is not as powerful as it seems
7	At the front or end of a book	17	Chinese lantern
8	Flock	18	Serviette
9	Lennon and McCartney	19	Wernham Hogg
10	Egypt	20	Twenty

1   What is the first name of Canadian singer Ms Lavigne?

2   What name is given to a tapering flag, particularly as used on a ship?

3   What is a waterfront promenade called in the USA?

4   *Wishing I Was Lucky* was a 1987 hit for which group?

5   On *Countdown*, how many letters are selected in each round?

6   The Pilgrims' Way runs from Winchester to which other city?

7   Which country has Tehran as its capital?

8   Retired swimmer Ian Thorpe had what nickname when he was competing?

9   Endocrinology is the study of what in the body?

10   Who played Tony Blair in the 2006 film *The Queen*?

11   Which chemical element has the symbol Sn?

12   Emma Hamilton was the mistress of which British naval hero?

13   What is the French term for dry or unsweetened sparkling wine?

14   In the British award, what does the "C" of CBE stand for?

15   *It's a Miracle* was a 1984 hit for which group?

16   Which type of drum has wires stretched across it?

17   The 2000 novel *The Amber Spyglass* was written by which author?

18   What attraction previously occupied the Legoland site in Berkshire?

19   What is the long, narrow pillow, often seen on a chaise longue, called?

20   Big Sur is a section of coast of which USA state?

Answers to QUIZ 285 – Pot Luck

1	Sylvester Stallone	11	Levi Strauss
2	Cardiff	12	Irish Sea
3	*Knots Landing*	13	Seal
4	Albania	14	Broadlands
5	Red and white	15	Artery
6	Ronaldo	16	Asterix
7	Phoebe	17	Naiad
8	Devon	18	Waterloo
9	Hollandaise	19	72
10	Allegro	20	Z

Easy

1 *Apache* was a hit for which group in 1960?

2 How were Davy Jones, Mickey Dolenz, Mike Nesmith and Peter Tork collectively known?

3 Levi Stubbs was the lead singer with which group?

4 *Little Red Rooster* was a 1964 chart-topper for which band?

5 *Pretty Flamingo* was a hit in 1966 for which group?

6 *Runaway* was a 1961 UK hit for which singer?

7 Which group had a 1964 hit with *The House of the Rising Sun*?

8 Who was the first singer to win the Eurovision Song Contest for the United Kingdom?

9 *With a Little Help from My Friends* was a 1968 chart-topper for which singer?

10 The name of which satellite gave The Tornados a 1962 UK hit?

11 What was the title of Roy Orbison's first UK hit?

Medium

12 Which group topped the charts in 1966 with *The Sun Ain't Gonna Shine Anymore*?

13 What was the title of Gerry and the Pacemaker's first UK single, which reached no.1?

14 *Cathy's Clown* was a 1960 hit for which duo?

15 What was the Beatles' second feature film?

16 Which group had a hit in 1965 with *Mr Tambourine Man*?

17 What was the subtitle of Elvis Presley's hit *It's Now or Never*?

18 *I Remember You* and *The Wayward Wind* were hits for which singer?

19 Which father and daughter topped the charts in 1967 with *Somethin' Stupid*?

20 *You Really Got Me* was a 1964 no.1 for which band?

Hard

Answers to QUIZ 286 – 1940s

1	Battle of the Bulge	11	1940
2	Orson Welles	12	Spain
3	McDonald's	13	A dance
4	Victory in Japan	14	*Hamlet*
5	James M Cain	15	London
6	*Woman's Hour*	16	Railways
7	Harry S Truman	17	1947
8	Pacific Ocean	18	Vienna
9	National Health Service	19	Food rationing
10	Ponte Vecchio	20	The Home Guard

1   Which scandal featured in the film *All the President's Men*?

2   Which anniversary celebrates 60 years of marriage?

3   What is the name of Tom Hanks' character in *The Da Vinci Code* and its sequels?

4   Kid Creole was backed by which group?

5   On which racecourse is Tattenham Corner?

6   Which group topped the charts in 2003 with *Crashed the Wedding*?

7   If you were born on November 1, what would your birth sign be?

8   What is the name of the *Children in Need* bear?

9   Which strait separates Hampshire from the Isle of Wight?

10 Richmal Crompton wrote which series of books about a mischievous schoolboy?

11 In which region of France is claret wine made?

12 Which soprano was known as "the Swedish nightingale"?

13 19th-century grocer John Walker established which famous drinks brand?

14 What name is given to a stone-worker?

15 What groups of animals are described as bovine?

16 Lewis and Harris are part of which island group?

17 In geometry, what term is used for a segment of a circle?

18 Ghana has which city as its capital?

19 What was Mozart's middle name?

20 Which European capital city sits at the mouth of the river Tagus?

Answers to QUIZ 287 – Pot Luck

1	Avril	11	Tin
2	Pennant	12	Horatio Nelson (Viscount Nelson)
3	Boardwalk	13	Brut
4	Wet Wet Wet	14	Commander
5	Nine	15	Culture Club
6	Canterbury	16	Snare drum
7	Iran	17	Philip Pullman
8	Thorpedo	18	Windsor Safari Park
9	Glands and hormones	19	Bolster
10	Michael Sheen	20	California

Easy

1. What name is given to a porter on a golf course?

2. How many players are in a basketball team?

3. What name is given to the area of the track from which the cars start a Grand Prix race?

4. What are the cross-pieces on a cricket wicket called?

5. Loose head and tight head define which position in a rugby team?

6. What is the surname of the brothers who took gold and silver in the 2016 Olympic triathlon?

7. What piece of classical music is associated with Torvill and Dean's 1984 Olympic win?

8. How many hurdles are there in a 110m hurdles race?

9. Who won the men's singles at Wimbledon in 1992?

10. In which annual event do teams take either the Middlesex station or the Surrey station?

Medium

11. What is a playing period in the game of polo called?

12. Which old name for England is associated with football team West Bromwich?

13. Where were the summer Olympic Games held in 1936?

14. Schuss and telemark are terms used in which winter sport?

15. In the Isle of Man TT races, what does "TT" stand for?

16. Which point follows deuce in a tennis match?

17. Which oriental martial art has a name meaning "empty hand"?

18. In 1981, who won the Grand National on Aldaniti?

19. In which field sport did Steve Backley compete for Great Britain?

20. Which legendary Victorian cricketer scored over 54,000 runs during his career?

Hard

Answers to QUIZ 288 – 1960s Music

1	The Shadows	11	*Only the Lonely*
2	The Monkees	12	Walker Brothers
3	The Four Tops	13	*How Do You Do It?*
4	The Rolling Stones	14	Everly Brothers
5	Manfred Mann	15	*Help!*
6	Del Shannon	16	The Byrds
7	The Animals	17	*O Sole Mio*
8	Sandie Shaw (*Puppet on a String*)	18	Frank Ifield
9	Joe Cocker	19	Frank and Nancy Sinatra
10	Telstar	20	The Kinks

ANSWERS ON PAGE **293**

1 Yogi Bear lives in which fictional park?

2 What name is given to a person who searches for water with a divining rod?

3 Who had hits with *Simply the Best* and *Private Dancer*?

4 Stops, pipes and pedals appear on which instrument?

5 Which is the smallest of the four main Channel Islands?

6 The UN flag features which two colours?

7 What is the term for a US legal panel, which usually has 23 members?

8 Businessman Samuel Ryder initiated a cup in which sport?

9 What is the Scottish term for the steep slope of a hillside?

10 Which single was the 1984 festive no.1?

11 What is the area of Cambridge behind the river, which shares its name with another name for defenders?

12 Contestants must speak "without hesitation, repetition or deviation" for a fixed period of time on which radio show?

13 In which film musical did Sir Rex Harrison play Professor Henry Higgins?

14 What is the name of the vast desert situated in China and southern Mongolia?

15 Who played Lewis to John Thaw's Morse?

16 The Roman numerals VII represent which number?

17 Who played Galadriel in the *Lord of the Rings* trilogy?

18 Which Asian country was formerly known as Kampuchea?

19 An eagle's nest is given what name?

20 Which item of furniture has a French name that means "office"?

Easy

Medium

Hard

Answers to QUIZ 289 – Pot Luck

1	Watergate	11	Bordeaux
2	Diamond	12	Jenny Lind
3	Robert Langdon	13	Johnnie Walker whisky
4	The Coconuts	14	Mason
5	Epsom	15	Cattle
6	Busted	16	Outer Hebrides (or Western Isles)
7	Scorpio	17	Arc
8	Pudsey	18	Accra
9	The Solent	19	Amadeus
10	*Just William*	20	Lisbon

Easy

1 How many years of bad luck are associated with breaking a mirror?

2 What is the name given to the phenomenon where a novice taking part in a new activity experiences unlikely success?

3 What item is considered unlucky to open indoors?

4 According to a well-known rhyme, what bird is considered unlucky when you view one, but lucky if you view two?

5 To break the bad luck when you spill salt, what are you required to do?

6 In which county is the village of Veryan, where a number of round houses were built so that the Devil had no corners in which to hide?

7 Which animal's foot is said to be lucky?

8 What four things are considered lucky for a bride to wear on her wedding day?

9 What item is considered lucky when nailed to a door?

10 To have good luck, what must one do when one finds a penny on the floor?

11 What chicken bone is it considered lucky to break with another?

12 It is considered unlucky to put what new items of clothing on a table?

Medium

13 Which number is generally thought to be the luckiest?

14 Which day is traditionally particularly unlucky if it falls on a Friday?

15 On a pavement, what is it considered unlucky to step on?

16 Touching an item made of which material is generally considered to bring good luck?

17 Which plant is said to be lucky when it has four leaves?

18 Which two words are often said to someone who has just sneezed?

19 In China, what colour is considered lucky?

20 What is it considered unlucky to walk beneath?

Hard

Answers to QUIZ 290 – Sport

1	Caddie	11	Chukka
2	Five	12	Albion
3	The grid	13	Berlin
4	Bails	14	Skiing
5	Prop	15	Tourist Trophy
6	Brownlee	16	Advantage
7	Bolero	17	Karate
8	Ten	18	Bob Champion
9	Andre Agassi	19	Javelin
10	The Boat Race	20	WG Grace

ANSWERS ON PAGE 295

1   Near which Scottish town would you find the sculptures called *The Kelpies*?

2   Which group backed Smokey Robinson?

3   In which event is "the Fosbury flop" a technique?

4   Which lough in Northern Ireland is the largest freshwater lake in the UK?

5   Pope Paul III took what action against King Henry VIII in 1538?

6   Which river flows through Durham?

7   What is the name of the Flintstones' daughter?

8   A clerical dignitary attached to a cathedral shares what name with a general rule or principle?

9   What was the title of George Michael's first solo album?

10   Which title is shared by a an old TV travel show, an album by Pink Floyd and a 1987 film starring Emily Lloyd?

11   In which county is Kettering?

12   What name is given to a writer of words for a song?

13   In 1989, what word was dropped from the title of soap opera *Emmerdale*?

14   Who wrote the play *Private Lives* (1930)?

15   What was the medieval knightly system of courtesy and consideration called?

16   Porridge has what main constituent?

17   Which unwanted plant, also known as convolvulus, twines around any support?

18   Qatar has what official language?

19   What is Whitehall's war memorial called?

20   In which James Bond film did Jane Seymour play a psychic?

Easy

Medium

Hard

Answers to QUIZ 291 – Pot Luck

1	Jellystone Park	11	Backs
2	Dowser	12	*Just a Minute*
3	Tina Turner	13	*My Fair Lady*
4	Organ	14	Gobi
5	Sark	15	Kevin Whately
6	Blue and white	16	Seven
7	Grand jury	17	Cate Blanchett
8	Golf	18	Cambodia
9	Brae	19	Eyrie
10	*Do They Know It's Christmas?*	20	Bureau

Easy

1 What new product did Apple release on April 24, 2015?

2 Which website featured in the film *The Social Network*?

3 What is the biggest key on a standard keyboard?

4 In which year was Twitter founded?

5 On mobile phones with a keypad on the handset, which letters appear on the number 8 key?

6 What name is given to the pen-like device used with a touchscreen computer?

7 What word is "app" short for?

8 Jimmy Wales was a co-founder of which website that launched in 2001?

9 Which mythological creature lends its name to a person who posts offensive messages on social media sites?

10 What long-handled device enables phone users to take wider photographs with their camera?

11 Which website was launched in 2010 to provide a "virtual pinboard" for users?

12 The ZX80 and the ZX Spectrum home computers were introduced in the early 1980s by which British inventor?

Medium

13 What on-line feature for discussions takes its name from an ancient Roman meeting place?

14 The Snapchat logo features what type of spooky character?

15 Which operating system has had versions called Lollipop and Marshmallow?

16 What does RAM stand for?

17 Martha Lane Fox and Brent Hoberman founded which internet company in 1998?

18 Which fruit and mathematical symbol combine to give the name of a basic computer used in education?

19 What does the "C" of ICT stand for?

20 What is COBOL an early example of?

Hard

Answers to QUIZ 292 – Superstitions

1	Seven years	11	Chicken wishbone
2	Beginner's luck	12	Pair of shoes
3	Umbrella	13	Seven
4	Magpie	14	13th
5	Throw salt over your shoulder	15	Cracks
6	Cornwall	16	Wood
7	Rabbit's foot	17	Clover
8	Something old, new, borrowed and blue	18	"Bless you"
9	Horseshoe	19	Red
10	Pick it up	20	A ladder

ANSWERS ON PAGE 297

1   Who created the characters of Wallace and Gromit?

2   In the TV series *Father Ted*, who played Mrs Doyle?

3   Which is the longest race in the decathlon?

4   Situated on the Mississippi, what is Tennessee's largest city?

5   What was the title of the 1983 hit duet by Kenny Rogers and Dolly Parton?

6   Which town is further south, Aberystwyth or Tenby?

7   *Toy Story*'s cowboy hero has what name?

8   How many degrees are there in half a circle?

9   What is the capital of Canada?

10 The 1964 film *Mary Poppins* starred which actress in the title role?

11 Who wrote the 1791 poem *The Banks o' Doon*?

12 On a standard Monopoly™ board, which property is the same colour as Park Lane?

13 What does the "D" of MOD stand for?

14 What is the name of Prospero's slave in Shakespeare's *The Tempest*?

15 The East Anglian town of Cromer is particularly associated with which type of seafood?

16 How many points does a snowflake have?

17 Which type of dagger is the tradional ceremonial sidearm of Scottish Highland regiment officers?

18 The Grand Union Canal links London with which other city?

19 Which 1960s puppet fought the Mysterons?

20 What is the Russian term for a country house or cottage?

Easy

Medium

Hard

Answers to QUIZ 293 – Pot Luck

1	Falkirk	11	Northamptonshire
2	The Miracles	12	Lyricist
3	The high jump	13	*Farm*
4	Neagh	14	Sir Noël Coward
5	Excommunicated him	15	Chivalry
6	Wear	16	Oats
7	Pebbles	17	Bindweed
8	Canon	18	Arabic
9	*Faith*	19	The Cenotaph
10	*Wish You Were Here*	20	*Live and Let Die*

Easy

1. Which river flows through Budapest and Belgrade?

2. What line on a map connects points of the same height?

3. What is the smallest kind of living creature?

4. In which two English counties is Romney Marsh?

5. By what other name is the great maple tree known?

6. Where would a troglodyte's home be found?

7. What large bodies of water can be Black, Red, White or Yellow?

8. Fort William is the nearest town to which Scottish mountain?

9. What name is given to the study of the earth's crust and rocks?

10. What is the largest freshwater lake in the world?

11. The area around the Pacific Ocean known for earthquakes and volcanic eruptions is given what name?

12. Which tree was famously affected by a "Dutch" disease?

13. What word is given to the point where the land and sky appear to meet?

14. Which island group lies north-west of the Shetlands?

Medium

15. Situated on the Peru/Bolivia border, which lake is the largest in South America?

16. What name is given to the hilly area of Yorkshire?

17. In which two parts of the world is the midnight sun visible in midsummer?

18. Which country has the longest coastline in the world?

19. The World Heritage Site of the Jurassic Coast lies within which two counties?

20. What is the name given to the point at which the Sun is at its highest?

Hard

Answers to QUIZ 294 – Technology

1	A watch	11	Pinterest
2	Facebook	12	Sir Clive Sinclair
3	Space bar	13	Forum
4	2006	14	Ghost
5	TUV	15	Android
6	Stylus	16	Random access memory
7	Application	17	Lastminute.com
8	Wikipedia	18	Raspberry Pi
9	Troll	19	Communications
10	Selfie stick	20	Programming language

1   In which season does the vernal equinox take place?

2   Alfred the Great's kingdom had which city as its capital?

3   Which word is used for fiscal studies on a large scale?

4   What was the title of the Jam's final single?

5   Jimmy Somerville left which band to form the Communards?

6   Who was president of the USA from 1974 to 1977?

7   The 2009 film *My Sister's Keeper* starred which actress as Sara Fitzgerald?

8   Who was Tina Turner's 1960s singing partner and former husband?

9   Spain and Portugal occupy which peninsula?

10 In which athletics event did Jonathan Edwards take the Olympic gold medal in 2000?

11 Which fish is cured to make a kipper?

12 What is the name of the water vole in *The Wind in the Willows* (1908)?

13 *Perfect Moment* was a hit for which ex-*EastEnders* actress in 1999?

14 Which children's series featured a pirate ship called *The Black Pig*?

15 Which architect designed Blenheim Palace?

16 Of what are ink-caps, death caps and puffballs all types?

17 *Nevermind* is a 1991 album by which band?

18 What term is given to the hammer used by judges and auctioneers?

19 Who played Sugar Kane Kowalczyk in the 1959 film *Some Like it Hot*?

20 What is an appaloosa?

Answers to QUIZ 295 – Pot Luck

1	Nick Park	11	Robert Burns
2	Pauline McLynn	12	Mayfair
3	1500m	13	Defence
4	Memphis	14	Caliban
5	*Islands in the Stream*	15	Crab
6	Tenby	16	Six
7	Woody	17	Dirk
8	180	18	Birmingham
9	Ottawa	19	Captain Scarlet
10	Dame Julie Andrews	20	Dacha

1   Who created the character of Bridget Jones, famous for her diary?

2   Which 1995 Nick Hornby novel's principal character was record shop owner Rob Fleming?

3   Which 2003 novel is told in a series of letters written by Eva Khatchadourian?

4   The characters of Sam Vimes and Granny Weatherwax were created by which author?

5   What type of supernatural creature was interviewed in the title of a 1994 novel by Anne Rice?

6   Emma Donoghue wrote which 2011 novel that was made into a 2015 film starring Brie Larson?

7   Which London street gave Monica Ali the title for her first novel?

8   What are the first names of the two main characters in the 2009 novel *One Day*?

9   Who wrote *The Lovely Bones*, later filmed starring Mark Wahlberg?

10 *The Postcard* (2016) and *Coming Home* (2018) are novels written by which TV presenter?

11 Whose wife is referenced in the title of a 2005 book by Audrey Niffenegger?

12 Which series of novels by George RR Martin is the basis for the TV series *Game of Thrones*?

13 Harry Bosch is the detective creation of which author?

14 Who wrote the award-winning 1995 novel *Behind the Scenes at the Museum*?

15 Which 2004 novel by David Mitchell consists of six stories which are interrupted then resumed later in the book?

16 Which of Henry VIII's wives was the subject of Philippa Gregory's 2015 novel *The Taming of the Queen*?

17 Dr Kay Scarpetta is the creation of which writer?

18 Who was the Irish writer of the 1990 novel *Circle of Friends*?

19 Which 1987 Stephen King novel featured the character of Paul Sheldon who was recovering from a car crash?

20 Khaled Hosseini's novel *The Kite Runner* features a family from which country?

Answers to QUIZ 296 – Natural World

1	Danube	11	Ring of Fire
2	A contour line	12	Elm
3	Amoeba	13	Horizon
4	Kent and East Sussex	14	Faroe Islands
5	Sycamore	15	Titicaca
6	In a cave or hole in the ground	16	The Dales
7	Seas	17	Arctic and Antarctic Circles
8	Ben Nevis	18	Canada
9	Geology	19	Devon and Dorset
10	Superior	20	Zenith

Easy

Medium

Hard

1   Who was the lead singer with Roxy Music?

2   In which Wiltshire town is STEAM, the Museum of the Great Western Railway?

3   Who played Annie in the 1994 film *Speed*?

4   Lanzarote lies north-east of which of the Canary Islands?

5   What is the set of three dots indicating an omission in writing called?

6   Mr Rochester appears in which classic 1847 novel?

7   Which cartoon series featured the character of Officer Dibble?

8   The play *A Doll's House* was written by which dramatist?

9   What caused the ill-fated Titanic to sink?

10   In the 1995 film *Se7en*, who played Brad Pitt's wife?

11   Which African country is separated from Spain by the Strait of Gibraltar?

12   What was the title of the 1980s yachting based TV series with Jan Harvey?

13   On which continent is the country of Iraq?

14   Which river in Devon gives its name to Devon's county town?

15   What sort of food is vichyssoise?

16   What, in cricket, is a run that is not credited to a batsman?

17   Which meat is obtained from deer?

18   Karl Marx is buried in which cemetery?

19   What name for the country is shown on Ireland's postage stamps?

20   Crathie Kirk is close to which royal residence?

Easy

Medium

Hard

Answers to QUIZ 297 – Pot Luck

1	Spring	11	Herring
2	Winchester	12	Ratty
3	Macroeconomics	13	Martine McCutcheon
4	*Beat Surrender*	14	*Captain Pugwash*
5	Bronski Beat	15	Sir John Vanbrugh
6	Gerald Ford	16	Fungi
7	Cameron Diaz	17	Nirvana
8	Ike	18	Gavel
9	Iberian	19	Marilyn Monroe
10	The triple jump	20	A horse

QUIZ 300 – Children's Television

ANSWERS ON PAGE 302

1 Which is the UK's longest-running children's television show?

2 Which cartoon hero has a sidekick called Penfold?

3 In *Thunderbirds*, which organisation do the Tracy family run?

4 What was the title of the series designed for hearing-impaired children, whose presenters included Tony Hart?

5 Which character wore a black suit and bowler hat when visiting a magic fancy-dress shop?

6 Which series that ran from 1965 to 1977 was based on a French stop-motion animation show?

7 The Sun Baby featured at the beginning and end of each episode in which series?

8 Which animated US series ran from 1985 to 1989 and included the characters Lion-O, Panthro and Jaga?

9 Which principal character in an animated series regularly fought the evil Skeletor?

10 What was the title of the stop-motion clay animated series which centred on a family of penguins?

11 Iggle Piggle and Upsy Daisy appeared in which series?

12 What type of animals were Pinky and Perky?

13 Which animated character was originally voiced by Neil Morrissey before the series was revamped in 2014?

14 In the series *Charlie and Lola*, what relation is Lola to Charlie?

15 Where did the Wombles carry out their litter-clearing activities?

16 Which stop-motion series was set in the fictional Welsh village of Pontypandy?

17 Which three words preceded "switch off your television set and go out and do something less boring instead" in the title of a long-running series?

18 In which series was the title pink-and-white-striped character owned by a young girl named Emily?

19 Which whistling creatures eat soup provided by the Soup Dragon?

20 Which presenter, who went on to join *Countryfile*, had a long-running *Newsround*?

Answers to QUIZ 298 – Modern Fiction

1	Helen Fielding	11	*The Time Traveler's Wife*
2	*High Fidelity*	12	*A Song of Ice and Fire*
3	*We Need to Talk about Kevin*	13	Michael Connelly
4	Sir Terry Pratchett	14	Kate Atkinson
5	Vampire	15	*Cloud Atlas*
6	*Room*	16	Catherine Parr
7	Brick Lane	17	Patricia Cornwell
8	Dexter and Emma	18	Maeve Binchy
9	Alice Sebold	19	*Misery*
10	Fern Britton	20	Afghanistan

1 Which Indian resort region once belonged to Portugal?

2 To which plant genus does the daffodil belong?

3 Which comedy film starring Bill Murray was based on *A Christmas Carol*?

4 Ronnie Corbett starred as Timothy Lumsden in which sitcom?

5 Which organ is affected by hepatitis?

6 In which Surrey town is the Sandown Park racecourse located?

7 Which city has the postcode prefix CF?

8 What is the large decorated goblet used in church for holding wine called?

9 The Model T was introduced by which car manufacturer in 1908?

10 Who accompanied Billy Preston on the 1979 duet *With You I'm Born Again*?

11 Which fruit is known as a bell pepper in the US?

12 What does Arthur Dent wear throughout *The Hitchhiker's Guide To The Galaxy*?

13 According to the Bible, which kind of people will inherit the Earth?

14 Which character did Ingrid Bergman play in the film *Casablanca* (1942)?

15 Where is the Isle of Wight regatta held?

16 The TV presenter and comedian brothers Jeremy and Tim have what surname?

17 What is the anatomical name for the large bone of the upper leg?

18 What sport is played by the Miami Dolphins?

19 What part of the proboscis monkey is most prominent?

20 Oslo is the capital city of which country?

Easy

Medium

Hard

Answers to QUIZ 299 – Pot Luck

1	Bryan Ferry	11	Morocco
2	Swindon	12	*Howards' Way*
3	Sandra Bullock	13	Asia
4	Fuerteventura	14	Exe
5	Ellipsis	15	Soup
6	*Jane Eyre*	16	An extra
7	*Top Cat*	17	Venison
8	Henrik Ibsen	18	Highgate Cemetery
9	It hit an iceberg	19	Eire
10	Gwyneth Paltrow	20	Balmoral

Easy

1 Which singer/songwriter topped the 2000 album charts with *White Ladder*?

2 What name is given to the steps set into a fence or wall to help people climb it?

3 "Walkies!" was the catchphrase of which dog trainer who featured on TV in the 1980s?

4 Fashion models parade on which raised platform?

5 Which was the title of the 2000 chart-topping single by Steps?

6 What is the American term for a careless pedestrian?

7 In which part of the body would a pacemaker be fitted?

8 Who had a Top Ten hit in 1968 with *Step Inside Love*?

9 A ladder might appear in which item of clothing?

10 Which walker, known as AW, is particularly associated with guides to the Lake District?

11 What symbols are embedded on Hollywood's Walk of Fame to honour people in the entertainment industry?

12 In the classic board game, if ladders help you reach the finish, which creatures present obstacles?

Medium

13 *Parisienne Walkways* was a hit in both 1979 and 1993 for which guitarist?

14 The UK code for pedestrians is named after which colour and symbol?

15 Who had a hit in 1960 with *Three Steps to Heaven*?

16 Which TV series features Andrew Lincoln as Sheriff Deputy Rick Grimes?

17 Who recounted his hiking adventures in 1998's *A Walk in the Woods...*?

18 ...and who played him in the 2015 film adaptation?

19 Who fronted the 1960s pop group the Pacemakers?

20 Which actor starred in the 1935 version of *The 39 Steps*?

Hard

Answers to QUIZ 300 – Children's Television

1	Blue Peter	11	In the Night Garden
2	Danger Mouse	12	Pigs
3	International Rescue	13	Bob the Builder
4	Vision On	14	Sister
5	Mr Benn	15	Wimbledon Common
6	The Magic Roundabout	16	Fireman Sam
7	Teletubbies	17	Why Don't You?
8	ThunderCats	18	Bagpuss
9	He-Man	19	The Clangers
10	Pingu	20	John Craven

ANSWERS ON PAGE 305

1 The duck-billed platypus is native to which country?

2 Which actress starred in the 2009 film *An Education*?

3 What is Captain Poldark's first name?

4 In which county is Blackburn?

5 Who had a 1988 hit with *One Moment in Time*?

6 Which grinning feline did Alice meet in Wonderland?

7 "The Sunshine State" is the nickname of which US state?

8 Who played Arnold Schwarzenegger's brother in the 1988 film *Twins*?

9 Which star sign is between Capricorn and Pisces?

10 Which small Cambridgeshire city is famed for its cathedral?

11 During the Falklands War, who was the UK Prime Minister?

12 Which sport featured in the 1996 film *Tin Cup*?

13 What is the outward motion of the tide called?

14 The NEC is located in which English city?

15 What cookery measure corresponds roughly to 5 millilitres?

16 Which one of the seven deadly sins involves eating to excess?

17 In *Absolutely Fabulous*, which character was played by Jennifer Saunders?

18 On which river does the annual ceremony of Swan Upping take place?

19 What type of creature is a Swaledale?

20 Which variety of curry is named after the wide, round-bottomed metal pan in which it is served?

Answers to QUIZ 301 – Pot Luck

1	Goa	11	Capsicum
2	*Narcissus*	12	A dressing-gown
3	*Scrooged*	13	The Meek
4	*Sorry!*	14	Ilsa Lund
5	The liver	15	Cowes
6	Esher	16	Vine
7	Cardiff	17	Femur
8	Chalice	18	American football
9	Henry Ford	19	Its nose
10	Syreeta	20	Norway

Easy

1. Who is the host of *8 Out of 10 Cats*?

2. Who is Jennifer Saunders' comedy partner?

3. What are the first names of Hale and Pace?

4. The BBC sitcom *Not Going Out* is written by and stars which comedian?

5. Which comedienne presented the Royal Variety Show in 2017, the first solo female to do so?

6. The topical show *The Last Leg* is hosted by which Australian comedian?

7. Which two comedians began presenting *The Great British Bake Off* in 2017?

8. Who are the two team captains of *Have I Got News For You*?

9. Who was Syd Little's comedy partner?

10. The series *Modern Life is Goodish* featured which comedian?

Medium

11. Who is the host of *Would I Lie to You*?

12. Richard Osman appears as a team captain against which comedian in *Insert Name Here*?

13. What is the name of Sue Perkins' long-time comedy partner?

14. Who is TV's *Chatty Man*?

15. Who co-hosted Robot Wars from 2016 to 2018?

16. In the TV series *The Young Ones*, who portrayed Rick?

17. Which comedian won *Celebrity MasterChef* in 2013?

18. Greg and Alan, the stars of *Man Down* and *Jonathan Creek* respectively, share which surname?

19. Which comedian starred in *Fresh Meat* and *Bad Education*?

20. What is the first name of Mr Hill, former host of *TV Burp*?

Hard

Answers to QUIZ 302 – Steps

1	David Gray	11	Stars
2	Stile	12	Snakes
3	Barbara Woodhouse	13	Gary Moore
4	Catwalk	14	Green cross code
5	*Stomp*	15	Eddie Cochran
6	Jaywalker	16	*The Walking Dead*
7	Heart	17	Bill Bryson
8	Cilla Black	18	Robert Redford
9	Tights or a stocking	19	Gerry Marsden
10	Alfred Wainwright	20	Robert Donat

1   Whom did Michelle Dotrice play in the TV series *Some Mothers Do 'Ave 'Em*?

2   Which dance is associated with the Moulin Rouge?

3   Who starred as John Nash in the 2001 film *A Beautiful Mind*?

4   *Love Will Tear Us Apart* was originally a hit for which band?

5   Which bodily organ was once considered the seat of melancholy?

6   What is the fruit of the wild rose called?

7   Dame Katherine Grainger won four Olympic medals for Great Britain in which sport?

8   What was the title of the 1981 Eurovision-winning song by Buck's Fizz?

9   What term is given to the release of a prisoner subject to a period of good behaviour?

10   How many blank tiles are there in a Scrabble® set?

11   In which county is Aylesbury?

12   What type of creature is an opossum?

13   The Royal Opera House is in which area of London?

14   Which Bond film features the bowler-hatted baddie Oddjob?

15   How are the US group of universities including Yale and Princeton known?

16   Which public school did actor Damian Lewis attend?

17   Who succeeded Ken Livingstone as London's mayor?

18   What is the alternate name for a castle in chess?

19   To what does the expression "the fourth estate" refer?

20   Which natural harbour of southern England contains Brownsea Island?

Easy

Medium

Hard

Answers to QUIZ 303 – Pot Luck

1	Australia	11	Margaret Thatcher (Baroness Thatcher)
2	Carey Mulligan	12	Golf
3	Ross	13	Ebb
4	Lancashire	14	Birmingham
5	Whitney Houston	15	Teaspoonful
6	Cheshire Cat	16	Gluttony
7	Florida	17	Edina Monsoon
8	Danny DeVito	18	Thames
9	Aquarius	19	A sheep
10	Ely	20	Balti

1 *Crème pâtissière* is a thick pastry cream similar to what sweet egg-based confection?

2 What dessert is made by mixing soft cooked fruit with whipped cream or custard?

3 What Italian dessert is usually composed of sponge fingers, coffee, mascarpone and chocolate?

4 An Apfelstrudel is a pastry containing which type of fruit?

5 How is the dessert *île flottante* known in English?

6 What brand-name powdered dessert is whisked with milk to create a mousse?

7 Which traditional English dessert contains sponge fingers soaked in sherry, fruit jelly, custard and cream?

8 The term for "sweetheart" in Cockney rhyming slang references which dessert?

9 What name is given to a dessert consisting of ice cream and cake, topped with meringue and then cooked?

10 What frozen dessert is made from sweetened water with flavouring, often fruit juice?

11 Neapolitan ice cream contains which three flavours?

12 What name is given to a brownie-like dessert that substitutes vanilla for the cocoa?

13 What baked, egg-based French dish is notoriously difficult to keep risen?

14 An upside-down cake traditionally features which tropical fruit?

15 What is the English translation of the name of the Italian dessert *panna cotta*?

16 "Banoffee" is a word combining which two main ingredients of banoffee pie?

17 Often used as a dessert fruit, which plant has edible pink stems and poisonous leaves?

18 Which fruit is associated with the dessert named after opera singer Dame Nellie Melba?

19 How is fruit cooked if it is served in a "compote"?

20 What does the name of the French dessert *parfait* mean in English?

Answers to QUIZ 304 – Comedians

1	Jimmy Carr	11	Rob Brydon
2	Dawn French	12	Josh Widdicombe
3	Gareth and Norman	13	Mel Giedroyc
4	Lee Mack	14	Alan Carr
5	Miranda Hart	15	Dara Ó Briain
6	Adam Hills	16	Rik Mayall
7	Sandi Toksvig and Noel Fielding	17	Adrian Edmondson
8	Paul Merton and Ian Hislop	18	Davies
9	Eddie Large	19	Jack Whitehall
10	Dave Gorman	20	Harry

1 What is the name of the Channel which forms the waterway between Wales and south-west England?

2 Which motorway is known as the London Orbital?

3 Which actor directed and starred in the 1998 film *The Horse Whisperer*?

4 In which country is the football team PSV Eindhoven based?

5 What was the name of the Beatles' record label?

6 Which film includes the song *White Christmas*?

7 What is the cube root of 1000?

8 *An Unexpected Journey* was the subtitle of which 2012 film?

9 Who wrote *How to be a Domestic Goddess*?

10 What is the meaning of the Latin phrase *ad nauseam*?

11 In the Bible, which of Jacob's sons was sold as a slave by his brothers?

12 Which trees feature in the name of the London district east of Battersea, Nine _?

13 What is a fox's tail called?

14 Who broadcast the radio series *Letter from America* from 1946 until 2004?

15 To which language family do Breton and Welsh belong?

16 Which military bugle call is played at the end of the day and during services of remembrance?

17 What is the term for a vast astronomical area containing many star systems?

18 An ibex is what type of animal?

19 Who is the trumpeter with a long hooked nose in *The Muppet Show*?

20 What is the word for pruning and sculpting of trees and shrubs into artistic shapes?

Easy

Medium

Hard

Answers to QUIZ 305 – Pot Luck

1	Betty	11	Buckinghamshire
2	Can-can	12	Marsupial
3	Russell Crowe	13	Covent Garden
4	Joy Division	14	*Goldfinger*
5	Spleen	15	Ivy League
6	Hip	16	Eton
7	Rowing	17	Boris Johnson
8	*Making Your Mind Up*	18	Rook
9	Probation	19	The press
10	Two	20	Poole

Easy

1   Which 1997 film was the first to be completely inspired by classical mythology rather than fairy tales?

2   The character named Mushu, voiced by Eddie Murphy, appears in which 1998 film based on a Chinese legend?

3   In which 1950 film do the stepsisters Drizella and Anastasia appear?

4   What is the title of the 1951 Disney film based on books by Lewis Carroll?

5   Which 1963 Disney film was based on the boyhood of King Arthur?

6   The song *Ev'rybody Wants to Be a Cat* features in which 1970 film?

7   What is the name of the title character from *The Hunchback of Notre Dame*?

8   Which film follows the adventures of an American cocker spaniel given by Jim Dear to his wife, Darling?

9   In *The Fox and the Hound,* is the character called Copper the fox or the hound?

10   In the 1942 film, what type of creature is Bambi?

11   What is the name of the wood-carver responsible for carving Pinocchio?

12   Who provided the voice of the genie in the 1992 film *Aladdin*?

Medium

13   Which 2017 film set in Mexico won the Best Animated Film and Best Original Song Oscars?

14   Which 1991 animated film was remade as a live-action film in 2017?

15   Based on a legendary British outlaw, which film was released in 1973 with a cartoon fox as the title character?

16   What was the name of Disney's first fully animated feature film to be released?

17   In which animated feature film does Mickey Mouse disastrously command a broom to do his chores?

18   Which was the last film to actually be produced by Walt Disney?

19   Which 1989 film based on a Danish fairytale was adapted into a musical in 2008?

20   In the 1994 film *The Lion King*, what is the name of the meerkat?

Answers to QUIZ 306 – Desserts

1	Custard	11	Strawberry, chocolate and vanilla
2	Fool	12	Blondie
3	Tiramisu	13	Soufflé
4	Apple	14	Pineapple
5	Floating island	15	Cooked cream
6	Angel Delight	16	Banana and toffee
7	Trifle	17	Rhubarb
8	Treacle tart	18	Peach
9	Baked Alaska	19	With syrup
10	Sorbet	20	Perfect

Hard

QUIZ 309 – Pot Luck

ANSWERS ON PAGE 311

1   By which abbreviated name is the central character of Dickens' *Great Expectations* known?

2   What kind of animal is a tench?

3   In human anatomy, what is the name of the tendon found down the back of the leg?

4   Which Latin word is used for an open-roofed entrance hall or central court in a building?

5   Which actor starred as Danny Trevanion in the TV series *Wild at Heart*?

6   The fermentation of sugar produces which substance found in beer and wine?

7   Which English city has Oxford Road, Victoria and Piccadilly railway stations?

8   Which Scottish loch is said to have "bonnie banks"?

9   What is the common abbreviated spelling of "boatswain"?

10   In which country did karaoke originate?

11   What is the nationality of a person from Tel Aviv?

12   Who had a hit in 1982 with *Heartbreaker*?

13   In which county is Saxmundham?

14   Which is the only surviving Wonder of the Ancient World?

15   Who played the title character in the 2001 film *Captain Corelli's Mandolin*?

16   Which football team's mascot is Stamford the Lion?

17   What does a vulcanologist study?

18   Which ancient site of a Greek sporting festival lends its name to a London exhibition hall?

19   Whose novels were set in the fictional Wessex?

20   Which country has the international car registration letter E?

Answers to QUIZ 307 – Pot Luck

1	Bristol	11	Joseph
2	M25	12	Elms (Nine Elms)
3	Robert Redford	13	A brush
4	The Netherlands	14	Alistair Cooke
5	Apple	15	Celtic
6	*Holiday Inn*	16	The Last Post
7	Ten	17	Galaxy
8	*The Hobbit*	18	Goat
9	Nigella Lawson	19	Gonzo
10	"To the point of sickness"	20	Topiary

Easy

1 Which London football team played home games at the Boleyn Ground at Upton Park until 2016?

2 Who became presenter of *Countdown* in 2012?

3 In which county is the town of Upton-upon-Severn?

4 Who played Lord Grantham in *Downton Abbey*?

5 Which Irish group covered Billy Joel's *Uptown Girl* in 2001?

6 A hoedown is what type of dance?

7 Which theatrical verb means to force someone else out of the limelight?

8 What betting items are said to be down at a critical moment?

9 Mark Ronson's *Uptown Funk* was the best-selling song in the UK in which year?

10 Which forest, covering both West and East Sussex, was the inspiration for the Winnie-the-Pooh stories?

Medium

11 Upsilon is a letter in which alphabet?

12 What term is given to the return of a spacecraft into the sea?

13 In the TV series *Up Pompeii!*, which comedian played Lurcio?

14 What term for a hand covering is proverbially thrown down in a challenge?

15 Which car manufacturer produces the "up!"?

16 In which two counties are the Blackdown Hills?

17 Which instrument can be upright or grand?

18 A modestly sized terraced house is often referred to as how many up and down?

19 With which bird is an early riser said to get up?

20 Which day of the week is often known as "dress-down"?

Hard

Answers to QUIZ 308 – Disney Films

1	Hercules	11	Geppetto
2	Mulan	12	Robin Williams
3	Cinderella	13	Coco
4	Alice in Wonderland	14	Beauty and the Beast
5	The Sword in the Stone	15	Robin Hood
6	The Aristocats	16	Snow White and the Seven Dwarfs
7	Quasimodo	17	Fantasia
8	Lady and the Tramp	18	The Jungle Book
9	Hound	19	The Little Mermaid
10	A deer	20	Timon

1 Which chart-topping group of the mid-1970s were noted for wearing tartan?

2 The 2002 series of *Celebrity Big Brother* was won by which singer?

3 What is the name of the annual American football championship game?

4 Who, in the Bible, was Esau's brother and the son of Isaac?

5 The inside of a pistachio nut is what colour?

6 Which branch of science studies viruses, bacteria etc?

7 Who directed the 2004 film *Million Dollar Baby*?

8 Catherine Parr was which of Henry VIII's wives?

9 The Radcliffe Road End is in which cricket ground?

10 What type of soil has a pH value of less than seven?

11 What is Winnie-the-Pooh's favourite food?

12 What prefix indicates 10^6?

13 Which Elvis single reached the top of the UK charts shortly after his death in 1977?

14 A purple emperor is what type of creature?

15 What is the main alcoholic ingredient in a margarita cocktail?

16 What is the term for a call made in a game of bridge?

17 According to the proverb, where does charity begin?

18 What word meaning a snooze also refers to the raised hairs on fabric?

19 According to the nursery rhyme, which child has "far to go"?

20 Which is the second largest city in the Netherlands?

Easy
Medium
Hard

Answers to QUIZ 309 – Pot Luck

1	Pip	11	Israeli
2	Fish	12	Dionne Warwick
3	Hamstring	13	Suffolk
4	Atrium	14	The Great Pyramid of Giza
5	Stephen Tompkinson	15	Nicolas Cage
6	Alcohol	16	Chelsea FC
7	Manchester	17	Volcanoes
8	Lomond	18	Olympia
9	Bosun	19	Thomas Hardy
10	Japan	20	Spain

Easy

1 The emperors of Germany were given which title?

2 Who was President of France from 2012 to 2017?

3 What is the lower house of Parliament in the Irish Republic?

4 Which Indian leader who advocated non-violent protest was assassinated in 1948?

5 China's Communist Party was led by which chairman until his death in 1976?

6 Which US President was involved in the Watergate scandal?

7 Who was President of Russia from 1991 to 1999?

8 The Isle of Man's parliament is given what name?

9 Who was Rhodesian Prime Minister when the country declared itself independent in 1965?

10 Which former British colony was returned to China in 1997?

Medium

11 Who was the emperor of Japan from 1926 to 1989?

12 From which country did the Democratic Republic of Congo gain freedom in 1960?

13 Who was President of Zimbabwe from 1987 until he resigned in 2017?

14 "The Iron Chancellor" was the nickname of which 19th-century German statesman?

15 Who was the 42nd President of the USA?

16 In 1960 which country became the first to have a female Prime Minister?

17 Who was the Israeli Prime Minister from 1969 to 1974?

18 The upper house of the US government is given what name?

19 What is the name for the medieval citadel in Moscow which is the centre of Russia's government?

20 Who was Prime Minister of Canada from 1968 to 1979 and 1980 to 1984?

Hard

Answers to QUIZ 310 – Up and Down

1	West Ham United	11	Greek
2	Nick Hewer	12	Splashdown
3	Worcestershire	13	Frankie Howerd
4	Hugh Bonneville	14	Gauntlet
5	Westlife	15	Volkswagen
6	Barn dance	16	Devon and Somerset
7	Upstage	17	Piano
8	The chips	18	Two up, two down
9	2015	19	The lark
10	Ashdown	20	Friday

1   What is the capital of Bosnia and Herzegovina?

2   Which duo sang *On Top of the World* in 1973?

3   Who sang *Going Underground* and *That's Entertainment*?

4   In what foreign country would one most likely encounter Cobra beer?

5   What is the first name of TV's Sergeant Bilko, played by Phil Silvers?

6   Which is the holiest city of Islam?

7   What was the surname of Samuel, the inventor of a famous pistol?

8   In the 1963 film *The Pink Panther*, who played Inspector Clouseau?

9   Who was in the charts in 2017 with *Human*?

10 Which small rodent appears in *Alice's Adventures in Wonderland*?

11 What was the name of Ronnie Barker's character in the TV series *Open All Hours*?

12 On a standard typewriter keyboard, which letter is to the right of H?

13 Who played Ellie Miller in the TV series *Broadchurch*?

14 King Duncan is a character in which Shakespeare play?

15 Which herb has the French name *persil*?

16 Of which Scottish islands is Kirkwall the capital?

17 Which biblical character provided a song title for Tom Jones?

18 Which character was played by Catherine Zeta-Jones in the televised adaptation of HE Bates' novel, *The Darling Buds of May*?

19 Which game show has been presented by many people over the years, including Carol Smillie and Nicky Campbell?

20 What does one proverbially wear on one's sleeve, if making one's feelings apparent?

Easy

Medium

Hard

Answers to QUIZ 311 – Pot Luck

1	Bay City Rollers	11	Honey
2	Mark Owen	12	Mega
3	Super Bowl	13	*Way Down*
4	Jacob	14	Butterfly
5	Green	15	Tequila
6	Microbiology	16	Bid
7	Clint Eastwood	17	At home
8	Sixth	18	Nap
9	Trent Bridge	19	Thursday's
10	Acid	20	Rotterdam

Easy

1. In which city was playwright Alan Bennett born?

2. Who is responsible for scenery changes during a production?

3. In which long-running musical is Cosette a central character?

4. Which country presents the Tony Awards?

5. What name is given to the area of a theatre in which tickets are sold?

6. Which character in *The Importance of Being Earnest* utters the words "A handbag?"?

7. Dramatist Ray Cooney is associated with what type of play?

8. What is the name of the area in which musicians perform in a theatre?

9. Which London theatre has been the venue for a number of TV variety shows, hosted in 2016 by Bradley Walsh?

10. Peter Shaffer wrote a 1979 play about which composer?

11. Which backstage member of staff may be credited in the programme as "continuity"?

12. Hollywood's Dolby theatre, formerly the Kodak theatre, is the venue for which annual awards?

13. Playwright August Strindberg was born in which country?

Medium

14. Who wrote the 1949 play *Death of a Salesman*?

15. What term is given to the text of a play?

16. Which Andrew Lloyd Webber (Baron Lloyd-Webber) stage musical featured a cast on roller skates?

17. What is "rep" short for in a theatrical context?

18. In which London park is there a famous open-air theatre?

19. Which US dramatist's plays include *The Odd Couple* and *The Sunshine Boys*?

20. "If music be the food of love" is the opening line of which Shakespeare play?

Hard

Answers to QUIZ 312 – World Politics

1	Kaiser	11	Hirohito
2	François Hollande	12	Belgium
3	Dáil	13	Robert Mugabe
4	Mahatma Gandhi	14	(Otto von) Bismarck
5	Mao	15	Bill Clinton
6	Richard Nixon	16	Sri Lanka (as Ceylon)
7	Boris Yeltsin	17	Golda Meir
8	Tynwald	18	Senate
9	Ian Smith	19	Kremlin
10	Hong Kong	20	Pierre Trudeau

1 According to the proverb, in what is it difficult to find a needle?

2 What are the surnames of *Grease* characters Danny and Sandy?

3 What nationality was composer Sergei Rachmaninov?

4 Which item of sporting equipment, hit with a racket, has "feathers"?

5 Which element, with the atomic number 10, is a noble gas used in fluorescent lighting?

6 Which Spanish word means an afternoon snooze?

7 What is loam?

8 What was the title of the Matt Lucas and David Walliams comedy show set in an airport?

9 What is the syrupy blackcurrant liqueur from France called?

10 Which south-east Devon village on Lyme Bay shares its name with a drink?

11 The comedian Groucho Marx had what real first name?

12 Who co starred with Richard Briers in the TV series *The Good Life*?

13 *Genie in a Bottle* and *Beautiful* were hits for which singer?

14 What sport does Bubba Watson play?

15 Which Kent coastal town shares its name with a transaction?

16 What is the internet country code for Germany?

17 In football, which set piece may be direct or indirect?

18 Who played Hyacinth Bucket in the TV series *Keeping Up Appearances*?

19 In which country are the Preseli Hills?

20 Which actress played Rose Tyler in *Doctor Who*?

Easy

Medium

Hard

Answers to QUIZ 313 – Pot Luck

1	Sarajevo	11	Arkwright
2	Carpenters	12	J
3	The Jam	13	Olivia Colman
4	India	14	*Macbeth*
5	Ernie	15	Parsley
6	Mecca	16	Orkneys
7	Colt	17	Delilah
8	Peter Sellers	18	Mariette Larkin
9	Rag'n'bone Man	19	*Wheel of Fortune*
10	Dormouse	20	One's heart

Easy

1 What is the ancient and modern language of Judaism?

2 By native speakers, what is the most spoken language in the world?

3 What is the name of the most widely spoken constructed language?

4 The *Star Trek* series popularised what fictional language?

5 What types of languages exclusively use manual communication?

6 The fictional language Na'vi is spoken by the aliens in which sci-fi film?

7 "Aloha" means both "hello" and "goodbye" in which language?

8 How many official languages are there of the United Nations?

9 Which two languages provide most of the influence for modern English?

10 What is the study of language called?

11 Old English is also referred to as which language?

12 What is the most spoken language in Mozambique?

13 What is the most translated book?

14 In which small enclaved country can you use an ATM in Latin?

Medium

15 *Fresa*, *plátano* and *manzana* are fruits in which language?

16 What does "dog-and-bone" mean in Cockney rhyming slang?

17 In Scandinavian countries, which language was spoken in medieval times?

18 Which country has the most official languages with 11?

19 What do Americans call a bathroom tap?

20 What is the profession of someone who converts one language to another?

Hard

Answers to QUIZ 314 – Theatre

1	Leeds	11	The prompt
2	Stage manager	12	Oscars
3	*Les Misérables*	13	Sweden
4	USA	14	Arthur Miller
5	Box office	15	Script
6	Lady Bracknell	16	*Starlight Express*
7	Farce	17	Repertory
8	Orchestra pit	18	Regent's Park
9	London Palladium	19	Neil Simon
10	Mozart (*Amadeus*)	20	*Twelfth Night*

QUIZ 317 – Pot Luck

1   Azure is a shade of which colour?

2   Which river flows through Shrewsbury?

3   Clark Gable played which character in *Gone with the Wind* (1939)?

4   In which US state is the city of Palm Springs?

5   What kind of spoon is described in Lear's *The Owl and the Pussycat*?

6   What was the first name of media mogul Baron Grade whose son Michael was Chairman of the BBC from 2004 to 2006?

7   Lancashire's council is based in which city?

8   Which city in Nevada was associated with quick divorces?

9   Frankie Goes to Hollywood and Jennifer Rush both had hits in the 1980s with which song title?

10 In Tandoori dishes, what is a tandoor?

11 Which cookery-based reality TV show has been fronted by Gordon Ramsay and Marco Pierre White, amongst others?

12 What is the international car registration letter for France?

13 Who was Nicole Kidman's co-star in *Moulin Rouge!*?

14 Which island borough contains New York's central business district?

15 K2 is in which mountain range?

16 How is the Left Bank area of Paris known in the local language?

17 In Scotland, which two teams are known as the "Old Firm"?

18 Who had a 1981 UK hit with *This Ole House*?

19 In which year did ABBA reach the top of the charts with their Eurovision Song Contest winner *Waterloo*?

20 What name is given to a ten-sided shape?

Answers to QUIZ 315 – Pot Luck

1	Haystack	11	Julius
2	Zuko and Olsson	12	Felicity Kendal
3	Russian	13	Christina Aguilera
4	A shuttlecock	14	Golf
5	Neon	15	Deal
6	*Siesta*	16	.de
7	Soil mixture of clay and sand	17	Free kick
8	*Come Fly with Me*	18	Dame Patricia Routledge
9	Crème de cassis	19	Wales
10	Beer	20	Billie Piper

Easy

1 What is the name of the famous big-eared mascot of the Walt Disney Company?

2 As at 2018, which former boxer held the record of being the youngest heavyweight champion in history?

3 Which English actor played the lead role of Charlie Croker in the 1969 film *The Italian Job*?

4 Who is best known for playing the starring role of Dexter Morgan in the US TV series *Dexter*?

5 Which Canadian singer released a 2016 album entitled *Nobody but Me*?

6 As at 2018, which retired US athlete held the record for winning the most Olympic gold medals?

7 Who played the lead role in the 1993 film *Falling Down* and the 1989 film *Black Rain*?

8 Which Formula 1 racing driver won seven championship titles between 1994 and 2004?

9 The 2004 documentary film *Fahrenheit 9/11* was by which American film-maker?

10 Who provides the voice of the title character in the *Shrek* series of films?

11 Who portrayed the title role in the 2015 film *Macbeth*?

Medium

12 Which retired professional basketball player (b.1963) played 15 seasons in the NBA for the Chicago Bulls and the Washington Wizards?

13 In the 2008 film *Frost/Nixon*, who played Sir David Frost?

14 Which Irish-born English actor took over the role of Professor Dumbledore in the final six *Harry Potter* films?

15 The *Transformers* series of films are produced and directed by which American film-maker?

16 *How Am I Supposed to Live Without You* was a 1989 hit for which singer?

17 Who played the title role in the 1988 film *Beetlejuice* and Tim Burton's *Batman* series of films?

18 From 1980 to 1983, who was the leader of the Labour party?

19 What is the name of the American actor noted for playing the role of prison inmate John Coffey in the 1999 film *The Green Mile*?

20 Who is noted for playing Gary Windass in the TV series *Coronation Street*?

Hard

Answers to QUIZ 316 – Languages

1	Hebrew	11	Anglo-Saxon
2	Mandarin	12	Portuguese
3	Esperanto	13	The Bible
4	Klingon	14	Vatican City
5	Sign languages	15	Spanish
6	*Avatar*	16	Phone
7	Hawaiian	17	Norse
8	Six (Arabic, Chinese, English, French, Russian and Spanish)	18	South Africa
9	Latin and French	19	A faucet
10	Linguistics	20	Translator

1 In which sporting event do competitors have to swim, cycle and run?

2 Which US state is bordered by Arizona to the south and Colorado to the east?

3 Which English player was Footballer of the Year in 1986 and 1992?

4 In *Little Women* (1868), what was the name of the eldest sister?

5 Which forearm bone lies parallel to the radius?

6 In the title of a play by John Webster, where was the duchess from?

7 Which ex-Neighbours actor topped the charts in 1989 with *Too Many Broken Hearts* and *Sealed with a Kiss*?

8 What is the name of the Narnia lion?

9 Which 1990s comedy drama was set in Cicely, Alaska?

10 What kind of animal gave Chas & Dave a 1981 hit?

11 Lindisfarne is off the coast of which county?

12 Whose first UK hit single was *Run To You*?

13 Which group had a hit with *Karma Chameleon* in 1983?

14 What was the title of the 1990 film featuring Johnny Depp as a fantasy hairdresser?

15 Totton is in which English county?

16 Which classic 1945 film starred Trevor Howard and Dame Celia Johnson?

17 What was the title of the 1981-83 drama series in which Wendy Craig cared for children?

18 A stonechat is what type of creature?

19 Which 1990s TV sleuth was played by Dame Patricia Routledge?

20 Which band had a no.1 hit in 1981 with *Ghost Town*?

Answers to QUIZ 317 – Pot Luck

1	Blue	11	*Hell's Kitchen*
2	Severn	12	F
3	Rhett Butler	13	Ewan McGregor
4	California	14	Manhattan
5	Runcible	15	Himalayas
6	Lew	16	Rive Gauche
7	Preston	17	Celtic and Rangers (from Glasgow)
8	Reno	18	Shakin' Stevens
9	*The Power of Love*	19	1974
10	Type of oven	20	Decagon

Easy

1 What is the first name of fashion designer Gaultier?

2 The 2017 film *Valerian and the City of a Thousand Planets* starred which English model (b.1992)?

3 What nationality is model Gigi Hadid?

4 Which British model (b.1970) appears on the international TV show *The Face*?

5 Who wore the controversial meat dress to the 2010 MTV Video Music Awards?

6 What nickname is English model Lesley Lawson (née Hornby) more widely known by?

7 "We don't wake up for less than $10,000 a day" was famously said by which Canadian model?

8 In what decade was the miniskirt designed?

9 What is the name of the fashion company known as "D&G"?

10 What is the name of the shoe company known by its logo of a star within a circle?

11 Which fashion company is known by its back-to-back C's logo?

12 In which country was Gucci founded?

13 Which actress and model starred in the 1961 film *Breakfast at Tiffany's*?

14 The word "chic" originates from which language?

15 What is the three-letter brand name of the sheepskin footwear of Antipodean origin?

16 Which two colours were most associated with the 1960s Mod style?

17 What international fashion and lifestyle magazine first ran in the United States in 1892?

18 Formerly known as *Gentleman's Quarterly*, what is now the name of the international men's fashion and lifestyle magazine?

19 Which American model (b.1966) is a host on MTV's *House of Style*?

20 Which men's trousers, originally popular in the 1920s, were named after an English city?

Medium

Hard

Answers to QUIZ 318 – Michaels

1	Mickey Mouse	11	Michael Fassbender
2	Mike Tyson	12	Michael Jordan
3	Sir Michael Caine	13	Michael Sheen
4	Michael C Hall	14	Sir Michael Gambon
5	Michael Bublé	15	Michael Bay
6	Michael Phelps	16	Michael Bolton
7	Michael Douglas	17	Michael Keaton
8	Michael Schumacher	18	Michael Foot
9	Michael Moore	19	Michael Clarke Duncan
10	Mike Myers	20	Mikey North

1   Which structure in Jerusalem is traditionally where Jews lament and pray?

2   What was Humphry Repton (b.1752) famous for creating?

3   What was the first name of 1930s Hollywood star Ms Harlow?

4   Stockard Channing played Betty Rizzo in which musical film?

5   Which member of Genesis had a solo hit with *One More Night*?

6   What term is given to a word that reads the same forwards and backwards?

7   Which of the BBC's TV channels began broadcasting in 1964?

8   In the 1973 film *Live and Let Die*, who played James Bond?

9   Which piece of cane or metal is used to produce sound from clarinets and oboes?

10 What is the name of Dame Emma Thompson's actress sister?

11 *You Wear It Well* and *Sailing* were 1970s hits for which singer?

12 What is the principal town of Portugal's Algarve?

13 What colour is saffron?

14 Which girl's name provided Barry Manilow with his debut hit?

15 A hydrangea's colour depends on what quality of the soil?

16 Which colour is that of unbleached linen?

17 Which Turkish city was formerly called Constantinople?

18 Which energy-generating machines are found in nuclear power stations?

19 The chain of small islands off the coast of South Florida are given what name?

20 In which US city is Madison Avenue, the street associated with advertising?

Answers to QUIZ 319 – Pot Luck

1	Triathlon	11	Northumberland
2	Utah	12	Bryan Adams
3	Gary Lineker	13	Culture Club
4	Meg	14	*Edward Scissorhands*
5	Ulna	15	Hampshire
6	Malfi (*The Duchess of Malfi*)	16	*Brief Encounter*
7	Jason Donovan	17	*Nanny*
8	Aslan	18	A bird
9	*Northern Exposure*	19	Hetty Wainthropp
10	Rabbit	20	The Specials

Easy

1 Which pink or white flower, also known as the chalk plant or baby's breath, is a favourite with flower arrangers?

2 The pansy is a member of which genus that shares its name with a musical instrument?

3 Which flower can be tea or floribunda?

4 The name of which water lily is also a sitting position in yoga?

5 "No flowers bloom, No wedding Saturday within the month of June" is a lyric from which song?

6 What is the male fertilising organ of a flower called?

7 In which decade did the slogan "Flower Power" become popular?

8 Which flower is also known as the "windflower"?

9 In which Shakespeare play does a character say "A rose by any other name would smell as sweet"?

10 From which flower is the drug opium obtained?

11 Who was entreated to "Give me your answer do" in a popular song?

12 With which country is heather associated?

Medium

13 In what form are daffodils and crocuses planted?

14 Which chef has children named Poppy Honey and Petal Blossom?

15 Lily flowers can be particularly toxic to which type of animal?

16 In which area of London does the title character sell flowers in the musical *My Fair Lady*?

17 Which group recorded *Flowers in the Rain* in 1967?

18 Off which Edinburgh thoroughfare is there a famous floral clock?

19 What is the most common colour for the cornflower?

20 Which flower is associated with the month of March?

Hard

Answers to QUIZ 320 – Fashion

1	Jean-Paul	11	(Coco) Chanel
2	Cara Delevingne	12	Italy
3	American	13	Audrey Hepburn
4	Naomi Campbell	14	French
5	Lady Gaga	15	Ugg® boots
6	Twiggy	16	Black and white
7	Linda Evangelista	17	*Vogue*
8	1960s	18	GQ
9	Dolce & Gabbana	19	Cindy Crawford
10	Converse	20	Oxford bags

1 Who backed the American singer Martha Reeves?

2 What is a female swan called?

3 "Mars ain't the kind of place to raise your kids" is a lyric from which song?

4 The South American agouti is related to which domestic animal?

5 Which group had a 1986 hit with *Through the Barricades*?

6 What animal group has a shorthorn variety?

7 The alligator pear is also known by what name?

8 The 1857 novel *Barchester Towers* was written by which author?

9 What is the internet country code for Switzerland?

10 Who was Shakespeare's Prince of Denmark?

11 Which English city has the postcode SO?

12 Which band had a 1981 hit with *Girls on Film*?

13 Purl, cable and rib are terms associated with which craft?

14 Which National Trust landmark is situated at Marazion in Cornwall?

15 A Gloucester Old Spot is what type of animal?

16 What is the largest county in Ireland?

17 What is the first name of the actor who played Renton in the *Trainspotting* films?

18 Which disease, once associated with sailors, is caused by vitamin C deficiency?

19 Which singer had hits with *Thank You*, *White Flag*, and *Life For Rent*?

20 Cliff Clavin and Carla Tortelli were characters in which show?

Answers to QUIZ 321 – Pot Luck

1	Wailing Wall	11	Sir Rod Stewart
2	Landscape gardens	12	Faro
3	Jean	13	Yellow
4	*Grease*	14	Mandy
5	Phil Collins	15	Acidity
6	Palindrome	16	Ecru
7	BBC2 (now BBC Two)	17	Istanbul
8	Sir Roger Moore	18	Reactors
9	Reed	19	The Florida Keys
10	Sophie	20	New York

1   Which city was Gene Pitney "twenty-four hours from"?

2   Which group's hits include *The Last Time* and *Honky Tonk Woman*?

3   In 1986, which song from the TV series *Spitting Image* topped the charts?

4   Who was *(Sittin' On) The Dock of the Bay* in 1968?

5   Marshall Mathers is better known by what name?

6   Which US family group sang *Love Me for a Reason* in 1974?

7   The Miami Sound Machine was the backing group for which singer?

8   Which group had a hit in 1995 with *Roll with It*?

9   Which "illness"'provided hits for Peggy Lee in 1958 and Madonna in 1993?

10 The 2002 film *Maid in Manhattan* starred which pop singer?

11 Who led Dozy, Beaky, Mick and Tich in a 1960s pop group?

12 Named after an aircraft, what was the title of the first big hit for Orchestral Manoeuvres in the Dark?

13 Which reptile is mentioned in the title of a 1956 hit by Bill Haley and the Comets?

14 Who is the lead singer with the Human League?

15 *Grace Kelly* was a 2007 hit for which singer?

16 Who had a 2006 hit with *Put Your Records On*?

17 Who had a hit in 1985 with *Everytime You Go Away*?

18 "I'm bulletproof nothing to lose, Fire away, fire away" are lyrics from which song?

19 *I Cry When I Laugh* was the 2015 debut album from which singer?

20 Who topped the UK singles charts in 2017 with *Sign of the Times*?

Answers to QUIZ 322 – Flowers

1	Gypsophila	11	Daisy
2	*Viola*	12	Scotland
3	Rose	13	Bulbs
4	Lotus	14	Jamie Oliver
5	*I Just Called to Say I Love You* (Stevie Wonder)	15	Cats
6	Stamen	16	Covent Garden
7	1960s	17	The Move
8	Anemone	18	Princes Street
9	*Romeo and Juliet*	19	Blue
10	Poppy	20	Daffodil

QUIZ 325 – Pot Luck

ANSWERS ON PAGE 327

1 Which singer had a hit with *Achy Breaky Heart* in 1992?

2 The Roman numerals XXXVIII equate to which number?

3 Next to which room in a house would you find a scullery?

4 Which actor starred in *Closer* and *Gattaca*?

5 Who played Baldrick in the TV series *Blackadder*?

6 What are male antelopes called?

7 *Band on the Run* was a 1973 hit for which band?

8 Which prehistoric animal group included the velociraptor and the triceratops?

9 What is the first name of Canadian singer Ms Furtado?

10 Tony Hancock's television place of residence was the East part of which town?

11 Which city was the capital of West Germany before reunification?

12 Robert Burns described which creature as a "Wee, sleekit, cowrin, tim'rous beastie"?

13 Which cartoon cat is Tweety Pie's arch-foe?

14 The Tintin cartoons were created by which Belgian cartoonist?

15 Which of Dexys Midnight Runners' no.1 hits in the UK was the only one to also top the US charts?

16 Which organisation was founded for those with high IQ scores?

17 If a Scottish person is "havering", what are they doing?

18 Who was the Beatles' manager until his death in 1967?

19 The rook and the raven belong to which family of birds?

20 Which actor starred as Ray Kinsella in the 1989 film *Field of Dreams*?

Answers to QUIZ 323 – Pot Luck

1 The Vandellas
2 Pen
3 *Rocket Man* (Sir Elton John)
4 Guinea pig
5 Spandau Ballet
6 Cattle
7 Avocado
8 Anthony Trollope
9 .ch
10 Hamlet
11 Southampton
12 Duran Duran
13 Knitting
14 St Michael's Mount
15 Pig
16 Cork
17 Ewan (McGregor)
18 Scurvy
19 Dido
20 *Cheers*

Easy

1 In which event did Carl Lewis win four Olympic Golds - in Los Angeles, Seoul, Barcelona and Atlanta?

2 In which country was Sir Mo Farah born?

3 In what do triple jump competitors land?

4 What are the two main categories of athletics?

5 In what event did Sally Gunnell win a gold medal at the 1992 Olympics in Barcelona?

6 Which former athlete became an MP in 1992?

7 The heptathlon is made up of how many events?

8 How many Olympic gold medals did Usain Bolt win?

9 Who won gold medals at both the 5000 metre and 10,000 metre events in the 1972 Summer Olympics?

10 With which field event was Geoff Capes particularly associated?

11 What is the nationality of athlete Donovan Bailey?

12 Who famously collided with Zola Budd in the 3000 metres in the Olympic Games in 1984?

Medium

13 Which athlete, portrayed by Ian Charleson in the film *Chariots of Fire*, refused to run on a Sunday?

14 In which year did the women's pole vault become an Olympic sport?

15 The Great North Run begins in which city?

16 Which event has an Ironman version?

17 What is the name of the stick passed between competitors in a relay race?

18 Which English female runner won the London Marathon three times from 2002 to 2005?

19 In which event did Colin Jackson specialise?

20 Which former leader of the Liberal Democrats competed at the Tokyo Olympics and was UK 100m record holder from 1967 to 1974?

Hard

Answers to QUIZ 324 – Pop Music

1	Tulsa	11	Dave Dee
2	The Rolling Stones	12	*Enola Gay*
3	*The Chicken Song*	13	Alligator (*See You Later, Alligator*)
4	Otis Redding	14	Phil Oakey
5	Eminem	15	Mika
6	Osmonds	16	Corinne Bailey Rae
7	Gloria Estefan	17	Paul Young
8	Oasis	18	*Titanium* (David Guetta featuring Sia)
9	Fever	19	Jess Glynne
10	Jennifer Lopez	20	Harry Styles

1   What is the capital of Nebraska?

2   What was the name of George Cole's character in the original TV series of *Minder*?

3   Which small snake is supposed to have killed Cleopatra?

4   Who wrote the 1912 play *Pygmalion*?

5   What breed of animal is a Munchkin?

6   Which friar was one of Robin Hood's Merry Men?

7   *Whiskey in the Jar* was a hit for which group in 1973?

8   On which day of the week was Solomon Grundy married?

9   What is the French clear meat-based soup called?

10 Leipzig and Dortmund are cities in which country?

11 Which actress was married to Tom Cruise from 2006 to 2012?

12 In Greek mythology, which Gorgon was slain by Perseus?

13 What name is given to the first four New Testament books of the Bible?

14 Which particle is formed by gaining or losing electrons?

15 Indira Gandhi International Airport is in which city?

16 Which duo had a hit with *This Town Ain't Big Enough for Both of Us* in 1974?

17 Which playwright wrote the 1891 play *Hedda Gabler*?

18 In which board game do players solve the murder of Dr Black?

19 Which notorious Russian monk was murdered in Moscow in 1916?

20 How many items are there in a brace?

Answers to QUIZ 325 – Pot Luck

1	Billy Ray Cyrus	11	Bonn
2	38	12	A mouse
3	The kitchen	13	Sylvester
4	Jude Law	14	Hergé
5	Sir Tony Robinson	15	*Come On Eileen*
6	Bucks	16	Mensa
7	Wings	17	Chattering foolishly
8	Dinosaur	18	Brian Epstein
9	Nelly	19	Crows (Corvids)
10	Cheam	20	Kevin Costner

1   Who had a hit in 2000 with *Reach*?

2   "The Stars and Stripes" is a name for the flag of which country?

3   What is the correct name for a star on a keypad and keyboard?

4   Whom did Cat Deeley replace (not in specials) as host of *Stars in Their Eyes*?

5   "Starry, starry night" are the opening words to which Don McLean song?

6   Which band released the single *A Sky Full of Stars* in 2014?

7   Who wrote the 2012 novel *The Fault in Our Stars...*?

8   ...and who provided the theme tune *All of the Stars* for the 2014 film adapation?

9   In which decade was *Stars on 45* and its follow-up hits?

10 Who presented the TV series *Shooting Stars*?

11 Which film company claimed to have "More stars than there are in heaven"?

12 If you were seeing stars, from what would you be suffering?

13 Who had a 1978 hit with *Lucky Stars*?

14 Which 2016 film musical featured the song *City of Stars*?

15 What feature of a newspaper is often referred to as "the stars"?

16 What device is used to get a better look at the stars?

17 *Dancing with the Stars* is the US version of which UK series?

18 Who said "We are all in the gutter, but some of us are looking at the stars"?

19 The 2018 song *All the Stars* by Kendrick Lamar and SZA featured in which superhero film?

20 Which is better, a four-star or a five-star hotel?

Answers to QUIZ 326 – Athletics

1	Long jump	11	Canadian
2	Somalia	12	Mary Decker
3	Sandpit	13	Eric Liddell
4	Track and field	14	2000
5	400m hurdles	15	Newcastle-upon-Tyne
6	Sebastian Coe (Baron Coe)	16	Triathlon
7	Seven	17	Baton
8	Eight	18	Paula Radcliffe
9	Lasse Viren	19	110m hurdles
10	Shot put	20	Menzies (Ming) Campbell

Easy
Medium
Hard

1   *Waterloo Sunset* reached no.2 in the charts in 1967 for which band?

2   Which actress played the Dowager Countess of Grantham in *Downton Abbey*?

3   Which word means "fear" in German, but "deep anxiety" in English?

4   What is the international car registration symbol for Brazil?

5   Camargue is a variety of which type of food?

6   If you sailed due west from Land's End, which country would you arrive at first?

7   Which revamped schoolchildren's game show was hosted by Simon Mayo in 2012?

8   Who sang the 1979 song *Brass in Pocket*?

9   What does the first "A" of ACAS stand for?

10 Which TV presenter joined *TV-am* as Scotland Correspondent in 1984?

11 *Mad World* and *Everybody Wants to Rule the World* were hits for which duo in the 1980s?

12 Which European republic may be described as Hellenic?

13 Which knighted British actor was born Maurice Micklewhite?

14 What species of camel has two humps?

15 In which town was Ricky Gervais' sitcom *The Office* set?

16 "I believe in angels, Something good in everything I see" is a lyric from which song?

17 Which city is the setting for the TV series *Hollyoaks*?

18 From which southern Rio neighbourhood was the girl in the Astrud Gilberto hit?

19 Diana Ross originally sang with which group?

20 What is the capital of Afghanistan?

Answers to QUIZ 327 – Pot Luck

1	Lincoln	11	Katie Holmes
2	Arthur Daley	12	Medusa
3	Asp	13	Gospels
4	George Bernard Shaw	14	Ion
5	A cat	15	Delhi
6	Friar Tuck	16	Sparks
7	Thin Lizzy	17	(Henrik) Ibsen
8	Wednesday	18	Cluedo®
9	Consommé	19	Rasputin
10	Germany	20	Two

Easy

1   In which 1988 comedy film did Tom Hanks star as a child trapped in an adult's body?

2   The phrase "Show me the money" featured in which 1996 Tom Cruise film?

3   What profession did Tom Hanks' character follow in the 1993 film *Philadelphia*?

4   Lestat, played by Tom Cruise in a 1994 film, was what type of supernatural creature?

5   Who played Tom Hanks' crime-fighting partner in the 1987 film *Dragnet*?

6   The 1993 Tom Cruise film *The Firm* was based on a novel by which author?

7   Which was the title of the second film starring Tom Hanks that was adapted from a Dan Brown novel?

8   Tom Cruise plays which character in the *Mission: Impossible* films?

9   What type of animal was Hooch in the 1989 film *Turner & Hooch*?

10 In which 2008 film did Tom Cruise play a German wartime officer?

11 Tom Hanks was on which "Road" in the title of a 2002 film?

12 What was Tom Cruise's call sign in the 1986 film *Top Gun*?

13 What was the name of the mermaid that Tom Hanks' character befriended in the 1984 film *Splash*?

Medium

14 The 1990 Tom Cruise film *Days of Thunder* featured which pursuit?

15 Which real-life person did Tom Hanks portray in the 2013 film *Saving Mr Banks*?

16 In which 1988 film did Tom Cruise play a bartender?

17 Which 1992 film features Tom Hanks as the manager of a baseball team?

18 Which day appears in the title of a 1989 film starring Tom Cruise as a war veteran?

19 Tom Hanks played which real-life person who was captured by pirates in a 2013 film?

20 In which 2005 film was Tom Cruise under attack by Martians?

Hard

Answers to QUIZ 328 – Stars

1	S Club 7	11	MGM
2	USA	12	Dizziness
3	Asterisk	13	Dean Friedman
4	Matthew Kelly	14	*La La Land*
5	*Vincent*	15	Horoscopes
6	Coldplay	16	Telescope
7	John Green	17	*Strictly Come Dancing*
8	Ed Sheeran	18	Oscar Wilde
9	1980s	19	*Black Panther*
10	Vic Reeves and Bob Mortimer	20	Five-star

1 The festive favourite *I Wish It Could Be Christmas Everyday* was a hit for which glam rock band?

2 What term is given to a solid figure with ten faces?

3 Leaves of which plant are traditionally used to relieve nettle stings?

4 Which word meaning "a snare" means "a piece" when read backwards?

5 *Every Little Thing She Does is Magic* was a 1981 hit for which group?

6 On which front was it *All Quiet* in the title of a 1930 film?

7 Who was Britain's first female radio disc jockey?

8 Whose second solo album, released in 1983, was *Hello I Must Be Going*?

9 Which is the largest of the Shetland Islands?

10 Coins are thrown into which Rome landmark, traditionally to guarantee one's return to the city?

11 In which Cairo suburb are the Pyramids located?

12 Which limb is affected by carpal tunnel syndrome?

13 What was a mangle used for?

14 Which thoroughfare in London is associated with the medical profession?

15 What is the surname of the hero of *The Thirty-Nine Steps*?

16 On a Monopoly™ board, what colour is the Old Kent Road?

17 Which fruit are used in a traditional Black Forest gateau?

18 The Bull represents which sign of the zodiac?

19 Which former Liverpool FC player was appointed manager of Glasgow Rangers in May 2018?

20 What is the name of the code used to access a cash machine?

Answers to QUIZ 329 – Pot Luck

1	The Kinks	11	Tears for Fears
2	Dame Maggie Smith	12	Greece
3	Angst	13	Sir Michael Caine
4	BR	14	Bactrian
5	Rice	15	Slough
6	Canada	16	*I Have a Dream* (ABBA)
7	*Blockbusters*	17	Chester
8	The Pretenders	18	Ipanema
9	Arbitration	19	The Supremes
10	Lorraine Kelly	20	Kabul

Easy

1   What is the capital of Cyprus?

2   In which county is the stately home of Hatfield House?

3   Mexico shares a border with how many US states?

4   In which country is the city of Volgograd?

5   The Brazilian flag has what background colour?

6   What is the Spanish word for a public square?

7   Which town in the Netherlands gives its name to blue and white earthenware?

8   In which county is Torquay?

9   On which north-east river does Middlesbrough stand?

10   In which US state did the Mormons settle?

11   Which county lies between Northamptonshire and Nottinghamshire?

12   The Australian state of Queensland was named after which queen?

13   Which Nebraskan city gave its name to one of the D-Day beaches?

14   The Welsh "Beacons" are near which historic market town?

Medium

15   What nationality is a native of Zagreb?

16   What is the currency unit of India?

17   Which island lies off the west coast of Malta?

18   Lausanne is located on which body of water on the Swiss-French border?

19   Which famous Australian beach is named after an Aboriginal weapon?

20   In which US state is the city of Seattle?

Hard

Answers to QUIZ 330 – Tom Tom

1	Big	11	Road to Perdition
2	Jerry Maguire	12	Maverick
3	Lawyer	13	Madison
4	Vampire	14	Stock car racing
5	Dan Aykroyd	15	Walt Disney
6	John Grisham	16	Cocktail
7	Angels & Demons	17	A League of Their Own
8	Ethan Hunt	18	Born on the Fourth of July
9	A dog	19	Captain Phillips
10	Valkyrie	20	War of the Worlds

1   What word meaning "genial" can also refer to a diluted fruit drink?

2   What name meaning "crown of the valley" is shared by cities in California and Texas?

3   Which English city has the postcode NR?

4   *Sweet Little Mystery* and *Sweet Surrender* were hits for which group in the 1980s?

5   An object described as "ovoid" has what shape?

6   How many metres are there in four kilometres?

7   In the TV series *Only Fools and Horses*, what was the name of Nicholas Lyndhurst's character?

8   What collective name was given to the nine goddesses of the arts in Greek mythology?

9   The Australian soap *Neighbours* is set in which fictional street?

10 Which opera is subtitled *The Lass that Loved a Sailor*?

11 Who played the title role in the TV series *McCloud*?

12 If a creature is described as "diurnal", when is it active?

13 Which New York borough lies north-east of Manhattan?

14 Which bird of the crow family is traditionally described as "thieving"?

15 Which organ of the body produces insulin?

16 Singers Kelly Clarkson and Jordin Sparks were discovered on which TV talent show?

17 How many sides does a pentagon have?

18 Who directed the 2012 film *Life of Pi*?

19 What is the collective term for a group of elephants?

20 Which Italian author wrote the 14th-century work *The Divine Comedy*?

Easy

Medium

Hard

Answers to QUIZ 331 – Pot Luck

1	Wizzard	11	Giza
2	Decahedron	12	Wrist and lower arm
3	Dock	13	Wringing clothes dry
4	Trap	14	Harley Street
5	The Police	15	(Richard) Hannay
6	The Western Front	16	Brown
7	Annie Nightingale	17	Cherries
8	Phil Collins	18	Taurus
9	Mainland	19	Steven Gerrard
10	Trevi Fountain	20	PIN

1 Who plays Demelza in the revived version of Poldark?

2 What were the names of the two cartoon mice who tormented Mr Jinks?

3 Which teen idol starred in the 1970s series *The Partridge Family*?

4 Which children's character has the catchphrase "Can we fix it?"?

5 The fictional London area of Walford is the setting for which long-running drama?

6 Which comedian is known for his *Good News*?

7 Who played Inspector Jack Frost on TV?

8 What nationality is actor Nikolaj Coster-Waldau?

9 Bryan Cranston and Aaron Paul played the lead roles in which American crime drama?

10 Which 1990s sitcom was set in the offices of GlobeLink News?

11 In the TV series *Mary, Mungo and Midge*, what type of creature was Midge?

12 What was the nickname of Roger Lloyd Pack's character in *Only Fools and Horses*?

13 Who played Uther Pendragon in the 2008 TV series *Merlin*?

14 *Tricks of the Mind* and *Confessions of a Conjuror* are books by which TV illusionist?

15 Which detective has been played on TV by both John Hannah and Ken Stott?

16 In which city was the police series *Taggart* set?

17 For what is Huw Edwards best known?

18 Evan Davis is the long-running presenter of which programme involving investors?

19 *The Durrells* stars which actress as Louisa?

20 Anne Robinson, Nicky Campbell and Matt Allwright have all been presenters on which consumer affairs programme?

Easy

Medium

Hard

Answers to QUIZ 332 – Geography

1	Nicosia	11	Leicestershire
2	Hertfordshire	12	Queen Victoria
3	Four (California, Arizona, New Mexico and Texas)	13	Omaha
4	Russia	14	Brecon
5	Green	15	Croat
6	Plaza	16	Rupee
7	Delft	17	Gozo
8	Devon	18	Lake Geneva
9	Tees	19	Bondi
10	Utah	20	Washington

1 What legal phrase means "done as a favour"?

2 In which country was the composer Grieg born?

3 Which group had a hit with *Le Freak* in 1978?

4 Which two words that sound the same but are spelt differently mean "to position" and "a fish"?

5 What was the name of the chief engineer in the original *Star Trek* series?

6 Madonna's *Into the Groove* featured in which 1985 film?

7 In which US city is Ghirardelli Square?

8 During which war did the Battle of Britain take place?

9 What word means "relating to the New Stone Age"?

10 Which musical instrument's name derives from the words "soft" and "loud"?

11 What is the internet country code for Portugal?

12 Which word can describe both a drinks container and an acrobat?

13 Which London financial institution is famous for its "Names"?

14 What is the first name of French actress Ms Tautou (b.1976)?

15 In equestrian terms, how many inches are measured by one hand?

16 What title was given to the heir to the French throne?

17 Which trio had their only UK chart-topper in 1974 with *When Will I See You Again*?

18 Which TV sitcom was set in a café in the French village of Nouvion?

19 In the cartoon *Tom and Jerry*, what type of creature is Jerry?

20 What is the royal house to which Queen Anne belonged?

Easy

Medium

Hard

Easy

1 Heather Small is the lead singer with which group?

2 In what sport do children compete in the Little League in the USA?

3 Petyr "Littlefinger" Baelish is a character from which TV series?

4 What is the smallest coin in the USA?

5 What name is given to small cubes of fried bread served with soup?

6 "It's a God-awful small affair" is the opening line from which song?

7 Who played James Herriot in the TV series *All Creatures Great and Small*?

8 The Swiss Guard is employed in which tiny state?

9 Which Charles Dickens story features the character Tiny Tim?

10 How is the constellation Ursa Minor better known?

11 Which legendary outlaw was a friend of Little John?

12 The Mini has been manufactured by which company since 2000?

13 Which of the Osmond brothers was known as "Little"?

14 What name is given to the longest part of the alimentary canal?

Medium

15 The "small screen" is another name for which household item?

16 Which group had hits in the 1960s with *Itchycoo Park* and *All or Nothing*?

17 London's Little Venice is close to which mainline train station?

18 *Shout Out to My Ex* was a 2016 UK chart-topper for which band?

19 What was the land of little people in Swift's *Gulliver's Travels*?

20 What type of creature was Stuart Little in the 1999 film?

Hard

Answers to QUIZ 334 – Television

1	Eleanor Tomlinson	11	Mouse
2	Pixie and Dixie	12	Trigger
3	David Cassidy	13	Anthony Head
4	Bob the Builder	14	Derren Brown
5	*EastEnders*	15	Rebus
6	Russell Howard	16	Glasgow
7	Sir David Jason	17	Reading the news
8	Danish	18	*Dragons' Den*
9	*Breaking Bad*	19	Keeley Hawes
10	*Drop the Dead Donkey*	20	*Watchdog*

Easy

1   The composer Chopin was what nationality?

2   Which two words that sound the same but are spelt differently mean "animal flesh" and "to encounter"?

3   What is the nationality of a native of Casablanca?

4   In which current-day National Park was the novel *Lorna Doone* set?

5   Who was the 40th US president?

6   Which series of films, based on a classic trilogy, starred Elijah Wood?

7   In a glacier, what name is given to a deep open split?

8   Which actress starred in the 1956 film *Bus Stop*?

9   What word can mean "concise" and "abrupt to the point of rudeness"?

10   What is the sacred river in Coleridge's poem *Kubla Khan*?

11   What name is given to the leaf of a fern?

12   Who had three top ten hits singing with Queen, Bing Crosby and Mick Jagger?

13   The liqueur Tia Maria® has what flavour?

14   Of which 1960s and 1970s group was Sheila Ferguson a member?

15   Which green plant is traditionally associated with St Patrick's Day?

16   A chalkhill blue is what type of creature?

17   What is the Latin word for "water"?

18   *Three Times a Lady* was a hit for which group in 1978?

19   Who wrote the 1968 novel *Airport*?

20   Which fish of the genus *Cyprinus* includes koi and silver varieties?

Medium

Hard

Answers to QUIZ 335 – Pot Luck

1	*Ex gratia*	11	.pt
2	Norway	12	Tumbler
3	Chic	13	Lloyd's of London
4	Place and plaice	14	Audrey
5	Scotty	15	Four inches
6	*Desperately Seeking Susan*	16	Dauphin
7	San Francisco	17	Three Degrees
8	WWII	18	'Allo 'Allo!
9	Neolithic	19	A mouse
10	Pianoforte	20	Stuart

Easy

1   Which weeding implement has a long handle?

2   What general name is given to the group of plants that grow high up on mountains?

3   *Ericaceous* plants are most suited to what type of soil?

4   What term is given to the glass or clear plastic cover put over young plants to protect them from the cold?

5   What is a trug used for?

6   The layer of earth nearest the surface in a garden is given what name?

7   Scarifying does what to soil?

8   What term is given to the act of removing old flowers from a plant?

9   For what are secateurs used?

10 What was the name of the garden makeover series that originally featured Alan Titchmarsh, Charlie Dimmock and Tommy Walsh?

Medium

11 What term is given to the process of growing more plants from an original?

12 In which decade was *Gardeners' World* first broadcast on the BBC?

13 For what is a riddle used?

14 What implement with a long curved blade is traditionally used for cutting grass?

15 Which annual national gardening competition began in 1963 and is now run by the RHS?

16 What name is given to the process of leaving garden waste to decay for future use on the garden?

17 What name is given to the perforated end of a watering can?

18 The *Big Dreams, Small Spaces* makeover show is presented by which TV gardener?

19 The practice of gardening in such as way as not to deplete the earth's natural resources is given what name?

20 What name is given to a fuchsia that is on a long stem?

Hard

Answers to QUIZ 336 – Little Things

1	M People	11	Robin Hood
2	Baseball	12	BMW
3	*Game of Thrones*	13	Jimmy Osmond
4	Cent	14	Small intestine
5	Croutons	15	Television
6	*Life on Mars?* (David Bowie)	16	The Small Faces
7	Christopher Timothy	17	Paddington
8	Vatican City	18	Little Mix
9	*A Christmas Carol*	19	Lilliput
10	Little Bear	20	A mouse

1   What is a firethorn?

2   What is the nickname of Batman's assistant Robin?

3   Which actress played Strawberry Fields in *Quantum of Solace*?

4   The title of which musical, based on the music of Borodin, means "destiny"?

5   Which forest features in Shakespeare's *As You Like It*?

6   The Sherlock Holmes novel *The Hound of the Baskervilles* is set in which part of Devon?

7   Which word meaning "at this moment" means "came first" when read backwards?

8   On the Crusaders' 1979 hit *Street Life*, who sang lead vocals?

9   What initials provided the late-night spin-off from the 1980s children's TV series *Tiswas*?

10 What type of creature is a blenny?

11 A bunion affects which part of the body?

12 Which group had a hit with *Automatic* in 1984?

13 What was the name of Helen Mirren's character in the TV series *Prime Suspect*?

14 Which 1980s police show starred Don Johnson as Crockett?

15 What is an amphora?

16 What is the word for a political party's statement of intent?

17 The country of Bangladesh lies in which continent?

18 What type of creature is a redstart?

19 Who painted *Rain, Steam and Speed - The Great Western Railway*?

20 What were the former divisions of Yorkshire called?

Easy

Medium

Hard

Answers to QUIZ 337 – Pot Luck

1	Polish	11	A frond
2	Meat and meet	12	David Bowie
3	Moroccan	13	Coffee
4	Exmoor	14	The Three Degrees
5	Ronald Reagan	15	Shamrock
6	*The Lord of the Rings*	16	Butterfly
7	Crevasse	17	*Aqua*
8	Marilyn Monroe	18	Commodores
9	Short	19	Arthur Halley
10	Alph	20	Carp

Easy

1 Which butterfly, with "eyes" on its wings, shares its name with a long-tailed bird?

2 If a bee has a Latin name beginning *Bombus*, to what family does it belong?

3 A Silver Y is what type of insect?

4 What common term for an insect also describes a computer error?

5 A leatherjacket is the larva of which insect?

6 What is the UK's largest wasp?

7 What family of butterflies share their name with a ship's captain?

8 A common darter is what type of insect?

9 Which large ladybird shares its name with a character usually dressed in a diamond-patterned costume?

10 Which insect is associated with biblical plagues?

11 What is the more common name for the aphid?

12 Which moth, seen in the UK, has a name that features two birds?

13 The Mexican song *La Cucaracha* is about which insect?

14 Which small biting insect is particularly associated with the west coast of Scotland?

Medium

15 A very thin person may be compared to which creature?

16 Which insects are the main food of the echidna?

17 How many legs does an insect have?

18 What are an insect's antennae better known as?

19 Which insect is associated with a popular "drive", where players aim to be the first to complete a cartoon drawing of it?

20 What name is given to the study of insects?

Hard

Answers to QUIZ 338 – Gardening

1	Hoe	11	Propagating
2	Alpines	12	1960s
3	Acidic	13	Sifting soil
4	Cloche	14	Scythe
5	Carrying flowers and produce (tray)	15	Britain in Bloom
6	Topsoil	16	Composting
7	Breaks it up	17	Rose
8	Deadheading	18	Monty Don
9	Pruning	19	Permaculture
10	*Ground Force*	20	Standard

1 What is the capital of Poland?

2 In *One Foot in the Grave*, who played Victor Meldrew?

3 What is cockney rhyming slang for "stairs"?

4 Which songbird was mentioned in the title of the long-running radio sitcom about the Royal Navy?

5 What is the device producing a fine spray for inhaling a medicinal drug called?

6 The drink perry is made from which fruit?

7 What word can refer both to a piece of foliage and part of a book?

8 In which section of the orchestra would you find a xylophone?

9 What type of creature is the misnamed slow-worm?

10 Which Italian smoked raw meat is also known as prosciutto?

11 Food prepared according to Jewish law is described by which word?

12 The town of Ilminster is in which English county?

13 Which guitarist covered Bob Dylan's *All Along the Watchtower* in 1968?

14 Who discovered penicillin in 1928?

15 *So Long, Farewell* is a song from which film and show?

16 He is the chemical symbol for which element?

17 *Young Guns (Go for It)* was a 1982 hit for which duo?

18 What is the main ingredient of the Indian dish dhal?

19 How many red balls are on the table at the start of a game of snooker?

20 What is the capital of South Korea?

Easy

Medium

Hard

Answers to QUIZ 339 – Pot Luck

1	A shrub	11	Toe
2	Boy Wonder	12	Pointer Sisters
3	Gemma Arterton	13	Jane Tennison
4	*Kismet*	14	*Miami Vice*
5	The Forest of Arden	15	A jar
6	Dartmoor	16	Manifesto
7	Now	17	Asia
8	Randy Crawford	18	A bird
9	OTT (Over the Top)	19	JMW Turner
10	Fish	20	Ridings

1 Who received the Ten Commandments?

2 Which version of the Bible is named after a British monarch?

3 In the New Testament story, what was turned into wine?

4 Who was the second son of Noah?

5 Which organisation, that offers a listening ear, takes its name from a helpful person in a New Testament parable?

6 According to the book of Matthew, what should you not cast before swine?

7 Which organisation is responsible for placing Bibles in hotel rooms?

8 In the New Testament gospels, how many were present at the Last Supper?

9 Which is the last book in the New Testament?

10 Which king ordered the Massacre of the Innocents?

11 In the New Testament Gospels, how many people were fed with five loaves and two fish?

12 In which country is there an area known as "the Bible belt"?

13 Which book of the Old Testament shares its name with a collection of wise sayings?

14 What term is given to a subdivision of a chapter in the Bible?

15 "The Lord is my shepherd, I shall not want" is the first line of which Psalm?

16 In the New Testament Gospels, in which river was Jesus baptised?

17 Which biblical tower was the scene of noise and confused languages?

18 What is the first book of the Old Testament?

19 Who was the wife of Abraham?

20 What term is given to the reading of a text from the Bible in church?

Answers to QUIZ 340 – Insects

1	Peacock	11	Greenfly
2	Bumble bees	12	Hummingbird hawk-moth
3	Moth	13	Cockroach
4	Bug	14	Midge
5	Daddy-long-legs (Crane fly)	15	Stick insect
6	Hornet	16	Ants and termites
7	Skipper	17	Six
8	Dragonfly	18	Feelers
9	Harlequin	19	Beetle
10	Locust	20	Entomology

1   On a map, which lines connect points of equal temperature?

2   What was the first name of George Gershwin's lyricist brother?

3   What is the radio code word that alphabetically follows Yankee?

4   Which Mexican state gives its name to a red peppery sauce?

5   In Shakespeare's *Twelfth Night*, what is the surname of Sir Toby?

6   If a creature is described as "piscivorous", on what does it feed?

7   Who replaced Len Goodman as *Strictly Come Dancing*'s head judge?

8   Which family troupe starred in the films *A Night at the Opera* and *A Day at the Races*?

9   What creature lends its name to farfalle pasta?

10 In which county is the town of Weybridge?

11 Which orange-seller became the mistress of King Charles II?

12 *Down Under* was a hit for which group in 1983?

13 Which musical term applies to a note half a tone higher than standard?

14 In 1982, which group's first hit was *Do You Really Want to Hurt Me?*

15 Which word can describe both a small glass toy and a type of stone?

16 What letter is horizontally next to "A" on a standard computer keyboard?

17 *Stand and Deliver* was a hit for which group in 1981?

18 What is the world's largest rodent?

19 The Sale Sharks play which sport?

20 Yul Brynner and Deborah Kerr starred in the 1956 film of which musical?

Answers to QUIZ 341 – Pot Luck

1	Warsaw	11	Kosher
2	Richard Wilson	12	Somerset
3	Apples and pears	13	Jimi Hendrix
4	Lark (*The Navy Lark*)	14	Sir Alexander Fleming
5	Nebuliser	15	*The Sound of Music*
6	Pears	16	Helium
7	Leaf	17	Wham!
8	Percussion	18	Lentils
9	Lizard	19	15
10	Parma ham	20	Seoul

1 Which astronaut wrote the 2016 book *Hello, is this Planet Earth?*

2 Which planet is eighth in distance from the Sun?

3 The brightest star in a constellation is designated by which Greek letter?

4 On which space mission did astronauts first set foot on the Moon...?

5 ...and what was the name of the rocket module, famously quoted as having landed?

6 Which "ology" is the study of the origin and nature of the universe?

7 The tagline "In space no-one can hear you scream" advertised which 1979 film?

8 What term is given to an artificial object launched into space orbit, for example, to provide communications?

9 In 1961, who became the first man in space?

10 Which planet is most famous for its rings?

11 Who was the commander of the Apollo 13 mission, played by Tom Hanks in the 1995 film?

12 NASA launched the InSight probe in 2018 to gather data about which planet?

13 What name is given to a building with a large telescope which is used for star-gazing?

14 Which word meaning "small" can be applied to stars, often also described with a colour?

15 Often given airplay in December, who sang the original version of *A Spaceman Came Travelling?*

16 In which century was the astronomer Copernicus born?

17 A large piece of rock or metal that has landed from space is given what name?

18 Who was the second man to walk on the moon?

19 What word is given to the path of an object travelling round a planet?

20 Which former commander of the ISS presented the BBC TV series *Astronauts: Do You Have What it Takes?*

Easy

Medium

Hard

Answers to QUIZ 342 – The Bible

1	Moses	11	5,000
2	King James Version	12	USA
3	Water	13	Proverbs
4	Ham	14	Verse
5	The Samaritans	15	23
6	Pearls	16	Jordan
7	Gideons	17	Babel
8	13	18	Genesis
9	Revelation	19	Sarah
10	Herod	20	Lesson

1   What is the name of the South Wales peninsula near Swansea?

2   Which is the most southerly state of the USA mainland?

3   Which strait of water runs through Istanbul?

4   "See the stone set in your eyes, See the thorn twist in your side" is a lyric from which song?

5   Who played Smithy in the TV series *Gavin & Stacey*?

6   What sport is played by the Chicago White Sox?

7   Which sculptor (b.1840) created the work *The Thinker*?

8   *Music*, released in 2000, was a hit album for which singer?

9   Tony Hadley and Martin Kemp were members of which New Romantic group?

10   Who composed *The Marriage of Figaro* (1786)?

11   What is Camp Coffee® flavoured with?

12   What is the instrument like a high-pitched flute, much used in military bands called?

13   In which county is Bishop's Stortford?

14   Who wrote *Moll Flanders* (1722)?

15   What was the code name for the Allied operation of which D-Day was the first phase?

16   What type of creature is a minke?

17   On which biblical character, noted for her dancing, did Oscar Wilde base a play in 1891?

18   Which word meaning "to boast" means "clothing" when read backwards?

19   What is the book of God's law in Judaism?

20   Which number is between 16 and 19 on a dartboard?

Answers to QUIZ 343 – Pot Luck

1	Isotherms	11	Nell Gwyn
2	Ira	12	Men at Work
3	Zulu	13	Sharp
4	Tabasco	14	Culture Club
5	Belch	15	Marble
6	Fish	16	S
7	Shirley Ballas	17	Adam and the Ants
8	Marx Brothers	18	Capybara
9	Butterfly	19	Rugby Union
10	Surrey	20	*The King and I*

Easy

Medium

Hard

1 What general term is given to cycle competitions that take place outdoors?

2 Which retired English superbike racer (b.1965) is nicknamed "Foggy"?

3 Christian Horner became principal of which team in January 2005?

4 What type of cars are used in Formula E racing?

5 From which famous royal palace did the time trial cycle races start and finish at the 2012 London Olympics?

6 Which cycle race awards the "King of the Mountains" title?

7 Which Spanish rider won the MotoGP World Championship four times between 2013 and 2017...?

8 ...and which other Spanish rider won the title three times between 2010 and 2015?

9 In which country is the Nürburgring circuit?

10 Which British driver won the Formula 1 World Championship in 1996?

11 What is "cc" an abbreviation for in reference to an engine?

12 How many Olympic gold medals did cyclist Sir Chris Hoy win?

13 In which county is the circuit of Thruxton?

14 Jason Plato and Matt Neal are previous British champions in which motorsport?

15 What does a black flag indicate in Formula 1 racing?

16 For what is BMX an abbreviation in relation to cycle competitions?

17 Which form of road racing involves driving between a number of stages?

18 In which country does the Indianapolis 500 take place?

19 Which Surrey hill was the highest point of the cycle route at the 2012 London Olympics?

20 Which Australian actor played James Hunt in the 2013 film *Rush*?

Answers to QUIZ 344 – Space

1	Tim Peake	11	Jim Lovell
2	Neptune	12	Mars
3	Alpha	13	Observatory
4	Apollo 11	14	Dwarf
5	*Eagle*	15	Chris de Burgh
6	Cosmology	16	15th century (1473)
7	*Alien*	17	Meteorite
8	Satellite	18	Buzz Aldrin
9	Yuri Gagarin	19	Orbit
10	Saturn	20	Chris Hadfield

ANSWERS ON PAGE **349**

1 In which county is the open-air Minack Theatre?

2 What is the word for a letter that is not a vowel?

3 Which musical direction means "softly"?

4 Zippy, George and Bungle featured in which children's TV series?

5 *Message in a Bottle* was which group's first UK no.1 hit in 1979?

6 What is the capital city of the Republic of Ireland?

7 Who owned Winnie-the-Pooh?

8 Which is the word for the loose rocks found on the side of a mountain?

9 *Because of You* and *Behind These Hazel Eyes* were hits for which US singer?

10 What term is given to a female elephant?

11 What colour fur does the mountain hare have in winter?

12 Boston is the capital of which US state?

13 Which instrument was used in a musical "duel" in the 1972 film *Deliverance*?

14 In which sport might you use a sabre or épée?

15 What is the name of the Dr Seuss character who "hears a Who"?

16 Which "Great" river flows into the Wash?

17 A gatekeeper is what type of insect?

18 What is the legal term for reported, rather than directly gathered, information?

19 Which group had hits with *Run* and *Chasing Cars*?

20 The Tour de Yorkshire features competitors in which sport?

Easy

Medium

Hard

Answers to QUIZ 345 – Pot Luck

1	Gower	11	Chicory
2	Florida	12	Fife
3	Bosporus	13	Hertfordshire
4	*With or Without You* (U2)	14	Daniel Defoe
5	James Corden	15	Overlord
6	Baseball	16	Whale
7	Auguste Rodin	17	Salome
8	Madonna	18	Brag
9	Spandau Ballet	19	The Torah
10	Mozart	20	Seven

Easy

1 Which musical, filmed in 1955 with Frank Sinatra and Marlon Brando, is based on stories by Damon Runyon?

2 Which song from the musical *Chess* was a hit for Elaine Paige and Barbara Dickson in 1985?

3 Which 1939 musical film features the Wicked Witch of the West?

4 *Hopelessly Devoted to You* is a song from which musical?

5 Which sport features in the 1958 film *Damn Yankees*?

6 Who played the title role in the 1980 remake of *The Jazz Singer*?

7 Ren McCormack and Ariel, daughter of a local church minister, are the central characters in which 1984 film?

8 Who starred in the 1972 film *Cabaret*?

9 Which 1975 musical featured the character of scientist Dr Frank N Furter?

10 In which 1971 film did Topol play the central character Tevye?

11 Which singer provided the voice of the plant in the 1986 film *Little Shop of Horrors*?

12 In the 2012 film *Les Misérables*, who played Fantine?

Medium

13 What was the name of Richard Gere's character in the 2002 film *Chicago*?

14 Who danced in bad weather in the 1952 film *Singin' in the Rain...*?

15 ...and which comedy duo performed a parody of it in their 1976 Christmas show?

16 Which 1983 film featured a welder who had aspirations to be a dancer?

17 *Defying Gravity* is a song from which 2003 musical?

18 Which 1961 film starring Natalie Wood and Richard Beymer was based on *Romeo and Juliet*?

19 The character of Jud Fry appears in which 1955 musical?

20 Which 1968 Broadway musical included the song *Aquarius*?

Hard

Answers to QUIZ 346 – Sport on Wheels

1	Road races	11	Cubic centimetres
2	Carl Fogarty	12	Six
3	Red Bull	13	Hampshire
4	Electric	14	Touring Cars
5	Hampton Court Palace	15	Unsafe behaviour
6	Tour de France	16	Bicycle motocross
7	Marc Márquez	17	Rallying
8	Jorge Lorenzo	18	USA
9	Germany	19	Box Hill
10	Damon Hill	20	Chris Hemsworth

1   Which member of the Addams Family is a disembodied hand?

2   In a bulb of garlic, what is an individual section called?

3   Which famous racing-car make is named after five Italian brothers?

4   Which 1980 comedy film starred Dan Aykroyd and John Belushi?

5   The Tooting Popular Front featured in which TV series?

6   What language of Belgium is almost identical to Dutch?

7   On which river is Baghdad located?

8   In which county is the town of Petersfield?

9   What type of amphibian has palmate and smooth species?

10 Which two words that sound the same but are spelt differently mean "an entrance room" and "to drag"?

11 The second and fourth of Henry VIII's six wives shared what name?

12 Krist Novoselic and Kurt Cobain formed which band in 1987?

13 Which actor starred in the 1977 film *The Deep*?

14 Who was Muttley's partner in the cartoon series *Wacky Races*?

15 What vessel is used for clearing mud from rivers?

16 By which name is the harebell more commonly known in Scotland?

17 What name is given to the branch of fiscal studies relating to individual households?

18 Which South Yorkshire city was the setting for the film *The Full Monty*?

19 Which sport was associated with the Surrey location of Brooklands?

20 Which long-running BBC feedback programme has been presented by Anne Robinson and Jeremy Vine, amongst others?

Easy

Medium

Hard

---

1 Where did the first Butlin's holiday camp open in 1936?

2 In 1930, who became emperor of Ethiopia?

3 Which fictional apeman was first played by Johnny Weissmuller in the 1930s?

4 Which ship became the world's largest liner when it was launched in 1938?

5 Born in 1932, which singer was also known as "The Man in Black"?

6 Which English composer, famous for the *Pomp and Circumstance Marches*, died in 1934?

7 In which month of 1939 did WWII start?

8 Which 1930s Brazilian actress was known for her fruit-laden headgear?

9 What sort of vehicle was *Mallard*, which set a new world speed record for its type in 1938?

10 In 1936, from which Tyneside town did workers march to London to protest against unemployment and poverty?

11 What type of insurance did the Road Traffic Act of 1930 make compulsory for drivers?

12 Which royal event was broadcast for the first time in December 1932?

13 What name was given to Franklin D Roosevelt's political programme of the mid-1930s?

14 In which sport was there a dispute over the "Bodyline" tactic during 1932-33?

15 Which actress was famously pursued by King Kong in the original film?

16 What term was given to the dry weather problems that damaged the ecology and agriculture of the North American prairies in the 1930s?

17 In which year did George VI become King?

18 Who wrote *The Big Sleep*, published in 1939?

19 Which English tennis player won three consecutive Wimbledon singles titles from 1934 to 1936?

20 In 1930, which skyscraper became the world's tallest building, until it was overtaken by the Empire State Building less than a year later?

Answers to QUIZ 348 – Musicals

1	*Guys and Dolls*	11	Levi Stubbs
2	*I Know Him So Well*	12	Anne Hathaway
3	*The Wizard of Oz*	13	Billy Flynn
4	*Grease*	14	Gene Kelly
5	Baseball	15	Morecambe and Wise
6	Neil Diamond	16	*Flashdance*
7	*Footloose*	17	*Wicked*
8	Liza Minnelli	18	*West Side Story*
9	*The Rocky Horror Picture Show*	19	*Oklahoma!*
10	*Fiddler on the Roof*	20	*Hair*

1   Which actress co-starred with Gerard Butler in the 2010 film *The Bounty Hunter*?

2   Who had a 1973 hit with *The Twelfth of Never*?

3   Elmer Fudd is the arch-enemy of which cartoon rabbit?

4   Who played the title role in the TV series *Buffy the Vampire Slayer*?

5   What name is given to a person who studies the environment?

6   An inhabitant of "the Granite City" is given what name?

7   What was Spandau Ballet's only no.1 hit?

8   Which Bond character was played by Donald Pleasence, amongst others?

9   What is the holy table in a church called?

10 Which group had a no.1 hit in 2007 with *Shine*?

11 What term was used to describe a group of anti-establishment writers in the 1950s, including such figures as John Osborne and Kingsley Amis?

12 What lost object did Pickles unearth in 1966?

13 Traditionally, what does a cooper make?

14 How many (including the cox) are in each boat in the annual Oxford and Cambridge Boat Race?

15 Who had a 1986 hit with *The Lady in Red*?

16 Which tree has a "wych" species?

17 What word can mean both a hanging ornament and a communications device?

18 What name is given to a male sheep?

19 The word "sinister" derives from the Latin for which side, left or right?

20 What is the name of the house in which the 1938 novel *Rebecca* is mainly set?

Easy

Medium

Hard

Answers to QUIZ 349 – Pot Luck

1	Thing	11	Anne
2	Clove	12	Nirvana
3	Maserati	13	Nick Nolte
4	*The Blues Brothers*	14	Dick Dastardly
5	*Citizen Smith*	15	Dredger
6	Flemish	16	Bluebell
7	The Tigris	17	Micro-economics
8	Hampshire	18	Sheffield
9	Newt	19	Motor racing
10	Hall and haul	20	*Points of View*

Easy

1. Which Spanish painter had a "blue period" from 1901 to 1904?
2. In which year did Spain first host the Summer Olympics?
3. Which ocean borders Spain?
4. In which city is the Sagrada Familia church?
5. Chorizo is what type of food?
6. The Vuelta a España is a race in which sport?
7. What currency is used in Spain?
8. Spain is bordered by which three European countries?
9. In which year did Spain win the FIFA World Cup for the first time?
10. What are the curved pieces of hollow wood that Spanish dancers click together to beat time to music?

Medium

11. Which Balearic island is famous for its club scene?
12. Sangria has which alcoholic drink as its basis?
13. *Jamón* is the Spanish word for which food item?
14. What is the Spanish top football division usually called?
15. What does the Spanish word *cruz* translate to in English?
16. What geographical feature is a "sierra"?
17. David Beckham played for which team from 2003 to 2007?
18. What colour are the stripes that appear on the Spanish flag?
19. Which city lends its name to a variety of bitter orange?
20. *Begin the Beguine* was a 1981 hit for which Spanish singer?

Hard

Answers to QUIZ 350 – 1930s

1	Skegness	11	Third party
2	Haile Selassie	12	Christmas message
3	Tarzan	13	New Deal
4	*RMS Queen Elizabeth*	14	Cricket
5	Johnny Cash	15	Fay Wray
6	Sir Edward Elgar	16	The Dust Bowl
7	September (3rd)	17	1936
8	Carmen Miranda	18	Raymond Chandler
9	Steam locomotive	19	Fred Perry
10	Jarrow	20	Chrysler Building

1   Which religious leader has the birth name Lhamo Thondup?

2   What was the name of King Arthur's magic sword?

3   Which barbarian was played on film by Arnold Schwarzenegger in 1982?

4   Hans Christian Andersen wrote about whose "new clothes"?

5   The chart-topping album ÷ (divide) was released by which singer in 2017?

6   Who wrote the 1964 novel *Chitty Chitty Bang Bang*?

7   What musical was based on the life of Argentina's Mrs Peron?

8   Which word meaning "to retain" means "a quick look" when read backwards?

9   Clovelly is in which county?

10 In which county is the theme park Alton Towers?

11 Which actor starred in the 1989 film *My Left Foot*?

12 What was the first name of singer Nilsson?

13 In which Brazilian city is Sugar Loaf Mountain?

14 .no is the internet code for which country?

15 Which bird is "ascending" in the famous work by Vaughan Williams?

16 Kelp is what type of plant?

17 *Angels* and *Old Before I Die* were 1997 hits for which singer?

18 Which British fighting service was formed in 1918?

19 Which word, the Latin for "load", is used to mean the burden of responsibility?

20 In the game of chess, which is the most powerful piece?

Easy

Medium

Hard

Answers to QUIZ 351 – Pot Luck

1	Jennifer Aniston	11	Angry Young Men
2	Donny Osmond	12	The Jules Rimet Trophy (FIFA World Cup)
3	Bugs Bunny	13	Barrels
4	Sarah Michelle Gellar	14	Nine
5	Ecologist	15	Chris de Burgh
6	Aberdonian	16	Elm
7	True	17	Mobile
8	Ernst Blofeld	18	Ram
9	Altar	19	Left
10	Take That	20	Manderley

Easy

1. Which term describes material that can be decomposed by natural means?
2. In the initials SSSI, what does the "I" stand for?
3. What is the word for the permanent disappearance of a species?
4. In a domestic residence, where are solar panels normally installed?
5. What colour is associated with the environmental movement?
6. The measurement of an individual's or company's carbon usage over a certain period of time has what two-word term?
7. Which chef and TV presenter mounted a campaign against single-use coffee cups in 2016?
8. Which measuring device can be installed in the home to track energy usage?
9. Discovered in the 1980s, there is a huge "garbage patch" in which ocean?
10. How is food described that has been grown without the use of pesticides?
11. In the phrase known as the "3 Rs of recycling", what are the first two Rs before "Recycle"?
12. Which 2017 series presented by Sir David Attenborough highlighted the problems of plastic items?

Medium

13. In which month each year does Earth Hour take place at 8.30pm local time?
14. The level of heat in a building is controlled by what device?
15. What is the controversial energy extraction method of hydraulic fracturing more commonly called?
16. What term is given to a car that combines an engine with an electric motor?
17. What function does a material such as mineral wool provide when laid in an attic?
18. The prefix "eco-" relates to which branch of science?
19. Other than black, which two colours appear on the Fairtrade logo?
20. What word describes the use of natural resources at a level that will not damage the natural environment?

Hard

Answers to QUIZ 352 – Spain

1	Pablo Picasso	11	Ibiza
2	1992 (Barcelona)	12	Red wine
3	Atlantic Ocean	13	Ham
4	Barcelona	14	La Liga
5	Sausage	15	Cross
6	Cycling	16	Mountain range
7	Euros	17	Real Madrid
8	France, Andorra, Portugal	18	Red and yellow
9	2010	19	Seville
10	Castanets	20	Julio Iglesias

1   Which vegetable is the main ingredient in coleslaw?

2   Who married Henry VII?

3   What completes the title official _, the person who winds up a company?

4   The Belfry is a venue for which sport?

5   What is the capital of New Mexico?

6   Is the town of Mold in North Wales or South Wales?

7   Which group had a hit with *I Don't Like Mondays*?

8   Who wrote the novel *Sons and Lovers*?

9   In *The Lord of the Rings* films, who played Legolas?

10 Carol Kirkwood is known for presenting what on TV?

11 Which UK coin, as of 2017, has twelve sides?

12 Which English city has the postcode CA?

13 What is five cubed?

14 From which country do borzoi dogs originate?

15 Hercules was said to have slain which many-headed monster?

16 Which herb is often associated with remembrance?

17 A large Roman building such as St Peter's in Rome is given what name?

18 Which actress played Muriel in the 1994 film *Muriel's Wedding*?

19 Who wrote *The Name of the Rose* (1980)?

20 What colour is a female blackbird?

Answers to QUIZ 353 – Pot Luck

1	The 14th Dalai Lama	11	Sir Daniel Day-Lewis
2	Excalibur	12	Harry
3	Conan	13	Rio de Janeiro
4	The Emperor's	14	Norway
5	Ed Sheeran	15	Lark
6	Ian Fleming	16	Seaweed
7	*Evita*	17	Robbie Williams
8	Keep	18	RAF
9	Devon	19	Onus
10	Staffordshire	20	Queen

ANSWERS ON PAGE **358**

Easy

1   Cindy Cunningham, played by Stephanie Waring, is a character from which long-running series?

2   Which programme did Geoff Hamilton present from 1979 until his death in 1996?

3   What is the name of Emilia Fox's character in *Silent Witness*?

4   In what area of England is *Emmerdale* set?

5   2017 *Strictly Come Dancing* winner Joe McFadden played Raf di Lucca in which hospital drama series?

6   Which daytime series is set in the fictional Midlands town of Letherbridge?

7   Laila Morse is best known for playing which *EastEnders* character?

8   Who was the original questionmaster on *University Challenge*?

9   Which production company makes *Coronation Street*?

10   Johnny Galecki and Jim Parsons play physicists in which US sitcom?

Medium

11   What relation is John Barnaby to John Nettles' Tom Barnaby in *Midsomer Murders*?

12   In what type of building did Jonathan Creek live in the early series?

13   What were the names of the Mitchell sisters who made their *EastEnders* debut in 2007 and exited ten years later?

14   Which US series featured the forensic anthropologist Dr Temperance Brennan?

15   In *Neighbours,* what is the name of the hotel complex?

16   In which decade was *The Antiques Roadshow* first screened?

17   Which actor is best known in the UK for the role of Alf Stewart in *Home and Away*?

18   In the name of the US series *Law & Order: SVU*, what does SVU stand for?

19   The Simpsons live in which town?

20   In which sci-fi series did a robotic dog called K9 appear?

Hard

Answers to QUIZ 354 – Environment

1	Biodegradable	11	Reduce and Reuse
2	Interest	12	*Blue Planet II*
3	Extinction	13	March
4	On the roof	14	Thermostat
5	Green	15	Fracking
6	Carbon footprint	16	Hybrid
7	Hugh Fearnley-Whittingstall	17	Insulation
8	Smart meter	18	Ecology
9	Pacific Ocean	19	Blue and green
10	Organic	20	Sustainable

1   Who directed the 2015 James Bond film *Spectre?*

2   What term describes British history from 1714 to 1830?

3   On Burns Night, which dish is traditionally "addressed"?

4   Morrissey was the lead singer of which band?

5   What is the second brightest object in the night sky?

6   What is the ninth letter of the Greek alphabet?

7   The Masai Mara wildlife reserve is in which country?

8   In which town was the TV series *Fawlty Towers* set?

9   What name is given to the sum payable to authors from their book sales?

10   Which 1968 Steppenwolf single featured in the film *Easy Rider?*

11   As seen on its stamps, what is "Switzerland" in Latin?

12   Which European country is indicated by the car registration letter P?

13   Who starred in the *Bridget Jones* films?

14   What term is given to a graduate's square cup?

15   In the TV crime series *Vera*, who plays the title role?

16   In which garden feature might you find blanket weed?

17   Which river of south-east Devon flows into Seaton Bay?

18   What style of spicy cuisine comes from the Deep South of the United States, especially Louisiana?

19   Who had a hit with *The Jean Genie* in 1972?

20   Michael Stipe was the lead singer of which group?

Answers to QUIZ 355 – Pot Luck

1	Cabbage	11	£1
2	Elizabeth of York	12	Carlisle
3	Receiver	13	125
4	Golf	14	Russia
5	Santa Fe	15	Hydra
6	North Wales	16	Rosemary
7	Boomtown Rats	17	Basilica
8	DH Lawrence	18	Toni Collette
9	Orlando Bloom	19	Umberto Eco
10	Weather forecast	20	Brown

Easy

1 How many ounces are there in a pound?

2 What number on a dartboard is between 11 and 16?

3 What is the sum of the digits one to nine inclusive?

4 In the game of bingo, what is the highest number?

5 How many centimetres are there in seven metres?

6 How many edges does a cube have?

7 What is 1/8 expressed as a percentage?

8 If it rains on St Swithin's Day, how many more days is it supposed to rain?

9 What is the next highest prime number above 23?

10 What is the value of pi to two decimal places?

11 How many ladies were dancing in *The Twelve Days of Christmas*?

12 Which imperial measure is equal to 1/20th of a ton?

13 How many court cards are there in a standard pack?

14 What is the square root of 49?

Medium

15 How many questions were there in the title of the Radio 4 guessing game?

16 What is thirty per cent of 600?

17 How many inches are there in six feet?

18 In which sequence, named after an Italian mathematician, do the numbers equate to the sum of the previous two numbers?

19 At what age is life said to begin?

20 What name is given to a chart showing the products of pairs of numbers?

Hard

Answers to QUIZ 356 – Long-Running Television Series

1	*Hollyoaks*	11	Cousin
2	*Gardeners' World*	12	A windmill
3	Dr Nikki Alexander	13	Ronnie and Roxy
4	Yorkshire Dales	14	*Bones*
5	*Holby City*	15	Lassiter's
6	*Doctors*	16	1970s (1979)
7	Mo Harris	17	Ray Meagher
8	Bamber Gascoigne	18	Special Victims Unit
9	Granada Television	19	Springfield
10	*The Big Bang Theory*	20	*Doctor Who*

1. What, in proof-reading, is an instruction to restore a correction called?

2. *Addicted To Love* was a 1986 hit for which musician?

3. What is the nautical term meaning "near or towards the stern of a boat"?

4. Which actor starred in the 1988 semi-animated film *Who Framed Roger Rabbit*?

5. Nathaniel Parker starred as which crime solver in a series beginning in 2001?

6. What is the usual form of address to an Italian man?

7. The name of which port provided a 1996 hit for the Beautiful South?

8. Brad Pitt and Orlando Bloom starred in which 2004 swords-and-sandals epic?

9. *Lucille* was a 1977 hit for which country singer?

10. The name of which public vehicle can be read backwards as the abbreviation for an underwater vessel?

11. Which city is home to the University of Strathclyde?

12. What name is given to Rome's underground cemeteries?

13. In the TV series *Doctor Who*, which actress played River Song?

14. What was the first name of *Shaft* theme music composer Hayes?

15. What is a horse's fastest pace?

16. By what name is a recently-graduated resident physician in a US hospital known?

17. What nationality is golfer Jordan Spieth?

18. Who wrote *Swallows and Amazons* (1930)?

19. How has a goujon been cooked?

20. In which county is the town of Redruth?

Answers to QUIZ 357 – Pot Luck

1	Sam Mendes	11	Helvetia
2	Georgian	12	Portugal
3	Haggis	13	Renée Zellweger
4	The Smiths	14	Mortar-board
5	Venus	15	Brenda Blethyn
6	Iota	16	A pond
7	Kenya	17	Axe
8	Torquay	18	Cajun
9	Royalty	19	David Bowie
10	*Born to be Wild*	20	REM

1 Who had hits in the 1960s with *Mustang Sally* and *In the Midnight Hour*?

2 What are dolly mixtures?

3 What type of object is a cherry picker?

4 In bingo, which number is traditionally called as Tom Mix?

5 Which *a cappella* vocal group, formed in the 1980s, took their name from the term for mobile protesters?

6 What is linctus also known as?

7 What are you said to pick up if you pay the bill in a restaurant?

8 Which 2014 sci-film featured an "Awesome Mix Tape"?

9 *Take Your Pick!* was the first British TV game show to give away what as a prize?

10 How many times did Martina Navratilova win a mixed doubles title at Wimbledon?

11 What is a winkle-picker?

12 A piece of art that uses varied materials is given which two-word term?

13 What is another name for the pick often used with a guitar?

14 Which washbasin fitting allows hot and cold water to be blended?

15 The town of Pickering is on the border of which English National Park?

16 What type of person would use a mixing desk?

17 What does the company Pickfords specialise in?

18 The Mastermixers backed which novelty pop act in the 1980s and 1990s?

19 Who issued the 2012 single *Picking Up the Pieces*?

20 Where does a mixologist work?

Answers to QUIZ 358 – Numbers

1	16	11	Nine
2	Eight	12	Hundredweight
3	45	13	12
4	90	14	Seven
5	700	15	20
6	12	16	180
7	12.5	17	72
8	40	18	Fibonacci sequence
9	29	19	40
10	3.14	20	Multiplication table

ANSWERS ON PAGE **363**

1   Which super heavy-weight boxer took the gold medal in Sydney in 2000?

2   What type of entertainment was featured in the TV series *The Good Old Days*?

3   Who was Cher's 1964-75 singing partner?

4   Who co-starred with Humphrey Bogart in the 1951 film *The African Queen*?

5   In the UK, what was the former name of the World Wide Fund for Nature?

6   What name is given to a biscuit containing a motto?

7   Which successful solo artist also recorded with The Yardbirds, Cream, Blind Faith and Derek and the Dominos?

8   Amsterdam is the largest city of which European country?

9   Which was the first grand slam tournament won by Sir Andy Murray?

10   Which is the largest of the Balearic Islands?

11   In the radio phonetic alphabet, what word is between "golf" and "India"?

12   Which film monster, back in cinemas in March 2017, first appeared on screen in 1933?

13   Which former member of Hear'Say co-presented *The One Show* in 2007?

14   The Amazon Rainforest is found on which continent?

15   Which river flows through Derby?

16   The clavicle has what common name?

17   Who played Detective Ken Hutchinson in the original *Starsky and Hutch* TV series?

18   *Slave to Love* was a hit for which singer in 1985?

19   What is the title of the classic 1881 children's book by Swiss author Johanna Spyri?

20   London Zoo is located in which park?

Easy

Medium

Hard

Answers to QUIZ 359 – Pot Luck

1	Stet	11	Glasgow
2	Robert Palmer	12	Catacombs
3	Aft	13	Alex Kingston
4	Bob Hoskins	14	Isaac
5	Inspector Lynley	15	Gallop
6	Signor	16	Intern
7	Rotterdam	17	American
8	*Troy*	18	Arthur Ransome
9	Kenny Rogers	19	Coated in breadcrumbs and deep-fried
10	Bus	20	Cornwall

Easy

1   On which TV show does Susie Dent appear?

2   Susan Sulley is a singer with which group formed in the 1980s?

3   In the 2017 series of *Strictly Come Dancing*, whom did Susan Calman partner?

4   Which fictional diarist was created by author Sue Townsend?

5   Susan Dey won a Golden Globe in 1988 for her role as Grace Van Owen in which US TV series?

6   Which novel is narrated by Susie Salmon?

7   What was the name of Susan Hampshire's character in the TV series *Monarch of the Glen*?

8   What is a lazy Susan?

9   In the TV series *Neighbours*, who plays the long-running character of Susan Kennedy?

10 In the 1981 film *Thelma & Louise*, which role did Susan Sarandon play?

Medium

11 *A Question of Sport* host Sue Barker played which sport from 1973 to 1984?

12 On which TV show did singer Susan Boyle find fame?

13 What was Little Susie told to do in the title of a 1957 Everly Brothers song?

14 What is a black-eyed Susan?

15 In the 1970s, which singer had hits with *Can the Can* and *Devil Gate Drive*?

16 Which TV presenter moved from the *BBC Breakfast* show to *Good Morning Britain* in 2014?

17 In *Coronation Street*, which character is played by Sue Cleaver?

18 Who wrote the chilling tale *The Woman in Black* (1983)?

19 The TV series *What Not to Wear* was co-presented by Susannah Constantine and which other fashion adviser?

20 Who played Susan in the TV series *Desperate Housewives*?

Hard

Answers to QUIZ 360 – Pick and Mix

1	Wilson Pickett	11	Pointed shoe or boot
2	Small sweets	12	Mixed media
3	A crane	13	Plectrum
4	Six	14	Mixer tap
5	The Flying Pickets	15	North York Moors
6	Cough mixture	16	A sound engineer
7	The tab	17	Moving (house)
8	*Guardians of the Galaxy*	18	Jive Bunny
9	Cash	19	Paloma Faith
10	Four times	20	Behind a bar

1 In which county is Kidderminster?

2 Which Swedish seaport faces Copenhagen?

3 Where would you find a dado rail?

4 Which nursery-rhyme shepherdess lost her sheep?

5 In the Bible, which disciple betrayed Jesus?

6 Which plant shares its name with a word meaning "to cut short"?

7 What is the watery component of blood?

8 *Oops Up Side Your Head* was a hit for which group in 1980?

9 Which 1999 film, set in London, starred Hugh Grant and Julia Roberts?

10 Which Robert directed *Gosford Park* and *Short Cuts*?

11 What is a saveloy?

12 In which city is England's National Railway Museum?

13 Which team won the women's FA Cup in 2018?

14 In 1989, which heavy metal band had a hit with *Paradise City*?

15 Who was Kim's partner in the TV series *How Clean Is Your House*?

16 Which constellation includes the Pole Star?

17 In which county is Leatherhead?

18 What is the laurel-like shrub with aromatic leaves used in cookery called?

19 New York City has what fruity nickname?

20 What is an Inuit snow house called?

Answers to QUIZ 361 – Pot Luck

1	Audley Harrison	11	Hotel
2	Music hall	12	King Kong
3	Sonny	13	Myleene Klass
4	Katharine Hepburn	14	South America
5	The World Wildlife Fund	15	Derwent
6	Fortune cookie	16	Collarbone
7	Eric Clapton	17	David Soul
8	The Netherlands	18	Bryan Ferry
9	US Open (2012)	19	*Heidi*
10	Majorca	20	Regent's Park

1   What term describes a group of companies banded together to monopolise a market?

2   In the UK, the RMT union covers workers in which sector?

3   Which colour is associated with stocks and shares that are considered to be a safe investment?

4   In a company P&L statement, what do P and L stand for?

5   Is a person who buys a franchise known as a franchisee or a franchiser?

6   What type of business is owned by the people who run it, who share its benefits and profits?

7   What name is given to the tax collected by the government on goods coming into a country?

8   The City of London is often known by what measurement?

9   A trade restriction on the quantity of goods that can be imported into a country is given what term?

10 What does the "R" stand for in the government department HMRC?

11 What was the standard VAT rate raised to in the UK in 2011?

12 The Hang Seng index relates to the stock market in which former British colony?

13 If goods are acknowledged by a Bill of Lading, on what type of transport have they travelled?

14 What type of event is an expo?

15 Which two-word term is given to an item that has been discounted to a level that will not make a profit but is intended to attract customers?

16 As from 2014, which government department has been responsible for preventing unfair business competition and consumer choice?

17 On which date does the British tax year end?

18 Which two animals are used to describe the state of the Stock Exchange market?

19 Introduced in the UK in 1999, what term is given to the lowest amount that a company can pay its workers?

20 What two-word term is given to the historical trade associations based in London?

Answers to QUIZ 362 – Susan and Friends

1	*Countdown*	11	Tennis
2	Human League	12	*Britain's Got Talent*
3	Kevin Clifton	13	Wake Up
4	Adrian Mole	14	A flower (of the sunflower family)
5	*LA Law*	15	Suzi Quatro
6	*The Lovely Bones* (Alice Sebold)	16	Susanna Reid
7	Molly MacDonald	17	Eileen Grimshaw
8	A revolving food tray or stand	18	Susan Hill
9	Jackie Woodburne	19	Trinny Woodall
10	Louise	20	Teri Hatcher

1 What was the Teenage Mutant Turtles' favourite food?

2 In which city can you visit Brunel's *SS Great Britain*?

3 Which 1980 film starring Irene Cara was remade in 2009?

4 What brand-name is give to one of the pleasure boats for sightseers in France's capital?

5 Which American humorist (b.1902), was noted for his unconventionally rhyming poetry published in the *New Yorker* magazine?

6 On a standard keyboard, which letter is to the immediate left of J?

7 In which US state is Fort Lauderdale?

8 What type of institution is Wormwood Scrubs?

9 Who captained the England team at the 2018 FIFA World Cup?

10 Jennifer Lawrence stars as Katniss Everdeen in which film franchise?

11 What was the surname of Patrick Macnee's character in *The Avengers*?

12 The traditional English dish of sausages and batter has what common name?

13 Which pioneering US four-piece punk rock band was formed in New York in 1974?

14 Which architectural style is characterised by rib vaults and flying buttresses?

15 What is the gelatinous dish made with cornflour and milk called?

16 A hairstreak is what type of creature?

17 Who wrote the novel *Twenty Thousand Leagues under the Sea* (1870)?

18 In 2018, who won the snooker World Championship title?

19 Which group had a 1982 no.1 hit with *Eye of the Tiger*?

20 Which is the second-smallest continent?

Easy

Medium

Hard

Answers to QUIZ 363 – Pot Luck

1	Worcestershire	11	A sausage
2	Malmö	12	York
3	On a wall	13	Chelsea
4	Little Bo-Peep	14	Guns N' Roses
5	Judas Iscariot	15	Aggie
6	Dock	16	Ursa Minor
7	Plasma	17	Surrey
8	Gap Band	18	Bay
9	*Notting Hill*	19	The Big Apple
10	Altman	20	Igloo

ANSWERS ON PAGE 368

Easy

1   Which actor starred as Jack in the 1985 film *Legend*?

2   *The Golden Compass* (2007) was adapated from a novel by which author?

3   Which fairy-tale was made into a 2015 live-action film starring Lily James?

4   Warwick Davis played the title character in which 1988 fantasy film?

5   Which animated film of 2013 features a snowman called Olaf?

6   David Bowie played Jareth the Goblin King in which 1986 film?

7   What profession does Bill Murray's character follow in the 1993 film *Groundhog Day*?

8   Who played the title role in the 1987 film *The Princess Bride*?

9   What was the 1984 sequel to *Conan the Barbarian*?

10   Who directed *Edward Scissorhands* (1990)?

Medium

11   In which 2016 film is Newt Scamander the main character?

12   Who played the title role in the 2014 film *Maleficent*?

13   What was the subtitle of the 2017 film in the *Jumanji* series?

14   In the second of the *Pirates of the Caribbean* films, what was the name of Bill Nighy's character?

15   Martin Freeman starred in which trilogy of fantasy films released between 2012 and 2014?

16   Which 1982 film directed by Jim Henson and Frank Oz featured a Gelfling called Jen as the main character?

17   Which 2007 fantasy film starred Claire Danes as a celestial body and Michelle Pfeiffer as a witch?

18   Who directed the 2017 film *King Arthur: Legend of the Sword*?

19   In the 2016 film *The BFG*, who provided the voice of the title character?

20   Who played Ron Weasley in the *Harry Potter* films?

Hard

Answers to QUIZ 364 – Business and Commerce

1	Cartel	11	20%
2	Transport	12	Hong Kong
3	Blue (chip)	13	Ship
4	Profit and loss	14	A trade fair
5	Franchisee	15	Loss leader
6	Cooperative	16	The Competition and Markets Authority
7	Tariff	17	April 5
8	Square Mile	18	Bear and bull
9	Quota	19	Minimum wage
10	Revenue	20	Livery companies

1   What was the title of the Avengers film released in the UK in April 2018?

2   A female rabbit is known by what name?

3   What birthday is the first for a nonagenarian?

4   An area of land described as a delta has what shape?

5   In which game would you have a pitcher's mound and an outfield?

6   Which group had a hit with *Common People* in 1995?

7   What type of food is grown in paddy fields?

8   In which soap did the character of Mike Baldwin appear?

9   Which fishing port lies on the Humber, near Cleethorpes?

10 *Discotheque* was a 1997 hit for which group?

11 Which zodiac sign is represented by two fish?

12 In which European capital city is there a statue of The Little Mermaid?

13 Dame Nellie Melba sang in which vocal range?

14 Which British actress appeared in the video of *Prince Charming* with Adam and the Ants?

15 Who played the title role in the TV series *Ironside*?

16 "Old Glory" is the nickname for which country's flag?

17 Which group was *Flying Without Wings* in 1999?

18 In bridge, who is the dummy's partner?

19 What are Jersey Royals?

20 Which month of the year was named after Julius Caesar?

Answers to QUIZ 365 – Pot Luck

1	Pizza	11	Steed (John)
2	Bristol	12	Toad-in-the-hole
3	*Fame*	13	Ramones
4	Bateau Mouche	14	Gothic
5	Ogden Nash	15	Blancmange
6	H	16	Butterfly
7	Florida	17	Jules Verne
8	Prison	18	Mark Williams
9	Harry Kane	19	Survivor
10	*The Hunger Games*	20	Europe

Easy

1   What is the stage name of the lead guitarist with Guns N' Roses?

2   Who had a hit in 1983 with *Pipes of Peace*?

3   Yehudi Menuhin was associated with which instrument?

4   Which musician had a 1978 hit with an instrumental version of John Denver's *Annie's Song*?

5   Take That had a 1992 hit with a cover of which Barry Manilow song?

6   Who played Ray Charles in the 2004 film *Ray*?

7   Which supergroup was formed by Jeff Lynne, Roy Orbison, George Harrison, Tom Petty and Bob Dylan?

8   What is the home-made music of the 1950s, as played by Lonnie Donegan?

9   Which 1971 John Lennon classic song mused on a vision of an ideal world?

10 In 2006, which actress did country musician Keith Urban marry?

11 Whose released the album 25 in November 2015?

12 In which decade of the 20th century was Sir Elton John born?

13 "Slowhand" is the nickname of which guitarist?

14 Who had a 2009 hit with *Poker Face*?

Medium

15 Which musician (b.1958) changed his name to a symbol for several years during the 1990s?

16 Trumpeter Miles Davis was famous in which area of music?

17 "Flea" is the stage name of the bass guitarist with which group?

18 Which group had a 1977 hit with the instrumental *Fanfare for the Common Man*?

19 In which country was percussionist Dame Evelyn Glennie born?

20 Which name is shared by the drummers from Queen and Duran Duran?

Hard

Answers to QUIZ 366 – Fantasy Films

1	Tom Cruise	11	*Fantastic Beasts and Where to Find Them*
2	Philip Pullman	12	Angelina Jolie
3	*Cinderella*	13	*Welcome to the Jungle*
4	*Willow*	14	Davy Jones
5	*Frozen*	15	*The Hobbit*
6	*Labyrinth*	16	*The Dark Crystal*
7	Weatherman	17	*Stardust*
8	Robin Wright	18	Guy Ritchie
9	*Conan the Destroyer*	19	Sir Mark Rylance
10	Tim Burton	20	Rupert Grint

1   Which English city has the postcode LN?

2   Which 20th-century author wrote the amusing autobiography *My Family and Other Animals*?

3   The winner of a British boxing title fight is awarded which belt?

4   Where was the treaty signed that established the EEC?

5   What sort of fruit is a Worcester Pearmain?

6   *You're So Vain* was a 1972 hit for which singer/songwriter?

7   Which naval officer ranking is between a rear admiral and a captain?

8   Who is Ernie's pal in the TV series *Sesame Street*?

9   Little Rock is the capital of which US state?

10 Who wrote the 19th-century novel *Vanity Fair*?

11 *The Ugly Duckling* was a tale written by which author?

12 *It Takes Two* was a 1990 hit for Sir Rod Stewart and which female singer?

13 Which actress starred in the 1990 film *Truly, Madly, Deeply*?

14 For which duke was Blenheim Palace built?

15 Which 1990 film featured the characters of Brontë and Georges?

16 In which country is the Firth of Forth?

17 What is the Chinese dish of poultry with pancakes, spring onion and hoisin sauce called?

18 The character of Uriah Heep features in which Dickens novel?

19 What is the second largest of the Balearic Islands?

20 Which word can mean both "atmosphere" and "to broadcast"?

Easy

Medium

Hard

Answers to QUIZ 367 – Pot Luck

1	*Avengers: Infinity War*	11	Pisces
2	Doe	12	Copenhagen
3	90th	13	Soprano
4	Triangular	14	Diana Dors
5	Baseball	15	Raymond Burr
6	Pulp	16	USA
7	Rice	17	Westlife
8	*Coronation Street*	18	Declarer
9	Grimsby	19	Potatoes
10	U2	20	July

Easy

1   South Wales is separated from Devon by which stretch of water?

2   Which saint features in the name of Exeter's railway station?

3   What nickname is given to the South Devon district of Torbay?

4   In which South Devon town is the Royal Naval College located?

5   What medal did Plymouth-born diver Tom Daley win in the 2012 London Olympics?

6   In which century was Sir Francis Drake born?

7   Which Devon football team are nicknamed "The Pilgrims"?

8   Which item is usually put on the scone first in a Devon cream tea, the jam or the cream?

9   Woolacombe and Croyde in North Devon are popular destinations for which ocean-based sport?

10 Which Devon-born author created Hercule Poirot?

Medium

11 What is the name of the National Park that includes areas of both Devon and Somerset?

12 The Devon-based Dartington company is famous for making what two products?

13 In which Devon seaside town did storms wash away a section of the railway track in 2014?

14 Which ornamental material is associated with the town of Honiton?

15 Newton Abbot is famous for hosting what type of sport?

16 In which market town of South Devon was the environmental Transition Network founded?

17 As well as Somerset, which two counties border Devon?

18 Which comedian who grew up in Devon appears on the TV programme *The Last Leg*?

19 What type of buildings are Berry Pomeroy and Powderham?

20 What method of transport links the villages of Lynton and Lynmouth in North Devon?

Hard

Answers to QUIZ 368 – Musicians

1	Slash	11	Adele
2	Sir Paul McCartney	12	1940s
3	Violin	13	Eric Clapton
4	James Galway	14	Lady Gaga
5	*Could It Be Magic*	15	Prince
6	Jamie Foxx	16	Jazz
7	Traveling Wilburys	17	Red Hot Chili Peppers
8	Skiffle	18	ELP (Emerson, Lake and Palmer)
9	*Imagine*	19	Scotland
10	Nicole Kidman	20	Roger Taylor

1   What is the stake put up before a new deal in poker called?

2   Through which county does the River Medway run?

3   Who was the 44th president of the USA?

4   What is the capital and chief port of Wales?

5   "I made it through the wilderness, Somehow I made it through" are lyrics from which song?

6   What type of animal was TV's Skippy?

7   How is "in the year of our Lord" written in Latin?

8   What is the fatty substance found in the cavities of bones?

9   The Pentland Firth separates which group of islands from the northern tip of Scotland?

10 *Love is the Drug* was a 1975 single by which band?

11 Kathmandu is the capital of which country?

12 "Richard of York gained battles in vain" is an acronym for what?

13 Which large Mediterranean island has Cagliari as its capital?

14 Which title is given to the ruling monarch's daughter in Spain?

15 *Losing My Religion* was a 1991 hit for which rock band?

16 Which Caribbean capital lends its name to a type of cigar?

17 What do Americans call an underground railway system?

18 At which Berkshire racecourse will the Royal Enclosure be found?

19 Which North American national park is famous for its geysers?

20 Ewan McGregor and Tara Fitzgerald starred in which 1996 film about a colliery band?

Answers to QUIZ 369 – Pot Luck

1	Lincoln	11	Hans Christian Andersen
2	Gerald Durrell	12	Tina Turner
3	Lonsdale Belt	13	Juliet Stevenson
4	Rome (1957)	14	Duke of Marlborough
5	Apple	15	*Green Card*
6	Carly Simon	16	Scotland
7	Commodore	17	Peking duck
8	Bert	18	*David Copperfield*
9	Arkansas	19	Minorca
10	William Makepeace Thackeray	20	Air

ANSWERS ON PAGE **374**

Easy

1 Which king was restored to the throne in 1660 after the English Civil War?

2 Alfred the Great was king of which region?

3 Who was King of Spain from 1975 until he abdicated in 2014?

4 What nickname was given to Louis XIV of France?

5 To which queen was William of Orange married?

6 Which man's name is the Latin word for "king"?

7 Who was Britain's last Stuart monarch?

8 Carl XVI Gustaf became king of which Scandinavian country in 1973?

9 Named after William IV's wife, what is the capital city of South Australia?

10 Which king was nicknamed "Farmer George"?

11 "Gloriana" was the nickname of which monarch?

Medium

12 King Constantine II was monarch of which country from 1964 until the monarchy was abolished in 1973?

13 Which figure in American history became known in song as "The King of the Wild Frontier"?

14 To which royal house did Queen Victoria belong?

15 Which English king utters the words "Now is the winter of our discontent" in a play by William Shakespeare?

16 Willem-Alexander became King of which European country in 2013 when his mother abdicated?

17 What religion was Queen Mary I?

18 Which king was Queen Elizabeth II's grandfather?

19 Edward VI was the son of which monarch?

20 Sweyn Forkbeard was king of which country from 986 to 1014?

Hard

Answers to QUIZ 370 – Devon

1	Bristol Channel	11	Exmoor
2	St David	12	Glass and crystal
3	English Riviera	13	Dawlish
4	Dartmouth	14	Lace
5	Bronze	15	Horse racing
6	16th century (1540)	16	Totnes
7	Plymouth Argyle	17	Cornwall and Dorset
8	Cream	18	Josh Widdicombe
9	Surfing	19	Castles
10	Dame Agatha Christie	20	Cliff railway (funicular)

1. Which seaport is the largest city in Alaska?

2. What was the surname of Lorenz, the lyric-writing partner of Richard Rodgers?

3. A twelve-sided solid shape is given what name?

4. Which North Wales resort is flanked by the Great and Little Orme headlands?

5. On the 1982 hit *Ebony and Ivory*, who duetted with Sir Paul McCartney?

6. What is the second letter of the Greek alphabet?

7. Which US state lies immediately north of Louisiana?

8. What is the highest volcano in Europe?

9. The Eustachian tube is between which two parts of the body?

10. Humphrey Bogart married which actress in 1945?

11. Which river joins the Trent to form the Humber Estuary?

12. What word can mean both "the underground part of a plant" and "to search"?

13. Which glam rock group had a hit in 1973 with *Blockbuster!*?

14. The animated film *Happy Feet* features which birds?

15. In cookery, what word is abbreviated to "tsp"?

16. Who was Henry VIII's second wife?

17. What is the first name of *The One Show* presenter Ms Jones?

18. In terms of a computer, what is meant by the initials ROM?

19. What condiment has cider, malt and wine varieties?

20. Which sport takes place in a velodrome?

Answers to QUIZ 371 – Pot Luck

1	Ante	11	Nepal
2	Kent	12	The colours of the rainbow
3	Barack Obama	13	Sardinia
4	Cardiff	14	Infanta
5	*Like a Virgin* (Madonna)	15	REM
6	A kangaroo	16	Havana
7	*Anno Domini*	17	Subway
8	Marrow	18	Ascot
9	The Orkney islands	19	Yellowstone
10	Roxy Music	20	*Brassed Off*

1. Which snack food is created by heating maize grains until they burst?
2. In Germany, what is a *bratwurst*?
3. What is the crisp disc often served at the start of an Indian meal?
4. Which snack shares its name with the ritual of raising a glass at a wedding?
5. Clusters of which fruit are sometimes called a "hand"?
6. In its native language, what snack is known as *pommes de terre frites*?
7. By what other name is a Scotch pie known, referencing the meat it may contain?
8. Which popular US snack food is often shaped like a knot?
9. What part of a plant is the misnamed pine nut?
10. A raisin is a dried version of which fruit?
11. The "Salt and Lineker" crisp was a special edition by which company?
12. What type of fruit is a Cox's orange pippin?
13. Which items sold in bags have given their name to a term for a small sum of money?
14. Ardennes and Brussels are varieties of which snack food?

15. Which green or black fruits are often eaten as part of a tapas selection?
16. Made from corn, which branded snack is shaped like the foot of a large creature?
17. What do Americans call crisps?
18. In the title of a 1982 book, which snack was it claimed that real men don't eat?
19. What is the translation of the pizza variety *quattro stagioni*?
20. Rice crackers are associated with which country?

Answers to QUIZ 372 – Kings and Queens

1	Charles II	11	Queen Elizabeth I
2	Wessex	12	Greece
3	Juan Carlos	13	Davy Crockett
4	The Sun King	14	Hanover
5	Mary II	15	Richard III
6	Rex	16	The Netherlands
7	Anne	17	Catholic
8	Sweden	18	George V
9	Adelaide	19	Henry VIII
10	George III	20	Denmark

1. For what man-made feature is Ribblehead most famous?

2. Which football commentator known as "Motty" retired at the end of the 2017-18 season?

3. In which county is the National Botanic Garden of Wales?

4. What was the name of the paranoid android in the cult series *The Hitch-Hiker's Guide to the Galaxy*?

5. The characters of Florence and Dougal featured in which children's TV series and film?

6. Watford Gap was the first British site of what in 1959?

7. Which Polish seaport was originally named Danzig?

8. Which Central American island was mentioned in Madonna's 1987 hit *La Isla Bonita*?

9. In the TV series *Frasier*, what was the name of Martin's dog?

10. Which state of north-east India is known for its tea production?

11. Which London art institution holds a "Summer Exhibition" every year which is open to all artists?

12. Which Oliver Stone film starred Gary Oldman as Lee Harvey Oswald?

13. On which bay is Aberystwyth located?

14. What is the common name of the shrub buddleia?

15. In 1996, *Wannabe* was the first hit for which girl group?

16. Which word can mean both "a door opener" and "crucial"?

17. Which trademarked business binder became popular in the 1980s?

18. Of all land plants, which is the fastest growing?

19. Which sport is nicknamed "the Sport of Kings"?

20. Who created the character of Mr Bean?

Answers to QUIZ 373 – Pot Luck

1	Anchorage	11	Ouse
2	Hart	12	Root
3	Dodecahedron	13	The Sweet
4	Llandudno	14	Penguins
5	Stevie Wonder	15	Teaspoon (or teaspoonful)
6	Beta	16	Anne Boleyn
7	Arkansas	17	Alex
8	Etna	18	Read Only Memory
9	Pharynx to the middle ear	19	Vinegar
10	Lauren Bacall	20	Cycling

Easy

1   What sort of work does Widow Twankey do?

2   If a pantomime character says "Oh no it isn't", what is the traditional response?

3   Who is Prince Charming's aide in *Cinderella*?

4   What does the goose lay in *Jack and the Beanstalk*?

5   Alphabetically, who is the first of Snow White's Seven Dwarfs?

6   What type of creature is the villain in Dick Whittington...?

7   ...and what type of creature is Dick Whittington's companion?

8   How long does the title character in *Sleeping Beauty* sleep for when under a spell?

9   Which pantomime hero is a sailor from Middle Eastern tales?

10 Maid Marian features in which pantomime?

Medium

11 What name is given to the hero of a pantomime, traditionally played by a female actor?

12 Goldilocks samples what food in the bears' house?

13 Which feline in footwear appears in the title of a pantomime?

14 Who does the wolf pretend to be in *Little Red Riding Hood*?

15 How many people usually play the pantomime cow or horse?

16 Michael and John Darling appear in which pantomime?

17 Who is the villain in *Aladdin*?

18 In *Jack and the Beanstalk*, which character cries "Fee-fi-fo-fum!"?

19 What poisoned fruit does Snow White eat?

20 Which maternal character's stories and rhymes provide the basis for a pantomime?

Hard

Answers to QUIZ 374 – Snacks

1	Popcorn	11	Walkers
2	A sausage	12	Apple
3	Poppadom	13	Peanuts
4	Toast	14	Pâté
5	Bananas	15	Olives
6	French fries	16	Monster Munch™
7	Mutton pie	17	Potato chips
8	Pretzel	18	Quiche
9	Seed	19	Four seasons
10	Grape	20	Japan

1 Which superhero lives by the mantra "with great power comes great responsibility"?

2 Who starred as Rooster Cogburn in the 1969 western *True Grit*?

3 Which Russian spirit is distilled from grain or potatoes?

4 In TV's *M*A*S*H*, who played "Hot Lips" Houlihan?

5 Who had a hit in 1999 with *Man! I Feel Like a Woman*?

6 Jakarta is the capital of which country?

7 Which taxi driver famously won *Mastermind* in 1980?

8 Australian tennis champion Evonne Cawley had what maiden name?

9 Who topped the charts in 1972 with *Puppy Love*?

10 Where would you find a rhizome?

11 In which year did Frankie Goes to Hollywood top the UK charts three times?

12 "Look at the stars, Look how they shine for you" is a lyric from which song?

13 Cantaloupe and honeydew are varieties of which type of fruit?

14 Someone called "Brummie" comes from which city?

15 What was the name of Tom Barnaby's wife in *Midsomer Murders*?

16 Which Roman emperor who died in 138 AD had a wall named in his honour in Great Britain?

17 Phoenix is the capital of which US state?

18 Which Shropshire new town was named after a famous Scottish civil engineer?

19 Henry Cooper was a champion in which sport?

20 What was the first name of *Golden Girls* actress Ms Arthur?

Easy

Medium

Hard

Answers to QUIZ 375 – Pot Luck

1	A viaduct (railway)	11	The Royal Academy
2	John Motson	12	JFK
3	Carmarthenshire	13	Cardigan Bay
4	Marvin	14	Butterfly bush
5	*The Magic Roundabout*	15	The Spice Girls
6	Motorway service station	16	Key
7	Gdansk	17	Filofax®
8	San Pedro	18	Bamboo
9	Eddie	19	Horse racing
10	Assam	20	Rowan Atkinson

Easy

1   What is the Welsh name for Wales?

2   In which Welsh village was the 1960s TV series *The Prisoner* mostly filmed?

3   On which day is St David's Day celebrated?

4   Which earthwork once formed the boundary between England and Wales?

5   Who was appointed manager of the Welsh national football team in January 2018?

6   Which Welsh singer had a 2008 hit with *Mercy*?

7   The National Library of Wales in is which university town?

8   Which North Wales village, featuring the Swallow Falls, is known as the "Gateway to Snowdonia"?

9   In 2016, which comedian took over hosting duties on *The Apprentice: You're Fired!*?

10 Which South Wales town is noted for its steelworks?

11 In the 1970s, which Welsh snooker player won six World Championship titles?

12 What is the name of the coastal National Park in the south of Wales?

13 In 2012 which North Wales town was officially granted city status?

14 Which motorway links London with South Wales?

Medium

15 In 2017 who became the first Welsh golfer to be inducted into the Golf Hall of Fame?

16 What title is given to the premier political figure in Wales...?

17 ...and what name is given to the governing body of the country?

18 Which headland includes Rhossili Bay and the "Worm's Head"?

19 What is the name of the national rugby ground in the Welsh capital?

20 From which port do boats depart for the Irish port of Rosslare?

Hard

Answers to QUIZ 376 – Pantomime

1	Laundry manager	11	Principal boy
2	"Oh yes it is"	12	Porridge
3	Dandini	13	*Puss in Boots*
4	Golden eggs	14	Her grandmother
5	Bashful	15	Two
6	A rat (King Rat)	16	*Peter Pan*
7	A cat	17	Abanazar
8	100 years	18	The giant (Blunderbore)
9	Sinbad	19	Apple
10	*Robin Hood*	20	Mother Goose

1 In which county is the seaside town of Southwold?

2 In the TV series *New Tricks*, who played Brian Lane?

3 What church-related nickname is given to an overnight period of employment?

4 Who was the star of the TV series *Dixon of Dock Green*?

5 What surname was adopted by author Charles Dodgson?

6 On a dartboard, which number is between 4 and 6?

7 Which actor played the title role in the original 1981 film *Arthur*?

8 In what drama series did Terence Alexander play Charlie Hungerford?

9 Which Kent spa town has the prefix "Royal" and the suffix "Wells"?

10 What is the principal religion of Indonesia?

11 Which creature was the enemy of the Three Little Pigs?

12 In which century was Isambard Kingdom Brunel born?

13 *Uptown Girl* was written by Billy Joel about which model?

14 Which scanning technique uses a magnetic field and radio waves to create detailed images of the body?

15 *Five Colours in Her Hair* was a 2004 hit for which group?

16 What term is given to the science and art of growing plants?

17 *Funky Gibbon* was a 1975 hit for which trio?

18 Known for its connections with the army, the town of Aldershot is in which county?

19 On which river are Düsseldorf, Mainz, Strasbourg and Rotterdam?

20 Which country hosted the 1998 FIFA World Cup?

Easy

Medium

Hard

Answers to QUIZ 377 – Pot Luck

1	Spider-Man	11	1984
2	John Wayne	12	*Yellow* (Coldplay)
3	Vodka	13	Melon
4	Loretta Swit	14	Birmingham
5	Shania Twain	15	Joyce
6	Indonesia	16	Hadrian
7	Fred Housego	17	Arizona
8	Goolagong	18	Telford
9	Donny Osmond	19	Boxing
10	On or below the earth (underground stem)	20	Bea

1 What colour plumage do egrets usually have?

2 Which sea duck has famously downy feathers used in bed coverings?

3 A kittiwake is what type of waterbird?

4 Which English island is known as "Puffin Island"?

5 A young goose is given what name?

6 In relation to waterbirds, what do the initials WWT stand for?

7 Which pink wading bird is often seen standing on one leg?

8 A white species of domesticated duck was named after which south-east county town?

9 Which wading bird has a name indicating that its beak is shaped like a piece of cutlery?

10 In the UK, which is the most common colour for a heron?

11 Which North American wading bird has a "whooping" species?

12 Which small fish-eating bird found in the UK is famous for its bright blue and orange plumage?

13 How many swans are a-swimming in the song *The Twelve Days of Christmas*?

14 Which is the largest species of penguin?

15 A shade of greenish-blue takes its name from which small duck?

16 In Europe, which wading bird is known for nesting on cartwheels that home owners place on top of their houses?

17 Which waterbird is often mentioned when referring to baldness?

18 On what type of terrain do guillemots nest?

19 Which diving bird's species include "great crested" and "little"?

20 Avocets have what two colours as their plumage?

Answers to QUIZ 378 – Wales

1	Cymru	11	Ray Reardon
2	Portmeirion	12	Pembrokeshire National Park
3	March 1	13	St Asaph
4	Offa's Dyke	14	M4
5	Ryan Giggs	15	Ian Woosnam
6	Duffy	16	First Minister
7	Aberystwyth	17	Welsh Assembly
8	Betws-y-Coed	18	Gower Peninsula
9	Rhod Gilbert	19	Principality Stadium
10	Port Talbot	20	Fishguard

1 The funnel-web spider is native to which country?

2 What is the surname of the actress Kathy who starred in the 1995 film *Dolores Claiborne*?

3 Which character lived on a dump in the 1963 children's book?

4 Which bird lays its eggs in another's nest?

5 *Knock Three Times* was a 1971 hit for which group?

6 What is the county town of Kent?

7 Which professional skateboarder has given his name to a series of video games?

8 Which 1979 film of a Thomas Hardy novel starred Nastassja Kinski in the title role?

9 The 1989 novel *The Remains of the Day* was written by which author?

10 Whose gang included Choo Choo, Spook and Benny the Ball?

11 *Coward of the County* was a 1980 hit for which singer?

12 What is the name of the very thin slices of toast named after a famous singer?

13 Which legendary poet wrote the *Iliad*?

14 Of which part of the body is nephrology a study?

15 Which band's first album *Definitely, Maybe* was released in 1994?

16 In which county is Okehampton?

17 How is Birmingham comedian Robert Davis better known?

18 Which Caribbean island has Kingston as its capital?

19 In *Gavin & Stacey*, what was the name of Rob Brydon's character?

20 What are the sweets "bootlaces" made from?

Answers to QUIZ 379 – Pot Luck

1	Suffolk	11	Big Bad Wolf
2	Alun Armstrong	12	19th century (1806)
3	Graveyard shift	13	Christie Brinkley
4	Jack Warner	14	MRI
5	(Lewis) Carroll	15	McFly
6	13	16	Horticulture
7	Dudley Moore	17	The Goodies
8	*Bergerac*	18	Hampshire
9	Tunbridge	19	Rhine
10	Islam	20	France

1. In which country was inventor Alexander Graham Bell born?

2. Which part of a whistle shares its name with a vegetable?

3. What term is given to naval trousers that are very wide at the end?

4. The song *Give a Little Whistle* features in which Disney film?

5. How many bells tolled in the title of the 1966 Alistair MacLean novel?

6. Which kitchen appliance sometimes whistles when its job is complete?

7. Who wrote the semi-autobiographical novel entitled *The Bell Jar*?

8. What name is given to a tour involving short stops at many different places?

9. *Ring My Bell* was a 1979 hit for which singer?

10. What would you do to wet your whistle?

11. Kristen Bell voiced which character in the 2013 film *Frozen*?

12. *I Whistle a Happy Tune* is from which musical?

13. Which former reporter was MP for Tatton from 1997 to 2001?

14. What is the penny whistle or tin whistle also known as?

15. The fairy Tinker Bell appears in which story?

16. What term is given to someone who exposes a company's often illegal secrets?

17. Where would you see a bell curve?

18. In which country is the ski resort of Whistler?

19. What are the first four words in the song *Jingle Bells*?

20. The novel *Whistle Down the Wind* by was made into a film in 1961 starring which actress, a daughter of the author?

Answers to QUIZ 380 – Waterbirds

1	White	11	Crane
2	Eider duck	12	Kingfisher
3	Gull	13	Seven
4	Lundy	14	Emperor
5	Gosling	15	Teal
6	Wildfowl and Wetlands Trust	16	Stork
7	Flamingo	17	Coot
8	Aylesbury	18	Cliffs
9	Spoonbill	19	Grebe
10	Grey	20	Black and white

1 Which comedian played Rufus T Firefly in the 1939 film *Duck Soup*?

2 What is the Latin for "earth"?

3 *The Radio Ham* and *The Blood Donor* were famous episodes from which show?

4 Which jazz pianist (b.1904) was nicknamed "Count"?

5 What is the metric measure of volume, equivalent to 1.76 pints?

6 In the 1970s and 1980s, which band had hits with *So You Win Again* and *It Started with a Kiss*?

7 Which highly toxic protein is derived from the castor oil plant?

8 Konungariket Sverige is the official name of which country?

9 What is the crime of having more than one spouse?

10 Which zoologist wrote the 1967 book *The Naked Ape*?

11 What fruity sauce is traditionally served with turkey?

12 On which Hawaiian island is the state capital Honolulu situated?

13 The city of Bristol stands on which river?

14 Which two words that sound the same but are spelt differently mean "to be tedious" and "a male animal"?

15 In the Disney version of *Pinocchio*, what sort of creature is Monstro?

16 What was the title of The Police's first UK hit?

17 Edinburgh doctor Joseph Bell was the inspiration for which character created by Sir Arthur Conan Doyle?

18 Which semi-precious stone is associated with Whitby?

19 Which actress duetted with Robbie Williams in 2001 on *Somethin' Stupid*?

20 Which Portuguese river is also the name of a wine region?

Easy

Medium

Hard

Answers to QUIZ 381 – Pot Luck

1	Australia	11	Kenny Rogers
2	Bates	12	Melba toast
3	Stig	13	Homer
4	Cuckoo	14	The kidneys
5	Dawn	15	Oasis
6	Maidstone	16	Devon
7	Tony Hawk	17	Jasper Carrott
8	*Tess*	18	Jamaica
9	Kazuo Ishiguro	19	Bryn
10	Top Cat	20	Liquorice

1   Which TV cook is also known for her involvement with Norwich City FC?

2   Which Italian chef presents the *Italian Escape* TV series?

3   Gordon Ramsay is the long-running host of which American culinary competition?

4   Who became the judges of *MasterChef* when it was revived in 2005?

5   How are TV foodies David Myers and Simon King better known?

6   Which chef, a regular on ITV's *This Morning*, married Fern Britton in 2000?

7   The *River Cottage* series was hosted by which chef?

8   Which chef launched the "Feed Me Better" campaign in 2005 to improve school dinners?

9   What is the name of Courteney Cox's chef character in *Friends*?

10 In 2015, who won the sixth series of *The Great British Bake Off* and has gone on to be a TV presenter?

11 Which gourmet and food writer is the daughter of Nigel, a former Chancellor of the Exchequer?

12 Which chef is associated with the hotel-restaurant Le Manoir aux Quat'Saisons?

13 The former host of the TV series *The Delicious Miss Dahl* has what first name?

14 Who took over from Michel Roux Jr as judge on *MasterChef: the Professionals*?

15 Which chef presented the 2018 TV series *Lose Weight for Good* after shedding 12 stone himself?

16 Which chef co-presents *Amazing Hotels: Life Beyond the Lobby* with Giles Coren?

17 In which BBC competition do professional chefs aim to cook at a banquet at the end of the series?

18 Who presented the series *Saturday Kitchen* from 2006 to 2016?

19 Which chef opened The Fat Duck restaurant in 1995?

20 What nationality is the Muppets' chef?

Answers to QUIZ 382 – Bells and Whistles

1	Scotland	11	Anna
2	Pea	12	*The King and I*
3	Bell-bottoms	13	Martin Bell
4	*Pinocchio*	14	Flageolet
5	Eight	15	*Peter Pan*
6	Kettle	16	Whistle-blower
7	Sylvia Plath	17	On a graph
8	Whisle-stop tour	18	Canada
9	Anita Ward	19	Dashing through the snow
10	Have a drink	20	Hayley Mills

1 Gin and vermouth are mixed to make which cocktail?

2 What is the name of the parrot owned by Doctor Dolittle?

3 What is the tip of an ink pen called?

4 In the radio alphabet, which word lies between India and kilo?

5 Which llama-like animal is prized for its soft wool?

6 *Everybody Hurts* was a 1992 hit for which group?

7 Stefan Dennis is best known for playing which *Neighbours* character?

8 What is the fifth colour of the rainbow?

9 Who duetted with George Michael in 1991 on *Don't Let the Sun go Down on Me*?

10 With which meat is apple sauce traditionally served?

11 Which musical notes equals half a minim?

12 *First Among Equals* is a 1984 novel by which author?

13 What name is given to the cycle of four operas by Wagner?

14 Australia has which two letters as its internet country code?

15 The concluding section of a play or book is given what name?

16 What is the French word for "yes"?

17 What do Americans call a caravan site?

18 Alexandra Burke topped the charts with which classic song after winning *The X Factor*?

19 The atria are in which organ of the body?

20 Which actress starred in the 1993 film *Indecent Proposal*?

Easy

Medium

Hard

Answers to QUIZ 383 – Pot Luck

1	Groucho Marx	11	Cranberry
2	*Terra*	12	Oahu
3	*Hancock's Half Hour*	13	Avon
4	William Basie	14	Bore and boar
5	Litre	15	A whale
6	Hot Chocolate	16	*Roxanne*
7	Ricin	17	Sherlock Holmes
8	Sweden	18	Jet
9	Bigamy	19	Nicole Kidman
10	Desmond Morris	20	Douro

Easy

1 What type of drink is arabica?

2 Bob Cratchit appears in which Charles Dickens novel?

3 Which part of the body is affected by colic?

4 Which part of London is famous for its diamond trade?

5 In which country is Entebbe?

6 Which DJ (d.2006) was nicknamed "Fluff"?

7 The Oxfordshire village of Goring is on which river?

8 "Hammersmith Palais" was one of the *Reasons to be Cheerful* for which singer?

9 What does the French word *ici* mean in English?

10 In which year did Jessie J top the charts with *Price Tag* and *Domino*?

11 Which American inventor founded the Kodak camera company?

12 Limassol is a port on which Mediterranean island?

13 As what was the Millennium Dome in Greenwich renamed in 2005?

14 In which county is the town of Newlyn?

Medium

15 What type of drink is oloroso?

16 Which team won rugby's Aviva Premiership in the 2016-17 season?

17 A ringmaster presents what type of entertainment?

18 What other playground equipment is paired with "swings" to describe changes in fortune?

19 Chris Tarrant was the original host of which game show that began in 1998?

20 What is another name for the Australian landmark Uluru?

Hard

Answers to QUIZ 384 – Chefs and Cooks

1	Delia Smith	11	Nigella Lawson
2	Gino D'Acampo	12	Raymond Blanc
3	*Hell's Kitchen USA*	13	Sophie
4	Gregg Wallace and John Torode	14	Marcus Wareing
5	The Hairy Bikers	15	Tom Kerridge
6	Phil Vickery	16	Monica Galetti
7	Hugh Fearnley-Whittingstall	17	*Great British Menu*
8	Jamie Oliver	18	James Martin
9	Monica Geller	19	Heston Blumenthal
10	Nadiya Hussain	20	Swedish

1   What name is given to the mixture of butter and flour used to thicken sauces?

2   *A New Hope* is the fourth episode in which film series?

3   Who sang *Don't Go Breaking My Heart* with Sir Elton John in 1976?

4   The zodiac sign Scorpio covers which two calendar months?

5   Which biblical boat carried two of each creature?

6   What is the name of the Muslim month of fasting?

7   "What's up, Doc?" is the catchphrase of which cartoon character?

8   Which word meaning "fuming" means "a river blockage" when read backwards?

9   Michael Bolton had a 1991 no.1 record with which song?

10   Which brand-name cooker is associated with the novels of Joanna Trollope?

11   Who composed the music for the 1889 ballet *Sleeping Beauty*?

12   Since 1967, what has been the capital of Pakistan?

13   What is the name of the small, toothed whale that resembles a dolphin?

14   Which stretch of shingle off the Dorset coast is 17 miles long?

15   The Penguin is an arch-enemy of which comic-book hero?

16   What is the surname of Kirstie, who starred in *Cheers* and the *Look Who's Talking* films?

17   The personal finance programme *Money Box* appears on which radio station?

18   Who is the star of the *Johnny English* films?

19   *We Are the Champions* was a 1977 hit for which band?

20   Which knitted woollen jacket was named after an earl?

Answers to QUIZ 385 – Pot Luck

1	Martini	11	Crotchet
2	Polynesia	12	Jeffrey Archer
3	Nib	13	*The Ring*
4	Juliet	14	.au
5	Alpaca	15	Epilogue
6	REM	16	*Oui*
7	Paul Robinson	17	Trailer park
8	Blue	18	*Hallelujah*
9	Sir Elton John	19	The heart
10	Pork	20	Demi Moore

Easy

1   What is the ankle-length robe worn by members of the clergy, the name of which rhymes with the word for a prayer-cushion?

2   The poncho originates from which continent?

3   What is the modern one-word term for "fancy dress"?

4   Which US state is noted for its colourful shirts?

5   What Spanish word for twilled cotton cloth is used for a style of trousers?

6   On which part of the body would a wimple be worn?

7   Which casual cotton top takes its name from a sport played on horseback?

8   What name connects a large silky-haired hound with a 1970s sheepskin coat?

9   For what activity would you wear salopettes?

10 What is the name for a man's formal outfit worn at a wedding?

Medium

11 Which style of full-gathered skirt originates from Tyrolean peasant wear?

12 Gendarmes wear what flat-topped military hat?

13 Which two colours of tie lend their names to a formal dress code?

14 The word "jodphurs" originates from which country?

15 Which warm item of clothing shares its name with a species of cow?

16 Culottes are a short pair of trousers cut to look like which other item of clothing?

17 Which Spanish dance is also the name of a jacket?

18 What material are chaps made from?

19 Popular in the 1980s, which skirt shares its name with a type of fungus?

20 What is the long white clerical robe whose name derives from the Latin word for "white"?

Hard

Answers to QUIZ 386 – First and Last

1	Coffee	11	George Eastman
2	A Christmas Carol	12	Cyprus
3	Abdomen	13	The O2 Arena
4	Hatton Garden	14	Cornwall
5	Uganda	15	Sherry
6	Alan Freeman	16	Exeter Chiefs
7	Thames	17	Circus acts
8	Ian Dury	18	Roundabouts
9	Here	19	Who Wants to Be a Millionaire?
10	2011	20	Ayers Rock

1   Who had a hit in 1978 with *MacArthur Park*?

2   Who starred as Frank Chambers in the 1981 film *The Postman Always Rings Twice*?

3   Which former British ski jumper was the subject of a 2016 film, the title of which was his nickname?

4   Matt Baker and Ellie Harrison are presenters on which BBC rural affairs programme?

5   Which city hosted the Eurovision Song Contest in 2018?

6   Rudyard Kipling wrote which "exact-sounding" stories?

7   What was the title of the 2007 film in the *Bourne* series?

8   What name was given to the three Victorian Acts that amended the system of parliamentary representation?

9   Who had a 1976 hit with *Sir Duke*?

10 What term is given to a female fox?

11 In which county are the Mendip Hills located?

12 On the Japanese flag, what colour is the large circle?

13 Which bird is also known as the green plover or peewit?

14 What is the phrase for being held in custody awaiting trial?

15 Who plays Jackie in the TV series *Friday Night Dinner*?

16 Which Hebrew prophet was delivered from the lion's den?

17 *Swan Lake* was written by which Russian composer?

18 What is the Anglican tradition resembling Catholicism?

19 What is the world's second-largest ocean?

20 Which market city is near Fountains Abbey?

Easy
Medium
Hard

Answers to QUIZ 387 – Pot Luck

1	Roux	11	Tchaikovsky
2	*Star Wars*	12	Islamabad
3	Kiki Dee	13	Porpoise
4	October and November	14	Chesil Beach
5	Noah's Ark	15	Batman
6	Ramadan	16	Alley
7	Bugs Bunny	17	Radio 4
8	Mad	18	Rowan Atkinson
9	*When a Man Loves a Woman*	19	Queen
10	Aga (Aga Saga)	20	Cardigan

Easy

1 Which actor starred as Steve Austin in *The Six Million Dollar Man* in the 1970s?

2 For what did the letters UXB stand in *Danger UXB*?

3 Who played Ria in the TV series *Butterflies* which began in 1978?

4 Which long-running series featured the character Cliff Barnes?

5 Who was the first presenter of *Give Us A Clue*?

6 In which 1970s sitcom did Dame Penelope Keith play Margo?

7 Which 1978-88 quiz show featured Dusty Bin?

8 Who starred in the original TV series of *Police Woman*?

9 What was the name of Brian Wilde's prison officer in *Porridge*?

10 Which spin-off from *Man About the House* starred Richard O'Sullivan as a chef?

11 How were Kate Jackson, Jaclyn Smith and Farrah Fawcett collectively known in the 1970s?

12 Which US crime series featured the catchphrase "Who loves ya, baby?"?

13 In which US sitcom did Suzi Quatro appear as "Leather" Tuscadero?

Medium

14 Which singer was the star of the TV series *Budgie*?

15 John-Boy, Olivia and Jason were members of which family?

16 The main characters in *The Sweeney* worked for which branch of the Met Police?

17 Captain Dobey was the boss of which two crime-fighters?

18 Which US series featured Bo and Luke and their cousin Daisy?

19 Who played private investigator James Rockford?

20 Which duo signed off each programme with "It's goodnight from me. And it's goodnight from him"?

Hard

Answers to QUIZ 388 – Clothing

1	Cassock	11	Dirndl
2	South America	12	Kepi
3	Cosplay	13	Black and white
4	Hawaii	14	Indian
5	Chino	15	Jersey
6	Head	16	Skirt
7	Polo shirt	17	Bolero
8	Afghan	18	Leather
9	Skiing	19	Puffball
10	Morning dress	20	Alb

ANSWERS ON PAGE 393

1   What is the fifth note of the tonic sol-fa scale?

2   The Costa del Sol is in which country?

3   Which long-running Radio 4 show is "an everyday story of country folk"?

4   Prince Rainier of Monaco married which film star?

5   Which former star of *Doctor Who* also played the title role in the TV series *Worzel Gummidge*?

6   In the name of the US TV network, what do the initials HBO stand for?

7   Who played Captain Von Trapp in the 1965 film *The Sound of Music*?

8   Which animal is known for constructing dams and lodges?

9   What is the capital city of Australia?

10 What is an Aberdeen Angus?

11 The acre was replaced by which metric measurement?

12 In what year did Austria regain full independence?

13 Who composed the music for *Cats* and *Evita*?

14 What was the nationality of philosopher/mathematician René Descartes (b.1596)?

15 The town of Bicester is in which county?

16 The Swiss ski resort of Zermatt is near the foot of which mountain?

17 Which Algarve coastal town shares a name with Nigeria's largest city?

18 In which poem does the shooting of an albatross cause bad luck?

19 Who had a 1980 hit with *Brass in Pocket*?

20 Which actress starred as Becky Sharp in the 2004 film *Vanity Fair*?

Easy
Medium
Hard

Answers to QUIZ 389 – Pot Luck

1	Donna Summer	11	Somerset
2	Jack Nicholson	12	Red
3	"Eddie" Edwards (Eddie the Eagle)	13	Lapwing
4	*Countryfile*	14	On remand
5	Lisbon	15	Tamsin Greig
6	*Just So*	16	Daniel
7	*The Bourne Ultimatum*	17	Tchaikovsky
8	Reform Acts	18	High Church
9	Stevie Wonder	19	Atlantic
10	Vixen	20	Ripon

ANSWERS ON PAGE 394

1   What name is given to a carved or paper band high up in a room?

2   For what is a bracket used?

3   A hod is used for carrying which items?

4   What mixture is used to fill in the spaces between tiles?

5   What type of soap is used for cleaning paintwork?

6   Which preparation material shares its name with a book containing basic facts about a subject?

7   The layer of material placed between a floor and a carpet is given what term?

8   What would an interior designer use a mood board for?

9   How is paint applied if it is "stippled"?

10   What term is give to one of four vertical surfaces in a room that has been decorated in a more noticeable manner than the rest?

11   A decorative centrepiece on the upper surface of a room has what flowery name?

12   Which device is used in checking the setting of horizontal surfaces?

13   A popular neutral paint colour shares its name with which spring-flowering shrub?

14   Which wooden style of furniture with a simple design takes its name from an American religious group?

15   Pencil pleat and eyelet are types of which soft furnishing?

16   Which style of decorating is based on making the furniture look old in an attractive way?

17   What method of decorating involves applying paint to a cut-out template?

18   A piece of string with a weight on it, used to check vertical angles, has what two-word name?

19   What type of hammer is used for extracting nails?

20   Which type of paint sounds like it is a natural casing?

Easy

Medium

Hard

Answers to QUIZ 390 – 1970s Television

1	Lee Majors	11	Charlie's Angels
2	Unexploded Bomb	12	*Kojak*
3	Wendy Craig	13	*Happy Days*
4	*Dallas*	14	Adam Faith
5	Michael Aspel	15	The Waltons
6	*The Good Life*	16	Flying Squad
7	3-2-1	17	Starsky and Hutch
8	Angie Dickinson	18	*The Dukes of Hazzard*
9	Mr Barrowclough	19	James Garner
10	*Robin's Nest*	20	The Two Ronnies

1 What is the surname of André, the famous Dutch violinist?

2 Toni Basil reached no.2 in the UK charts in 1982 with which song?

3 Which actress was painted gold in the 1964 film *Goldfinger*?

4 *Sound of the Underground* (2002) was the first hit for which group?

5 Which alloy of copper, tin and zinc was originally used for making firearms?

6 Oxbridge sportsmen and women are associated with which colour?

7 What is the title of the Channel 4 TV series which features people watching television?

8 The skull of Yorick features in which Shakespeare play?

9 Which group topped the UK singles chart in 1975 with *Bye Bye Baby* and *Give A Little Love*?

10 In which board game are the letters Z and Q worth ten points each?

11 With which industry is Julien MacDonald associated?

12 Which Parisian thoroughfare leads up to the Arc de Triomphe?

13 Barbara Vine was a pseudonym for which crime author?

14 Which country did Mats Wilander represent in tennis?

15 According to the song, how many trombones were there in the big parade?

16 In which county is the town of Corsham?

17 Which town near Hastings in East Sussex is the location of a famous abbey?

18 Who starred in the 1970s sitcom *Citizen Smith*?

19 Which company created the *Super Mario* series of games?

20 The Who and Sir Elton John both had hits with which song from the film *Tommy*?

Easy

Medium

Hard

Answers to QUIZ 391 – Pot Luck

1	Soh	11	Hectare
2	Spain	12	1955
3	*The Archers*	13	Andrew Lloyd Webber (Baron Lloyd-Webber)
4	Grace Kelly	14	French
5	Jon Pertwee	15	Oxfordshire
6	Home Box Office	16	Matterhorn
7	Christopher Plummer	17	Lagos
8	A beaver	18	*The Rime of The Ancient Mariner*
9	Canberra	19	The Pretenders
10	Breed of cattle	20	Reese Witherspoon

393

1 Which duo had a hit in 1982 with *Say Hello, Wave Goodbye*?

2 *Leave Right Now* was a 2003 hit for which singer?

3 *Gudbuy T'Jane* was a 1972 single by which glam rock band?

4 Which band recorded the 1982 single *See You*?

5 Who topped the UK singles charts in 2017 with *Too Good at Goodbyes*?

6 "I just can't stand the pain. Girl I'm leaving you tomorrow" is a lyric from which 1977 song?

7 1967's *Hello, Goodbye* was taken from which Beatles album?

8 How many ways did Paul Simon say there were to leave your lover?

9 *The Last Farewell* was a 1975 hit for which singer?

10 In which year did The Spice Girls top the charts with *Goodbye*?

11 *Don't Leave Me This Way* was in the charts in 1977 for both Harold Melvin and the Bluenotes and which female singer?

12 Sir Elton John said *Goodbye* to which thoroughfare in a 1973 song?

13 *Another Suitcase in Another Hall* is a song from which musical?

14 Sarah Brightman duetted with which opera singer on 1997's *Time to Say Goodbye*?

15 Who sang *Farewell My Summer Love* in 1984?

16 *Ready To Go* was a 1990s single by which English band?

17 *Too Late for Goodbyes* was a 1984 single by which singer?

18 What was the title of the band Chicago's only UK no.1 single?

19 Which heavy metal band released the 1982 single *Run to the Hills*?

20 The album *All That You Can't Leave Behind* was a chart-topper for which band?

Answers to QUIZ 392 – DIY and Decorating

1	Frieze	11	Ceiling rose
2	Supporting a shelf	12	Spirit level
3	Bricks	13	Magnolia
4	Grout	14	Shaker
5	Sugar soap	15	Curtains
6	Primer	16	Shabby chic
7	Underlay	17	Stencilling
8	Displaying samples of colour and texture	18	Plumb line
9	Dabbed on	19	Claw hammer
10	Feature wall	20	Eggshell

1 Which organisation was featured in the TV series *Jam & Jerusalem*?

2 Which group had a hit in 1980 with *Super Trouper*?

3 In a four-man bobsleigh team, where does the "brakeman" sit?

4 Who was Lou Costello's comedy partner?

5 What is the most common freestyle swimming stroke?

6 The original fairy tale of *Thumbelina* was written by which author?

7 Which Asian country has over thirteen thousand equatorial islands?

8 Which English king was executed in 1649?

9 *Oh, I Wish I'd Looked After Me Teeth* is by which writer of comic verse?

10 Which singer had a hit with *Walking on Broken Glass* in 1992?

11 Which river flows through Sheffield and Rotherham?

12 What was the surname of *The Likely Lads* actor Rodney?

13 Patrick Swayze and Demi Moore starred in whch romantic film of 1990?

14 Who played JR in TV's *Dallas*?

15 Which is the most northerly British town?

16 *Under Your Thumb* was a hit for which two former members of the band 10cc?

17 Who is best known for playing David Platt in *Coronation Street*?

18 The word "fritillary" can apply to a plant and to which insect?

19 Dustin Johnson (b.1984) plays which sport?

20 Where in California is the hottest part of the USA?

Answers to QUIZ 393 – Pot Luck

1	Rieu	11	Fashion
2	*Mickey*	12	Champs-Élysées
3	Shirley Eaton	13	Baroness Ruth Rendell
4	Girls Aloud	14	Sweden
5	Gunmetal	15	76
6	Blue	16	Wiltshire
7	*Gogglebox*	17	Battle
8	*Hamlet*	18	Robert Lindsay
9	Bay City Rollers	19	Nintendo®
10	Scrabble®	20	*Pinball Wizard*

Easy

1. What term is given to the upper chamber of the UK parliament?
2. In which county is Ilfracombe?
3. Which legendary British film company is famous for its horror films?
4. Which bridge on the Thames is closest to the Tower of London?
5. In which region of Scotland is Dunfermline?
6. What is the colloquial name for female members of the Royal Navy?
7. How is the Feast of St Stephen better known in the UK?
8. In which county is the Welsh town of Brecon?
9. What name links a classic Epsom horse race and a Midlands city on the River Derwent?
10. Which Upper Deeside village near Balmoral is famous for its annual Highland Games?

Medium

11. The Pennines are crossed by which motorway?
12. A parish minister of the Church of Scotland lives in what residence?
13. Which Dartmoor village is famous for a traditional ballad about its fair?
14. Who composed *Rule Britannia*?
15. Every October, which event of medieval origin takes place in Nottingham?
16. Which writer had a home at Hill Top in the Lake District?
17. In which Northern Ireland county is the Giant's Causeway?
18. Which Brixton avenue did Eddy Grant name in a 1983 hit?
19. In an English trial, how many people sit on the jury?
20. Which Dorset port and resort is famous for its Cobb?

Hard

1 What is the world's lowest lake?

2 Of which type of composition is Handel's *Messiah* an example?

3 Which Dutch explorer gave his name to an Australian island state?

4 Who wrote *Treasure Island* (1883)?

5 Which glam rock group sang the festive favourite *Merry Christmas Everybody*?

6 The 2008 film *Quantum of Solace* starred which actor as James Bond?

7 Which pale yellow beverage is often drunk with Chinese meals?

8 CDN is the international vehicle registration code for which country?

9 Which group had a 1979 hit with *Cool for Cats*?

10 What was the first name of the "King of Swing" jazz musician Mr Goodman?

11 The Hungarian language is known by what name in Hungarian?

12 Which gemstone is traditionally associated with the month of February?

13 What is the protective covering on the nose-cone of a spacecraft called?

14 Erinsborough is the setting for which long-running series?

15 The 1960s band the Dreamers had who as their frontman?

16 Which Chinese exercise system translates in English as "supreme ultimate"?

17 What is the reef material made by tiny aquatic animals?

18 Andy and Lance were played by Mackenzie Crook and Toby Jones in which comedy series?

19 In which county is Margate?

20 What is the American term for an overnight plane journey called?

Easy

Medium

Hard

Answers to QUIZ 395 – Pot Luck

1	Women's Institute	11	Don
2	ABBA	12	Bewes
3	At the rear	13	*Ghost*
4	Bud Abbott	14	Larry Hagman
5	Crawl	15	Lerwick (Shetland Islands)
6	Hans Christian Andersen	16	Godley and Creme
7	Indonesia	17	Jack P Shepherd
8	Charles I	18	Butterfly
9	Pam Ayres	19	Golf
10	Annie Lennox	20	Death Valley

Easy

1 Who co-starred with Michael Douglas in *Romancing the Stone*?

2 Which Scottish comedian co-starred with Dame Judi Dench in the 1997 film *Mrs Brown*?

3 In the 1988 thriller *Tequila Sunrise*, which actress co-starred with Mel Gibson?

4 Rebecca De Mornay co-starred with which actor in the 1983 film *Risky Business*?

5 Which member of the cast of *Friends* starred with Bruce Willis in *The Whole Nine Yards*?

6 Who was Nicole Kidman's co-star in the 2005 film *The Interpreter*?

7 Which 1999 adventure film starred Brendan Fraser and Rachel Weisz?

8 Who were the two stars of the 2016 film *La La Land*?

9 Which 2008 film set in Tudor times starred Scarlett Johansson and Natalie Portman?

10 How many *First Dates* did Drew Barrymore and Adam Sandler have in the title of a 2004 film?

11 Who directed Tom Hanks and Meg Ryan in *You've Got Mail*?

Medium

12 Chris O'Donnell played Robin to which star's Batman in the 1997 film *Batman & Robin*?

13 Which 1994 suspense film starred Keanu Reeves and Sandra Bullock?

14 Who co-starred with Leonardo DiCaprio in *Revolutionary Road* (2008)?

15 Which 1999 film was the second to co-star Julia Roberts and Richard Gere?

16 In the 1967 film, who played Bonnie and Clyde?

17 Who co-starred with Meryl Streep in the 1985 film *Out of Africa*?

18 Which 1995 crime thriller starred Al Pacino and Robert De Niro?

19 In the 1994 film *Four Weddings and a Funeral*, who played Charles and Carrie?

20 Which famous co-stars married in 1964 and again in 1975?

Hard

Answers to QUIZ 396 – The UK

1	House of Lords	11	M62
2	Devon	12	A manse
3	Hammer	13	Widecombe
4	Tower Bridge	14	Thomas Arne
5	Fife	15	Goose Fair
6	Wrens	16	Beatrix Potter
7	Boxing Day	17	Antrim
8	Powys	18	Electric Avenue
9	Derby	19	12
10	Braemar	20	Lyme Regis

ANSWERS ON PAGE 401

1 On which Scottish island is the town of Tobermory?

2 Which Raymond presented TV's new-technology programme *Tomorrow's World* from 1965 until 1977?

3 Which part of speech is the word "under"?

4 "They think it's all over. It is now" was said by which commentator in the 1966 FIFA World Cup Final?

5 Which sinister French cardinal features in the adventures of the Three Musketeers?

6 Which town in Kent adjoins Walmer?

7 Who was the British prime minister from 1974 to 1976?

8 In *The Wizard of Oz*, which of Dorothy's companions wanted a heart?

9 Which group had a hit in 1964 with *I Get Around*?

10 What was the first name of children's book illustrator Lucie Attwell?

11 The BBC's *Later...* TV series is presented by which musician?

12 Dean Gaffney is best known for playing which character in *EastEnders*?

13 What do the initials HGV stand for?

14 According to the rhyme, what happened to Solomon Grundy on Tuesday?

15 Which city is the capital of Bangladesh?

16 In the House of Lords, what colour are the seats?

17 Which is the USA's "Beehive State"?

18 The theme to which film gave Olivia Newton-John and ELO a 1980 no.1?

19 Bombay Duck is what type of food?

20 Galatasaray football team is based in which country?

Easy

Medium

Hard

Answers to QUIZ 397 – Pot Luck

1	Dead Sea	11	Magyar
2	Oratorio	12	Amethyst
3	Abel Tasman (Tasmania)	13	Heat shield
4	Robert Louis Stevenson	14	*Neighbours*
5	Slade	15	Freddie (Garrity)
6	Daniel Craig	16	Tai chi
7	Jasmine tea	17	Coral
8	Canada	18	*Detectorists*
9	Squeeze	19	Kent
10	Benny	20	Red-eye

Easy

1. On the Beaufort Scale, what type of tropical storm has the highest-speed wind?

2. The French word *neige* indicates what type of weather?

3. In which decade was the world's first successful weather satellite launched?

4. What name is given to the warming of part of the Pacific that happens every few years and affects weather patterns?

5. Does a warm front indicate a future drop in temperature or rise in temperature?

6. Which "ology" is the study of weather?

7. In the Solar UV index, what does "UV" stand for?

8. Which device measures air pressure to show when the weather is changing?

9. What term is given to the measure of the amount of water in the air?

10. How is visibility of less than 1 km described in weather reports?

11. A severe weather warning indicating "be aware" is shown as which colour?

12. What is a dust devil?

13. What term is given to the general weather conditions of a place?

Medium

14. Exposure to sunlight produces which vitamin?

15. Which Charles Dickens character gave her name to an inelegant umbrella?

16. What type of weather is indicated by a symbol of a cloud with one raindrop and one snowflake below it?

17. Which colour comes after green in the rainbow?

18. What term is given to the central part of a storm?

19. Does a northerly wind blow from the north or towards the north?

20. If the pollen count is shown as orange, how is it described?

Hard

Answers to QUIZ 398 – Co-Stars

1	Kathleen Turner	11	Nora Ephron
2	Sir Billy Connolly	12	George Clooney
3	Michelle Pfeiffer	13	*Speed*
4	Tom Cruise	14	Kate Winslet
5	Matthew Perry	15	*Runaway Bride*
6	Sean Penn	16	Faye Dunaway and Warren Beatty
7	*The Mummy*	17	Robert Redford
8	Emma Stone and Ryan Gosling	18	*Heat*
9	*The Other Boleyn Girl*	19	Hugh Grant and Andie MacDowell
10	*50*	20	Elizabeth Taylor and Richard Burton

1   In Europe, which era followed the Neolithic?

2   Which writers created the series *Dad's Army*?

3   Of which Gulf state is Muscat the capital?

4   What was the name of Stephen Hawking's first wife, on whose book the 2014 film *The Theory of Everything* was based?

5   Which elaborate structure did Daedalus build for King Minos of Crete?

6   *The Lion Sleeps Tonight* was a chart-topping hit for which group in 1982?

7   Which actress starred in the 2002 film *Bend it Like Beckham*?

8   What name is given to any surgical device used to tie blood vessels to stop bleeding?

9   The opera *Dido and Aeneas* (1680) was written by which English composer?

10   Which Venice landmark is known in Italian as "Ponte dei Sospiri"?

11   James Earl Jones provided the voice of which *Star Wars* character?

12   What is the title of the Fred Astaire musical which includes the song *Cheek to Cheek*?

13   What literary form does *The Pilgrim's Progress* (1678) take?

14   Which Essex town was granted city status in 2012?

15   What is the tenth letter of the Greek alphabet?

16   Declan MacManus was the original name of which singer?

17   What name is given to volcanic glass formed from lava?

18   Joseph Smith founded which religion?

19   Whose theory of the solar system was published in 1543 just before his death?

20   Which book of the Bible tells of the birth of Moses?

Easy

Medium

Hard

Answers to QUIZ 399 – Pot Luck

1	Mull	11	Jools Holland
2	Baxter	12	Robbie Jackson
3	Preposition	13	Heavy Goods Vehicle
4	Kenneth Wolstenholme	14	He was Christened
5	Cardinal Richelieu	15	Dhaka
6	Deal	16	Red
7	Harold Wilson (Baron Wilson of Rievaulx)	17	Utah
8	Tin Man	18	*Xanadu*
9	The Beach Boys	19	Fish
10	Mabel	20	Turkey

Easy

1   By what name is artist Jack Hoggan better known?

2   Which artist painted *The Garden of Earthly Delights*?

3   Which German Renaissance artist (b.1471) was famous for his woodcuts?

4   What title precedes the names of the artists Angelico and Filippo Lippi?

5   Bridget Riley is particularly known for which type of creative design?

6   Who painted *Bar at the Folies-Bergère* (1882)?

7   A picture painted on a wall before the plaster is dry is given what term?

8   Which artist was the first president of the Royal Academy?

9   In which town of Provence, in 1888, did Van Gogh share a house with Gauguin?

10 Who was Augustus John's painter sister?

11 Which British artist designed the lions in Trafalgar Square?

Medium

12 *Saturn Devouring His Son* was painted by which artist (b.1746)?

13 What were the first two names of artist LS Lowry?

14 In which city was David Hockney born?

15 Which Suffolk river provides the setting for the painting *The Hay Wain*?

16 Which Austrian painter Gustav was best known for his early 20th-century painting *The Kiss*?

17 Who created the art installation *Another Place*, featuring 100 statues?

18 In which Spanish city was Picasso born?

19 Which painter born in Latvia in 1903 was known for his large hazy rectangles of colour?

20 What is the term for a painting or design intended to deceive the eye?

Hard

Answers to QUIZ 400 – Weather

1	Hurricane	11	Yellow
2	Snow	12	A small whirlwind
3	1960s	13	Climate
4	El Niño	14	Vitamin D
5	Rise in temperature	15	Mrs Gamp
6	Meteorology	16	Sleet
7	Ultraviolet	17	Blue
8	Barometer	18	Eye
9	Humidity	19	From the north
10	Very poor	20	Moderate

ANSWERS ON PAGE 405

1   What was the nationality of the psychologist Jean Piaget?

2   On which island does the annual Battle of Flowers take place?

3   Which part of the body is affected by Crohn's Disease?

4   Which battle of 1346 between England and France involved the Black Prince?

5   On which river does Winchester stand?

6   In which year was Helen Shapiro *Walking Back to Happiness* at the top of the UK charts?

7   Which river flows through Canterbury?

8   Which French name is given to a large decorative wardrobe?

9   Which of the Haven Ports is the northernmost coastal town in Essex?

10 In literature, what was the name of adventurer Phileas Fogg's manservant?

11 Which band had a hit in 1972 with *Children of the Revolution*?

12 In which year did Sir Edmund Hillary and Tenzing Norgay become the first people to climb Mount Everest?

13 Which US comedian, born in Eltham in London, died in 2003 aged 100?

14 What was the title of the 1983 Heaven 17 hit that was also a hit when it was re-mixed and released in 1992?

15 Which actress starred in *Ninotchka* (1939)?

16 What is the second largest lake in the Lake District?

17 A Cuba libre cocktail has what type of alcohol as its basis?

18 Which group had a 1974 hit with *Teenage Rampage*?

19 Which country is home to the Korat cat?

20 In which year did banking via the Internet first become available in the UK?

Easy

Medium

Hard

Answers to QUIZ 401 – Pot Luck

1	Bronze Age	11	Darth Vader
2	Jimmy Perry and David Croft	12	*Top Hat*
3	Oman	13	Allegory
4	Jane	14	Chelmsford
5	Labyrinth	15	Kappa
6	Tight Fit	16	Elvis Costello
7	Keira Knightley	17	Obsidian
8	A ligature	18	Mormonism
9	Henry Purcell	19	Nicolaus Copernicus
10	Bridge of Sighs	20	Exodus

1 Gophers are native to which continent?

2 *Corvus frugilegus* is the Latin name of which bird of the crow family?

3 What term is given to a colony of baboons?

4 What secretion do honey bees produce to feed their larvae?

5 Collectively, how is a group of rhinoceroses referred to?

6 Which animal is known in America as the caribou?

7 The term "ursine" relates to which type of animal?

8 What is a baby pigeon called?

9 Which cod-like fish is also known as saithe?

10 Which part of a horse's mane falls in front between the ears?

11 How many legs does a katydid have?

12 "Forest person" is the meaning of the name of which ape found in Borneo?

13 Which is the fastest member of the animal kingdom?

14 Which river animal has been reintroduced to Knapdale in Scotland and is now a protected species?

15 "Reynard" is a old name for which animal?

16 A gadwall is what type of animal?

17 The egg-laying mammal called the spiny anteater has what other one-word name?

18 What term is given to a female badger?

19 What is the middle section of an insect?

20 The water ouzel is an alternative name for which bird?

Answers to QUIZ 402 – Art

1	Jack Vettriano	11	Sir Edwin Landseer
2	Hieronymus Bosch	12	Francisco Goya
3	Albrecht Dürer	13	Laurence Stephen
4	Fra	14	Bradford
5	Op art	15	Stour
6	Édouard Manet	16	Klimt
7	Fresco	17	Sir Antony Gormley
8	Sir Joshua Reynolds	18	Málaga
9	Arles	19	Mark Rothko
10	Gwen	20	*Trompe l'oeil*

1   Which 18th-century economist wrote *The Wealth of Nations?*

2   Which museum is located at Cosford in Shropshire?

3   Often used as a thickening agent, which cereal is obtained from the root of the cassava plant?

4   Which Swiss resort lies at the northern end of Lake Maggiore?

5   Which singer's debut album *In The Lonely Hour* was released in 2014?

6   What form of Buddhism featured in the title of Robert M Pirsig's 1974 bestseller?

7   *Setting Sons* was a 1979 album by which band?

8   What is the monetary unit of Vietnam?

9   *You Make Me Feel Brand New* was a hit for which 1970s soul band?

10   Which 1987 Michael Jackson album featured the song *Man in the Mirror?*

11   Who wrote the 1939 novel *After Many a Summer?*

12   Which beverage is made from the dried leaves of *Camellia sinensis?*

13   Which legal term means "not open to appeal"?

14   On which lake does Milwaukee stand?

15   In which Suffolk location was a Viking burial ship discovered in 1939?

16   First aired in 1953, to what did the radio programme *What Do You Know?* change its name in 1967?

17   What was Pakistan's first capital city?

18   Which Irish city stands at the head of the Shannon estuary?

19   *The Last Kiss* was a 1985 single by which former teen idol?

20   Which English king died in 1087 after falling off his horse?

Answers to QUIZ 403 – Pot Luck

1	Swiss	11	T Rex
2	Jersey	12	1953
3	The intestines (especially the colon)	13	Bob Hope
4	Crécy	14	*Temptation*
5	Itchen	15	Greta Garbo
6	1961	16	Ullswater
7	Stour	17	Rum
8	Armoire	18	The Sweet
9	Harwich	19	Thailand
10	Passepartout	20	1997

Easy

1. What was the surname of the French brothers who made the first piloted ascent in an air balloon in 1783?

2. Which German-born Count pioneered airship development from the late 19th century?

3. In which year did the *Hindenberg* disaster happen?

4. Who invented the modern helicopter and later designed the R-4, the world's first mass-produced helicopter?

5. What do the initials IATA stand for?

6. What is the name of Russia's national airline?

7. In which London borough is London City Airport?

8. What is the name of the English entrepreneur who completed the longest flight in a hot air-balloon, between Japan and Canada in 1991?

9. On which island is Cristiano Ronaldo Airport?

Medium

10. What is the average in-flight altitude of passenger aeroplanes?

11. CBR is the code for which international airport?

12. ESTA is a system used when travelling to which country?

13. What do the initials LAPL stand for in relation to aviation?

14. What type of vehicle is a sailplane?

15. Which airport formerly had terminals named Europa and Oceanic?

16. Which town in West Sussex hosts the International Birdman Competition?

17. The first female flight attendant was hired by which airline?

18. Which two of London's international airports are situated in Essex?

19. Which city is served by an airport located at Dyce?

20. In 2012, who jumped to Earth from a helium balloon in the stratosphere?

Hard

Answers to QUIZ 404 – Animal World

1	North America	11	Six (a cricket)
2	Rook	12	Orang-utan
3	Troop	13	Peregrine falcon
4	Royal jelly	14	Beaver
5	Crash	15	A fox
6	Reindeer	16	A duck
7	Bear	17	Echidna
8	Squab	18	Sow
9	Coley	19	Thorax
10	Forelock	20	Dipper

1 On the Beatles' *White Album*, who played lead guitar on *While My Guitar Gently Weeps*?

2 What feature has a palmiped bird?

3 Michael Brandon and Glynis Barber starred in which 1980s TV police series?

4 Which English city was called Glevum by the Romans?

5 Which Coldplay album did the single *Yellow* first appear on?

6 Bright's disease affects which organ of the body?

7 Which foodstuff was known as "hokey-pokey" in the late 19th century?

8 Which amateur detective was played by Tom Bosley on TV from 1989 to 1991?

9 Turpentine is obtained from the resin of which tree?

10 What is the capital city of Ukraine?

11 What was Elvis Presley's first UK no.1?

12 *Candy Girl* was a hit for which group in 1983?

13 What was the public space for markets in ancient Greece called?

14 Which bird has the largest wingspan of any living bird?

15 An annelid is what type of creature?

16 Which poet wrote the 1919 poem *The Second Coming*?

17 What term is given to crushed stone or gravel used to make concrete?

18 From 1999 to 2003, who captained the England cricket team?

19 Who wrote the *Twilight* series of novels?

20 Who first vaccinated people and animals against rabies, in 1885?

Answers to QUIZ 405 – Pot Luck

1	Adam Smith	11	Aldous Huxley
2	Royal Air Force Museum	12	Tea
3	Tapioca	13	Peremptory
4	Locarno	14	Lake Michigan
5	Sam Smith	15	Sutton Hoo
6	Zen (*Zen and the Art of Motorcycle Maintenance*)	16	*Brain of Britain*
7	The Jam	17	Karachi
8	Dong	18	Limerick
9	Stylistics	19	David Cassidy
10	*Bad*	20	William I

Easy

1 Who played Sarah Lund in the Danish series *The Killing*?

2 In which fictional town is *Inspector Montalbano* set?

3 What was the name of Sidse Babett Knudsen's prime minister in *Borgen*?

4 Who starred as Saga Norén in *The Bridge*?

5 What is the English title of the Swedish series centred around a guesthouse on the Åland Islands?

6 In which city is the French series *Spiral* set?

7 Krister Henriksson played which Swedish detective from 2005 to 2014?

8 Which Swedish actor starred as Christer Wijk in the *Crimes of Passion* series?

9 The thriller series *Salamander* is from which country?

10 The first series of which Danish drama series focused on the financial affairs of the fictional company Energreen?

11 Detective Sandra Winckler features in which French thriller series?

12 The series *Trapped* is set in which country?

13 What is the title of the series set in the Spanish prison called Cruz del Sur?

Medium

14 Which Danish series followed the fortunes of the Grønnegaard family?

15 The 2012-16 French series *Les Hommes de l'ombre* was broadcast in the UK under what title?

16 Foreign series are shown on Channel 4 and its related channels under what general name?

17 What is the English title of the French series *Les Revenants*?

18 What is the title of the English and French series inspired by *The Bridge*?

19 Who is Inspector Montalbano's long-suffering girlfriend?

20 Which year provided the title of a 2014 Danish drama series about a war?

Hard

Answers to QUIZ 406 – Air Travel

1	Montgolfier	11	Canberra
2	Ferdinand von Zeppelin	12	USA
3	1937	13	Light aircraft pilot licence
4	Igor Sikorsky	14	Glider
5	International Air Transport Association	15	Heathrow
6	Aeroflot	16	Bognor Regis
7	Newham	17	United Airlines
8	Sir Richard Branson	18	Stansted and Southend
9	Madeira	19	Aberdeen
10	35,000 feet	20	Felix Baumgartner

1   The song *He is an Englishman* appears in which Gilbert and Sullivan opera?

2   Which Canadian province has Winnipeg as its capital?

3   Which actor starred as Klaatu in the 2008 remake of *The Day the Earth Stood Still*?

4   *Low, Right Round* and *Wild Ones* have been hits for whch US rapper?

5   Who invented the vacuum flask?

6   With which motor vehicle manufacturer is Elon Musk associated?

7   Grace Road is the home of which county cricket club?

8   Which quiz programme was hosted by Hughie Green from 1955 to 1968?

9   What Latin term is given to a work of art reminding people that they will die?

10 Russian and Ukrainian belong to which family of languages?

11 The name of which shrub means "rose tree" in Greek?

12 Who developed the ideas of the collective unconscious and of the archetype?

13 Which group had hits in the 1980s with *Mirror Man* and *Open Your Heart*?

14 The character of Martin Riggs was played by Mel Gibson in which series of films?

15 What type of creature is a cowrie?

16 Writers Virginia Woolf, Leonard Woolf, John Maynard Keynes, Desmond Maccarthy and others were collectively known as what?

17 Which band was formed by Paul Weller and Mick Talbot in 1983?

18 In which British city is the Sheldonian Theatre?

19 What title was inherited by Frances Hodgson Burnett's character, Cedric Errol, an American boy?

20 Which singer has released albums entitled *Alf* and *Hoodoo*?

Answers to QUIZ 407 – Pot Luck

1	Eric Clapton	11	*All Shook Up*
2	Webbed feet	12	New Edition
3	*Dempsey and Makepeace*	13	Agora
4	Gloucester	14	Wandering (or snowy) albatross
5	*Parachutes*	15	A worm
6	Kidneys	16	WB Yeats
7	Ice cream	17	Aggregate
8	Father Dowling	18	Nasser Hussein
9	Pine	19	Stephenie Meyer
10	Kiev	20	Louis Pasteur (with Émile Roux)

1 Before their marriage, what relation to Prince Albert was Queen Victoria?

2 Which Greek island was the centre of the Minoan civilisation?

3 Which region of central Spain was a separate kingdom until 1479?

4 Of which historic region of Germany is Dresden the capital?

5 Who was the first Englishman to circumnavigate the world?

6 Where was the Temple of Artemis (or Diana), one of the Seven Wonders of the Ancient World, situated?

7 King Zog once ruled which country?

8 Which extinct species of early human takes its name from a valley in Germany?

9 Which cathedral city of Andalusia was the capital of Moorish Spain?

10 From where did Concorde's first test flight take off?

11 Which city was the northern capital of the historical Kingdom of the Two Sicilies?

12 Which French province was an English possession from 1154 to 1204?

13 Ragusa is the former name of which Croatian port?

14 Leonidas was king of which ancient Greek city?

15 Which crime-stopping organisation was set up in Vienna in 1923?

16 The explorer Christopher Columbus was born in which city?

17 In 1327, who became King of England?

18 Which Austrian archduke died at Mayerling in 1889?

19 Between 1871 and 1919, which region of north-east France was under German control?

20 Which city was the first capital of a unified Italy in 1861?

Answers to QUIZ 408 – Foreign Language Television

1	Sofie Gråbøl	11	*Witnesses*
2	Vigàta	12	Iceland
3	Birgitte Nyborg	13	*Locked Up*
4	Sofia Helin	14	*The Legacy*
5	*Thicker Than Water*	15	*Spin*
6	Paris	16	*Walter Presents*
7	Kurt Wallander	17	*The Returned*
8	Ola Rapace	18	*The Tunnel*
9	Belgium	19	*Livia*
10	*Follow the Money*	20	1864

1   Blondie's *Call Me* was used in which 1980 film?

2   Which group topped the UK singles chart in 2003 with *Crashed the Wedding*?

3   On which sea is the city of Sevastopol?

4   In which county is the town of Kirkby Lonsdale?

5   Ramsons is a member of which plant family?

6   In which country do Kaiserslautern football team play?

7   What is the capital of Ecuador?

8   The TV series *Diagnosis: Murder* starred which actor as Dr Mark Sloan?

9   Who wrote the 1998 play *Copenhagen*?

10 What was the name of the duo formed by Siobhan Fahey and Marcella Detroit?

11 What sport is played at Walton Heath?

12 What do the "RR" of JRR Tolkien's initials stand for?

13 How many Odes did Keats write where "*Ode*" appears in the title of the poem?

14 Which famous actor was born Ramón Antonio Gerard Estévez?

15 Who played Batman in the 2008 film *The Dark Knight*?

16 Jim Kerr is the frontman for which Scottish band?

17 In which Irish county is Tralee?

18 Which was the first nation to host the FIFA World Cup for a second time?

19 Which penguin species has yellow and black plumes on its head?

20 *Party Girl* was a 2010 hit for which band?

Answers to QUIZ 409 – Pot Luck

1	*HMS Pinafore*	11	Rhododendron
2	Manitoba	12	Carl Jung
3	Keanu Reeves	13	Human League
4	Flo Rida	14	*Lethal Weapon*
5	James Dewar	15	Mollusc
6	Tesla	16	The Bloomsbury Group
7	Leicestershire	17	The Style Council
8	*Double Your Money*	18	Oxford
9	*Memento mori*	19	Lord Fauntleroy
10	Slavonic	20	Alison Moyet

1   What is the name of the clock tower of the Houses of Parliament?

2   Is Uruguay ahead of or behind Greenwich Mean Time?

3   What luxury watchmaker company was founded in London in 1905?

4   Which book by George Orwell opens with a clock tolling 13 times...?

5   ...and in which children's book by Philippa Pearce does the clock strike 13 times?

6   Which English sports ground has a weather vane in the shape of Father Time?

7   In Doctor Who, what do the initials TARDIS stand for?

8   In Sir Terry Pratchett's *Discworld* novels, which character's home has a life-timer room?

9   Who played the character of Bill Nighy's son in the 2013 film *About Time*?

10 Which 2003 novel features the characters of Henry DeTamble and Clare Abshire?

11 Who had a 1986 hit with *My Favourite Waste of Time*?

12 At which British standards establishment was the first atomic clock built?

13 In which year did the Beautiful South top the charts with *A Little Time*?

14 What is the name of the underground-dwelling creatures in the 1895 novel *The Time Machine*?

15 Who wrote the 1986 book *The Blind Watchmaker*?

16 In which European capital city is there a giant sandglass known as the Timewheel?

17 Which singer starred in the 2011 film sci-fi film *In Time*?

18 Which country has three time zones, eight to ten hours ahead of GMT?

19 Before widespread adoption of alarm clocks, what profession would be responsible for waking people up in the morning?

20 In which cathedral is the large bell called "Great Tom"?

Answers to QUIZ 410 – European History

1	First cousin	11	Naples
2	Crete	12	Anjou
3	Castile	13	Dubrovnik
4	Saxony	14	Sparta
5	Sir Francis Drake	15	Interpol
6	Ephesus	16	Genoa
7	Albania	17	Edward III
8	Neanderthal	18	Rudolf
9	Córdoba	19	Lorraine
10	Filton (near Bristol)	20	Turin

ANSWERS ON PAGE 415

1   What does an ungulate animal have?

2   Which US company collapsed in a 2001 scandal?

3   Which singer/songwriter first found fame by writing *I'm a Believer* for the Monkees?

4   Who wrote the novel *A Town Like Alice* (1950)?

5   "'O where are you going?' said reader to rider" was written by which poet?

6   Which actor starred in the 2008 film *The Wrestler*?

7   In the Old Testament, who was the third son of Adam and Eve?

8   Which town is situated on County Westmeath's border with Roscommon?

9   What travels at approximately 186,000 miles per second?

10 In the game of Scrabble®, what is the points bonus for putting down all seven letters at once?

11 Which bird was considered sacred by the Incas?

12 Which central European country borders Hungary, Ukraine and Poland?

13 In the 2009 film *Avatar*, what was the name of the planet?

14 What tree of genus *Adansonia* is also known as the monkey-bread tree?

15 In which ocean is Christmas Island, now called Kiribati?

16 *Video Games* was a 2011 single for which singer?

17 Who played Captain Mainwaring in the 2016 film version of *Dad's Army*?

18 In the 1966 World Cup Final, who scored for England other than Geoff Hurst?

19 In relation to birds, what is a "lek"?

20 North Sea Gas was first produced in which year?

Answers to QUIZ 411 – Pot Luck

1	*American Gigolo*	11	Golf
2	Busted	12	Ronald Reuel
3	The Black Sea	13	Five
4	Cumbria	14	Martin Sheen
5	*Allium* (garlic)	15	Christian Bale
6	Germany	16	Simple Minds
7	Quito	17	Kerry
8	Dick Van Dyke	18	Mexico (1970 and 1986)
9	Michael Frayn	19	Macaroni
10	Shakespear's Sister	20	McFly

ANSWERS ON PAGE 416

1 Gaborone is the capital of which African country?

2 Which landlocked country borders Georgia?

3 In which American state is Harvard University located?

4 In which Irish county is the site of Newgrange?

5 Which river flows through Berlin?

6 The island state of Nauru lies in which ocean?

7 Which is the northernmost of the Central American republics?

8 The River Tay flows into which sea?

9 Which is Japan's second-largest city?

10 In which region of France is Strasbourg located?

11 The "Medway Towns" are Gillingham, Rochester, Strood, Rainham and which other town?

12 Which river forms the border between Germany and Poland?

13 The Vale of Eden is in which county?

14 In which city is the United Nations Headquarters building located?

15 What is the capital of the Falkland Islands?

16 The ruins of ancient Persepolis are found in which country?

17 What is the unit of currency in Thailand?

18 What name is shared by a Brittany seaport and a Belarus city near the Polish border?

19 In which US state is Cincinnati?

20 Karachi is in which province of Pakistan?

Answers to QUIZ 412 – Time

1	Elizabeth Tower (Big Ben is the bell)	11	Owen Paul
2	Behind	12	National Physical Laboratory
3	Rolex	13	1990
4	*Nineteen Eighty-Four*	14	Morlocks
5	*Tom's Midnight Garden*	15	Richard Dawkins
6	Lord's cricket ground	16	Budapest
7	Time and Relative Dimension in Space	17	Justin Timberlake
8	Death	18	Australia
9	Domhnall Gleeson	19	Knocker-up
10	*The Time Traveler's Wife*	20	Lincoln Cathedral

ANSWERS ON PAGE 417

1   With which instrument was Bert Weedon associated?

2   Heraklion is the capital of which Greek island?

3   What is the more common word for the process of parturition?

4   Pendennis Castle is situated in which Cornish town?

5   What type of animal is a Dandie Dinmont?

6   Who had a hit in 1990 with *Tears on My Pillow*?

7   How is chicken shawarma cooked?

8   Who was president of the USA during the earlier years of the Great Depression, 1929-33?

9   What was the title of the USA for Africa 1985 charity record?

10 What name is given to the part of a stem at which a leaf grows?

11 In which year was the Kingdom of Great Britain formed by the Act of Union?

12 Along with potatoes, which vegetable is a key ingredient of aloo gobi?

13 Which independence leader gave his name to a landlocked South American country?

14 Baku is the capital city of which country on the Caspian Sea?

15 Which traditional board game is set in Tudor Mansions?

16 In which county is Bishop Auckland?

17 Which bird can fly backwards?

18 The Moselle joins which other river at Koblenz?

19 What was the title applied to Siddhartha Gautama, founder of a major Eastern religion?

20 Which acid is the most predominant in the stomach?

Easy

Medium

Hard

Answers to QUIZ 413 – Pot Luck

1	Hooves	11	The condor
2	Enron	12	Slovakia
3	Neil Diamond	13	Pandora
4	Nevil Shute	14	Baobab
5	WH Auden	15	Pacific
6	Mickey Rourke	16	Lana Del Rey
7	Seth	17	Toby Jones
8	Athlone	18	Martin Peters
9	Light	19	A display area
10	50	20	1967

1 Who played Brian Hope in the 1990 film *Nuns on the Run*?

2 In which decade of the 20th century was Warren Beatty born?

3 How were Susan Sarandon and Goldie Hawn known in the title of a 2002 film?

4 What is the name of Andy Serkis' character in the *Planet of the Apes* series of films?

5 In which 1986 film do Tom Hanks and Shelley Long buy an ageing mansion?

6 Which Elvis Presley film features the name of a Mexican resort in its title?

7 In which 1994 film did Arnold Schwarzenegger co-star with Jamie Lee Curtis?

8 Which cult film of 1973 is set on the Scottish island of Summerisle?

9 What was the title of the first *Carry On* film, released in 1958?

10 Sigourney Weaver portrayed which real-life scientist in the 1988 film *Gorillas in the Mist*?

11 Which actress starred alongside Sir Sean Connery in the 1999 thriller *Entrapment*?

12 Which US film company has the motto *Ars gratia artis*?

13 In which 1959 film does Peter Sellers play a shop steward and Ian Carmichael a naïve worker?

14 Who was the star of the 1971 film *Fiddler on the Roof*?

15 The 2009 film *In the Loop* was based on which TV series?

16 What was the name of Scaramanga's servant in *The Man with the Golden Gun* (1974)?

17 Which actress played Melissa Lewis in the 2015 film *The Martian*?

18 Who directed the 1976 film *Bugsy Malone*?

19 The film *The Philadelphia Story* was remade as which musical?

20 Which actor starred in the 2003 film *Master and Commander*?

Answers to QUIZ 414 – Geography

1	Botswana	11	Chatham
2	Armenia	12	Oder
3	Massachusetts	13	Cumbria
4	Meath	14	New York
5	Spree	15	Port Stanley
6	Pacific	16	Iran
7	Belize	17	Baht
8	The North Sea	18	Brest
9	Yokohama	19	Ohio
10	Alsace	20	Sindh

ANSWERS ON PAGE 419

1   Which part of the calyx of a flower encloses the petals?

2   Which Spanish region includes Seville and Granada?

3   *In The Summertime* was a 1970 hit for which group?

4   Which actor starred in the 2004 remake of *The Manchurian Candidate*?

5   What name is given to a Scottish barrister?

6   *Ride a White Swan* was a 1970 hit for which group?

7   What did the chemist John Dalton define as the smallest particle of substance?

8   Of which US state is Cheyenne the capital?

9   Oberon is a moon of which planet in the solar system?

10 Who was Hero's lover, in Greek mythology?

11 Who was the first English Christian martyr?

12 Eric Hill created which cartoon dog?

13 On a fish, where is the dorsal fin?

14 What name is given to a plant growth induced by another organism, often a wasp?

15 Which are the most ancient of the sacred Hindu writings?

16 Dr Zamenhof devised which international language in 1887?

17 Which grade of army officer is next above a colonel?

18 Which naval base and dockyard lies on the north bank of the Firth of Forth?

19 What is the capital of Venezuela?

20 Sir Rod Stewart had a successful trial with which London football club?

Easy

Medium

Hard

Answers to QUIZ 415 – Pot Luck

1	Guitar	11	1707
2	Crete	12	Cauliflower
3	Childbirth	13	Simón Bolivar
4	Falmouth	14	Azerbaijan
5	Dog (terrier)	15	Cluedo®
6	Kylie Minogue	16	County Durham
7	Grilled on a spit	17	Hummingbird
8	Herbert Hoover	18	Rhine
9	*We Are the World*	19	Buddha
10	Node	20	Hydrochloric

Easy

1   What is the title of the novel by HG Wells on which *Half a Sixpence* is based?

2   "The mirror crack'd from side to side" is a line from which Tennyson poem?

3   Who wrote *The Blind Assassin* (2000)?

4   Which George Eliot novel features Dorothea Brooke?

5   SJ Watson wrote which novel that was filmed in 2014 starring Nicole Kidman and Colin Firth?

6   Which war was the subject of the *Iliad*?

7   *Open the Cage, Murphy!* is a memoir by which TV presenter?

8   What was the first name of writer AA Milne?

9   According to Wordsworth, who "dwelt among the untrodden ways"?

10   In which decade was the Guinness Book of Records first published?

Medium

11   What term is given to poetry that has lines that do not rhyme?

12   Bathsheba Everdene appears in which classic novel?

13   What is didactic literature intended to do?

14   What was the name of the Brontë sisters' brother?

15   *Tarka the Otter* was set on which two Devon rivers?

16   Who wrote the poem *The Wreck of the Hesperus* (1842)?

17   Which book by Rudyard Kipling is the story of an orphaned son of a soldier stationed in India?

18   Who wrote the 1930 Sam Spade novel *The Maltese Falcon*?

19   Charles Lamb adopted what pen-name?

20   Who wrote *The Gulag Archipelago*?

Hard

Answers to QUIZ 416 – Film

1	Eric Idle	11	Catherine Zeta-Jones
2	1930s (1937)	12	MGM
3	*The Banger Sisters*	13	*I'm All Right Jack*
4	Caesar	14	Topol
5	*The Money Pit*	15	*The Thick of It*
6	*Fun in Acapulco*	16	Nick Nack
7	*True Lies*	17	Jessica Chastain
8	*The Wicker Man*	18	Alan Parker
9	*Carry On Sergeant*	19	*High Society*
10	Dian Fossey	20	Russell Crowe

ANSWERS ON PAGE 421

1   Which British swimmer won the gold medal for the 100m breaststroke at the 1988 Olympics?

2   In Egyptian mythology, who was the mother of Horus?

3   What is the name of Leonato's daughter in Shakespeare's *Much Ado about Nothing*?

4   Which southern Asian country has been a republic since 2008?

5   The 1993 film *Free Willy* featured which type of creature?

6   Which singer had a hit in 2003 with *The Voice Within*?

7   Cedar Rapids is in which US state?

8   Which London Underground line stops at Morden?

9   What is a native of the country once called Mesopotamia called?

10 The 1990s TV series *Cadfael* starred which actor in the title role?

11 Who is the patron saint of the Czechia (Czech Republic)?

12 Which actress starred as Chuck Charles in the TV series *Pushing Daisies*?

13 What style of music is associated with John Lee Hooker and Muddy Waters?

14 In which month does the London to Brighton veteran and vintage car rally take place?

15 Which French dramatist penned *Tartuffe* (1664)?

16 By which name is the plant belladonna more widely known?

17 Who wrote the *No. 1 Ladies Detective Agency* series?

18 What is the amount by which the cost of imports exceeds the value of imports called?

19 *In Three Men in a Boat (To Say Nothing of the Dog)* (1889), what is the name of the dog?

20 Which actor starred in the 1967 film *Cool Hand Luke*?

Easy

Medium

Hard

Answers to QUIZ 417 – Pot Luck

1	Sepal	11	St Alban
2	Andalusia	12	Spot
3	Mungo Jerry	13	On its back
4	Denzel Washington	14	Gall
5	Advocate	15	The *Veda* writings
6	T Rex	16	Esperanto
7	The atom	17	Brigadier
8	Wyoming	18	Rosyth
9	Uranus	19	Caracas
10	Leander	20	Brentford FC

Easy

1. Which green liqueur was once made from wormwood?
2. Lumache pasta is named after which creature?
3. What is the prime cut of beef taken from the upper middle of the body called?
4. Cookery writer Mrs Beeton had what first name?
5. Which gas mark setting is the equivalent of 200 degrees Celsius?
6. Which type of restaurant takes its name from the French word for "brewery"?
7. What is the main ingredient in laver bread?
8. Duxelles is a paste made from shallots, herbs and which other foodstuff?
9. What type of food is produced from the sumac shrub?
10. The Irish dish colcannon is made from potatoes and which other vegetable?
11. Which region of Guyana gives its name to a variety of sugar?
12. A Manhattan cocktail has which spirit as its base?
13. Which small fruit has the Latin name *Prunus armeniaca*?
14. What is the scale used to measure the heat of chillies?

Medium

15. Sage Derby is what type of food?
16. Which girl's name is given to a steak dish seasoned with Worcestershire sauce?
17. What colour is a persimmon?
18. What type of fruit is an ugli fruit?
19. Traditional balsamic vinegar is made from which fruit?
20. What are you eating if you have a "Finnan Haddie"?

Hard

Answers to QUIZ 418 – Literature

1	*Kipps*	11	Blank verse
2	*The Lady of Shalott*	12	*Far from the Madding Crowd* (Thomas Hardy)
3	Margaret Atwood	13	Instruct
4	*Middlemarch*	14	Branwell
5	*Before I Go to Sleep*	15	Taw and Torridge
6	Trojan War	16	Henry Wadsworth Longfellow
7	Paul O'Grady	17	*Kim*
8	Alan	18	Dashiel Hammett
9	Lucy	19	*Elia*
10	1950s (1955)	20	Aleksandr Solzhenitsyn

ANSWERS ON PAGE **423**

1   Which river rises in the Pennines and flows into the North Sea between Hartlepool and Redcar?

2   W is the symbol for which chemical element?

3   Father and son doctors, Toby and Tom Latimer featured in which sitcom?

4   What type of creature is an agouti?

5   Which horse colouring consists of a brown body with black legs, mane and tail?

6   In the 2007 film *Music and Lyrics*, which actress co-starred with Hugh Grant?

7   Which dramatist wrote the play *Peer Gynt*?

8   Which actor played Dr Wilbur Larch in the film *The Cider House Rules*?

9   In which year was the first Wimpy® restaurant opened?

10 Which athlete was known as "the Flying Finn"?

11 The 1999 film *The Hurricane* starred which actor?

12 What was the title of Michael Jackson's 1995 Christmas hit?

13 Which body part is swollen if a person is suffering from myelitis?

14 *Mouldy Old Dough* was a 1972 hit for which band?

15 The ancient Chinese used clove oil as a remedy for which complaint?

16 Who wrote the play *Lady Windermere's Fan* (1892)?

17 Which queen succeeded William III?

18 Car manufacturer Dacia is based in which country?

19 What is the province of Greece in which Athens is located?

20 In which country is the port of Odessa?

Answers to QUIZ 419 – Pot Luck

1	Adrian Moorhouse	11	Wenceslas
2	Isis	12	Anna Friel
3	Hero	13	Blues
4	Nepal	14	November
5	Killer whale (orca)	15	Molière
6	Christina Aguilera	16	Deadly nightshade
7	Iowa	17	Alexander McCall Smith
8	Northern	18	Trade gap
9	Iraqi	19	Montmorency
10	Sir Derek Jacobi	20	Paul Newman

1 James Newell Osterberg Jr is known by which stage name?

2 Who were the Four Tops telling to *Walk Away* in their 1967 hit?

3 Which group had a 1974 hit with *The Cat Crept In*?

4 Who won the Eurovision Song Contest in 1980 and 1987, and wrote the winning song in 1992?

5 *I Owe You Nothing* is the autobiography of which singer?

6 Under what name does singer Derek Dick perform?

7 The Average White Band hit *Let's Go Round Again* was also a hit for which singer in 1997?

8 *Sorry Not Sorry* was a 2017 single by which singer?

9 Who has released albums entitled *Yours Truly* and *My Everything*?

10 Which group had a hit in 1981 with *The Land of Make Believe*?

11 By what name is musician and actor Ben Drew better known?

12 Who were *Uptown Top Ranking* in 1978?

13 In which decade of the 20th century was Sir Mick Jagger born?

14 Which former *Neighbours* actress had hits with *Born to Try* and *Lost Without You*?

15 *The Long and Winding Road* appears on which Beatles album?

16 Which group had the UK Christmas no.1 in 1996, 1997 and 1998?

17 What was Blur's first Top Ten hit?

18 Which singer/songwriter had a 2005 hit with *The One I Love*?

19 How is singer Rory Charles Graham better known?

20 Who sang *Drop the Pilot* in 1983?

Answers to QUIZ 420 – Food and Drink

1	Absinthe	11	Demerara
2	Snail	12	Whisky
3	Sirloin	13	Apricot
4	Isabella	14	Scoville scale
5	Gas Mark 6	15	Cheese
6	Brasserie	16	Diane
7	Seaweed	17	Orange (fruit)
8	Mushrooms	18	Citrus
9	Spice	19	Grapes
10	Cabbage	20	Smoked haddock

1 Which 2000 thriller starred Harrison Ford and Michelle Pfeiffer?

2 In which ocean is the Sargasso Sea?

3 Which French composer wrote the *Gymnopédies*?

4 What was an old measure of weight equal to a quarter of a bushel?

5 The Jerusalem artichoke is a member of which family of plants?

6 A hat called a toque would be worn by which professional?

7 Which Rodgers and Hammerstein musical was filmed in 1955?

8 Which 1999 remake of a Steve McQueen film featured Pierce Brosnan in the title role?

9 In which US state is Pittsburgh?

10 Who played speech therapist Lionel Logue in the 2010 film *The King's Speech*?

11 If something is described as "vitreous", from what is it made?

12 Who was Dr Samuel Johnson's biographer?

13 Who captained the England rugby team when they won the Grand Slam in 1980?

14 Which actor starred as William of Baskerville in the 1986 film *The Name of the Rose*?

15 Which group had a UK hit with *Leader of the Pack* in 1965, 1972 and 1976?

16 Which classic novel is narrated by Nick Carraway?

17 In which TV series did Elisabeth Moss play the character of Peggy Olson?

18 In human anatomy, what is the lowest part of the trunk?

19 Polyphemus was a member of which mythical one-eyed race of giants?

20 What is the title of the best-seller about punctuation written by Lynne Truss?

Easy

Medium

Hard

Answers to QUIZ 421 – Pot Luck

1	Tees	11	Denzel Washington
2	Tungsten	12	*Earth Song*
3	*Don't Wait Up*	13	The spinal cord
4	Rodent	14	Lieutenant Pigeon
5	Bay	15	Toothache
6	Drew Barrymore	16	Oscar Wilde
7	Henrik Ibsen	17	Anne
8	Sir Michael Caine	18	Romania
9	1954	19	Attica
10	Paavo Nurmi	20	Ukraine

1. What is the name of Indiana Jones' father?

2. Which fictional doctor is flatmates with Dr Leonard Hofstadter in the American sitcom *The Big Bang Theory*?

3. In the *Jurassic Park* novel and films, what is the name of the geneticist responsible for the cloning of the dinosaurs?

4. Who played Dr Curt Connors in the 2012 film *The Amazing Spider-Man*?

5. Which infamous doctor does Edward Prendick meet on an island in a 1896 HG Wells sci-fi novel?

6. In which US TV series did the characters Dr Cox and Dr Kelso work at the same hospital?

7. What is the name of Lucy Liu's character in the American TV series *Elementary*?

8. What infamous fictional doctor is first introduced in the 1981 novel *Red Dragon*?

9. GPs Daniel Granger and Heston Carter appear in which TV series?

10. Who played Dr Joel Fleischman in the TV series *Northern Exposure*?

11. Which doctor practised medicine in the town of Tannochbrae?

12. In which Shakespearean play does a doctor state "What is it she does now? Look how she rubs her hands"?

13. What pen name did crime writer Arthur Sarsfield Ward use for his novels featuring Dr Fu Manchu?

14. Dr Hugo Z Hackenbush appears in which 1937 film?

15. In which TV series did Dr Sarah Tancredi appear?

16. Clare Holman played which forensic pathologist in *Inspector Morse* and *Lewis*?

17. In which remade sci-fi series was Dr Gaius Baltar a central character?

18. Who played psychiatrist Dr Ben Sobel in the 1999 film *Analyze This*?

19. Dr Henry Higgins first appeared in which 1913 play?

20. In which series of sci-fi films did the character of Dr Emmett Brown feature?

Answers to QUIZ 422 – Pop Music

1	Iggy Pop	11	Plan B
2	Renée	12	Althea & Donna
3	Mud	13	1940s (1943)
4	Johnny Logan	14	Delta Goodrem
5	Luke Goss (of Bros)	15	*Let It Be*
6	Fish	16	The Spice Girls
7	Louise	17	*There's No Other Way*
8	Demi Lovato	18	David Gray
9	Ariana Grande	19	Rag'n'Bone Man
10	Bucks Fizz	20	Joan Armatrading

Easy

Medium

Hard

1 Which fictional soap opera was linked to the TV series *Moving Wallpaper*?

2 What is the Chinese geometrical puzzle of seven differently shaped pieces called?

3 Rachael Stirling is the daughter of which actress?

4 What was the title of Stephen King's first novel?

5 Which Australian train service was previously known as "The Afghan Express"?

6 On which island is Mauna Loa?

7 Who had a hit in 2006 with *Jump in My Car*?

8 Which Hampshire town lies between Portsmouth and Chichester?

9 What prefix indicates 10^9?

10 Which South American country borders Peru and Colombia?

11 What is the chemical formula for alcohol?

12 In the TV series, who is the major adversary of the *Terrahawks*?

13 What was the title of the 1975 hit single by Telly Savalas?

14 Who won the Best Actor Oscar for the 2002 film *The Pianist*?

15 What is the largest Bronze Age archaeological site on the island of Crete?

16 A "charm" is a collective noun for which birds?

17 Who might be interested in a "Cape triangular"?

18 Of which American state is Madison the capital?

19 In which city did the TV detective Piet Van der Valk operate?

20 The island of Komodo, famous for its "dragons", is in which country?

Answers to QUIZ 423 – Pot Luck

1	*What Lies Beneath*	11	Glass
2	The North Atlantic	12	James Boswell
3	Erik Satie	13	Bill Beaumont
4	Peck	14	Sir Sean Connery
5	Sunflower	15	Shangri-Las
6	Chef	16	*The Great Gatsby*
7	*Oklahoma!*	17	*Mad Men*
8	*The Thomas Crown Affair*	18	The pelvis
9	Pennsylvania	19	Cyclopes
10	Geoffrey Rush	20	*Eats, Shoots and Leaves*

Easy

Medium

Hard

Easy

1 The omnium is an event in which sport?

2 Which system of Japanese fighting has a name meaning "the way of gentleness"?

3 How many players are there in a baseball team?

4 Which snooker player won the World Grand Prix title in February 2017?

5 Figure skater Katarina Witt represented which country at the 1984 Winter Olympics?

6 The 2014 Ryder Cup took place on which course?

7 Which sport is played on the largest pitch?

8 In which year did Martina Navratilova win her last singles title at Wimbledon?

9 The wood of which tree is used to make bows for archery?

10 How many inches from the ground are the bails of a wicket?

11 Which sport is played by the Florida Panthers?

12 In which country is the Interlagos motor racing circuit?

13 Turf Moor is the home ground of which football team?

14 Which distance was first run by Pheidippides in 490 BC?

15 What is the name of Cambridge University's reserve rowing crew?

16 In which field event did Jesse Owens set a record that stood from 1935 to 1960?

17 The racecourse known as the Roodee is in which English city?

18 Who won the Formula 1 World Championship in 1962 and 1968?

19 What was the first name of 1950s Czechia (Czech Republic) runner Zátopek?

20 The 1952 summer Olympic Games were held in which city?

Answers to QUIZ 424 – Fictional Doctors

1	Professor Henry Jones	11	Dr Finlay
2	Dr Sheldon Cooper	12	*Macbeth*
3	Dr Henry Wu	13	Sax Rohmer
4	Rhys Ifan	14	*A Day at the Races*
5	Dr Moreau	15	*Prison Break*
6	*Scrubs*	16	Dr Laura Hobson
7	Dr Joan Watson	17	*Battlestar Galactica*
8	Dr Hannibal Lecter	18	Billy Crystal
9	*Doctors*	19	*Pygmalion*
10	Rob Morrow	20	*Back to the Future*

ANSWERS ON PAGE 429

1   The VW Beetle was designed by which sports-car manufacturer?

2   Which place of pilgrimage is in County Mayo, Ireland?

3   What was Elvis Presley's second UK no.1?

4   In Greek myth, what name is given to the blood of the gods?

5   What device is used for measuring wind speed?

6   Which artist was associated with the Catalonian town of Figueres?

7   Who wrote a *Christmas Oratorio* in 1734?

8   In the TV series *Grey's Anatomy*, who plays the title character?

9   Where in the body are the islets of Langerhans located?

10 Which bird is known as a "laughing jackass"?

11 In the title of a Dame Agatha Christie novel, what time is the train from Paddington?

12 Who wrote the novel *The Guns of Navarone*?

13 On which continent is the Tukano language spoken?

14 Which Hungarian virtuoso composer and pianist lived from 1811 to 1886?

15 What was the title of Diana Ross's first UK no.1 single?

16 Which Cumbrian river flows through Appleby and Carlisle?

17 Which is the second largest of the Shetland Islands?

18 In Shakespeare's *Twelfth Night*, what is the name of the Duke of Illyria?

19 Which English king first enclosed the New Forest as a hunting area?

20 Who wrote *The Commitments*, part of *The Barrytown Trilogy*?

Easy

Medium

Hard

Answers to QUIZ 425 – Pot Luck

1	*Echo Beach*	11	C_2H_5O
2	Tangram	12	Zelda
3	Dame Diana Rigg	13	*If*
4	*Carrie*	14	Adrien Brody
5	The Ghan	15	Knossos
6	Hawaii	16	Goldfinches
7	David Hasselhoff	17	A stamp collector
8	Havant	18	Wisconsin
9	Giga	19	Amsterdam
10	Ecuador	20	Indonesia

Easy

1 Who was the Roman goddess of handicrafts and equivalent of the Greek Athena?

2 Which *Cold Feet* actress played DI Martha Bellamy in the TV series *Suspects*?

3 How many points are there in a perfect hand at cribbage?

4 What does the Statue of Liberty wear on her feet?

5 Which Beatle played guitar left-handed?

6 How many cubic feet are there in a cubic yard?

7 At which racecourse is the Lincoln Handicap held?

8 How many toes does a camel have on each foot?

9 In which century was George Frederick Handel born?

10 What is the legendary creature Bigfoot also called in North America?

11 What is the name for someone who studies handwriting?

Medium

12 In *One Foot in the Grave*, what was the first name of Angus Deayton's character?

13 Sir Elton John had a double-A side no.1 with *Healing Hands* and which other song?

14 In which century was Harold Harefoot king of England?

15 Which king does Ned Stark become Hand of the King to in *Game of Thrones*?

16 Where in a house would you find the footings?

17 What was the nickname of the handyman in the TV programme *Changing Rooms*?

18 "Come and meet those dancing feet" is a lyric from the title song to which musical?

19 In which sport is it forbidden for anyone to play left-handed?

20 Who co-starred with Humphrey Bogart in the 1954 film *The Barefoot Contessa*?

Hard

Answers to QUIZ 426 – Sport

1	Track cycling	11	Ice hockey
2	Judo	12	Brazil
3	Nine	13	Burnley
4	Barry Hawkins	14	Marathon
5	East Germany	15	Goldie
6	Gleneagles	16	Long jump
7	Polo (275m x 145m)	17	Chester
8	1990	18	Graham Hill
9	Yew	19	Emil
10	28	20	Helsinki

1 Of what is hypnophobia a fear?

2 What is the name of the princess in the ballet *Swan Lake*?

3 Who wrote *The Fall of the House of Usher* (1839)?

4 What type of institution is run by Mrs Clonkers in Roald Dahl's *The BFG*?

5 Castlebar is the main town in which Irish county?

6 Who wrote the 1970 chart-topper *Woodstock*?

7 Which country forms the southern border of Tajikistan?

8 *Virginia Plain* was a 1972 hit for which group?

9 For which professional football team was chef Gordon Ramsay an apprentice?

10 What was the Rolling Stones' first UK no.1 single?

11 The freesia is a member of which family?

12 The musical *Sunshine on Leith* features the songs of which duo?

13 Ailsa Craig granite is used to make which sporting items?

14 Which fruit is the base for slivovitz?

15 Who won the Best Actress Oscar for the 2009 film *The Blind Side*?

16 How many points are awarded for a touchdown in American football?

17 Which group had a 1993 hit with *One Night in Heaven*?

18 What type of creature is a ruby tiger?

19 The sika deer is native to which continent?

20 From what is the Indonesian dish tempeh made?

Answers to QUIZ 427 – Pot Luck

1	Ferdinand Porsche	11	4:50
2	Knock	12	Alistair MacLean
3	*Jailhouse Rock*	13	South America
4	Ichor	14	Franz Liszt
5	Anemometer	15	*I'm Still Waiting*
6	Salvador Dali	16	Eden
7	JS Bach	17	Yell
8	Ellen Pompeo	18	Orsino
9	The pancreas	19	William I (the Conqueror)
10	Kookaburra	20	Roddy Doyle

Easy

1   What was the former name of the English National Ballet?

2   What French word, from ballet terminology, is given to a triple-step dance step?

3   How was the English ballerina Margaret Hookham better known?

4   Which ballet includes the characters Lescaut and Des Grieux?

5   In which city is the Northern Ballet company based?

6   Sir Matthew Bourne's ballet *The Car Man* was inspired by which opera and ballet?

7   In which country was ballerina Marianela Núñez born?

8   Who composed the original music for the ballet *Giselle*?

9   Who played the title role in the 2010 film *The Black Swan*?

10 Which horse, winner of the Derby in 1970, was named after a dancer and choreographer?

Medium

11 In which decade did Rudolf Nureyev defect from the Soviet Union?

12 What is the term given to the ballet position of supporting the weight on the toes?

13 In *The Nutcracker*, what is the name of Clara's godfather?

14 Who was the principal choreographer of the Royal Ballet from 1977 to 1992?

15 Who painted *Dancing Class* (1871) and *Ballet Rehearsal* (1873)?

16 What is the title of the three-act ballet by George Balanchine that was inspired by gemstones?

17 In which city is the Ballet Rambert based?

18 Who starred in the 1948 film *The Red Shoes*?

19 What is the French term for a ballerina's knee-bend?

20 Which former ballet dancer appeared in the 2018 series of *Celebrity Big Brother*?

Hard

Answers to QUIZ 428 – Hands and Feet

1	Minerva	11	Graphologist
2	Fay Ripley	12	Patrick (Trench)
3	29	13	*Sacrifice*
4	Sandals	14	11th century (1035-40)
5	Sir Paul McCartney	15	Robert Baratheon
6	27	16	In the foundations
7	Doncaster	17	Handy Andy
8	Two	18	*42nd Street*
9	17th century (1685)	19	Polo
10	Sasquatch	20	Ava Gardner

1   Which Egyptian god had the head of a jackal?

2   What was the name of Schumann's wife, a felllow pianist and composer?

3   Who was the hero of the 1960s puppet series *Stingray*?

4   *Ode on a Grecian Urn* (1819) was written by which English poet?

5   Which US group released the 1976 single *More Than a Feeling*?

6   Which Old Testament book precedes Job?

7   The name of which US city gave Scott McKenzie a 1967 UK no.1?

8   How are beetles of the family *Coccinellidae* better known?

9   Filbert and cobnut are alternative names for the fruit of which tree?

10 Which celebrity won the 2010 series of *Strictly Come Dancing*?

11 In April 2004, who became only the second person ever to score two triple centuries in Test cricket?

12 Which 1955 Dirk Bogarde comedy was based on a ship?

13 What was the middle name of Russian composer Tchaikovsky?

14 In the game of 8-ball pool, what is the colour of the last ball to be pocketed?

15 What is the cartel operated by oil-producing nations called?

16 Which flower gets its name from the Turkish word for "turban"?

17 Betsey Trotwood and Edward Murdstone feature in which Dickens novel?

18 Which author wrote the 1962 futuristic novel *A Clockwork Orange*?

19 Janus is a moon of which planet in the solar system?

20 What is the name for the left side of the tennis court for each player?

Answers to QUIZ 429 – Pot Luck

1	Sleep	11	Iridaceae (Iris)
2	Odette	12	The Proclaimers
3	Edgar Allan Poe	13	Curling stones
4	Orphanage	14	Plum
5	Mayo	15	Sandra Bullock
6	Joni Mitchell	16	Six
7	Afghanistan	17	M People
8	Roxy Music	18	A moth
9	Glasgow Rangers	19	Asia
10	*It's All Over Now*	20	Soya bcans

Easy

1   Cat breeds called "Rex" are associated with which two English counties?

2   In which city was the first official cat show held in 1791?

3   What is notable about the Sphynx cat?

4   Jon Arbuckle owns which fictional cat?

5   Which cat became chief mouser to 10 Downing Street in 2011?

6   What colour was Custard the cat in the animated series *Roobarb and Custard*?

7   By what name is the tortoishell cat known in America?

8   The snow leopard is native to which continent?

9   Which author (b.1899) was noted for keeping cats at his Florida home?

10 From which country does the Ocicat originate?

Medium

11 Which breed is nicknamed "the swimming cat"?

12 Which cat, named after a US state, is one of the largest domesticated cats?

13 A cat's vibrissae are more commonly referred to by what name?

14 Which cat breed takes its name from characters in *The Wizard of Oz*?

15 Which artist and inventor (b.1452) said "The smallest feline is a masterpiece"?

16 In a series of children's books by Kathleen Hale, what was the name of the "marmalade cat"?

17 Which Monopoly™ token was replaced by a cat in 2013?

18 Bastet the cat goddess features in which mythology?

19 Who starred as the cat in the 2003 film *The Cat in the Hat*?

20 What is the gestation period of a domestic cat?

Hard

Answers to QUIZ 430 – Ballet

1	Festival Ballet	11	1960s (1961)
2	Chassé	12	*En pointe*
3	Dame Margot Fonteyn	13	Drosselmeyer
4	*Manon*	14	Sir Kenneth MacMillan
5	Leeds	15	Edgar Degas
6	*Carmen*	16	*Jewels*
7	Argentina	17	London
8	Adolphe Adam	18	Moira Shearer
9	Mila Kunis	19	Plié
10	Nijinsky	20	Wayne Sleep

1   Which band's first UK hit was *Black Night*?

2   What is purslane?

3   Who starred as Jim Hacker in the TV series *Yes, Minister* and *Yes, Prime Minister*?

4   Oolong is what type of drink?

5   What is the county town of East Sussex?

6   In which US state is the Petrified Forest National Park?

7   Which dance shares its name with the state capital of West Virginia?

8   *Maid of Orleans* was a 1982 hit for which duo?

9   Which actor played Aragorn in *The Lord of the Rings* trilogy?

10 "Land of Enchantment" is the nickname for which US state?

11 Who had a 1981 no.1 with *Being with You*?

12 What term did WWII Allied pilots give to UFOs?

13 Banjul is the capital of which West African republic?

14 Who directed the 2016 film *Hacksaw Ridge*?

15 Which small Derbyshire settlement is known as "the plague village"?

16 Formerly known as Salisbury, what is the capital of Zimbabwe?

17 Who wrote "There shall be In that rich earth a richer dust concealed"?

18 Who topped the charts in 1975 with *January*?

19 The Mexican fir tree *Abies religiosa* is the preferred overwintering ground of which creature?

20 Rita Tushingham starred in which 1961 film set in Salford?

Answers to QUIZ 431 – Pot Luck

1	Anubis	11	Brian Lara
2	Clara	12	*Doctor at Sea*
3	Troy Tempest	13	Ilyich
4	Keats	14	Black
5	Boston	15	OPEC
6	Esther	16	Tulip
7	San Francisco	17	*David Copperfield*
8	Ladybirds	18	Anthony Burgess
9	The hazel	19	Saturn
10	Kara Tointon	20	The ad (advantage) court

1   Who invented the mercury thermometer?

2   The process of evaporation of water from a plant is known by what name?

3   Which colourless, odourless, inert gas found in the Earth's atmosphere has the atomic number 18?

4   The European Space Agency has its headquarters in which capital city?

5   Where in the body would you find the malleus?

6   Which layer of the Earth lies between the crust and the core?

7   Which unit of power is equivalent to one joule per second?

8   Who was the founder of modern systematic botany and zoology?

9   In hexadecimal, what number does the letter D represent?

10 Which synthetic pain relief compound was introduced by Bayer in 1899?

11 What is the ring of light around the Sun called?

12 What is the science of the measuring of the intensity of earthquakes called?

13 In the human body, what system includes all the glands and the hormones they produce?

14 What name is given to the clockwork model of the solar system devised in the early 18th century?

15 Amoxicillin is a type of what medicine?

16 Which layer of the Earth's atmosphere lies between 10km and 50km above the planet?

17 Iron pyrites is known by what common name?

18 Which essential nutrient is also known as retinol?

19 In which year was the first manned space flight?

20 Which is the lowest taxonomic classification?

Answers to QUIZ 432 – Cats

1	Devon and Cornwall	11	Turkish Van
2	London	12	Maine Coon
3	It has no hair	13	Whiskers
4	Garfield	14	Munchkin
5	Larry	15	Leonardo da Vinci
6	Pink	16	Orlando
7	Calico cat	17	An iron
8	Asia	18	Egyptian
9	Ernest Hemingway	19	Mike Myers
10	USA	20	$8\frac{1}{2}$ to $9\frac{1}{2}$ weeks

1   Who recorded the 2008 album *I Am...Sasha Fierce*?

2   The Arctic char is a member of which family of fish?

3   Who was the first chair of Radio 4's *The News Quiz* in 1977?

4   Which is the oldest Cambridge college?

5   Which mammals belong to the genus *ovis*?

6   From which country does the word "gymkhana" originate?

7   Which 1958 musical starring Leslie Caron and Maurice Chevalier won nine Oscars?

8   Who directed the 1990s films *Total Recall* and *Starship Troopers*?

9   Which shipping area lies south of Fastnet and Shannon?

10 Dudley Moore starred as an elf called Patch in which 1985 film?

11 Who wrote the plays *Loot* and *What the Butler Saw*?

12 Author Margaret Atwood was born in which country?

13 Which actress starred with Bing Crosby and Bob Hope in the *Road* films?

14 What was the name of Billy J Kramer's backing group?

15 Which country beat West Germany to win the 1982 FIFA World Cup?

16 In which English county is the feature known as the Hog's Back?

17 Who was the ancient Greek god of war?

18 How many vertebrae are there in a giraffe's neck?

19 Who co-starred with Dame Judi Dench in the film *Notes on a Scandal*?

20 Which river flows from the Cambrian Mountains and has tributaries called the Vernwy, Teme and Leadon?

Easy

Medium

Hard

Answers to QUIZ 433 – Pot Luck

1	Deep Purple	11	Smokey Robinson
2	A plant (in marshy regions)	12	Foo fighters
3	Paul Eddington	13	Gambia
4	Tea	14	Mel Gibson
5	Lewes	15	Eyam
6	Arizona	16	Harare
7	Charleston	17	Rupert Brooke (*The Soldier*)
8	Orchestral Manoeuvres in the Dark (OMD)	18	Pilot
9	Viggo Mortensen	19	Monarch butterfly
10	New Mexico	20	*A Taste Of Honey*

1   What was the name of the character played by Jack Lord in the original series of *Hawaii Five-o*?

2   *A Moment Like This* was the first chart-topper for which winner of *The X Factor*?

3   Which 1960s animated character chewed oxygum?

4   Who narrated the 1999 TV series *Walking with Dinosaurs*?

5   In the series *Z Cars*, who played DCI Charlie Barlow?

6   Which of the Monkees featured in *Coronation Street* as the grandson of Ena Sharples?

7   Who created the series *In the Club* and *Fat Friends*?

8   In the series *Dad's Army*, what was Private Pike's first name?

9   Which TV presenter and traveller (b.1972) has presented the series *Tropic of Cancer* and *Tropic of Capricorn*?

10 What was the name of the character played by Bruce Willis in *Moonlighting*?

11 Which "superhero" lives at 29 Acacia Road?

12 In the TV series *Waking the Dead*, who played Grace Foley?

13 What was the name of Jim Caviezel's character in the series *Person of Interest*?

14 In which decade of the 20th century was Joanna Lumley born?

15 Who was the first presenter of *Celebrity Squares*?

16 In the TV series *Glee*, which actress played Sue Sylvester?

17 Which *Friends* star appeared in the mini-series *Band of Brothers*?

18 Who plays the title role in the *Strike* series?

19 Spotty Dog featured in which children's puppet show?

20 What is the make and model of the car used since 2017 in the *Top Gear* segment *Star in a Reasonably Fast Car*?

Answers to QUIZ 434 – Science

1	(Daniel) Fahrenheit	11	Corona
2	Transpiration	12	Seismography
3	Argon	13	Endocrine system
4	Paris	14	Orrery
5	(Middle) ear	15	Antibiotic
6	Mantle	16	Stratosphere
7	Watt	17	Fool's gold
8	Carl Linnaeus	18	Vitamin A (Vitamin A_1)
9	13	19	1961
10	Aspirin	20	Species

1　Which politician was awarded the Nobel Peace Prize in 2009?

2　In the *UFO* TV series, which secret organisation defended the Earth?

3　Which of these ranks is the highest: brigadier in the army, group captain in the RAF or commander in the Navy?

4　What were the first two names of poet WH Auden?

5　The staff from Grace Brothers (*Are You Being Served?*) went on to run a country hotel in which series?

6　Which African country north-east of Botswana was formerly called Rhodesia?

7　Which organism is composed of both a fungi and an alga?

8　In the 1945 novel *Animal Farm*, what is the name of the industrious horse?

9　Which South African seaport and resort was previously called Port Natal?

10　How many pairs of walking legs has a sea spider?

11　Who was the lead vocalist with the 1970s group Dawn?

12　Weasels and stoats belong to which family of creatures?

13　Which one of these Republic of Ireland counties has a different name to its county town: Kildare, Kilkenny, Wexford or Wicklow?

14　A fashionable country club in a park in New York gave its name to which item of men's clothing?

15　Who co-starred with John Candy in the 1987 film *Planes, Trains & Automobiles*?

16　The wine-producing district of Médoc is in which region of France?

17　Who starred in the 1947 version of *The Secret Life of Walter Mitty*?

18　Which vegetable is known as the oyster plant?

19　What term is given to the young of a dragonfly after it hatches from the egg?

20　How was 1980s singer Chris Hamill better known?

Answers to QUIZ 435 – Pot Luck

1	Beyoncé	11	Joe Orton
2	Salmon	12	Canada
3	Barry Norman	13	Dorothy Lamour
4	Peterhouse (founded in 1284)	14	The Dakotas
5	Sheep	15	Italy
6	India	16	Surrey
7	*Gigi*	17	Ares
8	Paul Verhoeven	18	Seven (same as humans!)
9	Sole	19	Cate Blanchett
10	*Santa Claus*	20	The Severn

ANSWERS ON PAGE 440

Easy

1   The 1645 English Civil War battle of Naseby took place in which county?

2   What was a commoner of ancient Rome called?

3   In which year was the Festival of Britain held?

4   Which Scandinavian capital was formerly known as Christiania?

5   Verulamium was the Roman name for which English city?

6   In which month did the Great Fire of London break out in 1666?

7   In 1911, which London Underground station was the first to have an escalator installed?

8   In which month did the Boston Tea Party take place?

9   Who was Edward VII's queen consort?

10 Which Greek city fought Athens in the Peloponnesian War?

11 Who became president of the Soviet Union in 1977?

12 In 1883, which New York bridge became the first example of a steel wire suspension bridge?

13 Which religion was founded by L Ron Hubbard?

Medium

14 In which year did the *Amoco Cadiz* run aground off Brittany?

15 In which country did the Boxer Rebellion take place?

16 Which African country was formerly known as Northern Rhodesia?

17 What was the name of the ship that rescued survivors from the *Titanic*?

18 In 1996, which Welsh county was replaced by Denbighshire and Flintshire and became a "preserved" county?

19 What nationality was Pope Adrian IV?

20 Which English king was also known as Henry Bolingbroke?

Hard

Answers to QUIZ 436 – Television

1	(Detective) Steve McGarrett	11	Bananaman
2	Leona Lewis	12	Sue Johnston
3	Marine Boy	13	John Reese
4	Sir Kenneth Branagh	14	1940s (1946)
5	Stratford Johns	15	Bob Monkhouse
6	Davy Jones	16	Jane Lynch
7	Kay Mellor	17	David Schwimmer
8	Frank	18	Tom Burke
9	Simon Reeve	19	*The Woodentops*
10	David Addison	20	Toyota GT86

QUIZ 439 – Pot Luck

ANSWERS ON PAGE 441

1   In which year did Bill Haley release *Rock Around the Clock*?

2   Which oil-bearing Moroccan tree is often climbed by goats?

3   Which radio show featured characters including Julian and Sandy and Rambling Syd Rumpo?

4   On which Eminem hit, released in December 2000, did Dido sing?

5   Which author wrote the novels *Flaubert's Parrot* and *The Noise of Time*?

6   What was the nickname of the racehouse Corbiere?

7   Which country lies north of Israel?

8   *I Will Never Let You Down* was a no.1 for which singer in 2014?

9   To which family of plants does kale belong?

10 What is the legal term for an obligation to corroborate allegations?

11 Who starred as Alex in the 1983 film *Flashdance*?

12 In which county is the town of Rothbury?

13 Which African country lies west of Botswana?

14 Which actor played Roux in the 2000 film *Chocolat*?

15 In which Lakeland village is William Wordsworth buried?

16 Which Shakespearean character is the son of Queen Gertrude?

17 In 2001, New Orleans International Airport was re-named after which musician?

18 What is the currency unit of Pakistan?

19 Which creature has species including Daubenton's and serotine?

20 In which country are the cities of Harbin, Wuhan and Shenyang?

Answers to QUIZ 437 – Pot Luck

1	Barack Obama	11	Tony Orlando
2	SHADO	12	Mustelids
3	Brigadier	13	Kildare (Naas)
4	Wystan Hugh	14	The Tuxedo
5	*Grace & Favour*	15	Steve Martin
6	Zimbabwe	16	Bordeaux
7	Lichen	17	Danny Kaye
8	Boxer	18	Salsify (the root)
9	Durban	19	Nymph
10	Eight	20	Limahl

ANSWERS ON PAGE 442

Easy

1 What does DMA stand for in computing?

2 The letter M is on which row of a computer keyboard?

3 Which version of the Windows® operating system was released in 2007?

4 "Wi-fi" is a combination of which two words?

5 What type of online resource is DuckDuckGo?

6 What name was given to the forerunner of the emoji, used in texts and emails?

7 The logo of which on-line company consists of a globe of jigsaw pieces containing characters?

8 What is the full name of the company usually referred to as HP?

9 What term is given to code or software that anyone may modify?

10 In a computing context, what is LISP?

Medium

11 Which English mathematician is widely considered to be "the father of modern computer science"?

12 In which year was the first *Halo* video game released?

13 What does the "s" stand for in "laser"?

14 At which location did the English National Museum of Computing open in 2007?

15 In the name of the Intel Corporation, for which two words does "Intel" stand?

16 Which microblogging site was founded by David Karp in 2007?

17 What does USB stand for?

18 In which country is the Baidu technology company based?

19 Which computer, sold from 1998 to 2003, was available in a range of colours including blueberry, strawberry and grape?

20 What phrase applies to graphics programs which interact with people?

Hard

Answers to QUIZ 438 – History

1	Northamptonshire	11	Leonid Brezhnev
2	Plebeian	12	Brooklyn Bridge
3	1951	13	Church of Scientology
4	Oslo	14	1978
5	St Albans	15	China
6	September	16	Zambia
7	Earl's Court	17	*Carpathia*
8	December	18	Clwyd
9	Alexandra (of Denmark)	19	English
10	Sparta	20	Henry IV

1   Who was Stefanie Powers' co-star in the TV series *Hart to Hart*?

2   Who was the first person to be buried at Poets' Corner in Westminster Abbey?

3   Brasenose College is part of which university?

4   What is a flock of partridges called?

5   Who was the first person to win European Footballer of the Year in three successive years?

6   In which novel by Charles Dickens was Dick Swiveller a clerk to Sampson Brass?

7   Which fruit can be found on the top of the trophy for the men's singles title at Wimbledon?

8   In the novel *Treasure Island*, what is the name of Long John Silver's parrot?

9   Which singer starred in the 1986 film *Shanghai Surprise*?

10 Who was the first ever Formula 1 World Champion?

11 Which Northern Ireland county is the only one not to adjoin Lough Neagh?

12 As well as scales, what does the blindfolded figure of Justice carry?

13 *In the Hall of the Mountain King* is a piece from which classical suite?

14 Who co-starred with Dawn French in the TV series *Roger & Val Have Just Got In*?

15 On which British island is Fingal's Cave?

16 Who discovered the planet Uranus?

17 What is a more common name for coquille Saint-Jacques?

18 Thornton Wilder's play *The Matchmaker* was the basis for which musical?

19 Which herb has the Latin name *Salvia officinalis*?

20 What is the cold winter wind that blows down from the mountains onto the eastern Adriatic coast?

Easy

Medium

Hard

Answers to QUIZ 439 – Pot Luck

1	1954	11	Jennifer Beals
2	Argan	12	Northumberland
3	*Round the Horne*	13	Namibia
4	*Stan*	14	Johnny Depp
5	Julian Barnes	15	Grasmere
6	Corky	16	Hamlet
7	Lebanon	17	Louis Armstrong
8	Rita Ora	18	Pakistani rupee
9	Brassica	19	Bat
10	Burden of proof	20	China

Easy

1 What was the name of St Petersburg from 1914 to 1924?

2 Who created the character of Lord Peter Wimsey?

3 Which constituency did Baron Peter Mandelson represent from 1992 to 2004?

4 By what other name are "St Peter's fish" known, so-called because of the black spot on each side, said to be St Peter's thumbprints?

5 In which 1959 film did Peter Sellers play three roles?

6 By what name is London's Collegiate Church of St Peter better known?

7 The song *Puff the Magic Dragon* was originally performed by which group?

8 Which 1964 film about a jewel robbery featured Peter Ustinov?

9 Which TV series initially starred Stephen Tompkinson as Father Peter Clifford?

10 Peter Sallis voiced which animated character up until 2010?

11 In which London borough is Petersham?

12 Peter Davison played which incarnation of the Doctor in *Doctor Who*?

13 Who directed the *Lord of the Rings* and the *Hobbit* trilogies?

Medium

14 Which football team did Peter Crouch play for from 1998 to 2000 and 2009 to 2011?

15 In which sci-fi series did Milo Ventimiglia play Peter Petrelli?

16 Peter Griffin is the main character in which animated series?

17 In which county is Peterborough?

18 Which duo topped the charts in 1973 with *Welcome Home*?

19 Which National Hunt jockey retired in 1993, setting a then all-time record for the most number of wins?

20 Who played Peter in the 1992 British comedy *Peter's Friends*?

Hard

Answers to QUIZ 440 – Technology

1	Direct memory access	11	Alan Turing
2	Bottom	12	2001
3	Windows Vista®	13	Stimulated
4	Wireless Fidelity	14	Bletchley Park
5	Search engine	15	Intelligent Electronics
6	Emoticon	16	Tumblr
7	Wikipedia®	17	Universal Serial Bus
8	Hewlett-Packard	18	China
9	Open source	19	iMac G3
10	Programming language	20	Virtual reality

1. Which American paediatrician wrote the 1946 *Common Sense Book of Baby and Child Care?*

2. What do the letters HDPE stand for when seen on a plastic item?

3. What is the smallest species of British deer?

4. In which country is the wine-growing Barossa Valley?

5. In which US state is Newark the largest city?

6. What term is given to the study of fish?

7. In which city did Shakespeare set *Measure for Measure?*

8. Which coastal footpath links Amroth to St Dogmaels?

9. What is the name of the oldest bridge in Britain?

10. King Power Stadium is the home ground for which football club?

11. The moons called Phobos and Deimos belong to which planet of our solar system?

12. Which group topped the charts in 1974 with *Billy Don't Be a Hero?*

13. Which country is landlocked between China, Vietnam, Cambodia, Thailand and Burma?

14. Brent Spiner played which android character in *Star Trek: The Next Generation?*

15. By what title was the fictional character Michael Henchard known?

16. What type of creature is a bullhead?

17. In Formula 1, what does KERS stand for?

18. Which vitamin is found in milk, wheatgerm and meat?

19. The 1930s documentary film *Night Mail* featured which form of transport?

20. Which 1990s comedy drama series featured a Canadian Mountie in the USA?

Easy

Medium

Hard

Answers to QUIZ 441 – Pot Luck

1	Robert Wagner	11	Fermanagh
2	Geoffrey Chaucer	12	A sword
3	Oxford	13	*Peer Gynt* (Suite no.1)
4	A covey	14	Alfred Molina
5	Michel Platini (1983-85)	15	Staffa
6	*The Old Curiosity Shop*	16	William Herschel
7	Pineapple	17	Scallops
8	Captain Flint	18	*Hello, Dolly!*
9	Madonna	19	Sage
10	Nino Farina (1950)	20	Bora

1 What covers 85% of Algeria?

2 The Victoria Falls is on the border of which two countries?

3 Under what pen name did Karen Blixen write *Out of Africa*?

4 Which is Africa's third longest river?

5 Timbuktu is in which country?

6 To what was the Republic of Upper Volta renamed in 1984?

7 The Serengeti National Park is in which country?

8 Which country used to be known as the Gold Coast?

9 Which Nigerian city became the country's capital in 1991?

10 Who won a Best Actor Oscar for his role in *The African Queen* (1951)?

11 Who became President of South Africa in February 2018?

12 Eritrea, Ethiopia and Somalia border which small republic?

13 What is the former name of the South African province prefixed with "KwaZulu" in 1994?

14 In which country are the ruins of ancient Carthage?

15 The Mediterranean and the Red Sea are linked by which waterway of 100 miles?

16 What does ANC stand for?

17 Which African desert is home to the bushmen?

18 Situated off the coast of south-east Africa, which island provided the title for a 2005 animated film?

19 What is the capital of Rwanda?

20 What was Ethiopia's former name?

Answers to QUIZ 442 – Peter

1	Petrograd	11	Richmond upon Thames
2	Dorothy L Sayers	12	Fifth
3	Hartlepool	13	Peter Jackson
4	John Dory	14	Tottenham Hotspur
5	*The Mouse That Roared*	15	*Heroes*
6	Westminster Abbey	16	*Family Guy*
7	Peter, Paul and Mary	17	Cambridgeshire
8	*Topkapi*	18	Peters and Lee
9	*Ballykissangel*	19	Peter Scudamore
10	Wallace	20	Stephen Fry

1   What colour are the flowers of the mock orange, *Philadelphus*?

2   In mythology, who was the lover of the Carthaginian queen Dido?

3   Who co-starred with Ben Stiller in the 2004 film *Along Came Polly*?

4   Which river runs through Leicester?

5   Who was the French composer of the music for the ballet *Coppélia*?

6   Which country singer had a 1961 hit with *Crazy*?

7   The TV series *Detectorists* was set in which fictional village?

8   What do the initials FIA stand for in the context of motor sport?

9   What is the name of the Middle Eastern waters between Iran and Saudi Arabia?

10   Zeno of Citium founded which ancient Greek school of philosophy?

11   What is the name of Bob the Builder's cat?

12   What is Israel's chief seaport?

13   In the TV series *The Golden Girls*, who played Sophia?

14   What gives English mustard its colour?

15   Which sea separates Scandinavia from Germany?

16   Zennor Head is found in which English county?

17   Who wrote the 1759 novel *Tristram Shandy*?

18   Psittacosis is a disease found in which animals?

19   Which Spanish airport is indicated by the code ALC?

20   How is the gooney bird better known?

Answers to QUIZ 443 – Pot Luck

1	Dr Benjamin Spock	11	Mars
2	High Density Polyethylene	12	Paper Lace
3	Muntjac	13	Laos
4	Australia	14	Data
5	New Jersey	15	The Mayor of Casterbridge
6	Ichthyology	16	Fish
7	Vienna	17	Kinetic Energy Recovery System
8	Pembrokeshire	18	Niacin
9	Tarr Steps	19	Train
10	Leicester City	20	*Due South*

Easy

1 What is the square root of 256?

2 How many pounds are there in a hundredweight?

3 Moving anticlockwise on a dartboard, which number is next to 9?

4 How many sides has a trapezium?

5 In geometry, how many minutes are there in a degree?

6 How many hours are there in April?

7 In imperial measurement, how many yards are in a chain?

8 How many old pence were there in £1?

9 A regular tetrahedron has how many faces?

10 What is the number on the black ball in a game of pool?

11 Which number is traditionally called as "The Brighton Line" in bingo?

12 Which number is *undici* in Italian?

13 An emerald anniversary celebrates how many years of marriage?

14 How many number slots, including 0, are there on a UK roulette wheel?

Medium

15 What is the next highest prime number above 53?

16 How many ounces are there in a stone?

17 If a billion is written in digits, how many zeros are there?

18 How many yards are there in a furlong?

19 In a quarter of an hour, how many seconds are there?

20 How many acres are there in a square mile?

Hard

Answers to QUIZ 444 – Africa

1	The Sahara Desert	11	Cyril Ramaphosa
2	Zambia and Zimbabwe	12	Djibouti
3	Isak Dinesen	13	Natal
4	Niger	14	Tunisia
5	Mali	15	Suez Canal
6	Burkina Faso	16	African National Congress
7	Tanzania	17	The Kalahari
8	Ghana	18	Madagascar
9	Abuja	19	Kigali
10	Humphrey Bogart	20	Abyssinia

1. What is the SI unit of force?

2. In 2000, which former Spice Girl had a solo hit with *I Turn To You*?

3. What is the third book of the Old Testament?

4. Which canal was opened in 1869?

5. Who recorded the 1976 disco hit *More More More*?

6. Periwinkle is the name of both a flower and which type of creature?

7. What is the shipping forecast area north-west of Dogger?

8. How many eyes has a bee?

9. Who had a hit in 2001 with *Fallin'*?

10. Which poem begins "The curfew tolls the knell of parting day"?

11. What is the county town of Fermanagh?

12. Dr Samuel Johnson was famous for compiling what sort of book?

13. In which year did Premium Bonds first go on sale?

14. Which is the largest species of crocodile?

15. Which group of islands was formerly known as the Sandwich Islands?

16. What was the British Royal Family's house before it adopted the name Windsor in 1917?

17. Dr Cockroach, Insectosaurus and Missing Link all feature in which 2009 animated sci-fi film?

18. In which country is Cape Wrath?

19. Which actor starred in the 2012 film *Arbitrage*?

20. With which band was Roland Gift the lead vocalist in the mid-1980s?

Answers to QUIZ 445 – Pot Luck

1	White	11	Pilchard
2	Aeneas	12	Haifa
3	Jennifer Aniston	13	Estelle Getty
4	Soar	14	Turmeric
5	Delibes	15	Baltic
6	Patsy Cline	16	Cornwall
7	Danebury	17	Laurence Sterne
8	Fédération Internationale de l'Automobile	18	Birds (communicable from parrots)
9	The Gulf (also known as the Persian Gulf or the Arabian Gulf)	19	Alicante-Elche Airport
10	Stoicism	20	Albatross

1 What is the former name of Lake Malawi?

2 Which river lies between lakes Erie and Ontario?

3 Which series of films centres around Camp Crystal Lake?

4 In which Scottish region is Loch Fyne?

5 How long is Lake Windermere, in miles?

6 Drumnadrochit is on the shore of which loch?

7 Where were the Winter Olympics held in 1980?

8 What term is given to a small curved lake that lies on the flood plain of a river?

9 Which small lake is situated close to Grasmere in the Lake District?

10 What is unusual about the Scottish body of water on which Port of Menteith is situated?

11 The lake Königssee is in which region of Germany?

12 Lake Tahoe is on the border of which two US states?

13 The lochs of Coriusk and Snizort are on which Scottish island?

14 Which is Africa's longest lake?

15 What Spanish word for "beach" also denotes a dry lake bed in an arid region?

16 The *Salzkammergut* is known as the Lake District of which country?

17 Which French lakeside town is referred to as "the Venice of the Alps"?

18 In which country does the Euphrates river flow through Lake Assad?

19 Which is Africa's largest lake?

20 Montreux is located on which lake?

Answers to QUIZ 446 – Numbers

1	16	11	59
2	112	12	11
3	14	13	55
4	Four	14	37
5	60	15	59
6	720	16	224
7	22	17	Nine
8	240	18	220
9	Four (three sides and a triangular base)	19	900
10	Eight	20	640

1   Who starred alongside Cher in the 1983 film *Silkwood*?

2   What sort of food is Neufchâtel?

3   Which horse breed was formerly reared to pull carriages?

4   Who was the front man with 1970s band Sweet?

5   In pre-decimal currency, which coin was worth the equivalent of 25p?

6   Which California town at the foot of Mount Wilson features in the title of a 1948 Humphrey Bogart film?

7   What is the capital city of Colombia?

8   Mary, Queen of Scots was born in which palace?

9   In which county are the Bedruthan Steps?

10   From which English city would you catch a ferry to Le Havre?

11   What was the name of the horse on which Lester Piggott first won the Derby?

12   Who composed *Finlandia* (1899)?

13   In Marvel's *Iron Man* films, what is the name of Tony Stark's personal AI system?

14   A person suffering from pruritus has an overwhelming urge to do what?

15   Singer Engelbert Humperdinck had what original name?

16   Which actor starred in the 2008 film *The Curious Case of Benjamin Button*?

17   Who was the British Prime Minister during the short reign of Edward VIII?

18   Which lake is known to the French as Lac Leman?

19   How many symphonies did the composer Beethoven complete?

20   Where did General Montgomery defeat General Rommel?

Answers to QUIZ 447 – Pot Luck

1	Newton	11	Enniskillen
2	Melanie Chisholm (Mel C)	12	English dictionary
3	Leviticus	13	1956
4	Suez	14	Saltwater crocodile
5	Andrea True Connection	15	Hawaii
6	Mollusc	16	Saxe-Coburg-Gotha
7	Forth	17	*Monsters vs. Aliens*
8	Five	18	Scotland
9	Alicia Keys	19	Richard Gere
10	Thomas Gray's *Elegy*	20	Fine Young Cannibals

Easy

1   In a game of water polo, what is the colour of the cap worn by the goalkeeper?

2   Which round-the-world yachtsman was rescued after four days upside down in his boat in 1996?

3   The bucket turn is used to change to breaststroke from which other swimming stroke?

4   In 2017, who was appointed chair of UK Sport?

5   The four shapes used in diving competitions are free, straight, pike and which other?

6   In which country was swimmer Hannah Miley born?

7   Which former British swimmer-turned-commentator appeared in the sixth series of *Strictly Come Dancing*?

8   Which relatively new watersport was added to the Olympics in 1984?

9   How many oars does each rower have in a sweep boat?

10 What is the highest height of a diving board used in competition?

11 At the 2012 Olympics, in which body of water did the open water swimming competitions take place?

Medium

12 In which year did Sir Matthew Pinsent win his fourth Olympic gold medal?

13 What term is used in rowing to describe older competitors?

14 In which discipline did Ed McKeever win an Olympic gold medal in 2012?

15 How long does each quarter of a water polo match usually last?

16 The Dorney Lake rowing lake, owned by Eton College, is in which county?

17 What is the name of Oxford University's reserve rowing team?

18 Women were first allowed to swim in the Olympics in which decade?

19 How long is the Oxford-Cambridge Boat Race in miles?

20 Which Scottish swimmer won the 200m breaststroke gold medal at the 1976 summer Olympic Games?

Hard

ANSWERS ON PAGE 453

1   Which 2001 crime thriller starred Gene Hackman and Danny DeVito?

2   The song *On the Street Where You Live* features in which musical?

3   Which band had albums entitled *The Great Escape* and *Modern Life Is Rubbish*?

4   Which amount is equivalent to the pre-1971 shilling?

5   What is the literal meaning of "Algarve"?

6   The Victoria Jubilee Bridge in Canada spans which river?

7   On the Beaufort Scale, what is Force 8 called?

8   Which actress starred in the 1989 film *Dead Calm*?

9   Who designed the Lloyd's building in London?

10 How are Jake, Milo, Bella and Fizz known collectively?

11 Which port is part of the city of Edinburgh?

12 What is the capital of the US state of Delaware?

13 A chemical reaction that absorbs heat is described by what word?

14 How is the bell tower in the Piazza dei Miracoli famously known?

15 Which city was the birthplace of Dylan Thomas?

16 What is the animal symbol for Scotland?

17 Which West Indian island has Bridgetown as its capital?

18 The Kennet and Avon canal links which city and town?

19 In September 1996, which jockey won all seven races in one day at Ascot?

20 At which Channel port does the Sussex Ouse flow into the English Channel?

Easy

Medium

Hard

Answers to QUIZ 449 – Pot Luck

1	Meryl Streep	11	Never Say Die
2	Cheese	12	Jean Sibelius
3	Hackney	13	JARVIS
4	Brian Connolly	14	Scratch
5	Crown	15	Arnold Dorsey
6	Sierra Madre	16	Brad Pitt
7	Bogotá	17	Stanley Baldwin
8	Linlithgow Palace	18	Lake Geneva
9	Cornwall	19	Nine
10	Portsmouth	20	El Alamein

ANSWERS ON PAGE 454

1   In which county is the racecourse of Redcar?

2   What was the surname of the baroness who wrote *The Scarlet Pimpernel*?

3   What was the title of the first single released by Simply Red?

4   Whom did Amanda Redman play in the TV series *New Tricks*?

5   In which Olympic Games did Sir Steve Redgrave win his fifth consecutive gold medal?

6   What is a red-hot poker, if it is not a fire implement?

7   Which actress starred in the 2018 film *Red Sparrow*?

8   In US voting, a "red state" is one where people predominately voted for which party?

9   What is the setting for the 1995 film *Crimson Tide*?

10 What did the *Red Light* spell in the title of a 1977 hit for Billy Ocean?

11 Which actress starred in the 1985 film *Red Sonja*?

12 After which US state is a "red" breed of chicken named?

13 What is the name of Danny John-Jules' character in the TV series *Red Dwarf*?

14 What type of creature is a redpoll?

15 Which Irish province has the Red Hand as its symbol?

16 How many times did Sebastian Vettel win the Formula 1 World Championship with the Red Bull team?

17 Which strait separates Egypt and Saudi Arabia?

18 Which Neil Diamond song was a no.1 for UB40?

19 Who wrote the 1847 poem *Now Sleeps the Crimson Petal*?

20 Who trained the Grand National winner Red Rum?

Answers to QUIZ 450 – Water Sports

1	Red	11	Serpentine
2	Tony Bullimore	12	2004
3	Backstroke	13	Masters
4	Dame Katherine Grainger	14	Kayaking
5	Tuck	15	Eight minutes
6	Scotland	16	Buckinghamshire
7	Mark Foster	17	Isis
8	Synchronised swimming	18	1910s (1912)
9	One	19	Just under 4.25 miles
10	10m	20	David Wilkie

ANSWERS ON PAGE 456

1   Which coast runs from Salerno to Sorrento?

2   Which is the largest country in Central America?

3   By which more common name is the plant of the genus *Aquilegia* known?

4   Which member of Humble Pie had a solo hit with *Show Me the Way* in 1975?

5   Which dry white Italian wine is from the area near Verona?

6   Who had a hit in 1987 with the record *Nothing's Gonna Stop Us Now*?

7   *Express Yourself* and *Dear Jessie* are tracks on which Madonna album?

8   In which city was Sir Andy Murray born?

9   The song *Wand'rin' Star* is from which musical?

10 In the US National Football League, The Bears are a team from which city?

11 On which island was retired footballer Matt Le Tissier born?

12 A funambulist is more usually referred to by what two-word name?

13 What is the name of the lough in County Fermanagh with Enniskillen on its shore?

14 Who wrote the 1991 novel *The Famished Road*?

15 Which word meaning "therefore" spells out a fairy-tale character when read backwards?

16 A frugivorous animal eats what as the main part of its diet?

17 The Erskine Bridge spans which river?

18 A googol is the number one followed by how many zeros?

19 What is the capital of the Canadian province of New Brunswick?

20 Who wrote the 1990 novel *Possession*?

Answers to QUIZ 451 – Pot Luck

1	*Heist*	11	Leith
2	*My Fair Lady*	12	Dover
3	Blur	13	Endothermic
4	Five pence	14	Leaning Tower of Pisa
5	The West	15	Swansea
6	St Lawrence	16	Unicorn
7	Gale	17	Barbados
8	Nicole Kidman	18	Bristol and Reading
9	Richard Rogers (Baron Rogers of Riverside)	19	Frankie Dettori
10	The Tweenies	20	Newhaven

Easy

1. The first series of *Strictly Come Dancing* was won by which professional dancer?

2. Who was the original host of *Stars in Their Eyes*?

3. Who was the first dancer to win *Britain's Got Talent*?

4. The series *America's Next Top Model* was created by which former model?

5. What was the title of the 2008 show that was searching for a Nancy for *Oliver!*?

6. Who was the original presenter of the talent show *Fame Academy*?

7. Davina McCall hosted which dance show from 2009 to 2014?

8. Which rock star was on the *American Idol* judging panel from 2011 to 2012?

9. Which act was the runner-up in the first series of *The X Factor*?

10. Which talent show gave Showaddywaddy their big break?

11. How many people were on the judging panel for the 2018 talent show *All Together Now*?

Medium

12. Who won the second series of *The Voice UK*?

13. Which group won the 2015 *a cappella* competition *The Naked Choir*?

14. What was the name of the short-lived boy band created as a result of *Popstars: the Rivals*?

15. Who won the second series of *Pop Idol*?

16. The 1999 BBC talent show *Get Your Act Together* was hosted by which singer?

17. Edd Kimber won the first series of which competition?

18. Bonnie Langford first found fame on which talent show?

19. With which winning dance troupe is Ashley Banjo associated?

20. For how many years did *Strictly Come Dancing* former winner Alesha Dixon appear on the judging panel?

Answers to QUIZ 452 – Red

1	North Yorkshire	11	Brigitte Nielsen
2	Orczy	12	Rhode Island
3	*Money's Too Tight (to Mention)*	13	The Cat
4	Sandra Pullman	14	Bird
5	2000 (Sydney)	15	Ulster
6	A flower	16	Four
7	Jennifer Lawrence	17	The Red Sea
8	Republicans	18	*Red Red Wine*
9	Nuclear submarine	19	Alfred, Lord Tennyson
10	*Danger*	20	Ginger McCain

Hard

1 In which US city is the Liberty Bell located?

2 Who won the BBC Overseas Sports Personality of the Year in 2016?

3 The theme song from the TV series *Boon* was a 1986 hit for which singer?

4 Who starred with Sandra Bullock in the 2006 film *The Lake House*?

5 Spain and France are bordered by which Atlantic bay?

6 Which of the Apollo 11 astronauts did not walk on the moon?

7 Who is the third god of the Hindu trinity?

8 Which UK shipping area lies directly south of Viking?

9 *The Darkling Thrush* is a 1900 poem by which writer?

10 Who wrote the 1944 play *The Glass Menagerie*?

11 In 1961, the Nobel Peace Prize was awarded to which secretary-general of the United Nations?

12 Who wrote the 1816 poem *On First Looking into Chapman's Homer"*?

13 In which year did the UK introduce self-adhesive stamps?

14 Calico cloth originated in which country?

15 How did the TV characters the *Tomorrow People* refer to teleportation?

16 What title was given to a magistrate ranking next after a consul in Ancient Rome?

17 What name was given to the series of 1970s space probes that provided pictures of Jupiter and Saturn?

18 In which year did Eurostar first run a service from London?

19 Which novelist created the character of Jason Bourne?

20 At which English racecourse are the Coventry Stakes run?

Answers to QUIZ 453 – Pot Luck

1	Amalfi Coast	11	Guernsey
2	Nicaragua	12	Tightrope walker
3	Columbine	13	Erne
4	Peter Frampton	14	Ben Okri
5	Soave	15	Ergo
6	Starship	16	Fruit
7	*Like A Prayer*	17	Clyde
8	Glasgow	18	100
9	*Paint Your Wagon*	19	Fredericton
10	Chicago	20	AS Byatt

Easy

1   In which century was Chopin born?

2   Benjamin Britten (Baron Britten) and Sir Peter Pears established which annual Suffolk music festival?

3   What was the first name of the composer Rimsky-Korsakov?

4   What does *Lieder Ohne Worte* mean?

5   Who composed *The Rite of Spring* (1913)?

6   In a standard modern symphony orchestra which two brass instruments are in the back row?

7   King Ludwig II of Bavaria was the patron of which German composer?

8   Who wrote two operas based on the Shakespeare plays *Macbeth* and *Othello*, and another on the Shakespearean character Falstaff?

9   How is *The Marriage of Figaro* known in Italian?

10   Which conductor became Music Director of the London Symphony Orchestra in 2017?

Medium

11   Which instrument usually has 47 strings?

12   Anne-Sophie Mutter is associated with which instrument?

13   Which Beethoven piece is the anthem of the European Union and Council of Europe?

14   In which city is the opera *Carmen* set?

15   Which three-act Puccini opera was first performed in 1900?

16   What was the nationality of composer Jean Sibelius?

17   Which two conductors founded the London Philharmonic Orchestra?

18   *The Bartered Bride* was written by which Czech composer?

19   In which London street would you find the Royal Opera House?

20   How many *Brandenburg Concertos* did Bach compose?

Hard

Answers to QUIZ 454 – Talent Shows

1	Brendan Cole	11	100
2	Leslie Crowther	12	Andrea Begley
3	George Sampson	13	The Sons of Pitches
4	Tyra Banks	14	One True Voice
5	*I'd Do Anything*	15	Michelle McManus
6	Patrick Kielty	16	Ronan Keating
7	*Got to Dance*	17	*The Great British Bake Off*
8	Steven Tyler	18	*Opportunity Knocks*
9	G4	19	Diversity
10	*New Faces*	20	Three

QUIZ 457 – Pot Luck

ANSWERS ON PAGE 459

1 Who performed the title track to the sitcom *The Royle Family*?

2 What is the capital of the Democratic Republic of the Congo?

3 What old horse-drawn cab was named after its architect inventor?

4 Miss Moneypenny was first played by which actress in the 1995 film Bond film *GoldenEye*?

5 Which 2007 animated film featured the voices of Jerry Seinfeld and Renée Zellweger?

6 Who won a diving gold medal at the 1988 Olympics, despite hitting his head on the board performing a reverse 2½ pike?

7 What word is used in Buddhism to indicate the ideal truth as set forth by Buddha?

8 The former EU scheme of "set aside" applied to which type of business?

9 Who was Mike Chapman's most famous co-producer on many 1970s records?

10 The Cape Verde islands are in which ocean?

11 "Hoosier State" is the nickname of which US state?

12 *Love Letters in the Sand* was a 1957 hit for which singer?

13 What name is given to biblical writings that are not part of the accepted Scriptures?

14 What does the expression *Ecce homo* mean?

15 In the TV series *The Avengers*, who played Emma Peel?

16 Which country has "Suomi" on its coins and stamps?

17 In which US state is Lake Placid?

18 Which Lerner and Loewe musical is based on a novel by Colette?

19 Which actor's first name means "cool breeze over the mountains" in Hawaiian?

20 How many hearts has an octopus?

Answers to QUIZ 455 – Pot Luck

1	Philadelphia	11	Dag Hammarskjöld
2	Simone Biles	12	Keats
3	Jim Diamond	13	1993
4	Keanu Reeves	14	India
5	Biscay	15	Jaunting
6	Michael Collins	16	Praetor
7	Shiva	17	*Pioneer*
8	Forties	18	1994
9	Thomas Hardy	19	Robert Ludlum
10	Tennessee Williams	20	Ascot

Easy

1 In the 12th century Blondel was the legendary minstrel of which king?

2 What was the profession of Queen Elizabeth II's cousin Lord Lichfield?

3 Of which country was King Farouk the leader from 1936 to 1952?

4 Which English monarch married Eleanor of Aquitaine?

5 In 1831, Leopold I became the first monarch of which country?

6 Madame de Pompadour was a mistress to which French king?

7 Margaret of Anjou was the wife of which English king?

8 Which plot led to the execution of Mary, Queen of Scots?

9 Windsor Castle was built by which English king?

10 In which year did the royal yacht *Britannia* make her final voyage?

11 Sir Anthony Van Dyck was court painter to which English king?

12 In which European city is the royal palace of Belvedere?

13 Which law excluded women from succeeding to the throne of some European countries?

Medium

14 The Palace of Versailles gardens were designed at the behest of which 17th-century monarch?

15 Geoffrey Plantagenet, Count of Anjou (b.1113) was the father of which English king?

16 Which English monarch reputedly lost some of the Crown Jewels in The Wash?

17 Who was the last Queen of France before the revolution?

18 The House of Grimaldi is associated with which European principality?

19 Who was the last ruler of the House of Plantagenet?

20 Kenneth I and Kenneth II were kings of which country?

Hard

Answers to QUIZ 456 – Classical Music

1	19th century (1810)	11	Harp
2	Aldeburgh	12	Violin
3	Nikolai	13	*Ode to Joy*
4	Song without words	14	Seville
5	Igor Stravinsky	15	*Tosca*
6	Trombones and tubas	16	Finnish
7	Richard Wagner	17	Sir Thomas Beecham and Sir Malcolm Sargent
8	Verdi	18	Bedřich Smetana
9	*Le Nozze di Figaro*	19	Bow Street
10	Sir Simon Rattle	20	Six

1   Which group had a hit record in 1969 with *Bad Moon Rising*?

2   Which 1960s TV series starred Sir Roger Moore as Simon Templar?

3   What type of creature is a noctule?

4   Rose Byrne played Ellen Parsons in which legal drama series?

5   Which Portuguese archipelago lies 600 miles north-west of Madeira?

6   In which country would you find Mount Logan?

7   The Den is the home ground of which football team?

8   What is the capital of the Australian state of Victoria?

9   In the original TV series *Thunderbirds*, who provided the voice of Lady Penelope?

10 Who played Eric's sister in the TV series *Sykes*?

11 Which are the two Outer Hebridean islands separated by Benbecula?

12 In which Scottish town is McCaig's Tower?

13 Coir is a natural fibre from which plant?

14 Who represented the UK in the 1992 Eurovision Song Contest with *One Step Out of Time*?

15 What is the study of birds' eggs called?

16 *Girl on Fire* was a single in September 2012 for which singer?

17 In which country is Isfahan?

18 What name is given to the region to the east of the Mediterranean Sea?

19 Which stringed instrument features prominently in Dixieland and bluegrass music?

20 In which year was the debit card launched in the UK?

Answers to QUIZ 457 – Pot Luck

1	Oasis	11	Indiana
2	Kinshasa	12	Pat Boone
3	Hansom	13	Apocrypha
4	Samantha Bond	14	Behold the man
5	*Bee Movie*	15	Dame Diana Rigg
6	Greg Louganis	16	Finland
7	Dharma	17	New York
8	Agriculture	18	*Gigi*
9	Nicky Chinn	19	Keanu Reeves
10	Atlantic	20	Three

Easy

1   What is the name of the most famous geothermal spa in Iceland?

2   In which decade was IKEA founded?

3   In which year did Denmark win the European Football championships after initially failing to qualify?

4   Which capital city is the most populated city in Scandinavia...?

5   ...and what is the most populated Scandinavian country?

6   Which two colours appear on the flag of Denmark?

7   The Faroe Islands are situated about halfway between which two countries?

8   What is the international car registration code for Sweden?

9   In which ocean is the Norwegian archipelago of Svalbard?

10 What were Scandinavian pirates more commonly known as?

11 In which city is the Tivoli amusement park?

12 Sonja Henie was a Norwegian Olympic champion in which sport?

13 What is the airport code for Copenhagen?

14 The Danish pastry was introduced to Denmark by bakers from which country?

15 Which two sports do Nordic Combined competitors take part in?

16 By which country was Finland governed from the 17th to the 19th century?

17 In local usage, which three countries does "Scandinavia" usually refer to?

18 Which masked Finnish rock group won the Eurovision Song Contest in 2006?

19 In which decade of the 20th century was Björn Borg born?

20 Which Scandinavian country was the setting for Disney's *Frozen*?

Medium

Hard

Answers to QUIZ 458 – Royalty

1	Richard I (The Lionheart)	11	Charles I
2	Photographer	12	Vienna
3	Egypt	13	Salic law
4	Henry II	14	Louis XIV
5	Belgium	15	Henry II
6	Louis XV	16	King John
7	Henry VI	17	Marie Antoinette
8	The Babington Plot	18	Monaco
9	William the Conqueror	19	Richard III
10	1997	20	Scotland

QUIZ 461 – Pot Luck

ANSWERS ON PAGE 463

1   Retired racing driver Nelson Piquet was born in which country?

2   What is another name for the honey badger?

3   Which actress starred in the film *The Piano*?

4   Which fruit flavours the Belgian beer *Kriek lambic*?

5   The novelty record *Shaddup You Face* kept which single from reaching the top of the charts in 1981?

6   "Anything can happen in the next half hour" was the announcement at the start of which popular children's TV series?

7   Radicchio is a variety of which salad plant?

8   Which African country between Nigeria and Gabon has Yaoundé as its capital?

9   What is the term used for a wide railway track?

10 In which area of Russia is Lake Baikal?

11 What type of bridge is the Forth Railway Bridge?

12 Rothesay is the main town on which Scottish island?

13 Which Dame Daphne Du Maurier novel was filmed by Sir Alfred Hitchcock in 1940?

14 Who wrote the collection of poems entitled *Songs of Innocence and of Experience*?

15 Which group recorded the 1987 album *Tango in the Night*?

16 In which branch of the arts was Sir Frederick Ashton famous?

17 Which Asian river forms much of the border between Laos and Thailand?

18 What name is given to the vertical divide on a window?

19 The 1976 book *The Selfish Gene* was written by which author?

20 Which Greek philosopher was a student of Plato and taught Alexander the Great?

Easy

Medium

Hard

Answers to QUIZ 459 – Pot Luck

1	Credence Clearwater Revival	11	North Uist and South Uist
2	*The Saint*	12	Oban
3	Bat	13	Coconut
4	*Damages*	14	Michael Ball
5	Azores	15	Oology
6	Canada	16	Alicia Keys
7	Millwall FC	17	Iran
8	Melbourne	18	Levant
9	Sylvia Anderson	19	Banjo
10	Hattie Jacques	20	1987

1   In which year was *Heart of Glass* the first UK no.1 hit for Blondie?

2   What, in military parlance, is a "glasshouse"?

3   What eye condition is indicated if a prescription for glasses includes numbers relating to "spherical", "cylinder" and "axis"?

4   Who wrote the 1994 novel *The Glass Lake*?

5   How many 250ml glasses are there in a jeroboam?

6   Who released the 1980 song *We are Glass*?

7   What is the title of the 1972 sequel to *Charlie and the Chocolate Factory*?

8   What is the name of the small magnifying glass used by jewellers?

9   The 1965 spy novel *The Looking Glass War* was written by which author?

10 Noted for its stained glass, in which area of Paris is Sainte-Chapelle?

11 Which Italian island is famous for its glass-making?

12 Under what name did Baroness Ruth Rendell write the 1990 novel *Gallowglass*?

13 Glass noodles originate from which continent?

14 What two-word term is given to a product such as Google Glass?

15 Singer Bono wears his trademark sunglasses due to having which eye condition?

16 Who played the title role in the 2016 film *Alice Through the Looking Glass*?

17 Which glass-making company has its headquarters in St Helens?

18 In which country was the composer Philip Glass born?

19 In which year was the Kirk Douglas version of the film *The Glass Menagerie* released?

20 Who had a 1978 hit with *I Love the Sound of Breaking Glass*?

Answers to QUIZ 460 – Scandinavia

1	Blue Lagoon	11	Copenhagen
2	1940s (1943)	12	Figure skating
3	1992	13	CPH
4	Stockholm	14	Austria
5	Sweden	15	Cross-country skiing and ski jumping
6	Red and white	16	Sweden
7	Norway and Iceland	17	Denmark, Norway and Sweden
8	S	18	Lordi
9	Arctic Ocean	19	1950s (1956)
10	Vikings	20	Norway

1 What is the literal meaning of "spaghetti"?

2 Which is Turkey's second-largest city?

3 What was the name of the first manned spacecraft to orbit the Moon?

4 *Working My Way Back to You* was a hit for which group in 1980?

5 What did the initials UNCLE stand for in The *Man from UNCLE*?

6 Tulsa is in which US state?

7 Who was leader of the Labour Party when it adopted the Red Rose as its emblem?

8 Which comedy series featured the Brockman family?

9 Movable metal type was invented by which German printer of bibles?

10 What is the fifth letter of the Greek alphabet?

11 What is the study of the flight of projectiles?

12 Which English city traditionally holds a Miners' Gala every July?

13 Bangladesh has which official language?

14 Which former *Blue Peter* presenter was appointed Chief Scout in 2004?

15 Which celebrated mystic published his *Les Prophéties* in 1555?

16 In the 1990s, which comedian wrote the novels *Blast From the Past* and *Inconceivable*?

17 Which Germanic people invaded the Roman Empire between the third and fifth centuries?

18 In 1988, who achieved a "Golden Slam" by winning all four Grand Slam titles plus the Olympic Gold?

19 In which year were contactless payments introduced in the UK?

20 What behaviour characterises somebody named as a *flâneur*?

Easy

Medium

Hard

Answers to QUIZ 461 – Pot Luck

1	Brazil	11	Cantilever
2	Ratel	12	Bute
3	Holly Hunter	13	*Rebecca*
4	Cherry	14	William Blake
5	*Vienna* (by Ultravox)	15	Fleetwood Mac
6	*Stingray*	16	Dance (choreography)
7	Chicory	17	Mekong
8	Cameroon	18	Mullion
9	Broad gauge	19	Richard Dawkins
10	Siberia	20	Aristotle

Easy

1. Hoylake is the home of which golf club?

2. Who won the US Masters tournament in 2018?

3. In the 2014 BBC Sports Personality of the Year Award, which golfer was runner-up?

4. What nationality is Rickie Fowler?

5. Which Spanish course hosted the first Ryder Cup in mainland Europe in 1997?

6. In which month is The Open championship played?

7. What is the real first name of Fuzzy Zoeller?

8. On which course is the hole known as "the Postage Stamp"?

9. Which golf club was used to hit the three golf balls on the Moon?

10. Which of the four major tournaments is the only one to be held at the same location each year?

Medium

11. What are the first names of the two Molinari brothers?

12. What is the maximum number of clubs that a golfer is permitted to carry at any one time?

13. In which year did the "Miracle at Medinah" mark Europe's comeback in the Ryder Cup?

14. The Royal Lytham & St Anne's golf club is in which county?

15. Anchoring strokes using which long-handled club was banned at the start of 2016?

16. Which Spanish golfer (b.1964) is noted for his love of cigars?

17. What nationality is Inbee Park?

18. In 1990, who became the first international player to be named PGA of America Player of the Year?

19. How long can a golfer look for a ball before it is deemed to be lost?

20. Which golfer won The Open in 2017?

Hard

Answers to QUIZ 462 – Glass

1	1979	11	Murano
2	Military prison	12	Barbara Vine
3	Astigmatism	13	Asia
4	Maeve Binchy	14	Smart glasses
5	12	15	Glaucoma
6	Gary Numan	16	Mia Wasikowska
7	*Charlie and the Great Glass Elevator*	17	Pilkington
8	Loupe	18	USA
9	John le Carré	19	1950
10	Île de la Cité	20	Nick Lowe

ANSWERS ON PAGE **467**

1   What is the Chinese *Book of Changes* more usually called?

2   In the TV series *Ever Decreasing Circles*, who played Martin's wife?

3   What is the name for a mixture of beer and cider?

4   Who was Formula 1 World Champion in 1998, 1990 and 1991?

5   In which year was Catherine the Great born?

6   Which type of insect has a "peppered" variety?

7   Which actress won an Oscar for her portrayal of a woman with Alzheimer's disease in *Still Alice* (2014)?

8   What is the name of the pub in the radio series *The Archers*?

9   Who played Mr Gruber in the 2017 film *Paddington 2*?

10   The 1975 film *Picnic at Hanging Rock* is set in which country?

11   Baron Greenback is an adversary of which TV character?

12   Which sea lies to the east of Italy?

13   Who starred as Jack Harper in the 2013 film *Oblivion*?

14   Which river of Switzerland and France flows into the Camargue delta?

15   In Greek mythology, who was the mother of Eros?

16   Who was the lead singer with the band Bread?

17   Boston crab is a term used in which sport?

18   Which term refers to waves of a frequency below the range of human hearing?

19   Who captained the 2016 European Ryder Cup team?

20   In which UK city is Queen Street station?

Easy

Medium

Hard

Answers to QUIZ 463 – Pot Luck

1	LIttle strings	11	Ballistics
2	Ankara	12	Durham
3	Apollo 8	13	Bengali
4	The Detroit Spinners	14	Peter Duncan
5	United Network Command for Law Enforcement	15	Nostradamus
6	Oklahoma	16	Ben Elton
7	Neil Kinnock (Baron Kinnock)	17	Goths
8	*Outnumbered*	18	Steffi Graf
9	Gutenberg	19	2007
10	Epsilon	20	Idleness

1 Benedict Cumberbatch portrayed which mathematician in the 2014 film *The Imitation Game*?

2 Who directed the 1982 film *Gandhi*?

3 Which 2015 film featuring Jake Gyllenhaal portrayed members of an ill-fated 1996 expedition?

4 Which singer did Sissy Spacek play in the 1980 film *Coal Miner's Daughter*?

5 *Amazing Grace* (2006) featured which actor as William Wilberforce?

6 Who starred in the 1953 film *Calamity Jane*?

7 Kurt Russell and Kevin Costner both portrayed which lawman in the mid-1990s?

8 Which Tudor figure is the main character in *A Man For All Seasons* (1966)?

9 Sir Daniel Day-Lewis won his first Oscar for portraying which artist in 1989?

10 In the 1994 film *Ed Wood*, who played the title role?

11 Who played the title role in the 1952 film *Hans Christian Andersen*?

12 *The Spirit of St Louis* (1957) told the story of which aviator?

13 Who played figure skater Tonya Harding in the 2017 film *I, Tonya*?

14 Which 2013 film tells the story of Solomon Northup?

15 Which of Henry VIII's wives was featured in a 1969 film?

16 In the 2011 film *My Week with Marilyn*, who played Marilyn Monroe?

17 Who was the *Funny Girl* in the title of the 1968 musical film?

18 Bushranger Ned Kelly was played by which singer in a 1970 film?

19 Which Irish singer was the subject of the 1991 film *Hear My Song*?

20 Who played George Adamson in the 1966 film *Born Free*?

Answers to QUIZ 464 – Golf

1	Royal Liverpool	11	Edoardo and Francesco
2	Patrick Reed	12	14
3	Rory McIlroy	13	2012
4	American	14	Lancashire
5	Valderrama	15	Belly putter
6	July	16	Miguel Ángel Jiménez
7	Frank	17	South Korean
8	Royal Troon	18	Nick Faldo
9	Six iron	19	Five minutes
10	The Masters (Augusta)	20	Jordan Spieth

1   Who was the lead singer with Led Zeppelin?

2   Who played Julius Caesar in *Carry on Cleo* and Judge Burke in *Carry on Cowboy*?

3   Who won the Best Supporting Actor Oscar for his role in the 1993 film *The Fugitive*?

4   Retired American footballer William Perry had what nickname when he was playing?

5   *I Want Your Love* and *Baby I Don't Care* were 1980s hits for which group?

6   Which programme has been presented at different times by Anne, Kenneth, Robert and Tony Robinson?

7   *I've Never Been to Me* was a hit for which singer in 1982?

8   Who wrote *The Invisible Man* (1897)?

9   Which white wine grape variety is most widely planted in California?

10   What is the title of the 1981 Stephen King novel about a killer dog?

11   The Sperrin Mountains are in which country?

12   Who is the Greek goddess of hunting?

13   What was Frank Sinatra's middle name?

14   Who was King of Macedonia from 336 to 323 BC?

15   Which white cheese is named after a South Wales town?

16   What is the seventh letter of the Greek alphabet?

17   Hamilton is the capital of which British dependency in the western Atlantic?

18   What name is given to a triangle with all sides unequal?

19   *He's So Fine* was a US no.1 hit for which group?

20   Which city was Australia's capital from 1901 to 1927?

Easy

Medium

Hard

Answers to QUIZ 465 – Pot Luck

1	I Ching	11	Danger Mouse
2	Dame Penelope Wilton	12	Adriatic
3	Snakebite	13	Tom Cruise
4	Ayrton Senna	14	Rhône
5	1729	15	Aphrodite
6	Moth	16	David Gates
7	Julianne Moore	17	Wrestling
8	The Bull	18	Infrasonic or subsonic
9	Jim Broadbent	19	Darren Clarke
10	Australia	20	Glasgow

1   What is the literal meaning of "karaoke"?

2   Which prefix indicates 10^{-9}?

3   From which language is the word "ghetto" derived?

4   Bathophobia is a fear of what?

5   What name is used in Britain for the vegetable that Americans called rutabaga?

6   What is the meaning of the word "grockle"?

7   Which two words that sound the same but are spelt differently mean "a car make" and "to grade"?

8   The French word *cheveux* has what English translation?

9   Which Latin phrase means "genuine" or "in good faith"?

10 What in animal terms, is a bellwether?

11 The Spanish word *manzana* refers to which fruit?

12 What word can refer to both a bird and a frilly collar?

13 Of what is speleology the study?

14 What is a peruke?

15 If someone is described as "bibulous", what do they like to do?

16 What word meaning "to steal" means "a piece of equipment" when read backwards?

17 Which card game derives its name from the Spanish word for basket?

18 The American word "bullhorn" has what British equivalent?

19 From which language does the word "smithereens" originate?

20 What is the term for words that mean the opposite of each other?

Easy

Medium

Hard

1   Which German dramatist wrote *The Caucasian Chalk Circle* (1948)?

2   Peter Noone was the lead singer with which group?

3   Which TV series starring Neil Pearson and Sarah Lancashire featured two rival choirs?

4   Lyn Paul and Eve Graham were members of which 1970s group?

5   What type of animal is a macaque?

6   Which musical includes the song *Happy Talk*?

7   In which county is the town of Cricklade?

8   *Say You Won't Let Go* was a 2016 hit for which singer?

9   Which character in ancient myth was visited by Zeus in the form of a swan?

10 Which US state lies to the south of the Beaufort Sea?

11 How many rounds are there in a woman's Olympic boxing match?

12 What type of creature is a gurnard?

13 "The Baggies" is the nickname of which football team?

14 Which fabric did chemist Joseph Shivers invent in 1958?

15 2240lb is the same as which imperial weight?

16 What type of rock is created by a structural change from pressure or heat?

17 Who starred in the 1970s TV series *Cannon*?

18 The juice of which fruit is used in a whiskey sling?

19 Who played the young Han Solo in the film *Solo: A Star Wars Story*?

20 Which country both hosted and won the first ever football World Cup in 1930?

Answers to QUIZ 467 – Pot Luck

1	Robert Plant	11	Northern Ireland
2	Kenneth Williams	12	Artemis
3	Tommy Lee Jones	13	Albert
4	The Fridge	14	Alexander the Great
5	Transvision Vamp	15	Caerphilly
6	*Points of View*	16	Eta
7	Charlene	17	Bermuda
8	HG Wells	18	Scalene
9	Chardonnay	19	The Chiffons
10	*Cujo*	20	Melbourne

1. Where in the human body is the plantar fascia?

2. Referred to as "good cholesterol", what do the initials HDL stand for?

3. In which part of the body would you find the pineal gland?

4. Who developed a vaccine against smallpox in 1796?

5. What is the largest organ of the human body?

6. How many milk teeth do humans normally develop?

7. What is the more common name of the disease pertussis?

8. Where in the body is the incus?

9. Which part of the body is affected by osteomyelitis?

10. What is the third portion of the small intestine?

11. Where would you find something that is said to be subcutaneous?

12. Episcleritis affects which part of the body?

13. What term is given to a tube inserted into the body for the delivery or removal of fluid?

14. William Harvey was the first person to describe what body process in detail?

15. What name is given to the fused vertebrae at the base of the spinal column?

16. The ethmoid, vomer and zygomatic bones can all be found in which part of the body?

17. Which bony tissue forms the bulk of a tooth?

18. How many pairs of ribs does an adult normally have?

19. Which glands are found immediately above the kidneys in the human body?

20. Where in the human body would you find metacarpal bones?

Answers to QUIZ 468 – Words

1	Empty orchestra	11	Apple
2	Nano	12	Ruff
3	Italian	13	Caves
4	Depth	14	(Old style) wig
5	Swede	15	Drink (alcohol)
6	Tourist (in Devon or Cornwall)	16	Loot
7	Marque and mark	17	Canasta
8	Hair	18	Loudhailer or megaphone
9	*Bona fide*	19	Irish Gaelic
10	A sheep that leads the flock	20	Antonyms

1   In which county is the National Trust stately home of Wallington?

2   What is the capital of Lithuania?

3   Which wind instrument was played by jazz musician Benny Goodman?

4   Gilbert O'Sullivan had a 1972 hit with which girl's name?

5   Which actor starred in the 1984 thriller *Tightrope*?

6   Who is the Earl of Gloucester's son in Shakespeare's *King Lear*?

7   In the *X-Men* series of films, who starred as Mystique?

8   Which strait separates Alaska from Russia?

9   Who was the first person to fly around the world solo?

10 The Black Country museum is in which town?

11 Which actress played the title role in the 1998 film *Little Voice*?

12 Originally a hit for Dusty Springfield, what was the title of the last UK top 10 hit for the Bay City Rollers?

13 Which industrial city of north-east Mexico lies at the foothills of the Sierra Madre Oriental mountains?

14 Which was the title of the Beatles' debut studio album?

15 Who had a 1983 hit with *Give It Up*?

16 San Juan is the capital of which Caribbean island?

17 How long does each round of men's boxing last at the Olympics?

18 Which 1990s sitcom about an airline crew starred Alan Cumming?

19 Which French artist, first name Henri, died in 1954?

20 The Eurovision Song Contest was won for the first time by which country in 2017?

1 Who was President of South Africa before FW de Klerk?

2 Which US President declared that "The ballot is stronger than the bullet"?

3 In elections, for what do the letters STV stand?

4 Who was British Prime Minister four times between 1868 and 1894?

5 In which decade of the 20th century was Bill Clinton born?

6 The famous concert pianist Ignace Paderewski became Prime Minister of which country in 1919?

7 Where exactly would one find the Resolute desk?

8 Who was the first Labour Party Prime Minister?

9 In which year did minister John Profumo resign, admitting that he had misled the House of Commons regarding his relationship with Christine Keeler?

10 Robert Menzies was twice the Prime Minister of which country?

11 Which public school did Sir Winston Churchill attend from 1888 to 1892?

12 Who was the first Egyptian leader to visit Israel and to address the Knesset (parliament) there?

13 In which year was the minimum voting age in the UK lowered from 21 to 18 years of age?

14 Of which country was Hosni Mubarak the president from 1981 until 2011?

15 In 1959, who deposed dictator Fulgencio Batista?

16 What does the Serjeant at Arms carry into and out of the debating chamber of the House of Commons each day?

17 Which party did Robert Mugabe represent when he became Zimbabwe's first executive president?

18 Who was the first Prime Minister to make use of Chequers?

19 Of which country was Nawaz Sharif the Prime Minister from 1990 to 1999 and 2013 to 2017?

20 The Cortes is the parliament of which country?

Answers to QUIZ 470 – Human Biology

1	The foot (band of tissue)	11	Under the skin
2	High-density lipoprotein	12	Eye
3	In the brain	13	Cannula
4	Edward Jenner	14	The circulation of the blood
5	Skin	15	The coccyx
6	20	16	The skull
7	Whooping cough	17	Dentine
8	Ear (middle ear bone)	18	12
9	Bones	19	Adrenal glands
10	Ileum	20	Hand

ANSWERS ON PAGE 475

1   In which county is the Forestry Commission site of Westonbirt?

2   The Annapurna ridge is in which mountain range?

3   What is the name of the square cap worn by the Catholic clergy?

4   Jenever is a drink from which country?

5   The late 14th-century soldier Sir Henry Percy had what nickname?

6   What were the first names of author DH Lawrence?

7   The Savill garden is part of which park?

8   Which number is next to 5 reading anticlockwise on a dartboard?

9   Who played Lt Daniel Kaffee in the 1992 film *A Few Good Men*?

10 The Monach Isles belong to which country?

11 In and around which town does the action of the 1977 film *A Bridge Too Far* take place?

12 Which actor starred in the 1996 flm *Broken Arrow*?

13 The ski resort of Verbier is in which country?

14 The radio station Classic FM launched in which year?

15 Who had a hit in 1999 with *Beautiful Stranger*?

16 Which US state lies immediately south of Iowa?

17 In the TV series *Jemima Shore Investigates*, which actress played the title role?

18 Which group had hits in the 1990s with *Fall at Your Feet* and *Weather with You*?

19 Furze and whin are other names for which shrub?

20 Who is the Roman goddess of agriculture?

Answers to QUIZ 471 – Pot Luck

1	Northumberland (near Morpeth)	11	Jane Horrocks
2	Vilnius	12	*I Only Want to Be With You*
3	Clarinet	13	Monterrey
4	Clair	14	*Please, Please Me*
5	Clint Eastwood	15	KC and the Sunshine Band
6	Edgar	16	Puerto Rico
7	Jennifer Lawrence	17	Two minutes
8	The Bering Strait	18	*The High Life*
9	Wiley Post (in 1933)	19	Matisse
10	Dudley	20	Portugal

Easy

1. What is the highest rank in the British Army?

2. In pre-decimal currency, what was one-fortieth of a pound?

3. Which is the second-largest island of the Inner Hebrides?

4. Which vegetable's UK season officially runs from 23rd April to Midsummer's Day?

5. In which year was the London Marathon first run?

6. The highest point of which range of hills is at Cross Fell?

7. In which year did the Church of England's parliament vote by a narrow margin to allow women to be ordained as priests?

8. Which company developed the pottery called Jasperware?

9. Which city is served by an airport located at Ringway?

10. What is the Welsh word for "valley"?

11. A famous oyster festival takes place in which Essex town?

12. What title is given to the head of a Scottish municipal corporation?

13. What is the county town of Somerset?

14. Who laid the foundation stone at Coventry Cathedral in 1956?

15. The ship "Cutty Sark" carried what as its cargo?

16. Which is London's oldest theatre site?

17. In which year was the bimetallic £2 coin first issued into general circulation?

18. What does it mean if the Union Jack is flown upside down from a ship?

19. The first Chelsea Flower Show was held in which decade?

20. Which two rivers flow through Aberdeen?

Medium

Hard

Answers to QUIZ 472 – World Politics

1	PW Botha	11	Harrow
2	Abraham Lincoln	12	Anwar Sadat
3	Single Transferable Vote	13	1969
4	William Gladstone	14	Egypt
5	1940s (1946)	15	Fidel Castro
6	Poland	16	The mace
7	The Oval Office	17	ZANU
8	Ramsay MacDonald	18	David Lloyd George (First Earl Lloyd-George of Dwyfor)
9	1963	19	Pakistan
10	Australia	20	Spain

1 Jeremy Bentham was associated with which set of principles?

2 Which word for a mischievous person is derived from the Old French word for "rabble"?

3 In which year did the Beatles disband?

4 The plant *Myosotis* is better known by what name?

5 Which river runs through the centre of Warsaw?

6 Who had a hit with *Your Game* in 2004?

7 The *kabuki* style of drama is associated with which country?

8 Tiffi and Mr Yeti are characters from which game?

9 Who played Edward Cullen in the *Twilight* films?

10 Which Catholic organisation is mentioned in the novel *The Da Vinci Code*?

11 In which 2002 biopic did Salma Hayek play a Mexican artist?

12 *Sad Sweet Dreamer* was a 1974 hit for which group?

13 Who played Reggie Perrin's wife in the 2009 remake of the classic series?

14 What is the state capital of South Dakota?

15 Which fruit has a variety called Ellison's orange?

16 Which author lived at Abbotsford House near Melrose?

17 Who sang *One Man Band* in 1974?

18 What is the chief port of Senegal?

19 Los Barcos was the setting for which 1990s soap?

20 A bundt cake is baked in a mould of what shape?

Answers to QUIZ 473 – Pot Luck

1	Gloucestershire	11	Arnhem
2	Himalayas	12	John Travolta
3	Biretta	13	Switzerland
4	The Netherlands	14	1992
5	Hotspur	15	Madonna
6	David Herbert	16	Missouri
7	Windsor Great Park	17	Patricia Hodge
8	12	18	Crowded House
9	Tom Cruise	19	Gorse
10	Scotland	20	Ceres

Easy

1. What was notable about a football game played at Bramall Lane on October 14, 1878?

2. The Golden Cage is a goalkeeping award in which European country?

3. Who won the BBC Women's Footballer of the Year 2017?

4. In the 1956 FA Cup Final, which goalkeeper played the end of the match with a broken neck?

5. Who was the first goalkeeper to captain a FIFA World Cup winning team?

6. Which was the first team to be managed by Brian Clough?

7. Who captained Tottenham Hotspur FC during the double-winning season of 1961?

8. Beating Inter Milan 2-1 in Lisbon, in which year did Celtic become the first British football club to win the European Cup?

9. On retiring from playing football, which team did Peter Shilton manage from 1992 to 1995?

10. In which country do the teams Omonia, Enosis and Anorthosis play?

11. In 1957, who became the first player to twice be named the Football Writers' Association Footballer of the Year?

Medium

12. Which major UK football club was founded as Dial Square?

13. Against which team did Archie Gemmill score his famous goal at the 1978 FIFA World Cup?

14. In which decade did Everton FC play their first game at Goodison Park?

15. Who won English football's Premier League Golden Boot award in 2010?

16. Which was the first purpose-built all-seater football stadium in Scotland?

17. How old was Pelé when he won his first World Cup?

18. Northern Ireland lost out to which country in the 2018 World Cup play-offs?

19. Billy Bremner and Graeme Souness both received how many caps for Scotland?

20. Which was Luis Figo's last club before retiring from playing football in 2009?

Hard

Answers to QUIZ 474 – The UK

1	Field marshal	11	Colchester
2	Sixpence	12	Lord Provost
3	Mull	13	Taunton
4	Asparagus	14	Queen Elizabeth II
5	1981	15	Tea
6	Pennines	16	Theatre Royal, Drury Lane
7	1992	17	1998
8	Wedgwood	18	A distress signal
9	Manchester	19	1910s (1912)
10	Cwm	20	The Dee and the Don

1   Which Hollywood actor changed his name from Eric Bishop?

2   Which authoress challenged the traditional roles of women in the book *The Second Sex*?

3   The Sutherland Falls lie between Lake Quill and Arthur River in which country?

4   What was the theme song to the TV series *Boon*?

5   What is King Alfred's Cake?

6   *Have I the Right* was a 1964 hit for which group?

7   Which poet (d.1529) wrote the work *Phillip Sparrow*?

8   Skokholm island lies off the coast of which country?

9   What is the capital of Qatar?

10 Who wrote the 1791 book *The Rights of Man*?

11 *Nights in the Gardens of Spain* (1916) was written by which composer?

12 For what is an Aldis lamp used?

13 Who was the Greek Muse of love poetry?

14 Manama is the capital of which Gulf state?

15 Of what is anuptaphobia a fear?

16 What trade does Omar Khayyam's surname imply?

17 Which Normandy city is the burial place of William the Conqueror?

18 In John le Carre's book, what was the name of the *Spy Who Came in From the Cold*?

19 Which football team plays at Oakwell?

20 Who was Composer to the Chapel Royal and, from 1679, organist at Westminster Abbey?

Easy

Medium

Hard

Answers to QUIZ 475 – Pot Luck

1	Utilitarianism	11	*Frida*
2	Rascal	12	Sweet Sensation
3	1970	13	Fay Ripley
4	Forget-me-not	14	Pierre
5	Vistula	15	Apple
6	Will Young	16	Sir Walter Scott
7	Japan	17	Leo Sayer
8	*Candy Crush Saga*	18	Dakar
9	Robert Pattinson	19	*Eldorado*
10	Opus Dei	20	Ring

Easy

1. What was the name of the cat in the TV series *Rising Damp*?

2. In the US TV series *Numb3rs*, who played maths genius Charlie Eppes?

3. In which fictional village was the series *Hamish Macbeth* set?

4. Who won the first series of *The Voice UK*?

5. What was the title of the 2000-02 drama series about an internet start-up company?

6. Christopher Trace and Leila Williams were the first presenters of which long-running series?

7. What was the name of Aiden Gillen's character in the series *The Wire*?

8. In which year was *Casualty* first broadcast?

9. Who presented the UK version of the TV adventure show *The Mole*?

10. Which *EastEnders* character was originally played by Jo Warne for ten episodes in 1991 before returning with a new actress in 1994?

Medium

11. For what was the TV character of Kristin Shepard famous?

12. Who played Chloe O'Brian in the series *24*?

13. Carbide and Eruption were amongst the winners of which TV competition?

14. Chris Lintott has presented on which programme since 2000?

15. Who hosted *Crackerjack* in its 1980s format?

16. The character of Helen Flynn, played by Lisa Faulkner, was controversially killed off in the second ever episode of which series?

17. Who is best known for playing Sandor "The Hound" in *Game of Thrones*?

18. The fictional research project The Dharma Initiative featured on which TV series?

19. Who played Pierre Bezukhof in the 2016 TV adaptation of *War and Peace*?

20. In which series did Amy Acker play Samantha Groves, nicknamed "Root"?

Hard

Answers to QUIZ 476 – Football

1	It was the first floodlit match	11	Tom Finney
2	Denmark	12	Arsenal FC
3	Ada Hegerberg	13	The Netherlands
4	Bert Trautmann	14	1890s (1892)
5	Gianpiero Combi (1934)	15	Didier Drogba
6	Hartlepool United	16	McDiarmid Park
7	Danny Blanchflower	17	17
8	1967	18	Switzerland
9	Plymouth Argyle	19	54
10	Cyprus	20	Internazionale

1   Who wrote "Hope springs eternal in the human breast"?

2   Which French general became Supreme Commander of all Allied Forces on the Western Front in the First World War in 1918?

3   "The woods decay, the woods decay and fall" is the first line of which Tennyson poem?

4   What was the title of the first record to be released on the Virgin record label?

5   Which American singer/songwriter's real name is Robert James Ritchie?

6   In which year was the speaking clock introduced in the UK?

7   Which environmentalist published *The End of Nature* in 1989?

8   Wat Chaiwatthanaram is a tourist attraction in which country?

9   In which year was Canada founded?

10   *What A Girl Wants* was a hit for Christina Aguilera in which year?

11   Lentigines is the medical term applied to what?

12   What is a sea lemon?

13   Who wrote *Sylvie and Bruno* (1889), a work which evolved from a short story entitled *Bruno's Revenge*?

14   Which play by Sheridan features Lydia Languish?

15   What kind of creature would be described as lumbricoid?

16   *A Moon Shaped Pool* is a 2016 album by which band?

17   In which country is Arlanda International Airport?

18   What is the capital city of Burkina Faso?

19   Which former Prime Minister once played cricket for Middlesex?

20   What is the name of the flying island in *Gulliver's Travels* (1726)?

Easy

Medium

Hard

Answers to QUIZ 477 – Pot Luck

1	Jamie Foxx	11	Manuel de Falla
2	Simone de Beauvoir	12	Signalling
3	New Zealand	13	Erato
4	*Hi Ho Silver*	14	Bahrain
5	Fungus	15	Staying single
6	The Honeycombs	16	Tent maker
7	John Skelton	17	Caen
8	South Wales	18	Alec Leamas
9	Doha	19	Barnsley FC
10	Thomas Paine	20	Henry Purcell

Easy

1 Who founded the American environmental organisation The Sierra Club?

2 On Heard Island in the southern Indian Ocean, what is Big Ben?

3 What type of creature is a gelada?

4 Which is Scotland's deepest loch?

5 In which archipelago are Terceira, Pico, Faial, São Jorge and Flores?

6 Martha, who died in Cincinnati Zoo in 1914, was the last living example of which bird?

7 The Itatinga waterfall is in which country?

8 What is Spain's highest mountain, on the island of Tenerife?

9 Which is the main island of the Seychelles?

10 What is the "Alpide Belt" noted for?

11 A Pacific sea wasp is what type of creature?

12 What acid gives nettles their sting?

13 In which decade was the Great Barrier Reef listed as a World Heritage Site?

Medium

14 Which geological period immediately followed the Cambrian period?

15 The type of abalone known as a "paua" is found in which country?

16 Of which mountain range is Narodnaya the highest peak?

17 In which US state is the Mammoth Cave National Park?

18 The "Gaia hypothesis" is associated with which environmentalist?

19 Which is the longest river in Canada?

20 Which feathery-leaved plant is also known as milfoil?

Hard

Answers to QUIZ 478 –Television

1	Vienna	11	She shot JR in *Dallas*
2	David Krumholtz	12	Mary Lynn Rajskub
3	Lochdubh	13	*Robot Wars*
4	Leanne Mitchell	14	*The Sky at Night*
5	*Attachments*	15	Stu Francis
6	*Blue Peter*	16	*Spooks*
7	Tommy Carcetti	17	Rory McCann
8	1986	18	*Lost*
9	Glenn Hugill	19	Paul Dano
10	Peggy Mitchell	20	*Person of Interest*

1 In which year did Frank Bruno win the WBC heavyweight title?

2 Who won four successive Olympic gold medals in the discus from 1956 to 1968?

3 Which Australian folk group had a hit in 1965 with *The Carnival is Over*?

4 Which geological period immediately followed the Carboniferous period?

5 Who wrote the play *Who's Afraid of Virginia Woolf* (1962)?

6 Which British composer wrote the 1968 opera *Punch and Judy*?

7 The Preakness Stakes, Belmont Stakes plus which other race make up the American Triple Crown?

8 *Who You Are* is a 2011 album by which singer?

9 What term was given to the 16th-century belief that herbs resembling specific body parts could be used to treat ailments in those body parts?

10 What is the flat rock on which tools are sharpened called?

11 Which 1957 Patrick White novel describes a journey into the Australian interior?

12 If you have coryza, from what are you suffering?

13 Who wrote the 1921 play *Six Characters in Search of an Author*?

14 What is a calpac?

15 What was the title of Britney Spears' fourth album?

16 The National Trust property of Erddig is on the outskirts of which town?

17 The sacred Hindu text *Bhagavad Gita* was incorporated into which epic poem?

18 Who topped the singles charts in 1970 with *Woodstock*?

19 Which French author wrote the 1949 novel *The Thief's Journal*?

20 What is the primary collection of sacred texts in Zoroastrianism?

Answers to QUIZ 479 – Pot Luck

1	Alexander Pope	11	Freckles
2	Ferdinand Foch	12	A sea slug
3	*Tithonus*	13	Lewis Carroll
4	*Tubular Bells* (Mike Oldfield)	14	*The Rivals*
5	Kid Rock	15	Worm
6	1936	16	Radiohead
7	Bill McKibben	17	Sweden (Stockholm)
8	Thailand (Buddhist temple)	18	Ouagadougou
9	1867	19	Sir Alec Douglas-Home
10	2000	20	Laputa

Easy

1. Who wrote the 1794 poem *The Clod and the Pebble*?

2. *Tall, Dark and Gruesome* is the 1977 autobiography by which actor?

3. Which James Hilton novel is set in the fictional location of Shangri-La?

4. What is the name of Heidi's invalid companion in the classic 1881 children's novel?

5. In 1938, who was awarded the Nobel Prize in Literature?

6. *The Rachel Papers* (1973) was the first novel by which author?

7. What was author Ian Fleming's middle name?

8. The 2005 novel *The Book Thief* was written by which Australian author?

9. In 1935, which British publisher launched the first range of Penguin titles?

10. Although not made an official position until 1668, who became the first Poet Laureate in 1616?

11. Who created the Chinese detective Charlie Chan?

12. What are the forenames of Scottish author JM Barrie?

13. In 1697, who published *Mother Goose's Fairy Tales*?

14. Which literary figure was born in 1809 at Somersby Rectory in Lincolnshire?

15. What was the first name of writer F Scott Fitzgerald's wife?

16. The 2017 Man Booker Prize was won by which author for *Lincoln in the Bardo*?

17. Which hat is named after an 1894 novel by George du Maurier?

18. In Rider Haggard's 1887 novel *She*, who is the immortal queen?

19. Who wrote the 1961 sci-fi novel *Solaris*?

20. Which 1938 Evelyn Waugh novel features Lord Copper?

Answers to QUIZ 480 – Planet Earth

1	John Muir	11	Jellyfish
2	A volcano	12	Formic acid
3	Monkey (baboon)	13	1980s (1981)
4	Morar	14	Ordovician
5	Azores	15	New Zealand
6	Passenger pigeon	16	Urals
7	Brazil	17	Kentucky
8	Teide	18	James Lovelock
9	Mahé	19	The Mackenzie
10	Earthquakes	20	Yarrow

1. In which country did the Morito and Chupaderos meteorites both land?
2. Who wrote *The Adventures of Peregrine Pickle* (1751)?
3. Which actor won Best Supporting Actor Oscars for *Spartacus* and *Topkapi*?
4. What is Peru's currency unit?
5. During the two World Wars of the last century, at which course was the Derby held?
6. Which singer topped the UK singles charts in 2015 with *Don't Be So Hard on Yourself*?
7. What is a cariole?
8. In July 2011, which space shuttle made its final flight?
9. Which football team plays at Kenilworth Road?
10. For what is oakum used on a ship?
11. What is the King of Naples' name in Shakespeare's *The Tempest*?
12. By what name is Bechuanaland now known?
13. What type of creature is a true lover's knot?
14. If someone is pandiculating, what are they doing?
15. What is a tava?
16. Which South Pacific island state was once called the New Hebrides?
17. In which city are football team PFC CSKA based?
18. Who won the Booker Prize in 1971 with *In a Free State*?
19. Which actress took the leading role in DW Griffiths 1915 film *The Birth of a Nation*?
20. In which city is the Mariinsky Ballet based?

Easy

Medium

Hard

Answers to QUIZ 481 – Pot Luck

1	1995	11	*Voss*
2	Al Oerter	12	Nasal inflammation caused by a cold
3	The Seekers	13	Luigi Pirandello
4	Permian	14	A hat (high-crowned cap)
5	Edward Albee	15	*In the Zone*
6	Harrison Birtwistle	16	Wrexham
7	Kentucky Derby	17	*Mahabharata*
8	Jessie J	18	Matthews' Southern Comfort
9	Doctrine of Signatures	19	Jean Genet
10	Oilstone	20	Avesta

ANSWERS ON PAGE 486

1   Who invented the carpet sweeper?

2   Anthony Trollope is famous as a novelist, but which item of "street furniture" did he invent?

3   What is the name of the French inventor of the parachute?

4   Which Italian is said to have invented the modern pianoforte?

5   In which decade was Coca-Cola® invented?

6   What is Swiss engineer George de Mestral best known for inventing after cleaning his dog in 1941?

7   In which country was snooker invented?

8   Which household item was invented by James Spangler in 1908?

9   Douglas Engelbart invented which item of computer hardware in 1963?

10 What did Evangelista Torricelli invent in 1643?

11 What is the name of the English inventor who is often known as "the father of aviation"?

12 Who invented the digital camera?

13 For what purpose was Alka-Seltzer® first marketed?

14 What invention first appeared around 3500 BC and was originally used to shape clay?

15 What did the US company Diablo Data Systems invent for use on typewriters?

16 Louis Moinet invented which time measurement device in 1816?

17 Who invented the bifocal lens?

18 Clergyman William Oughtred invented which aid to calculation in 1622?

19 What was invented by Walter Morrison in 1946?

20 Who is often known as "the Father of English Clockmaking"?

Answers to QUIZ 482 – Literature

1	William Blake	11	Earl D Biggers
2	Sir Christopher Lee	12	James Matthew
3	*Lost Horizon*	13	Charles Perrault
4	Clara	14	Alfred, Lord Tennyson
5	Pearl Buck	15	Zelda
6	Martin Amis	16	George Saunders
7	Lancaster	17	Trilby
8	Markus Zusak	18	Ayesha
9	Allen Lane	19	Stanislaw Lem
10	Ben Jonson	20	*Scoop*

Easy

Medium

Hard

ANSWERS ON PAGE **487**

1   Which German state has Wiesbaden as its capital?

2   Which British historian (b.1800) wrote *The Lays of Ancient Rome*?

3   Which country lies between Benin and Ghana?

4   What name is given to the small vestigial tube in the human intestine?

5   In which Scottish region is John o' Groats located?

6   Which Australian sportsman was nicknamed "The Rockhampton Rocket" in his playing days?

7   In 2001, the Gorillaz had a hit song about which actor?

8   Which rugby team played their home games at Knowsley Road until 2010?

9   What name is given to a clay tobacco pipe with a long, curved stem?

10 What type of creature is a great ramshorn?

11 In which year were the Dead Sea Scrolls found?

12 For which team did motor racing's John Surtees win his first Grand Prix?

13 Tristan Tzara is associated with which early 20th-century anarchist art movement?

14 Who was leader of the former state of Czechoslovakia from 1968 to 1969?

15 Which major river flows through France, Belgium and the Netherlands?

16 Which philosopher, author of *Also Sprach Zarathustra*, is known for his theories of the "superman"?

17 Andrássy Avenue is a World Heritage site in which European city?

18 On which Croatian peninsula are Pula and Rovinj located?

19 In which 1946 Hitchcock thriller did Cary Grant play a government agent called TR Devlin?

20 Which geological era saw the appearance of flowering plants and giant dinosaurs?

Answers to QUIZ 483 – Pot Luck

1	Mexico	11	Alonso
2	Tobias Smollett	12	Botswana
3	Peter Ustinov	13	Moth
4	Sol	14	Stretching while yawning
5	Newmarket	15	Frying pan (in Asia)
6	Jess Glynne	16	Vanuatu
7	A horse-drawn vehicle	17	Moscow
8	*Atlantis*	18	VS Naipaul
9	Luton Town FC	19	Lillian Gish
10	Waterproofing (also called caulking)	20	St Petersburg

Easy

1   Matthew McConaughey starred in which 1999 comedy film?

2   What was Walt Disney's middle name?

3   Which 1936 Hitchcock thriller is based on Joseph Conrad's *The Secret Agent*?

4   In the 2006 film *Factory Girl*, who played Andy Warhol?

5   What was the first name of Charlie Sheen's character in *Wall Street*?

6   Who directed the 1948 film *State of the Union*?

7   In the 1997 film *Anaconda*, which actress and singer played the lead role of Terri Flores?

8   What was the surname of silent-film star Theda?

9   Which 1973 film was Clint Eastwood's first western as a director?

10   In the film *Ghost*, what was Sam Wheat's profession?

11   Who played Rosalie Hale in the *Twilight* films?

Medium

12   Which film director was shot by an air rifle during a 2005 interview in Los Angeles with Mark Kermode?

13   Which actor won an Oscar for the 1952 film *Viva Zapata!*?

14   In the 2018 Marvel film *Black Panther*, who played the title role?

15   Who played Sarah Connor in the 2015 film *Terminator Genisys*?

16   Which Canadian actor played Evan in the 2007 film *Superbad*?

17   Which 2007 film featuring Emily Blunt was based on a novel by Karen Joy Fowler?

18   How was the actor Michel Shalhoub better known?

19   Who played Ted Striker in *Airplane!* (1980)?

20   For which film did Meryl Streep receive her first Oscar nomination?

Hard

Answers to QUIZ 484 – Inventors and Inventions

1	Melville Bissell	11	Sir George Cayley
2	Pillar box	12	Steven Sasson
3	André-Jacques Garnerin	13	Cold cure
4	Bartolomeo Cristofori	14	Wheel
5	1880s (1886)	15	Daisy wheel printer
6	Velcro®	16	Chronograph
7	India	17	Benjamin Franklin
8	Vacuum cleaner	18	The slide rule
9	The mouse	19	Frisbee
10	Barometer	20	Thomas Tompion

1   Lake Tanganyika is bordered by the Democratic Republic of the Congo, Tanzania, Zambia and which other country?

2   Who wrote the children's book *The Very Hungry Caterpillar*?

3   Loch Ness and Oregon thornless are varieties of which fruit?

4   Who wrote the 1916 play *Hobson's Choice*?

5   What is the surname of *A Good Man in Africa* author William?

6   Who wrote the play *Chips with Everything* (1962)?

7   The battery was invented by which physicist?

8   What is the name of Jean de Brunhoff's cartoon elephant?

9   Which English king was known as "Beauclerc"?

10 Ricoh Arena is the home ground of which football team?

11 What was the name of the world's first electronic computer?

12 The travel memoir *Au Maroc* was written by which French author (b.1850)?

13 Which tree is the main food of the brimstone butterfly in caterpillar form?

14 The character of Professor Challenger was created by which author (b.1859)?

15 What is the longitude of the International Date Line?

16 In which country is the River Jumna?

17 To which family of mammals do civets belong?

18 What is South Korea's chief port and second-largest city?

19 Who wrote the 1989 novel *The Cloning of Joanna May*?

20 Who played Bernie in the 1999 film *Notting Hill*?

Answers to QUIZ 485 – Pot Luck

1	Hesse (Hessen)	11	1947
2	Thomas Macaulay	12	Lotus
3	Togo	13	Dadaism
4	Appendix	14	Alexander Dubĉek
5	Highland	15	Meuse
6	Rod Laver	16	Friedrich Nietzsche
7	Clint Eastwood	17	Budapest
8	St Helens	18	Istria
9	A churchwarden	19	*Notorious*
10	Water snail	20	Mesozoic

Easy

1 What was the title of Evanescence's second studio album, released in 2006?

2 Which band's cover of *The Sound of Silence* reached no.29 in the UK charts in 2016?

3 The 1992 album *America's Least Wanted* was by which band?

4 In the band name Kings of Leon, who is "Leon"?

5 Singer Myles Kennedy teamed up with which famous guitarist to form the Conspirators?

6 Which band featured Tony Iommi and Geezer Butler in its line-up?

7 Who released a 2016 album entitled *Braver Than We Are*?

8 Who was the original lead singer of AC/DC?

9 St Jimmy and Whatsername are characters in a concept album by which band?

10 Which hard-rock band released the 2003 album *St Anger*?

11 *Badge* and *White Room* were singles by which late 1960s rock band?

Medium

12 Which original band member joined Jeff Lynne in 2014 when he re-formed ELO?

13 Which singer collaborated with Robert Plant on the 2007 album *Raising Sand*?

14 Nickelback's 2001 single *How You Remind Me* was taken from which album?

15 2007's *Favourite Worst Nightmare* was the second album by which band?

16 Whose first solo album was entitled *Vigil in a Wilderness of Mirrors*?

17 The 2009 Westlife hit *What About Now* was originally recorded by which US rock band?

18 What was the title of the 2006 only UK no.1 single for My Chemical Romance?

19 M Shadows and Synyster Gates are members of which US hard rock band?

20 Which band released the 1980s albums *British Steel* and *Screaming for Vengeance*?

Hard

1 The poisonous fungus *Amanita phalloides* is known by what common name?

2 Which London Tube station lies between Caledonian Road and Arsenal?

3 What is a jota?

4 Which branch of medicine is concerned with deformities of the bones caused by disease or injury?

5 Madeleine Wickham also writes "chick lit" under what pen name?

6 Between 1900 and 1908, which Olympic competitor won all the Olympic standing high-jump and standing long-jump events?

7 Which composer (b.1835) wrote the opera *Mademoiselle Fifi*?

8 In which country is the River Glåma?

9 What name is give to the principle that the simplest explanation is the most likely one?

10 Who scored two penalties in the 1994 FA Cup final?

11 Jimi Hendrix's former Mayfair house has two blue plaques honouring both him and which composer?

12 What was the first name of the sewing-machine inventor Singer?

13 "That is no country for old men" was written by which poet?

14 Which musician was backed by his Paramount Jazz Band?

15 Who wrote the 1911 novel *The Lair of the White Worm*?

16 In *Murders In The Rue Morgue*, who or what was the murderer?

17 Which UK group's first Top 5 hit was *Sha-La-La-La-Lee* in 1966?

18 Which French poet wrote the 1873 work *A Season in Hell*?

19 What is the largest freshwater lake in New Zealand?

20 In which East African country is the Ngorongoro Crater?

Easy

Medium

Hard

Answers to QUIZ 487 – Pot Luck

1	Burundi	11	Colossus
2	Eric Carle	12	Pierre Loti
3	Blackberry	13	Buckthorn
4	Harold Brighouse	14	Sir Arthur Conan Doyle
5	Boyd	15	180 degrees (with several deviations)
6	Arnold Wesker	16	India
7	Alessandro Volta	17	Viverridae
8	Babar	18	Busan
9	Henry I	19	Fay Weldon
10	Coventry City	20	Hugh Bonneville

Easy

1   In Greek mythology, what was Tiresias' profession?

2   The Egyptian god Sobek took the form of which creature?

3   Which Cypriot city is the mythical birthplace of Aphrodite?

4   The tale of Culhwch and Olwen was originally written in which language?

5   How many worlds are there in Norse mythology?

6   In Greek mythology, which nymph of Artemis was changed into a bear?

7   Ops was the wife of which Roman god?

8   Who or what is Yggdrasil in Norse mythology?

9   Which word can refer both to all the gods of a religion, or the place in which they were worshipped?

10 In which country's mythology does the Moon deity Thoth appear?

Medium

11 What name was given to the Roman rite where images of the gods were set out as if at a banquet?

12 What is the name of Thor's hammer?

13 Who was the queen of the winter in Scottish folklore?

14 In Greek mythology, what was used to suspend the Sword of Damocles?

15 Who was the goddess of the hearth and its fire in Ancient Rome?

16 In Egyptian mythology, what role did Anubis have?

17 The Edda is a collection of poems from which mythology?

18 Which Roman god of war later came to be identified with Romulus?

19 The Dagda appears in the mythology of which country?

20 In Greek mythology, who were the parents of Rhea?

Hard

Answers to QUIZ 488 – Rock Music

1	*The Open Door*	11	Cream
2	Disturbed	12	Richard Tandy
3	Ugly Kid Joe	13	Alison Krauss
4	Their grandfather	14	*Silver Side Up*
5	Slash	15	Arctic Monkeys
6	Black Sabbath	16	Fish
7	Meat Loaf	17	Daughtry
8	Bon Scott	18	*Welcome to the Black Parade*
9	Green Day	19	Avenged Sevenfold
10	Metallica	20	Judas Priest

1 What lived in the boiler of *Ivor the Engine*?

2 In the 1936 novel *Jamaica Inn*, what is the name of the vicar?

3 What is the alternative name for the earth-boring dung beetle?

4 Who was the French composer of *The Sorcerer's Apprentice* (1897)?

5 In which novel by Charles Dickens does the character Kit Nubbles appear?

6 Minestrone soup derives its name from the Italian "minestrare", which translates to what in English?

7 Who was the mythical wife of Odysseus?

8 Rarotonga is part of which island group?

9 In which US state is the Black Canyon?

10 Which ancient region and Roman province corresponds largely to modern Portugal?

11 What type of creature is a nyala?

12 The 1996 film *Up Close and Personal* featured which Celine Dion song?

13 Which group's first song was a no.1 hit entitled *Baby, Now That I've Found You* in 1967?

14 In which city is the Eden Park sports stadium?

15 Who wrote the 1739 work *A Treatise of Human Nature*?

16 In 1849, who invented the safety pin?

17 How was singer Dino Crocetti better known?

18 How many stomachs does a giraffe have?

19 *Blue Lines, Mezzanine* and *Heligoland* are albums by which group?

20 By what name has British Honduras been known since 1973?

Easy

Medium

Hard

Answers to QUIZ 489 – Pot Luck

1	Death cap	11	George Frederick Handel
2	Holloway Road	12	Isaac
3	A dance (from Spain)	13	WB Yeats (*Sailing to Byzantium*)
4	Orthopaedics	14	Acker Bilk
5	Sophie Kinsella	15	Bram Stoker
6	Ray Ewry	16	An orang-utan
7	César Cui	17	The Small Faces
8	Norway	18	Arthur Rimbaud
9	Occam's razor	19	Taupo
10	Eric Cantona	20	Tanzania

Easy

1 What was singer Perry Como's full first name?

2 Which baseball player was nicknamed "The Georgia Peach"?

3 How was singer and actor Terence Nelhams-Wright better known?

4 Which American state is nicknamed "the Garden State"?

5 What was the real name of Italian artist Botticelli?

6 Singer Frankie Vaughan had which original surname?

7 How was the consumer electronics company LG known before it shortened its name?

8 To what did Hollywood star Issur Danielovitch change his name?

9 What name did French playwright Jean-Baptiste Poquelin adopt as a pseudonym?

10 "The Land of the Long White Cloud" is the nickname of which country?

11 Betty Perske was the birth name of which American actress?

12 Which politician was born William Jefferson Blythe III?

13 By what name is Caryn Johnson (b.1955) better known?

14 Which UK city is also known as "the City of Discovery"?

Medium

15 What was the nickname of Edmund II, who was King of England for several months in 1016?

16 What were the first names of the author Baroness James of Holland Park?

17 Which creature is also known as the needlefish?

18 Whose Symphony No 4 is known as the "Italian" Symphony?

19 Which singer's birth name was Stevland Judkins?

20 The international CITES treaty is also known by what name, after the city in which it was created?

Hard

Answers to QUIZ 490 – Mythology

1	Soothsayer	11	Lectisternium
2	Crocodile	12	Mjölnir
3	Paphos	13	Beira
4	Welsh	14	A single horse hair
5	Nine	15	Vesta
6	Callisto	16	Leading the dead to judgement
7	Saturn	17	Norse (Icelandic literature)
8	A giant tree	18	Quirinus
9	Pantheon	19	Ireland
10	Egypt	20	Uranus and Gaia

ANSWERS ON PAGE 495

1   Lake Volta lies wholly within which African country?

2   What nationality was philosopher Arne Naess (b.1912)?

3   Which branch of theology is concerned with the end of the world?

4   In the 1999 sci-fi film *The Matrix*, what was the name of Neo's girlfriend?

5   What is the capital of the Isles of Scilly?

6   Victor Barna (b.1911) was five times world champion in which sport?

7   In which country did the game of chess originate?

8   What is the English translation of the title of the ballet *La Fille mal gardée*?

9   Grantley Adams Airport serves which island?

10 Which is the word for eleven bets, made up of six doubles, four trebles and an accumulator?

11 What is fear of rain called?

12 Colchester had what name in Roman times?

13 In sailing, what name is given to a lightweight, three-cornered headsail used to improve performance when sailing downwind?

14 The 1995 film *Sudden Death* featured which sport?

15 Which Czech city was the historical capital of Moravia?

16 Which freshwater mammal has the Latin name *Lutra lutra*?

17 In canoe polo, how many members of each team are in play at a time?

18 Who was the daughter of Oedipus and Jocasta in Greek mythology?

19 Menachem Begin founded which Israeli political party?

20 The Vagabonds are the backing band for which singer (b.1940)

Easy

Medium

Hard

Answers to QUIZ 491 – Pot Luck

1	Idris the Dragon	11	Antelope
2	Francis Davey	12	*Because You Loved Me*
3	Dor	13	The Foundations
4	Paul Dukas	14	Auckland
5	*The Old Curiosity Shop*	15	David Hume
6	Serve at table	16	Walter Hunt
7	Penelope	17	Dean Martin
8	The Cook Islands	18	Four
9	Colorado	19	Massive Attack
10	Lusitania	20	Belize

Easy

1. What is the capital city of Nicaragua?

2. In which country is the archaeological site of Chan Chan?

3. Sápmi is a region of Europe better known by what name in the UK?

4. What is the name of Melbourne's international airport?

5. Which Turkic language would be spoken by a native of Tashkent?

6. On the African mainland, which is the westernmost city?

7. The Devil's Beef Tub is one of the two sources of which Scottish river?

8. Which island off north-west France marks the southern entrance to the English Channel?

9. What is the name of the highest point in Yellowstone National Park?

10. What is the capital of Andorra?

11. Garuda is the national airline of which country?

12. The sand dunes of Maspalomas are on which holiday isle?

13. Which small Swiss canton lies between Zurich and Schwyz?

14. In Belgium, what is the capital of the region of Wallonia?

Medium

15. What is the highest mountain in Hokkaido, Japan?

16. Which South Pacific country was formerly called the Ellice Islands?

17. The kwacha is the currency unit of which country?

18. In which US city is the Gateway Arch?

19. On which island in the Tierra del Feugo archipelago is Cape Horn?

20. Which lough forms the boundary between the Irish counties of Longford and Roscommon?

Hard

Answers to QUIZ 492 – Also Known As

1	Pierino	11	Lauren Bacall
2	Ty Cobb	12	Bill Clinton
3	Adam Faith	13	Whoopi Goldberg
4	New Jersey	14	Dundee
5	Alessandro Filipepi	15	Ironside
6	Abelson	16	Phyllis Dorothy
7	Lucky Goldstar	17	Gar (or garfish)
8	Kirk Douglas	18	Mendelssohn
9	Molière	19	Stevie Wonder
10	New Zealand	20	The Washington Convention

1. Who wrote the two collections of poems entitled *A Boy's Will* and *North of Boston*?

2. On which British island is Sumburgh Head?

3. The Bosnia-Herzegovina flag has what main colour?

4. What is another name for the Spider Bridge in Sheffield?

5. Which is the highest mountain peak in Russia?

6. Johnson Beharry won which military award in 2005?

7. Who composed the 1821 opera Der *Freischütz*?

8. In which year was the Lonsdale Belt introduced as a boxing prize?

9. Which country has the internet country code .is?

10. What was the name of the family living at 1313 Mockingbird Lane, Mockingbird Heights?

11. *Christmas in the Heart* was a 2009 album by which singer?

12. What dinosaur's name means "deceptive lizard"?

13. Which Nottinghamshire abbey was the home of Lord Byron?

14. Sergei Diaghilev founded which ballet company?

15. What is the surname of Amyas, hero of Kingsley's *Westward Ho!*?

16. What are sufferers of Sjogren's syndrome unable to do?

17. Under what name did Alexei Maximovich Peshkov write?

18. Who wrote *Prayer Before Birth*, that begins: "I am not yet born; O hear me"?

19. Which singer's real name was Eleanora Fagan?

20. Which mythological daughter of Tantalus was turned into stone by Apollo and Artemis?

Easy

Medium

Hard

Answers to QUIZ 493 – Pot Luck

1	Ghana	11	Ombrophobia
2	Norwegian	12	Camulodunum
3	Eschatology	13	Spinnaker
4	Trinity	14	Ice hockey
5	Hugh Town	15	Brno
6	Table tennis	16	Otter
7	India	17	Five
8	*The Wayward Daughter*	18	Antigone
9	Barbados	19	Likud
10	Yankee	20	Jimmy James

Easy

1   In which year was the first trans-Atlantic radio communication sent and received?

2   Which comedian made the first "public" mobile phone call in Britain at St Katherine's Docks in 1985?

3   What does the "AM" stand for in the term AM radio?

4   Which English king established the first "Master of the Posts"...?

5   ...and which king opened up the postal service to the general public?

6   In which year did Royal Mail complete the national roll-out of postcodes?

7   What name was given to the first US space satellite launched in 1958?

8   Which London church is known as "the journalists' church"?

9   In digital communication terms what does MIME stand for?

10   Cuneiform script was invented by which civilisation?

11   "What hath God wrought" was an 1844 message sent by Samuel Morse by which form of communication?

12   The Token Ring method of communication was used in which form of technology?

13   What does DLP stand for in relation to projectors?

14   Claude Chappe (b.1763) invented which method of communication?

15   Who published the 1837 pamphlet *Post Office Reform: Its Importance and Practicability*?

16   By what title is *The Daily Universal Register* now known?

17   Which was the first legal commercial radio station on mainland Britain?

18   The world's first scheduled airmail service flew between which two towns?

19   In which year was the Office of Communications (OFCOM) launched?

20   With whom did Marconi share the 1909 Nobel Prize in Physics for work in wireless telegraphy?

Answers to QUIZ 494 – Geography

1	Managua	11	Indonesia
2	Peru	12	Gran Canaria
3	Lapland	13	Zug
4	Tullamarine	14	Namur
5	Uzbek	15	Asahi
6	Dakar	16	Tuvalu
7	Annan	17	Zambia
8	Ushant	18	St Louis
9	Eagle Peak	19	Hornos Island
10	Andorra la Vella	20	Ree

1 Who was the first player to win 20 titles at Wimbledon?

2 What technological item was invented in 1981 and named Osborne 1 by its creator Adam Osborne?

3 What is Bulgaria's currency unit?

4 What is the name of the desert region of southern Israel?

5 In *Under Milk Wood* (1954), what is the first name of the character Mr Bread?

6 What is the nineteenth book of the Old Testament?

7 A "muster" describes a group of which birds?

8 Which game was invented by unemployed Charles Darrow, that enabled him to retire a multi-millionaire?

9 What does the K stand for in the name of the author Jerome K Jerome?

10 On Glasgow's Subway, which station lies between St George's Cross and Buchanan Street?

11 Who was the human partner of Lenny the Lion?

12 What is the name of the U-shaped bone at the base of the tongue that supports the tongue muscles?

13 Which light cavalry regiment gives its name to a dance for eight or sixteen pairs?

14 Arrecife is a city on which island?

15 The choanoid muscles are found in which part of the body?

16 Who was the first female jockey to ride in the Grand National?

17 In the 1985 film *St Elmo's Fire*, who played Jules?

18 Who was the father of legendary Greek hero Ajax?

19 The Moluccas are part of which country?

20 St Anne is the administrative centre of which UK island?

Easy

Medium

Hard

Answers to QUIZ 495 – Pot Luck

1	Robert Frost	11	Bob Dylan
2	Mainland (Shetland)	12	Apatosaurus
3	Blue	13	Newstead Abbey
4	Cobweb Bridge	14	Ballet Russes
5	Mount Elbrus	15	Leigh
6	Victoria Cross	16	Cry
7	Carl Maria von Weber	17	Maxim Gorky
8	1909	18	Louis Macneice
9	Iceland	19	Billie Holiday
10	The Munsters	20	Niobe

1   The Volkswagen Golf was first introduced in which year?

2   Which make and model of car was named *Top Gear* Car of the Decade from 2000 to 2009?

3   Built in 1885, which vehicle is considered to be the world's first production automobile?

4   What make and model of car is Ecto-1 in the 1984 film *Ghostbusters*?

5   What is the full name of the company known as BMW?

6   The Lamborghini logo features which animal?

7   Which company is based in the town of Maranello?

8   Which manufacturer renamed its "Zhiguli" brand when exporting to other countries?

9   In which year was General Motors founded?

10   Which iconic British sports car was manufactured between 1961 and 1975?

11   The first model by which company was nicknamed "the Coal Scuttle"?

12   The company Nihon Sangyo, founded in 1928, used what name from the 1930s onwards?

13   What is the French name for the Citroën 2CV?

14   For what do the initials "Fiat" stand in the name of the car manufacturing company?

15   In the 2000 film *Gone in 60 Seconds*, what make and model is the car known as "Eleanor"?

16   Which car was awarded World Car of the Year and World Car Design of the Year in the 2016 World Car Awards?

17   In the 1974 film *The Blues Brothers*, what make and model of car is driven by Jake and Elwood Blues?

18   What model of car, made by Lotus Cars from 1996, was named after the granddaughter of the chairman of the company at that time?

19   The Vauxhall Astra was first introduced in which year?

20   What make and model of car, codenamed "BlueStar", was listed in *Time* Magazine's "Best 25 Inventions of 2017"?

Answers to QUIZ 496 – Communications

1	1901	11	Telegram
2	Ernie Wise	12	Local area networks (LANS)
3	Amplitude modulation	13	Digital Light Processing
4	Henry VIII (in 1516)	14	Semaphore visual telegraph
5	Charles I	15	Sir Rowland Hill
6	1972	16	*The Times*
7	*Explorer*	17	LBC
8	St Brides Church (Fleet Street)	18	Hendon and Windsor
9	Multipurpose Internet Mail Extensions	19	2003
10	The Sumerians	20	Karl Ferdinand Braun

1   Which TV couple lived at 1164 Morning Glory Circle, West Port, Connecticut?

2   Eating cheese late at night can cause nightmares as it contains large amounts of what substance which affects the nervous system?

3   The 1838 work *Kinderszenen* by Robert Schumann has what English name?

4   *Seven Tears* was a 1982 hit for which group?

5   In which country is the Belmont Stakes horse race run?

6   What subatomic particles take their name from a passage in James Joyce's *Finnegans Wake*?

7   Whose hit *5-4-3-2-1* was used as the introductory music to the TV pop programme *Ready Steady Go*?

8   Which stately home is the seat of the Marquess of Exeter?

9   Grévy's and Burchell's are species of which animal?

10 "Q" was the pseudonym of which writer?

11 Which Hollywood film company produced *Citizen Kane* and *King Kong*?

12 Who created the detective Albert Campion?

13 Judith Durham was the lead singer with which Australian group?

14 Which constellation contains the star Thuban?

15 The mineral cobalt is what colour?

16 Which Irish rider (b.1952) won the Prix de L'Arc de Triomphe four times?

17 Who played Sue Storm in the 2015 version of *Fantastic Four*?

18 The Mindbenders were the backing group for which singer in the 1960s?

19 At which public school was squash first played?

20 Who wrote the 1965 novel *The Magus*?

Easy

Medium

Hard

Easy

1   The Cretaceous period occurred during which geological era?

2   What does scotopic vision allow one to do?

3   In the 6th century BC, who realised the"Morning Star" and the "Evening Star" were one and the same?

4   What was astronaut Buzz Aldrin's original first name?

5   In a CAT scan, for what do the letters CAT stand?

6   What is the most abundant protein in the body?

7   What prefix indicates 10^{15}?

8   Sir Christopher Wren was a professor in which scientific field?

9   The lack of which vitamin causes the disease beriberi?

10 What is the name of the network of nerves and blood vessels behind the stomach?

Medium

11 In Einstein's formula $E = mc^2$, what does C stand for?

12 Which naturalist lived at Down House in Kent?

13 In 1938, which Italian-born physicist was awarded a Nobel Prize?

14 What is the SI unit of pressure?

15 In which year is Halley's comet next predicted to be visible from Earth?

16 What name is given to the minimum speed required to break free from gravity?

17 John Enders, Frederick Robbins and Thomas Weller jointly shared the Nobel Prize for Physiology and Medicine in 1954 for research into which disease?

18 Admiralty, cartridge and red are variations of which alloy?

19 Which is the largest object in the asteroid belt?

20 Which branch of medical science is concerned with muscles?

Hard

Answers to QUIZ 498 – Car Makes and Models

1	1974	11	Aston Martin
2	Bugatti Veyron EB 16.4	12	Nissan
3	Benz Patent-Motorwagen	13	Deux Chevaux (two horses)
4	Cadillac Miller-Meteor	14	Fabbrica Italiana Automobili Torino
5	Bayerische Motoren Werke	15	Ford Shelby Mustang GT500
6	Bull	16	Mazda MX-5
7	Ferrari	17	Dodge Monaco
8	Lada	18	Lotus Elise (after Elisa)
9	1908	19	1979
10	Jaguar E-Type	20	Tesla Model 3